TEXTBOOK

English and European Legal Systems

CONSULTANT EDITOR: LORD TEMPLEMAN
EDITOR: CHARLES P REED
LLB, Barrister

OLD BAILEY PRESS

OLD BAILEY PRESS
200 Greyhound Road, London W14 9RY

First edition 1999

© HLT Group Ltd 1999
Reprinted 2000

All Old Bailey Press publications enjoy copyright protection and the copyright belongs to the HLT Group Ltd.

All rights reserved. No part of this publication may be reproduced or transmitted in any form or by any means, electronic, mechanical, photocopying, recording or otherwise, or stored in any retrieval system of any nature without either the written permission of the copyright holder, application for which should be made to the Old Bailey Press, or a licence permitting restricted copying in the United Kingdom issued by the Copyright Licensing Agency.

Any person who infringes the above in relation to this publication may be liable to criminal prosecution and civil claims for damages.

ISBN 1 85836 351 9

British Library Cataloguing-in-Publication.
A CIP Catalogue record for this book is available from the British Library.

Acknowledgements

The publishers and author would like to thank the Incorporated Council of Law Reporting for England and Wales for kind permission to reproduce extracts from the Weekly Law Reports, and Butterworths for their kind permission to reproduce extracts from the All England Law Reports.

The author would like to thank Michael T Molan, the author of *Constitutional Law: The Machinery of Government* (2nd ed, 1999) Old Bailey Press, for the replication of Chapters 12, 17, 18, 19 and 20 of this textbook.

Printed and bound in Great Britain

Contents

Preface *vii*

Table of Cases *ix*

Table of Statutes and Other Materials *xvii*

Part I: Sources of Law

1 Introduction: Divisions and Sources of English Law *3*

Historical background: origins and development of common law and equity – The division between civil and criminal law – Law of tort – Law of contract – Law of property – Classification of sources – Custom – Legislation – Case law – European law

2 Interpretation of Legislation and Law Reform *24*

Introduction – The canons of interpretation – Other principles of construction – Aids to interpretation and construction – The influence of the European Convention on Human Rights and the likely impact of Human Rights Act 1998 – Judges as law reformers – Law reform bodies – Examples of reform – A Ministry of Justice?

3 The Doctrine of Precedent *42*

Introduction – Stare decisis: meaning – Principal elements of stare decisis – The operation of precedent within the hierarchy of the courts – The European Court of Justice (ECJ) – The European Court of Human Rights (ECHR) – The House of Lords – The Court of Appeal – The High Court – Other courts – Reform proposals

Part II: The Personnel of the Legal System

4 The Judiciary and the Magistracy *61*

Introduction: the concept of a career judiciary – Judicial offices and statistics – Appointment of judges – Training of judges – Removal and retirement – Immunity, independence and impartiality – Functions of a judge – Lay magistrates (Justices of the Peace) – Stipendiary magistrates

5 The Jury System *76*

The jury in civil cases – The jury in criminal cases – Arguments for and against the jury system – Reform proposals

6 The Legal Profession *86*

Introduction: the divided legal profession – Solicitors – Barristers – The Crown Prosecution Service – Reform of the legal profession

Part III: Methods of Adjudication and the Financing of Legal Services

7 Courts, Tribunals and Alternative Dispute Resolution *105*

Divisions of the courts – The main English courts – Tribunals and inquiries – Arbitration – Alternative dispute resolution (ADR) – Diagrams of the main English court structure

8 Funding of Legal Advice and Representation *118*

Introduction: the legal aid scheme – Legal advice and assistance: the green form scheme and ABWOR – Civil legal aid – Criminal legal aid – Costs – Alternative methods of funding: legal expenses insurance and conditional fees – Free legal services – Reform proposals: the Access to Justice Bill 1999

Part IV: Civil Proceedings

9 Civil Procedure in the High Court *135*

Procedure prior to 26 April 1999: Jurisdiction: High Court or county court? – Issue and service of the writ – Acknowledgement of service – Exchange of pleadings – Discovery – The summons for directions (O.25) – Interlocutory applications – Bringing proceedings to an end before trial – The trial – Judgment, interest and costs – Enforcement of judgments – A new approach to civil litigation – *Reform*: Recommendations of the Woolf Report – Reactions to the Woolf Report – *Procedure from 26 April 1999*: Introduction – Jurisdiction – Pre-action protocols – Judges as trial managers – Issue and service of proceedings – The defence's response – The allocation stage – Disclosure – Interlocutory applications – The listing questionnaire stage – Bringing proceedings to an end before trial – Sanctions – The trial – Judgment, interest and costs – Miscellaneous changes in terminology – Effect on precedents

10 Civil Procedure in the County Court *158*

Procedure prior to 26 April 1999: Jurisdiction: High Court or county court? – Bringing proceedings – Issue of proceedings (actions) and service – Pleadings – Automatic directions – Interlocutory applications – Bringing proceedings to an end before trial – The trial – Enforcement of judgments – Small claims procedure – *Procedure from 26 April 1999*: *Small claims*: Jurisdiction and allocation – Pre-trial procedure – The trial – Costs – Effect on precedents

11 Civil Appeals *166*

Introduction – Appeals from orders of masters, registrars, High Court judges, circuit judges and district judges – Appeals to the Court of Appeal (Civil Division) – Appeals to the House of Lords

Part V: Criminal Proceedings

12 Arrest, Search and Seizure and Interrogation *173*

Introduction – Police powers to stop and search – Conduct of searches under s1 of the 1984 Act – Other powers to stop and search – Road checks – Powers of entry, search and seizure on premises – Entry, search and seizure without warrant – Powers of seizure – Powers of arrest – Arrestable offences – Power to arrest for arrestable offences – Power to arrest for offences which are not arrestable – Information on arrest – Voluntary attendance at police station – Procedure following arrest – Appearance before magistrates following charge – Interrogation of suspects and the right to legal advice – Searches and fingerprinting following arrest – Confessions: general – The use of the caution and the right to silence – Challenging the admissibility of evidence

13 Criminal Procedure I: Preliminary Matters *219*

Prosecution: introduction – The prosecutors – The decision to prosecute – Commencing a prosecution – Bail: introduction – A right to bail? – Conditions of bail – Challenges to bail decisions – Effect of failure to surrender – Classification of offences – Determining the mode of trial – Committal proceedings; sending a case for trial

14 Criminal Procedure II: Summary Trial *238*

Introduction – Attendance and representation – The information – The trial procedure – Sentencing

15 Criminal Procedure III: Trial on Indictment *247*

Introduction – Representation – The plea; plea directions hearings; preparatory hearings; plea bargaining – Pre-trial disclosure – The trial procedure – Sentencing

16 Criminal Appeals *260*

Appeals following a summary trial – Appeals following trial on indictment – Miscarriages of justice: the historical position – The Criminal Cases Review Commission (CCRC)

Part VI: European Legal Systems

17 The European Community and European Union I *271*

Introduction – The institutions of the European Union – The sources of European Community law

18 The European Community and European Union II *295*

EC law in the United Kingdom – EC law and United Kingdom sovereignty – Conclusion

19 The European Convention on Human Rights *304*

Introduction: the political background – The rights protected under the ECHR – The Strasbourg machinery for enforcement – The place of the ECHR in English law – The Human Rights Act 1998

20 Recent Cases *326*

The European Community and the European Union – The European Convention on Human Rights

Index *333*

Preface

Old Bailey Press textbooks are written specifically for students. Whatever their course they will find our books clear and concise, providing comprehensive and up-to-date coverage. Written by specialists in their field, our textbooks are reviewed and updated on a regular basis. A companion Casebook, Revision WorkBook and Statutes are also published.

The traditional syllabus for English legal system has been expanded in recent times as a result of new modular courses being pioneered by higher education institutions. Such courses now include a heavy emphasis on European law and its influence on the English legal system. Consequently, to assist students on such courses this new edition has been re-titled and expanded to ensure comprehensive coverage of the European dimension.

Radical changes have also been made to many of the chapters on the English legal system, these being necessitated by rapid developments occurring during the past three years and by impending changes of considerable magnitude. Hence there are new chapters on the legal profession, the funding of legal advice and representation, civil procedure in the High Court and county court (a new civil justice system is implemented from 26 April 1999) and civil appeals.

In addition other chapters have been revised to include new cases in such areas as the doctrine of precedent and police powers. Knowledge of recent cases is extremely important as it demonstrates not only an active interest in the law as it develops but also the dynamic nature of the law which is constantly adapting to changing social and economic trends. Some chapters have been expanded to include other developments, such as the Labour government's reform proposals for the judiciary, the magistracy and the jury system. Again, keeping up to date with such information is essential to those studying for examinations.

The law is stated as at 1 January 1999, though some developments occurring after that date have been included, notably the implications for the judiciary in the ruling in *Re Pinochet Ugarte* (January 1999) and the publication of the new Legal Aid Eligibility rates (April 1999).

Table of Cases

Abbassy v MPC [1990] 1 WLR 385   *197*
Afzal v Ford Motor Co Ltd [1994] 4 All ER 720   *164*
Alderson v Booth [1969] 2 All ER 271   *192*
Allen v Emmerson [1944] KB 362   *32*
American Cyanamid Co v Ethicon Ltd [1975] AC 396; [1975] 1 All ER 504   *141*
Anderton v Ryan [1985] 2 All ER 335   *51*
Angus v Dalton (1877) 3 QBD 85   *15*
Anns v Merton London Borough [1977] 2 All ER 492   *48*
Anton Piller KG v Manufacturing Processes Ltd [1976] Ch 55   *7, 141*
Application for a warrant of further detention, In the matter of an [1988] Crim LR 296   *200*
Arab Bank plc v Mercantile Holdings Ltd [1994] 2 All ER 74   *33*
Armah v Government of Ghana [1968] AC 192   *35*
Ashville Investments v Elmer Contractors [1988] 3 WLR 867   *46*
Assam Railways and Trading Co Ltd v IRC [1935] AC 445   *36*
Associated Provincial Picture Houses Ltd v Wednesbury Corporation [1948] 1 KB 223   *193*
Attorney-General v Associated Newspapers Ltd [1994] 2 WLR 277; [1994] 1 All ER 556   *82*
Attorney-General v Jones [1990] 1 WLR 859   *30*
Attorney-General v Prince Ernest Augustus of Hanover [1957] AC 436 (HL)   *30, 31, 34*
Attorney-General for Canada v Attorney-General for Ontario [1937] AC 326   *18*
Attorney-General's Reference (No 14 of 1993) [1994] RTR 49   *266*

Bain v Fothergill (1874) LR 7 HL 158   *39*
Beckett (Alfred F) Ltd v Lyons [1967] 1 All ER 833   *16*
Behrens v Bertram Mills Circus Ltd [1957] 1 All ER 58   *46*
Beoco Ltd v Alfa Laval Co Ltd [1994] 4 All ER 464   *139*
Bidie, Re [1948] 2 All ER 995   *31*

Birkett v James [1977] 3 WLR 39   *143*
Black-Clawson International Ltd v Papierwerke Waldhof-Aschaffenburg AG [1975] AC 591; [1975] 1 All ER 810   *25, 27, 30, 36*
Bourgoin SA and Others v MAFF [1986] QB 716   *294*
Boys v Chaplin [1971] AC 356   *46*
Brannigan and McBride v United Kingdom (1993) 17 EHRR 539   *200*
Brasserie du Pêcheur SA v Federal Republic of Germany Case C–46/93 [1996] 2 WLR 506   *291, 328*
British Railways Board v Pickin [1974] AC 765   *18*
British Rail v Herrington [1972] AC 877   *52*
Bulmer (HP) Ltd v J Bollinger SA [1974] Ch 401; [1974] 3 WLR 202; [1974] 2 All ER 1226   *34, 296*

C v Director of Public Prosecutions [1995] 2 All ER 43; [1994] 3 All ER 190   *52*
CR v UK (1995) The Times 5 December   *52*
Cassell v Broome [1972] AC 1027   *49*
Castorina v Chief Constable of Surrey (1988) 138 NLJ 180   *193*
Central London Property Trust Ltd v High Trees House Ltd [1947] KB 130   *43*
Chapman v DPP (1989) 89 Cr App R 190   *186*
Chief Adjudication Officer v Foster [1993] 2 WLR 292   *37*
Christie v Leachinsky [1947] AC 573; [1947] 1 All ER 567   *193, 194*
Colchester Estates v Carlton Industries [1984] 2 All ER 601   *55*
Costa v ENEL Case 6/64 [1964] CMLR 425; [1964] ECR 585   *23, 284, 297*

D'Souza v Director of Public Prosecutions [1992] 1 WLR 1073; [1992] 4 All ER 545   *187*
Davis v Johnson [1979] AC 317; [1978] 2 WLR 553   *54*
Defrenne v SABENA [1976] ECR 455   *288*
Derbyshire County Council v Times Newspapers Ltd and Others [1993] 2 WLR 449   *315*

Director of Public Prosecutions v Hawkins [1988] 1 WLR 1166   *197*
Director of Public Prosecutions v Marshall [1988] 3 All ER 683   *215*
Director of Public Prosecutions v Nicholas [1987] Crim LR 474   *197*
Director of Public Prosecutions v Schildkamp [1971] AC 1   *32*
Director of Public Prosecutions v Tokai [1996] AC 856   *320*
Donnelly v Jackman [1970] 1 All ER 987   *175*
Donoghue v Stevenson [1932] AC 562   *43, 47*
Doughty v Rolls Royce [1992] CMLR 1045   *288*
Dowling, Re [1967] AC 725; [1967] 1 All ER 210   *51*
Duke v GEC Reliance Ltd [1988] 1 All ER 626   *300*
Duport Steels Ltd v Sirs [1980] 1 WLR 142   *28*

EC Commission v Italy Case 39/72 [1973] ECR 101   *280*
EC Commission v Italy [1989] 3 CMLR 25   *280*
Earl of Oxford's Case, The (1615) 1 Rep Ch 1   *9*
Eastman Photographic Materials Co Ltd v Comptroller General of Patents [1898] AC 571   *36*
Ecclesfield Inhabitants, Re (1818) 1 B & Ald 348   *15*
Edwards v Director of Public Prosecutions (1993) 97 Cr App R 301   *195*
El Cortes Ingles v Rivero [1996] 2 CMLR 507   *289*
Elder, Dempster & Co Ltd v Paterson, Zochonis & Co Ltd [1924] AC 522   *46*
Elguzouli-Daf v Commissioner of Police of the Metropolis [1995] 1 All ER 833   *223*
Evans v Bartlam [1937] AC 473; [1937] 2 All ER 646   *167*
Export Tax on Art Treasures (No 2), Re [1972] CMLR 699   *285, 297*

Faccini Dori v Recreb Srl Case C–91/92 [1995] CMLR 833   *289, 290*
Fisher v Bell [1961] 1 QB 394; [1960] 3 All ER 731   *25, 26, 29*
Foster v British Gas [1991] QB 405   *288*
Foulkes v Chief Constable of Merseyside Police [1998] 3 All ER 705   *189*
Francovich (and Others) v Italian Republic [1992] IRLR 84; [1991] ECR 1–5337   *287, 291, 292, 326, 327*

Furniss v Dawson [1984] 2 WLR 226   *19*

G v Superintendent of Police, Stroud (1985) The Times 29 November   *193*
Gallie v Lee [1969] 2 Ch 17   *45*
Gapper v Chief Constable of Avon and Somerset Constabulary [1998] 4 All ER 248   *190*
Garland v British Rail Engineering Ltd [1983] 2 AC 751   *34, 299*
Ghani v Jones [1970] 1 QB 693   *174*
Grey v Pearson (1857) 6 HL Cas 61   *29*
Griffith v Jenkins [1992] 2 WLR 28   *261*

H v Ministry of Defence [1991] 2 WLR 1192   *77*
Hadmor Productions Ltd v Hamilton [1983] 1 AC 191; [1982] 1 All ER 1042   *170*
Hamilton v Martell Securities [1984] 1 All ER 665   *55*
Hanlon v The Law Society [1981] AC 124; [1980] 2 All ER 199   *35, 124*
Hanning v Maitland (No 2) [1970] 1 QB 580   *125*
Harz v Deutsche Tradex GmbH [1984] ECR 1921   *289, 300*
Hastie and Jenkerson v McMahon [1991] 1 All ER 255   *137, 152*
Hedley Byrne v Heller & Partners Ltd [1963] 3 WLR 101   *47*
Henn and Darby v DPP [1981] AC 850   *283*
Heydon's Case (1584) 3 Co Rep 74   *30*
Hilder v Dexter [1902] AC 474   *27*
Horsler v Zorro [1975] Ch 302   *47*
Hughes v Kingston-upon-Hill City Council (1998) The Times 9 December   *49, 56, 126*
Hughes v Metropolitan Railway (1877) 2 App Cas 439   *43*
Hussien v Chong Fook Kam [1970] AC 942   *192*

Inland Revenue Commissioners v Hinchy [1960] AC 748   *26, 29*

Jeffrey v Black [1978] 1 All ER 555   *214*
Jeffrey S Levitt Ltd, Re [1992] 2 All ER 509   *55*
John v Mirror Group Newspapers Ltd [1996] 2 All ER 35   *77*
Johnson v Agnew [1979] 2 WLR 487   *47*
Johnstone v Chief Constable of the Royal Ulster Constabulary [1987] QB 129   *288*
Jones v Secretary of State for Social Services [1972] 2 WLR 210   *51, 57*

Joyce v Liverpool City Council [1995] 3 All ER 110   *163*
Joyce v Sengupta [1993] 1 WLR 337   *121*

Kenlin v Gardner [1987] 2 QB 510   *176*
Kennedy v Spratt [1972] AC 83; [1971] All ER 803   *107*
Kleinwort Benson Ltd v Lincoln City Council and Other Appeals [1998] 4 All ER 513   *53*
Kremzow v Republik Osterreich [1997] ECR 1–2629   *325*
Kruhlak v Kruhlak [1958] 2 QB 32   *30*
Kuruma, Son of Kania v R [1955] 1 All ER 236   *214*

Langley v North West Water Authority [1991] 1 WLR 697; [1991] 3 All ER 610   *53*
Letang v Cooper [1965] 1 QB 197   *36*
Lewis v Chief Constable of the South Wales Constabulary [1991] 1 All ER 206   *197*
Limb v Union Jack Removals Ltd [1998] 2 All ER 513   *55*
Lim Poh Choo v Camden & Islington Area Health Authority [1980] AC 174   *17*
Lister v Forth Dry Dock & Engineering Co Ltd [1990] 1 AC 546   *290, 300*
London Borough of Ealing v Woolworths plc [1995] Crim LR 58   *215*
London Street Tramways Co v London County Council [1898] AC 375   *50*
Lyons v Chief Constable of West Yorkshire (CCRTF 96/1379/C)   *193*

Macarthys Ltd v Wendy Smith [1979] 3 All ER 325   *297*
Macarthys Ltd v Wendy Smith [1980] ECR 1275   *299*
Macarthys Ltd v Wendy Smith [1981] QB 180   *299*
Magor and St Mellons Rural District Council v Newport Corporation [1952] AC 189; [1951] 2 All ER 839   *27, 29*
Malone v Metropolitan Police Commissioner [1979] Ch 344   *314*
Mareva Compania Naviera SA v International Bulk Carriers SA [1975] 2 Lloyd's Rep 509   *7, 141*
Marleasing SA v La Comercial Internacional de Alimentacion SA [1992] 1 CMLR 305   *290, 300*
Marshall v Southampton and South West Hampshire Area Health Authority [1986] QB 401   *288, 289*

Mercer v Chief Constable of Lancashire [1991] 2 All ER 504   *140*
Mighell v Reading and Another; Evans v Motor Insurers Bureau; White v White and Another (1998) The Times 12 October   *287, 326*
Miliangos v George Frank (Textiles) Ltd [1975] 3 WLR 758; [1975] 3 All ER 801   *48, 51, 56*
Mohammed-Holgate v Duke [1984] AC 437   *192*
Moodie v Inland Revenue Commissioners [1993] 1 WLR 266   *51*
Morelle Ltd v Wakeling [1955] 2 QB 379   *49*
Morris Angel and Son Ltd v Hollande [1993] 3 All ER 569   *34*
Mulder and Others v Council and Commission [1992] ECR 1–3061   *329*
Murphy v Brentwood District Council [1990] 3 WLR 414   *48*
Murphy v Director of Public Prosecutions [1990] 2 All ER 390   *230*
Murray v United Kingdom (1996) 22 EHRR 29   *211*

NWL Ltd v Woods [1979] 1 WLR 1294   *30*
Nash (Inspector of Taxes) v Tamplin & Sons Brewery (Brighton) Ltd [1952] AC 231   *45*
National Union of Teachers and Others v Governing Body of St Mary's Church of England (Aided) Junior School and Others (1996) The Times 16 December   *288*
Nokes v Doncaster Amalgamated Collieries [1940] AC 1014   *29*
Nothman v Barnet London Borough Council [1979] 1 All ER 142 (HL); [1978] 1 WLR 220 (CA)   *28*

O'Hara v Chief Constable of the Royal Ulster Constabularly [1997] 2 WLR 1; [1997] 1 All ER 129   *192*
O'Loughlin v Chief Constable of Essex (1997) The Times 12 December   *186*
Opinion No 2/94 [1996] ECR 1–1759   *324*
Osman, Re [1995] 1 WLR 1327   *79*

Page One Records v Britton [1967] 3 All ER 822   *9*
Parkes v R (1976) 64 Cr App R 25   *209*
Pepper v Hart [1993] 1 All ER 42   *26, 31, 33, 36, 37*
Pepper v Healey [1982] RTR 411   *164*
Pickstone v Freemans plc [1989] 1 AC 66   *300*
Pinochet Ugarte, Re [1999] NLJ Rep 88   *71, 170, 267*

Politi v Ministry of Finance [1971] ECR 1039 286
Powell v Kempton Park Racecourse Co [1899] AC 143 32
Practice Direction [1976] Crim LR 561 252
Practice Direction (Crown Court: Plea and Directions Hearings) [1995] 4 All ER 379 249
Practice Note [1962] 1 All ER 448 244
Practice Note [1988] 3 All ER 1086 80
Practice Note [1995] 1 All ER 385 115, 138, 145, 146
Practice Note [1996] 3 All ER 383 115
Practice Note (Court of Appeal: Procedure) [1999] 1 All ER 186 166, 168
Practice Statement [1966] 1 WLR 1234 50, 51, 54
Practice Statement [1994] 1 All ER 34 114
Practice Statement (Judgments) [1998] 2 All ER 667 43
Prudential Assurance Co v London Residuary Body [1992] 3 All ER 504 57
Pubblico Ministero v Ratti Case 148/78 [1979] ECR 1629 285

R v Absolam (1989) 88 Cr App R 322 204
R v Alladice (1988) 87 Cr App R 380; [1988] Crim LR 608 204, 210
R v Allen (1872) LR 1 CCR 367 29
R v Anderson [1993] Crim LR 448 205
R v Andrews (1998) The Times 15 October 81
R v Badham [1987] Crim LR 202 198
R v Bean [1991] Crim LR 843 82
R v Bentley (1998) The Times 31 July 264, 268
R v Berry (No 2) [1991] 1 WLR 125 267
R v Brosch [1988] Crim LR 743 192
R v Cadette [1995] Crim LR 229 215
R v Callender [1992] 3 All ER 51 35
R v Central Criminal Court, ex parte Guney [1996] 2 All ER 705 230
R v Chalkley; R v Jeffries [1998] 2 All ER 155 193, 263, 264
R v Chandler [1976] 1 WLR 585 210
R v Chelmsford Crown Court, ex parte Chief Constable of Essex Police [1994] 1 WLR 359 262
R v Chief Constable of Devon and Cornwall, ex parte Central Electricity Generating Board [1982] QB 458 192
R v Chief Constable of Lancashire, ex parte Parker [1993] 2 WLR 248; [1993] 2 All ER 56 184

R v Chief Constable of South Wales, ex parte Merrick [1994] 1 WLR 663; [1994] 2 All ER 560 205
R v Chief Constable of the Royal Ulster Constabulary, ex parte Begley; R v McWilliams [1997] 4 All ER 833 201
R v Christou [1992] 3 WLR 228 215
R v Clegg [1995] 1 All ER 334 52
R v Clinton [1993] 2 All ER 998 264
R v Comerford [1998] 1 All ER 823 80
R v Crook [1992] 2 All ER 687 247
R v Crown Court at Maidstone, ex parte Lever [1995] 2 All ER 35 227
R v Crown Court at Reading, ex parte Bello [1992] 3 All ER 353 227
R v Delaney [1989] Crim LR 39 175
R v Disciplinary Committee of the Jockey Club, ex parte The Aga Khan [1993] 1 WLR 909 318
R v Dunford (1990) 91 Cr App R 150 204
R v Ealing Magistrates, ex parte Dickson [1989] 2 All ER 1050 221
R v Eccles Justices, ex parte Farrelly (1992) The Times 17 June 74
R v Farrow (1998) The Times 20 October 263
R v Fisher [1969] 1 All ER 100 20
R v Ford [1989] 3 WLR 762; [1989] 3 All ER 445 81
R v Fulling [1987] 2 WLR 923; [1987] 2 All ER 65 213
R v Gilfoyle [1996] 3 All ER 883 264
R v Gough [1993] 2 WLR 883; [1993] 2 All ER 724 70, 80
R v Gould [1968] 1 All ER 849 54
R v Governor of Brockhill Prison, ex parte Evans [1997] 1 All ER 439 56
R v Grafton [1992] 4 All ER 609 247, 248, 255, 265
R v Graham (HK) and Others [1997] 1 Cr App Rep 302 265
R v Greater Manchester Coroner, ex parte Tal [1984] 3 WLR 643 56
R v Green [1992] Crim LR 292 82
R v Greenwich London Borough Council, ex parte Lovelace (No 2) [1992] 1 QB 155; [1992] 1 All ER 679 125
R v Harrow Crown Court, ex parte Dave [1994] 1 WLR 98 261
R v Hawkins (1993) The Times 29 June 256
R v Highbury Corner Magistrates' Court, ex parte Di Matteo [1991] 1 WLR 1374 32
R v HM Treasury, ex parte British Telecommunications plc [1996] 3 WLR 203 293

R v Home Secretary, ex parte Bhajam Singh [1976] QB 198   *314*
R v Horseferry Road Magistrates' Court, ex parte K [1996] 3 All ER 719   *233*
R v Horsman [1997] 3 All ER 385   *265*
R v Hughes [1995] Crim LR 407   *206*
R v Human Fertilisation and Embryology Authority, ex parte Blood [1997] 2 All ER 687   *72*
R v Insurance Ombudsman Bureau and the Insurance Ombudsman, ex parte Aegon Life (1994) The Independent 11 January   *318*
R v Ireland (1970) 126 CLR 321   *214*
R v Jones (Steven Martin) (1996) The Times 23 July   *265*
R v Judge of the City of London Court [1892] 1 QB 273   *26*
R v Keenan [1989] 3 All ER 598   *175*
R v Kelt [1977] 1 WLR 1365   *35*
R v Kelt [1994] 2 All ER 780   *207*
R v Khan [1993] Crim LR 54   *203*
R v Khan (Sultan) [1996] 3 WLR 162; [1996] 3 All ER 289   *216*
R v Kingston-upon-Thames Justices, ex parte Martin (1993) The Times 10 December   *244*
R v Kirk [1984] CMLR 522   *325*
R v Leatham (1861) 8 Cox CC 489   *214*
R v Lee [1984] 1 WLR 578   *262*
R v Longman [1988] Crim LR 534   *185*
R v MAFF, ex parte First City Trading and Others (1996) The Times 20 December   *302*
R v McFarlane [1994] 2 WLR 494   *35*
R v McIlkenny [1992] 2 All ER 417   *263*
R v McIvor (Neil) [1987] Crim LR 409   *182*
R v Maguire [1992] 2 All ER 433   *263*
R v Maloney (Peter James) (1996) The Times 25 March   *83*
R v Manchester City Stipendiary Magistrate, ex parte Snelson [1977] 1 WLR 911   *235*
R v Mandair [1994] 2 All ER 715   *267*
R v Maqsud Ali, R v Ashiq Hussain [1965] 2 All ER 464   *214*
R v Mason [1981] QB 881   *81*
R v Mason [1988] 1 WLR 139   *215*
R v Maxwell [1990] 1 All ER 801   *249*
R v Metropolitan Police Commissioner, ex parte Blackburn [1968] 2 WLR 893   *221*
R v Miah, R v Akhbar (1996) The Times 18 December   *83*
R v Ministry of Agriculture, ex parte Headley Lomas (Ireland) Ltd [1996] 3 WLR 787   *293*

R v Moore [1995] 4 All ER 843   *33*
R v Murphy [1965] NI 138   *214*
R v Murray [1994] 1 WLR 1   *211*
R v Newsome; R v Browne [1970] 2 QB 711   *54*
R v Obellim [1997] 1 Cr App Rep 355   *80*
R v Oliver (1995) The Times 6 December   *82*
R v Panel on Take-overs and Mergers, ex parte Datafin plc [1987] 2 WLR 699   *318*
R v Paris; R v Abdullahi; R v Miller (1993) 97 Cr App R 99   *213*
R v Parris (1989) 89 Cr App R 68   *205*
R v Pinfold [1988] 2 All ER 217   *267*
R v Pitman [1991] 1 All ER 468   *252*
R v Ponting [1985] Crim LR 318   *83*
R v Preddy [1996] 3 All ER 481   *265*
R v Preston [1993] 4 All ER 638   *252*
R v R (Rape: Marital Exemption) [1991] 4 All ER 481   *52*
R v Rafferty (1998) The Times 9 April   *232*
R v Redbridge Justices, ex parte Ram [1992] 1 All ER 652   *245*
R v Registrar-General, ex parte Smith [1991] 2 WLR 782   *31, 33*
R v Royle [1971] 3 All ER 1359   *25*
R v Samuel [1988] 2 WLR 920; [1988] 2 All ER 135   *203, 204*
R v Sang [1980] AC 402   *213*
R v Satpal Ram (1995) The Times 7 December   *264*
R v Saunders [1988] Crim LR 521   *175*
R v Secretary of State for Employment, ex parte Equal Opportunities Commission and Another [1994] 2 WLR 409   *294*
R v Secretary of State for Employment, ex parte Seymour Smith (1997) The Times 14 March   *289, 294*
R v Secretary of State for Foreign and Commonwealth Affairs, ex parte Rees-Mogg [1994] 2 WLR 115; [1994] 1 All ER 457   *34, 37, 274*
R v Secretary of State for the Home Department, ex parte Ahmed and Others (1998) The Times 15 October   *314*
R v Secretary of State for the Home Department, ex parte Al-Mehdawi [1989] 1 All ER 777   *54*
R v Secretary of State for the Home Department, ex parte Brind [1991] 2 WLR 588   *314*
R v Secretary of State for the Home Department, ex parte Flynn (1995) The Times 23 March   *286*
R v Secretary of State for Social Security, ex parte Sutton (1997) The Times 25 April   *292*

R v Secretary of State for Transport, ex parte Factortame Ltd and Others [1990] 2 AC 85 *327*
R v Secretary of State for Transport, ex parte Factortame Ltd and Others (No 2) [1991] 1 AC 603; [1990] 3 WLR 818 *300, 327*
R v Secretary of State for Transport, ex parte Factortame Ltd and Others (No 3) [1992] QB 680 *328*
R v Secretary of State for Transport, ex parte Factortame Ltd and Others (No 4) Case C–48/93 [1996] 2 WLR 506 *291, 328*
R v Secretary of State for Transport, ex parte Factortame Ltd and Others (No 5) (1998) The Times 28 April *293, 327*
R v Self [1992] 1 WLR 476; [1992] 3 All ER 476 *191*
R v Sheffield Crown Court, ex parte Brownlow [1980] 1 WLR 892 *81*
R v Shivpuri [1986] 2 WLR 988 *51*
R v Silcott (1991) The Times 9 December *205*
R v Slough Justices, ex parte Stirling [1987] Crim LR 576 *200*
R v Smith (Eric) [1987] Crim LR 579 *182*
R v Smurthwaite [1994] Crim LR 53 *215*
R v South Western Magistrates' Court, ex parte Cofie [1997] 1 WLR 885 *184*
R v Southwark Crown Court, ex parte Tawfick (1994) The Times 1 December *220*
R v Taylor [1950] 2 KB 368 *54*
R v Thompson [1962] 1 All ER 65 *83*
R v Thompson (1995) The Times 6 February *252*
R v Tower Bridge Metropolitan Stipendiary Magistrate, ex parte Chaudhry [1993] 3 WLR 1154 *220*
R v Turner [1970] 2 WLR 1093 *251*
R v W (1993) The Times 16 March *266*
R v Ward (Judith) [1993] 2 All ER 577 *253*
R v Warley Magistrates Court, ex parte Director of Public Prosecutions [1999] 1 All ER 251 *232*
R v Wood Green Crown Court, ex parte Howe [1992] 1 WLR 702 *227, 230*
R v Young [1995] 2 WLR 430 *82, 83*
Racal Communications Ltd, Re [1981] AC 374 *167*
Racz v Home Office [1994] 2 WLR 23 *76*
Rakhit v Carty [1990] 2 All ER 202 *54*
Rantzen v Mirror Group Newspapers [1993] 3 WLR 953 *77, 315*
Raymond v Honey [1983] 1 AC 1 *33*
Restick v Crickmore [1994] 1 WLR 420 *136*

Rice v Connolly [1966] 2 QB 414 *176*
Rickards v Rickards [1989] 3 WLR 748 *54*
Ridehalgh v Horsefield [1994] 3 WLR 462 *144*
River Wear Commissioners v Adamson (1877) 2 App Cas 743 *29*
Roache v News Group Newspapers Ltd (1992) The Times 23 November *143*
Roberts Petroleum Ltd v Bernard Kenny Ltd [1983] 2 AC 192; [1983] 2 WLR 305 *23, 43*
Robinson v The Queen [1985] AC 956 *320*
Roebuck v Mungovin [1994] 2 WLR 290 *143*
Rondel v Worsley [1969] 1 AC 191; [1967] 3 All ER 993 *97*
Rookes v Barnard [1964] AC 1129; [1964] 1 All ER 367 *49*
Ross v Caunters [1979] 3 WLR 605 *92*

Saif Ali v Sydney Mitchell & Co [1980] AC 198; [1978] 3 All ER 1033 *91, 97*
Scher v Policyholders Protection Board (No 2) [1993] 4 All ER 840 *36*
Schorsch Meier GmbH v Hennin [1975] QB 416 *48*
Scruttons Ltd v Midland Silicones Ltd [1962] 2 WLR 186 *46*
Seaford Court Estates Ltd v Asher [1949] 2 KB 481 *27*
Secretary of State for Trade and Industry v Desai (1991) The Times 5 December *49*
Shaw v Director of Public Prosecutions [1962] AC 220 *72*
Shtun v Zalejska [1996] 3 All ER 411 *143*
Sim v Stretch [1936] 2 All ER 1237 *84*
Sirros v Moore [1974] 3 WLR 459 *69*
Southern Water Authority v Nature Conservancy Council [1992] 3 All ER 481 *31*
Spicer v Holt [1976] 3 All ER 71 *197*
Srl CILFIT v Ministry of Health [1982] ECR 3415 *282*
Stafford v DPP [1974] AC 878; [1973] 3 All ER 762 *263*
Steel and Others v United Kingdom (1998) The Times 1 October *306, 329*
Stoke-on-Trent City Council v B & Q plc [1991] 2 WLR 42 *303*
Stoke-on-Trent City Council v B & Q (Retail) Ltd [1984] 2 All ER 332 *35*
Swain v The Law Society [1983] 1 AC 598 *126*
Swallow Securities v Brand (1983) 45 P & CR 328 *55*
Sweet v Parsley [1970] AC 132 *33*

Tanistry Case (1608) Dav Ir 28   *15, 16*
Thai Trading Co (A Firm) v Taylor [1998] 3 All ER 65   *126*
Thompson v Commissioner of Police of the Metropolis [1997] 2 All ER 762   *77*
Three Rivers District Council v Bank of England (No 2) [1996] 2 All ER 363   *37*
Three Rivers District Council v Bank of England (No 3) [1996] 3 All ER 558   *294*
Tolstoy-Miloslavsky v Lord Aldington [1996] 2 All ER 556   *144*
Tucker v Director of Public Prosecution [1992] 4 All ER 901   *261*

United Kingdom v Council of the European Union Case C–84/94 (1996) The Times 21 November   *281*
United Railways of Havana and Regla Warehouses Ltd, Re [1961] AC 1007   *48*
Universal Corporation v Five Ways Properties [1979] 1 All ER 552   *30*
Uppal v Home Office (1980) 3 EHRR 391   *314*

Van Duyn v Home Office Case 41/74 [1974] ECR 1337   *285, 286, 298*
Van Gend en Loos v Nederlandse Administratie der Belastingen [1963] ECR 1   *286*
Vince v Chief Constable of Dorset Police [1993] 1 WLR 415   *198*
Von Colson v Land Nordrhein-Westfalen [1984] ECR 1891   *289, 300*

Wagner Miret v Fondo de Garantia Salaria [1993] ECR 1–6911   *291, 327*

Walrave and Koch v Union Cycliste Internationale [1974] ECR 1405   *288*
Walsh v Lonsdale (1882) 21 Ch D 9   *8, 10*
Walters, Re [1987] Crim LR 577   *204*
Walters v W H Smith & Sons Ltd [1914] 1 KB 595   *191*
Waltham Forest London Borough Council v Thomas [1992] 3 WLR 131   *33*
Ward v James [1966] 1 QB 273; [1965] 1 All ER 563   *77, 84*
Webb v EMO Air Cargo Ltd (UK) (No 2) [1995] 1 WLR 1454   *290, 300*
Webster v Cecil (1861) 30 Beav 62   *7*
Westdeutsche Landesbank Girozentrale v Islington London Borough Council [1996] 2 All ER 961   *52*
Wheeler v Le Marchant (1881) 17 Ch D 675   *92*
Williams v Bedwellty Justices [1996] 3 All ER 737   *235*
Wilson v Dagnall [1972] 1 QB 509   *20*
Woking Urban District Council, Re [1914] 1 Ch 300   *35*
Wolstanton Ltd v Newcastle-under-Lyme Corporation [1940] 3 All ER 101   *16*
Woolwich Building Society v Inland Revenue Commissioners [1992] 3 WLR 366   *23*
Wychavon District Council v National Rivers Authority [1993] 2 All ER 440   *33*

Yonge v Toynbee [1910] 1 KB 215   *92*
Young v Bristol Aeroplane Co Ltd [1944] KB 718; [1946] AC 163   *48, 53, 54, 56, 57*
Younghusband v Luftig [1949] 2 All ER 72   *49, 56*

Table of Statutes and Other Materials

Access to Justice Bill 1999   *87, 88, 90, 95, 99, 100, 102, 127, 129*
Act of Settlement 1701   *69*
Administration of Justice Act 1969
    s12   *170*
    s13   *170*
Administration of Justice Act 1970   *108*
Amsterdam Treaty *see* Treaty on European Union 1997
Appellate Jurisdiction Act 1876   *106, 107, 217*
    s25   *63*
Arbitration Act 1996
    s69   *114*
Assize of Clarendon 1166   *4*
Assize of Northampton 1176   *4*
Assize of Windsor 1179   *4*

Bail Act 1976   *224, 228*
    s3   *227*
    s3(8)   *230*
    s4   *225*
    s5B   *228*
    s6(1)   *230*
    s7   *226, 227*
    s7(3)   *230*
    Schedule 1 Part I   *226*
    Schedule 1 Part II   *227, 228*
Bail (Amendment) Act 1993
    s1   *229*
Betting Act 1853   *32*
Bill of Rights 1689   *304*

Capital Transfer Tax Act 1984   *19*
Chancery Amendment Act 1858   *9*
Child Support Act 1991   *109*
Children Act 1989   *39, 112*
    s25   *166*
Children and Young Persons Act 1933
    s53(2)   *266*
Children and Young Persons Act 1969
    s28(2)   *189*
Civil Procedure Act 1997   *149, 150*

Civil Procedure Rules 1998   *149, 150, 155*
    Part 1   *151, 157, 165*
    Part 3   *151*
    Part 20   *153*
    Part 24   *155*
    Part 31   *153, 165*
    Part 36   *155*
Common Law Procedure Act 1852   *9*
Common Law Procedure Act 1854   *9*
Common Law Procedure Act 1860   *9*
Contempt of Court Act 1981
    s8   *82*
    s8(1)   *82*
Council Directive 64/221   *286*
Council Directive 68/151
    art 11   *290*
Council Directive 74/557/EEC   *293*
    art 34   *293*
County Court Rules   *158, 161*
County Courts Act 1984   *158*
Courts Act 1971   *64, 108, 110*
    Schedule 2 Part 1A   *65*
Courts and Legal Services Act 1990   *64, 87, 89, 95, 97, 101*
    s8   *77, 169*
    s19   *102*
    s20   *102*
    s21–26   *91*
    s27–33   *89*
    s27(2)   *220*
    s58   *125, 126*
    s61(1)   *97*
    s69(1)   *70*
    s71   *43, 63, 64, 65, 74, 75, 110, 111, 112*
    s71(2)   *63*
    s71(3)   *38*
    s74(1)   *65*
    s74(2)   *65*
    s108   *74*
    s115   *43*
    Part II   *70*

Courts and Legal Services Act 1990 (*contd.*)
    Schedule 2   *102*
    Schedule 10
        para 1   *63*
        para 31   *64*
Crime and Disorder Act 1998
    s25   *180*
    s34   *52*
    s49   *239*
    s50   *239*
    s51   *237*
    s52   *237*
    s53   *99*
    s54(2)   *228*
    s56   *225, 226*
    Schedule 3   *237*
Crime (Sentences) Act 1997
    s51   *232, 246*
Criminal Appeal Act 1968   *262, 263, 264*
    s2   *267*
    s2(1)   *263, 264*
    s3(1)   *265*
    s9   *266*
    s11   *266*
    s17   *267*
    s23   *264, 265*
Criminal Appeal Act 1995   *262, 264, 267, 268*
    s1(1)   *262*
    s2(1)   *263*
    s3   *268*
    s4(1)   *264, 265*
    ss8–14   *267*
    s13   *268*
    s16   *268*
    Schedule 1   *267*
Criminal Attempts Act 1981   *19*
    s2   *190*
Criminal Damage Act 1971
    s1   *234*
Criminal Evidence (Amendment) Act 1997   *207*
    Schedule 1   *207*
Criminal Evidence (Northern Ireland) Order 1988   *210, 211*
Criminal Justice Act 1967
    s11   *236, 253*
    s22   *229*
Criminal Justice Act 1972
    s36   *266*
Criminal Justice Act 1987   *235, 250*
Criminal Justice Act 1988   *202*
    s35   *266*
    s36   *266*
    s53   *265*

Criminal Justice Act 1988 (*contd.*)
    s118(1)   *79*
    s118(2)   *79*
    s120   *79*
    s140   *177*
Criminal Justice Act 1991   *235*
Criminal Justice and Public Order Act 1994   *174, 211*
    s25   *225, 229*
    s26   *226*
    s27   *224*
    s28   *199*
    s28(2)   *224*
    s30   *228*
    s32   *39*
    s33   *39*
    s34   *211*
    s35   *212*
    s36   *211*
    s37   *211*
    s37(a)   *174*
    s40   *78*
    s41   *79*
    s42   *79*
    s43   *82*
    s45   *240*
    s46   *234*
    s48   *251*
    s51   *83*
    s52   *65*
    s54   *207*
    s59   *206*
    s60   *179*
    s60(4A)   *180*
    s60(8)   *190*
    s81   *180*
    s85   *182*
    s142   *39*
    s166   *190*
    s167   *190*
    Schedule 5   *240*
Criminal Law Act 1967
    s6(1)   *249*
    s6(5)   *249*
Criminal Law Act 1977   *19*
    s6   *185*
    s7   *185*
    s8   *185*
    s10   *185*
Criminal Procedure and Investigations Act 1996   *235, 250, 252, 253, 254*
    s3   *252*
    ss3–11   *252*

Criminal Procedure and Investigations Act 1996 (*contd.*)
    s5   *252, 253*
    s5(7)   *236, 253*
    s7   *253*
    s23   *253*
    s29   *250*
    s40   *250, 251*
    s47   *235*
    s48   *240*
    s49   *231*
    s54   *83*
    Schedule 1   *235*
Crown Court, Rules of   *110*
Customs and Excise Management Act 1979
    s1(1)   *189*

Defamation Act 1996   *77*
Drug Trafficking Offences 1986
    s38(1)   *181*

EC Treaty 1957 *see* Treaty of Rome 1957
Education Act 1944   *310*
Education Act 1996
    s9   *310*
Equal Pay Act 1970   *297, 298*
Equal Treatment Directive
    art 6   *289*
European Coal and Steel Treaty 1951   *271*
European Communities Act 1972   *17, 284, 295, 298, 302, 303, 314, 324*
    s1   *296*
    s1(1)   *298*
    s2   *298, 299*
    s2(1)   *296, 298*
    s2(2)   *20, 296*
    s2(4)   *296, 297, 298, 300*
    s3(1)   *296*
European Communities (Amendment) Act 1993   *273*
European Convention on Human Rights   *23, 24, 37, 50, 52, 216, 218, 226, 274, 283, 304–325, 330*
    art 1   *311*
    art 2   *305, 311, 316*
    art 2(1)   *305*
    art 2(2)   *305*
    art 3   *305, 311, 316*
    art 4   *305, 316*
    art 4(1)   *311*
    art 5   *306, 316, 330*
    art 5(1)   *306, 329, 330, 331*
    art 5(2)   *196, 200, 306*

European Convention on Human Rights (*contd.*)
    art 5(3)   *194, 306, 311, 317*
    art 5(4)   *306*
    art 5(5)   *306*
    art 6   *211, 212, 307, 316, 330*
    art 6(1)   *307*
    art 6(2)   *212*
    art 6(3)   *307, 329*
    art 7   *307, 311, 316*
    art 7(2)   *307*
    art 8   *216, 218, 308, 314, 316, 319*
    art 8(1)   *308*
    art 8(2)   *308, 311*
    art 9   *308, 316*
    art 9(1)   *308*
    art 9(2)   *308, 311*
    art 10   *77, 308, 309, 314, 315, 316, 329, 330, 331*
    art 10(1)   *308*
    art 10(2)   *308, 311, 331*
    art 11   *308, 309, 316*
    art 11(1)   *309*
    art 11(2)   *309, 311*
    art 12   *309, 316*
    art 14   *309, 316*
    art 15   *311*
    art 15(1)   *311*
    art 16   *309, 317*
    art 17   *309, 317*
    art 18   *317*
    arts 19–56   *312*
    art 25   *312*
    art 26   *319*
    art 27(2)   *319*
    art 31   *319*
    art 34   *317*
    art 41   *322*
    art 46   *319*
    art 63(1)   *305*
    Protocol 1   *305, 309*
        art 1   *309, 316*
        art 2   *310, 316, 317*
        art 3   *310, 316*
    Protocol 4   *310*
    Protocol 6   *310*
        art 1   *316*
        art 2   *316*
    Protocol 7   *310*
    Protocol 11   *312*
    Section I   *313*
    Section II   *313*
    Section III   *313*

Family Law Act 1996   116
Finance Act 1975   19
Finance Act 1976
   s63   36
Firearms Act 1968
   s47   179
Football (Offences) Act 1991   190
Foreign Judgments (Reciprocal Enforcement) Act 1933
   s8   30

Government of Wales Act 1998   318
Grand Assize 1179   5

Human Rights Act 1998   23, 24, 37, 50, 175, 216, 218, 304, 305, 311, 313, 314, 315, 317, 318, 319, 321, 322, 323
   s1   316
   s2   50
   s2(1)   319
   s3   37
   s3(1)   319
   s3(2)   321
   s4(6)   321
   s5(1)   321
   s6(1)   318, 319
   s6(2)   319
   s6(3)   318
   s6(6)   318, 319
   s7   317
   s7(1)   317, 318
   s7(2)   317
   s7(3)   317
   s7(5)   317
   s7(6)   317
   s7(7)   317
   s7(9)   317
   s8(1)   322
   s8(2)   322
   s8(3)   322
   s9(1)   318
   s9(2)   318
   s10   322
   s10(1)   322
   s10(2)   322
   s11   320
   s12   320, 321
   s12(2)   321
   s12(3)   321
   s12(4)   320
   s13   321
   s18   316
   s19   323
   s20   316

Human Rights Act 1998 (*contd.*)
   s20(1)   322
   s21(5)   316
   Schedule 2   322, 323
   Schedule 4   318

Income Tax Act 1952
   s25(3)(a)   26
Intelligence Services Act 1994   217
Interception of Communications Act 1985   252
Interpretation Act 1978   19, 35

Judicature Act 1873   9, 106, 108
   s24   106
   s25   106
Judicature Act 1875   9, 108
Judicial Pensions and Retirement Act 1993   69
   s26   69
Juries Act 1974   78, 79
   s5(2)   80
   s8   79
   s9   79
   s9B   79
   s13   82
   s12(4)   79
   s17   82, 257
   s17(3)   83
   Schedule 1 Part I   79
   Schedule 1 Part II   78
   Schedule 1 Part III   79
Juries (Disqualifications) Act 1984   78
Justices of the Peace Act 1997   72

Law Commission Act 1965   38
Law of Property (Miscellaneous Provisions) Act 1989   39
Legal Advice and Assistance Act 1972   119
Legal Aid Act 1988   120
   s3   118
   s9   119
   s21(2)   123
   s22(2)   123
   Part III   119
   Part IV   121
   Part V   122
Local Government Act 1933   27
Local Government Act 1972
   s222   35
Lord Cairns' Act *see* Chancery Amendment Act 1858
Luxembourg Agreement 1966   276

Maastricht Treaty *see* Treaty on European Union 1992

Magistrates' Courts Act 1980   *238*
    s1   *189*
    s2(6)   *238*
    s6(1)   *235*
    s6(2)   *235*
    s11   *240*
    s11(1)   *240*
    s11(3)   *239, 240*
    s11(4)   *240*
    s12   *239, 240*
    s12A   *240*
    s13   *240*
    s13(1)   *240*
    s13(2)   *240*
    s13(2A)   *240*
    s13(2B)   *240*
    s15   *239*
    s17A   *231*
    s19–23   *232*
    s19(3)   *232*
    s25(2)   *233*
    s33   *189*
    s38   *232, 233, 246*
    s38A   *232, 246*
    s102   *236, 242, 255*
    s105   *242*
    s111(1)   *261*
    s127   *221*
    s142   *245*
    Schedule 1   *231*
Mental Health Act 1983   *187, 207*
    s17   *187*
Merchant Shipping Act 1988   *292, 293, 301, 327, 328, 329*
    Part II   *292, 300*
Minors' Contracts Act 1987   *39*
Misuse of Drugs Act 1971   *195*
    s23   *179*

New Zealand Bill of Rights Act 1990   *324*

Obscene Publications Act 1959
    s2   *190*
Offences Against the Person Act 1861
    s38   *191*
    s57   *29*
Official Secrets Act 1920   *189*
    s8(1)   *190*
    s8(4)   *190*
    s8(5)   *190*

Police Act 1964
    s51(1)   *176, 187*
    s51(3)   *176, 195*

Police Act 1997   *216*
    s91(1)   *217*
    s91(10)   *218*
    s93   *217*
    s93(2)   *217, 218*
    s93(4)   *217*
    s97(3)   *218*
    s101(1)   *218*
    s102   *218*
    s103(1)   *217*
    s104   *218*
    s104(1)   *218*
    s106   *218*
    Part III   *217*
Police and Criminal Evidence Act 1984   *19, 39, 174, 176, 177, 178, 179, 181, 188, 192, 201, 202, 206, 210, 213, 216*
    s1   *173, 176, 177, 178, 179*
    s1(1)   *176*
    s1(2)   *176*
    s1(3)   *176*
    s1(4)   *176, 182*
    s1(5)   *176, 182*
    s1(6)   *177*
    s1(7)   *177*
    s1(8)   *177*
    s1(9)   *177*
    s2   *178*
    s2(1)   *178*
    s2(2)   *178*
    s2(3)   *178*
    s2(6)   *179*
    s2(7)   *179*
    s2(8)   *179*
    s2(9)   *178*
    s4   *180*
    s4(3)   *180*
    s6   *180*
    s6(2)   *180*
    s8   *182*
    s8(1)   *182, 183*
    s8(2)   *185, 188*
    s8(3)   *182, 183*
    s10   *183*
    s11   *183*
    s14   *183*
    s15   *184*
    s15(5)   *184*
    s15(6)   *184*
    s15(7)   *184*
    s15(8)   *184*
    s16(3)   *184*
    s16(4)   *184*

Police and Criminal Evidence Act 1984 (*contd.*)
 s16(5) *184*
 s16(10) *184*
 s17 *185, 186, 187*
 s17(1) *186, 187*
 s17(6) *185*
 s18 *185, 187*
 s18(1) *187*
 s18(5) *187*
 s19 *188*
 s19(4) *188*
 s19(6) *188*
 s22 *188*
 s24 *177, 182, 189, 190, 194*
 s24(2) *190*
 s24(4) *191*
 s24(5) *191*
 s24(6) *186, 191, 192*
 s24(7) *192*
 s25 *176, 177, 190, 195, 196, 197*
 s25(1) *196*
 s25(2) *195*
 s25(3) *195, 196*
 s25(4) *195*
 s26 *190, 196*
 s28 *196*
 s28(1) *196*
 s28(3) *186, 197*
 s28(5) *196*
 s29 *197*
 s30(1) *198*
 s32(1) *198*
 s32(2) *198*
 s32(6) *198*
 s35 *198*
 s37 *199*
 s37(1) *198*
 s37(2) *198*
 s37(7) *198*
 s37(9) *198*
 s38 *199, 201, 224*
 s38(1) *199*
 s39 *201*
 s40 *201*
 s40(1) *199*
 s40(3) *199*
 s40(5) *199*
 s40(12) *199*
 s40(14) *199*
 s41 *199*
 s41(1) *199*
 s41(2) *199*
 s42 *200*
 s43 *200*

Police and Criminal Evidence Act 1984 (*contd.*)
 s43(7) *200*
 s44 *200*
 s46(2) *201*
 s46(3) *201*
 s46(4) *201*
 s46(5) *201*
 s46(6) *201*
 s46(7) *201*
 s46(8) *201*
 s46(9) *201*
 s54(3) *205*
 s54(4) *205*
 s55 *206*
 s55(8) *206*
 s55(9) *206*
 s56 *181, 201, 202*
 s56(5A) *202*
 s58 *181, 182, 202, 203, 204, 210*
 s58(1) *205*
 s58(5) *202*
 s58(8) *202, 203*
 s60 *202*
 s62 *207*
 s63 *206*
 s65 *207*
 s67(8) *174*
 s76 *209, 212, 215*
 s76(2) *212, 213, 215*
 s76(3) *213*
 s76(8) *213*
 s78 *175, 203, 205, 214, 215, 216*
 s82 *212*
 s116 *181*
 s116(6) *182*
 s117 *175*
 Part I *176, 182*
 Part II *182*
 Part IV *198*
 Schedule 1 *183*
 Schedule 2 *189, 190*
 Schedule 5 *181*
Policyholders Protection Act 1975 *37*
Powers of Criminal Courts Act 1973 *33*
 s42 *246*
 s43 *32*
Prevention of Terrorism (Temporary Provisions) Act 1984
 s2 *181*
 s8 *181*
 s9 *181*
 s10 *181*
 s11 *181*

Table of Statutes and Other Materials

Prevention of Terrorism (Temporary Provisions) Act 1989   *179*
    s13A   *180*
    s14   *200*
Prosecution of Offences Act 1985   *39, 98*
    s6   *220*
Protection of Children Act 1978
    s1   *190*
Public Order Act 1936
    s1   *185*
    s7(3)   *189*
Public Order Act 1986
    s4   *185*
    s19   *190*

Rehabilitation of Offenders Act 1974   *258*
Restriction of Offensive Weapons Act 1957   *25*
Road Traffic Act 1988   *231*

Sale of Goods Act 1893   *57*
Sale of Goods Act 1979   *12, 57*
Scotland Act 1998
    s29(2)   *318*
Second Council Directive (84/5/EEC)   *287, 326*
Sex Discrimination Act 1964
    s6(4)   *299*
Sex Discrimination Act 1975   *297, 298*
Sexual Offences Act 1956
    s14   *190*
    s22   *190*
    s23   *190*
    s30(1)   *35*
Single European Act 1986   *272, 275, 278, 279, 283, 324*
Statute Law (Repeals) Act 1989   *39*
Statute of Westminster I 1275   *15*
Supreme Court Act 1981   *69, 166*
    s28   *262*
    s28(1)   *261*
    s29   *262*
    s31   *262*
    s35   *301*
    s42   *30*
    s48(2)   *260*
    s49(1)   *9*
    s50   *9*
    s69   *71*
    s69(1)   *76*
    s69(3)   *76*
    s84   *110*
Supreme Court, Rules of   *161*
    O.13   *137*

Supreme Court, Rules of (*contd.*)
    O.14   *142, 155*
    O.18 r7   *138*
    O.19   *138*
    O.22   *142*
    O.24   *140*
    O.25   *140*
    O.29 r1   *141*
    O.38   *140*
    O.38 r2A   *140*
    O.62   *144*
    O.65 r4   *137*

Taxation of Chargeable Gains Act 1992   *19*
Theft Act 1968   *38, 57, 231*
    s1   *182*
    s12   *229*
    s12(1)   *190*
    s12A   *229*
    s16   *35*
    s16(2)(a)   *25*
    s24(2)   *177*
    s25(1)   *190*
Theft Act 1978   *25*
Trade Union and Labour Relations Act 1974
    Schedule 1, para 10   *28*
Treaty of Accession 1972   *295*
Treaty of Paris 1951   *271*
Treaty of Rome 1957   *271, 272, 275, 280, 281, 282, 284, 286, 288, 289, 291, 292, 297, 303, 314, 324, 325*
    art 2   *272*
    art 3   *272*
    art 6   *324*
    art 7   *324*
    art 10   *284, 289*
    art 48   *286*
    art 68   *280*
    art 141   *297, 298, 299*
    art 195   *278*
    art 202   *275*
    art 205   *275*
    art 222   *279*
    art 226   *276, 280*
    art 230   *280*
    art 233   *281*
    art 234   *50, 282, 286, 287, 298, 299, 300, 301*
    art 249   *284, 287*
    art 308   *325*
Treaty of Westminster 1949   *283*
Treaty on European Union 1992   *272, 273, 274, 278, 280*

Treaty on European Union 1992 (*contd.*)
    art F   *324*
    Title V   *274*
Treaty on European Union 1997   *272, 274, 275, 276, 278, 283*
    art F.1   *324*
Tribunals and Inquiries Act 1992   *113*

Universal Declaration of Human Rights 1948   *304*

Vagrancy Act 1824
    s6   *190*

Wildlife and Countryside Act 1981
    s28   *31*

Part I: Sources of Law

1

Introduction: Divisions and Sources of English Law

Divisions of English law

1.1 Historical background: origins and development of common law and equity

1.2 The division between civil and criminal law

1.3 Law of tort

1.4 Law of contract

1.5 Law of property

Sources of English law

1.6 Classification of sources

1.7 Custom

1.8 Legislation

1.9 Case law

1.10 European law

Divisions of English law

1.1 Historical background: origins and development of common law and equity

The Anglo-Saxon period prior to 1066

At this time the country was divided into various areas (or kingdoms) each with its own body of law based on the customs of the people who lived there. There was no uniform system of law because of the absence of any judicial machinery to require or produce it. Instead, the laws of Saxon and Danish kings were imposed on local traditions. These laws were known as 'dooms'.

These laws were conservative and harsh in character, reflecting a society in which violence, robbery and death dominated everyday life.

The effect of the Norman Conquest 1066

Social conditions did not change significantly after the Conquest because William I did not try to impose Norman law on local conditions or customs, at least not immediately. The process of change was gradual but nevertheless dramatic because of the introduction of the feudal system. Under this system all land was owned by the King, so that at a stroke the country became a united kingdom, replacing the local kingdoms that had existed prior to 1066.

In return for various services the King granted land to his barons and other followers. They in turn granted land to tenants in return for services. This process was known as 'subinfeudation'. The result was a single kingdom but one in which different laws continued to exist in different areas, eventually collected together in the Domesday Book 1086.

William I introduced a central government based at Westminster. His closest advisers were known as the King's Council or 'Curia Regis' (arguably an early precedent for the modern Cabinet system of government).

At first, the Council performed judicial functions as well as legislative and administrative ones, but gradually the judicial functions were delegated to committees of the Council, which became the royal courts of justice. The first court to emerge was the Court of Exchequer which dealt with the collection of taxation. The next was the Court of Common Pleas, which dealt with disputes between individuals such as contract and tort. The final court to appear was the Court of King's Bench, dealing with criminal law and also any civil matter of public importance affecting the King.

At first the royal courts sat only at Westminster Hall but, in order to maintain law and order throughout the kingdom, the practice arose of sending judges into the provinces on 'assize' or 'circuit'. These judges acted under the authority of various 'royal commissions' granted to them by the Norman kings in order to try criminals.

The reforms of Henry II (1154–1189)

Henry II, a lawyer by character, laid the foundations for a system of common law, through the following reforms:

1. *the Assize of Windsor (1179)*: this placed the circuit system on a regular and permanent basis;
2. *the Assizes of Clarendon (1166) and Northampton (1176)*: these established the system of criminal justice which brought about the development of trial by jury and the investigation by the royal judges of the charges made against offenders presented by the local courts – the origin of the committal system.

3. *the Grand Assize (1179)*: introduced a new method of trying cases of disputed ownership of land, leading to the modern system of determining title to land. The civilised nature of this system helped put a stop to the use of force by those claiming wrongful dispossession of their lands.

The circuit system of royal justice administered a system of national law which was not qualified in any way by local custom. The reforms of Henry II helped to develop a national legal system based on 'common law', a law common to all persons and parts of England and Wales. At regular periods the travelling judges, who were known as 'justices in eyre', held a 'General Eyre' in each locality dealing with all the legal and fiscal matters of that area in one sitting. The General Eyre gradually died out by the mid-fourteenth century but the regular circuit system survived into modern times.

Early common law and the forms of action

Early common law was characterised by an obsession with procedural law. A system developed whereby a civil dispute had to be brought before the appropriate royal court by a writ. Each writ was drawn up to fit the precise facts of that dispute and all writs were collected on a register of writs so as to provide precedents of procedure, known as 'forms of action'.

However, the system quickly became rigid because judges, fearing a flood of actions as a result of the popularity of royal justice, stopped the issue of new forms of action, so that a litigant only had a right of action if he could find a form to fit exactly the facts of his case. Later, the strictness of this approach was relaxed to allow the issue of writs which were reasonably similar to those already on the register of writs. Nevertheless, the obsession with preserving existing forms of action was a major obstacle to the development of new rules and principles, particularly in the fields of contract law and tort.

The early system was also extremely technical and if not followed precisely could lead to failure to obtain any remedy for the wrong suffered. Frustrated litigants sometimes petitioned the King for a remedy, because the King was the 'fountain of justice'. Some of these petitions were granted and the popularity of this led to an increase in the number of petitions. The King referred them to the Lord Chancellor, one of his closest advisers, who was not only a lawyer but also regarded as keeper of the King's conscience. It was not surprising therefore that the various Lord Chancellors decided cases as much on principles of morality as on strict law.

The origins and development of equity

The body of rules and principles developed by the Lord Chancellors became known as 'equity' because they were based on concepts of fairness and justice (from the Latin, 'aequitas'). They were applied in a special court of the Lord Chancellor known as the Court of Chancery which began to recognise and enforce new rights and duties, thus providing an alternative system of justice to that of the common law courts. New remedies were also developed by the Chancery Court. Among the new rights and remedies invented by Equity in early times were those listed below.

1. *The trust* (or 'use' in early times): Party A is given the legal title to property to hold it for the benefit of Party B.
2. *The equity of redemption*: the mortgagor has the right to regain his property from the mortgagee.
3. *The doctrine of part performance*: in certain situations the law requires written contracts. If there is no writing and yet one party performs his part of the contract, equity will compel the other party to perform his part of the contract.
4. *The equitable lease*: the law requires leases over three years long to be in a deed. Equity will enforce leases that do not meet this requirement.
5. *The doctrine of equitable estoppel*: a party to a contract informs the other party that he does not intend to rely on his strict legal rights. In certain circumstances he will not be able to go back on this undertaking (for the full story of how this important doctrine was developed in the twentieth century see Lord Denning's accounts in the *Discipline of Law* (1979), pp197–223, and *The Closing Chapter* (1983), pp254–257).
6. *Restrictive covenants*: equity will enforce restrictive covenants against parties who were not parties to the original agreement, hence circumventing the common law rule of privity of contract.
7. *Contractual licences*: these now give some right to remain in property.
8. *The remedy of injunction*: a mandatory injunction is an order to perform an act; a prohibitory injunction is an order not to perform an act; a 'quia timet' injunction is an order not to do an act that a party is planning to do in the future, ie it is based on speculative evidence and requires more proof than for an ordinary prohibitory injunction; and an 'interlocutory' injunction may be granted before the full trial to preserve the situation until the trial can be held.
9. *The remedy of specific performance*: an order to perform a contract; it is granted only where the common law remedy of damages would not be adequate compensation for the breach, eg a contract for the transfer of land or of a rare or personal chattel.
10. *The remedy of rectification*: a written document that does not reflect the true intention of the parties will be corrected in certain circumstances.
11. *The remedy of rescission*: a contract will be rescinded (ie set aside as if it had not been made) where one of the parties is the victim of some unfairness or wrongdoing.
12. *The remedy of account*: to return money fraudulently obtained.
13. *Delivery-up and cancellation of documents*: a document may be returned to court to be cancelled, eg a void lease, conveyance, negotiable instrument.
14. *The process of discovery of documents*: in civil litigation to require each side to

disclose to the other all relevant documents in their possession, custody or control. This has become 'automatic' in modern litigation and is based on the 'cards on the table' philosophy, discouraging trials by ambush and encouraging sensible evaluation of the strength of an opponent's case, sometimes resulting in an out-of-court settlement.
15. *The subpoena*: an order to compel the attendance of a witness at court.
16. *The appointment of a receiver*: after one side has obtained a judgment against the other side, a financial manager may be appointed to recover debts and administer affairs. This is known as 'equitable execution', but tends to be more expensive than other methods of enforcing judgment.

During modern times equity has demonstrated its potential to continue developing new rights and remedies. From the interlocutory injunction has developed the 'Anton Piller order' and the 'Mareva injunction'. The Anton Piller order allows inspection of and prevents disposal of goods, documents, etc that may be needed in evidence at the trial: *Anton Piller KG* v *Manufacturing Processes Ltd* [1976] Ch 55. The Mareva injunction prevents disposal of assets abroad, ie it has the dramatic effect of 'freezing assets' and preventing the normal conduct of the party's financial affairs; accordingly it may only be granted if it is established that there is a real danger of the party trying to avoid probable judgment at trial by getting rid of assets in the meantime: *Mareva Compania Naviera SA* v *International Bulk Carriers SA* [1975] 2 Lloyd's Rep 509.

The story of the Anton Piller order is told by Lord Denning in the *Due Process of Law* (1980) pp123–130 and in *The Closing Chapter* (1983) pp235–239. The story of the Mareva injunction is told in the *Due Process of Law* at pp133–151 and in *The Closing Chapter* at pp225–239.

All equitable remedies are discretionary, so that even if a litigant wins a case on the merits the remedy might be withheld if, for example, the winning litigant had himself been guilty of unconscionable conduct during the dispute. This became the maxim that '*He who comes to equity must come with clean hands*' and was applied in the case of *Webster* v *Cecil* (1861) 30 Beav 62, where Cecil had offered to sell certain property and stated that the price would be £1,100. He meant to write £2,100. Webster was well aware that Cecil had made a slip of the pen but he snapped up the offer and sued for specific performance. The court refused the remedy owing to his inequitable conduct.

Equity developed other maxims to emphasise its flexible character and its concern for fair dealing. Examples are given below.

Equity is equality
This can be illustrated by reference to tenancies. At common law, if property were given to A, B and C, they took a joint tenancy therein which meant that if A died his share passed to B and C, not to A's relatives. When B died, C became entitled to the whole interest. However, if the gift had been made to 'A, B and C as tenants in

common' A's interest on his death would pass under his will or intestacy; the same would happen to B's interest when B died and C's when C died. Equity preferred the tenancy in common and accordingly wherever possible would interpret words as creating such a tenancy even if common law would have interpreted them as creating a joint tenancy. Similarly, equity would construe a tenancy in common whenever two or more persons purchased property with money found in unequal shares or where two or more lend money upon a mortgage in equal or unequal shares, even though in each case the conveyance or mortgage was expressed as jointly, or as joint tenants.

Equity looks on as done that which ought to be done
This is well illustrated by the case of *Walsh* v *Lonsdale* (1882) 21 Ch D 9. Lonsdale had agreed to lease a mill to Walsh for a period of seven years, such agreement being in writing. The rent was to be paid quarterly in arrears but Lonsdale was entitled to demand one year's rent in advance if he so desired. No lease was ever actually executed but Walsh entered into possession and paid his rent as stipulated. Lonsdale then demanded a year's rent in advance. Walsh refused to pay. Lonsdale sued for specific performance and won because the court treated the agreement for the lease as being as good as the lease itself, as if it had been formally executed.

Equity looks to the intention rather than the form
Similar to the preceding maxim, it enables equity to disregard formal procedural requirements in order to ascertain and implement the real intention of the parties.

Equity acts in personam
This maxim emphasised that equity could act against the physical person of the defendant by imprisoning him for contempt of court if he failed to obey an injunction, or order for specific performance, etc. A consequence of the maxim is that equity will not entertain a suit unless the defendant is within the jurisdiction of the court and amenable to such orders.

Equity will not suffer a wrong to be without a remedy
This maxim was used to justify the invention of new rights and duties which would not otherwise be developed because of the rigidity of the common law system of forms of action. The trust is a shining example of the exercise of the maxim.

Equity does nothing in vain
Equity's jurisdiction was based on its integrity and therefore equity would not make an order likely to prove useless or unenforceable, eg an order for specific performance of a contract for personal services. Alternative remedies that might have the desired persuasive effect would be granted instead, eg an injunction preventing the party performing those services elsewhere, or imprisonment for contempt.

Hence, whereas common law remedies were granted as of right on the merits, equity was and is a discretionary system sometimes criticised for arbitrary decision-making. In early times it was said that 'equity varies with the length of the Chancellor's foot' (John Selden). In early times equity provoked a jealous reaction from the common law judges because, despite its potential for arbitrariness, equity proved popular with litigants and consequently the common law courts lost revenue to the Court of Chancery (in those early times courts were private enterprise institutions which charged fees for the dispensation of justice). The tension between the courts of common law and equity became serious when the Court of Chancery claimed exclusive jurisdiction over cases in which the defence was of an equitable nature, and the Court would issue a 'common injunction' against the plaintiff in such a case to prevent him from continuing the action at common law or, if he had already obtained a judgment in damages, from enforcing that judgment. Disobedience of the common injunction was punished by imprisonment for contempt of Chancery. The common law judges objected to the practice and eventually the dispute was referred to James I (1603–1625) in the *Earl of Oxford's Case* (1615) 1 Rep Ch 1. The King ruled that in all future cases of conflict between rules of common law and equity, equity should prevail, but that as far as possible equity should follow the rules of common law and only intervene where common law provided inadequate remedies. The compromise was accepted and it no longer became necessary to issue common injunctions.

Equity became a body of legal principles which were described by Maitland as a 'gloss on the common law' and by Hammond as 'supplemental and superior in quality to the common law'. During the nineteenth century a number of statutes were passed which were designed to harmonise the administration of the two systems of law. For example, the Common Law Procedure Acts 1852–1860 allowed common law courts to grant equitable remedies and the Chancery Amendment Act (Lord Cairns' Act) 1858 allowed the Court of Chancery to grant the common law remedy of damages in lieu of an injunction where appropriate. A modern illustration can be found in *Page One Records* v *Britton* [1967] 3 All ER 822 (pop group 'The Troggs' took on another manager in breach of a restrictive covenant with existing manager, who sought injunction. *Held* damages in lieu because Troggs could not survive without a manager). The relevant rule is now contained in the Supreme Court Act 1981, s50.

The harmonisation process culminated in the Judicature Acts 1873 and 1875 which restructured the court system and fused the administration of common law and equity. The courts of common law and the Court of Chancery became divisions of a single High Court with one set of procedures, under which common law and equitable principles and remedies could be applied in all divisions of the High Court. The rule that equity must prevail in the event of conflict was put into statutory form and is today contained in s49(1) Supreme Court Act 1981:

'Every court exercising jurisdiction in England and Wales in any civil cause or matter shall continue to administer law and equity on the basis that, whenever there is conflict or variance between the rules of equity and the rules of the common law, with reference to the same matter, the rules of equity shall prevail.'

The Judicature Acts did not fuse common law and equity, which remain distinct systems, as illustrated by the first case decided after those Acts which involved a conflict between the two systems: *Walsh* v *Lonsdale*, above. Consequently, equity has survived as a system capable of inventing new rights and remedies in areas where common law is deficient.

1.2 The division between civil and criminal law

A major division in English law is between criminal and civil law.

There is a fundamental distinction between crimes and civil wrongs which are dealt with by different courts and by very different procedures. Some of the main differences between criminal and civil cases are set out below.

While it is important to be able to tell whether an act is criminal or not it is not easy to define exactly what a crime is. There are certain tests which may be applied to distinguish criminal acts.

Criminal cases	*Civil cases*
1. In general any citizen can bring a criminal prosecution	Generally only the person wronged may sue.
2. Brought in the name of the Crown in trials on indictment and usually prosecuted by public authorities.	Brought by private individuals.
3. An individual cannot discontinue a prosecution at will as it is brought in the public interest.	The plaintiff may discontinue at any time.
4. The Crown may put an end to the prosecution by the entry of a nolle prosequi by the Attorney-General or by decision of the Crown Prosecution Service.	The Crown cannot interfere to prevent the maintenance of a civil case.
5. The Crown may pardon a crime.	The Crown cannot pardon a civil wrong.
6. The consent of the victim is usually irrelevant to a criminal charge, eg assault.	The consent of the 'victim' will in most cases prevent him from suing.

Criminal cases	*Civil cases*
7. Sanctions primarily intended to protect the community and punish the offender (although in some cases the court can compensate the victim as well).	Remedies primarily intended to compensate the victim (although in some cases extra damages are awarded as a punishment).
8. Criminal law attempts to regulate the behaviour of the whole community	Civil law attempts to regulate relationships and behaviour between individuals.

1.3 Law of tort

In general terms a tort is a civil wrong arising from a breach of duty created not by agreement but by operation of law.

Such a breach gives rise to a cause of action for unliquidated (ie unspecified in amount) damages. The law of tort enables compensation to be made to a person for damage caused to him by another, but not all damage is actionable. The law of tort specifies when a person who has suffered damage can sue for compensation.

While some torts are also crimes a tort has no general moral character. Not all anti-social conduct constitutes a tort (eg perjury which harms another), while some conduct is tortious even though it causes no harm (eg trespass).

In general when an act is both a crime and a tort both criminal and civil proceedings may be taken in respect of the same act. However, if the victim of a minor assault brings a summary prosecution against the offender no civil proceedings may subsequently be taken in respect of that assault whether or not the offender is convicted. This forces the victim to decide whether he wishes to institute civil or criminal proceedings and avoids unnecessary proceedings for a fairly minor wrong. The police do not usually take proceedings in such cases to allow the victim to make this choice.

1.4 Law of contract

While the modern law of contract developed from the same root as the law of tort, the old action of trespass, they are now significantly different. The important difference is that in contract the obligations are primarily fixed by the parties themselves whereas the duties enforced by the law of tort are imposed by the law, although they may be varied contractually.

Some conduct is both a breach of contract and a tort. Thus if a taxi driver causes an accident in which his passenger is injured he is both in breach of his contractual obligation to convey his passenger safely and in breach of his duty to take care imposed by the tort of negligence. It is not usually important to consider whether certain conduct is both a tort and a breach of contract. The plaintiff may pick which is the most advantageous to him or he may plead both in the alternative (but of course, he cannot have two lots of damages). In general it is more advantageous to sue in tort as the measure of damages is wider, aggravated damages might be recoverable, the limitation period operates from a later date and damages which may be too remote in contract may be recoverable in tort.

1.5 Law of property

The law of property in land is complex and has developed over many centuries, and there are now many legal and equitable interests which can exist in land. A freeholder, a lessee, a mortgagee and a neighbour whose drains run under the land in question all have different interests in the land. The law of property in goods is less complicated.

Goods

Ownership or title to goods is described as 'property'. Thus where the Sale of Goods Act 1979 refers to the transfer of ownership the words used are 'the transfer of the property in the goods'.

This is general property, and a legal interest in goods which is less than ownership is called special property. Examples are hirers and bailees, and these forms of special property are based on possession.

Distinguish between ownership, possession and custody as follows:

1. If I buy a book I have ownership of the book.
2. If I agree to lend you the book for a week you have possession of the book. This means that you have a legal right to have that book for the week.
3. If you take the book without asking my permission, you have custody of the book but you have no right to retain it.

Land

Land cannot be owned absolutely because in theory the Crown is the ultimate landowner. Individuals hold land from the Crown, and the form of holding is known as 'tenure'.

In the Middle Ages there were several forms of tenure but they are no longer of practical importance. While tenure relates to the relationship between the lord and his tenant, the interest which the latter has in his land is termed an 'estate'. There were many types of estate at common law, but since 1 January 1926 there are only two legal estates in land: (1) a fee simple absolute in possession (freehold); and (2) a term of years absolute in possession (leasehold). 'In possession' means that the estate owner is entitled now and does not have to wait for a future event, and it includes the right to rent and profits. Thus where land is leased the landlord freeholder has a legal fee simple and the tenant has a legal term of years. It is this possibility of several estates and interests co-existing in the same piece of land which makes the law of land more complicated than the law relating to property in goods.

Apart from the two legal estates there are many other legal and equitable interests in land.

Real and personal property

This is a classification of property which derives from an early legal procedure. At first the Royal courts were mainly interested in acquiring jurisdiction over pleas of the Crown (crimes) and disputes over land. The earliest forms of action were those directed to recovering land and were known as real actions, as the thing (in Latin, res) in dispute could actually be recovered. Interests protected by these actions were called real property, or realty.

Actions for dispute over chattels were known as personal actions because at first the plaintiff could not insist on the return of the thing itself, and the subject matter of such actions were known as personal property, or personalty. Until the fifteenth century leases were treated as purely contractual matters and were classed as personal property. This classification persists despite the fact that a lease can now be a legal estate in land.

The difference between real and personal property is of little importance since the property legislation of 1925.

Personal property can be divided into two classes:

1. Choses in possession, which are something capable of physical possession, such as goods.
2. Choses in action, which are rights in intangible property that can only be enforced by action (eg debts, copyrights, stocks and shares). Choses in action can only be transferred by some document or formality.

Sources of English law

1.6 Classification of sources

An important aspect of any legal system is its source of law, and the English legal system has many sources – their significance varying from area of law to area, and from one period of history to another. For example, in the Anglo-Saxon period prior to the Norman Conquest of England in 1066, law was largely customary and there was little interference in law by the Crown. A few hundred years later, there had been a momentous change and the common law, derived from the authority of case law, was becoming the dominant source. In the twentieth century, case law is still of great importance, but legislation has become very much more significant over the last century or so – a trend which has been increased by the United Kingdom's membership of the European Union.

There are numerous ways of classifying sources, not always distinct.

Formal sources

These are the sources from which a legal system ultimately derives its validity and effect: for example John Austin (1790–1859) saw laws as the commands of a sovereign, to whom a habit of obedience is owed, which are enforced by sanctions.

Historical sources

These are the historical origins and development of different rules of law, deriving from separate sources (eg the common law, equity, the Law Merchant, Roman Law, Canon Law, European Law, legislation and custom).

Legal sources

These are the authorities for existing rules of law (eg case law, legislation and custom). The comparative importance of these matters has varied greatly over the last thousand years – custom now having a very minor role to play in the law, though it was of prime importance before the development of the common law.

Literary sources

The written records of legal rules, such as statutes, European legislation, law reports, statutory instruments, and, to a lesser extent, legal textbooks.

1.7 Custom

In a wide sense of the word, custom is of great historical significance. Before the developing common law extinguished the local variations of law, English law was 'custom' in the sense that, with the exception of limited royal intervention, law varied from area to area, shire to shire, town to town.

These local customary laws were not written down and were administered by the local courts. However, with the rapid development of the royal courts and royal justice which provided a law 'common' to the entire realm (that is, it was of even application and did not vary with the locality), the local customary law went into a decline and disappeared. However, though not much is known about communal, customary justice, it is clear that parts of it did exert an influence on the developing common law.

In the modern law, custom has a very limited role to play and a narrower meaning: that is, a particular rule which has existed since 'time immemorial' and must have obtained legal status within a particular location. Custom should be distinguished from mere trade usage which is simply a factual question of usual practice within a given trade and which is not subject to the stringent tests for establishing custom providing the usage is legal and reasonable. One use for trade usage is to imply terms into contracts.

Basic definition

In the *Tanistry Case* (1608) Dav Ir 28 custom was defined as 'such usage as has obtained the force of law' and is binding as regards the particular places, persons and things with which it is concerned.

The main characteristics of custom are:

1. It must have existed in fact, or by presumption, since time immemorial, namely, 1189.
2. The custom must be local, that is, confined to a particular locality. A custom cannot exist in one place which purports to confer a right to something in a different locality: *Re Ecclesfield Inhabitants* (1818) 1 B & Ald 348 (Lord Ellenborough CJ). Contrast this with the common law which is not (within England and Wales) confined to any particular locality.
3. Custom is an exception to the normal operation of the common law – though many customs have been abolished by legislation.

Essential elements of custom

Time immemorial
The custom must be shown to have existed since 1189, the time fixed by the Statute of Westminster I, 1275 as 'time immemorial' (viz. the first year of the reign of Richard I). In some cases, it is sufficient to raise a presumption of antiquity, for example by showing that a continuous customary user has existed for as long as living memory can go: *Angus v Dalton* (1877) 3 QBD 85 at 103–104. Of course, such a presumption is open to rebuttal, such as by evidence indicating that the custom began after 1189.

Must be reasonable
This requirement means that if the alleged custom is without a legal reason, it will not be upheld. 'Unreasonableness' in this context can mean that the custom arose from accident or by the permission of another, for example from a royal grant and not from a right arising in ancient times. The reasonableness of a custom is to be

adjudged at the time it began, and a custom is not unreasonable merely because it is not consistent with the common law: *Tanistry Case*, above.

Further, if the custom is repugnant to the principles of the common law it will not be upheld, for example if it entails placing a disproportionate burden on some for the benefit of others: *Wolstanton Ltd* v *Newcastle-under-Lyme Corporation* [1940] 3 All ER 101 (HL).

Must be certain
The custom alleged must be clear and certain not only in respect of the nature of the right claimed but as to the custom itself. A custom must be certain:

1. as to its general nature;
2. as to the persons alleged to be affected; and
3. as to the locality in which it is alleged to be affected (eg a town, manor, parish or county).

Must be obligatory
Unless the custom carries with it obligatory force it will not be upheld, since in that case it does not have the characteristic of a rule of law.

Must not have been interrupted
To be valid a custom must have existed without interruption since time immemorial. A mere lack of use for a period does not necessarily mean that the custom has been extinguished, though it makes it more difficult to establish.

Creation and enjoyment

Provided that the requirements stated above have been fulfilled, it is unnecessary to prove how the custom originated. However, the right claimed by virtue of custom must be enjoyed as of right (viz by virtue of the custom) and without violence, secrecy or the permission of another (nec vi nec clam nec precario): *Alfred F Beckett Ltd* v *Lyons* [1967] 1 All ER 833 (CA).

As noted in the section above, non-user will not of itself extinguish the custom though it may raise an inference that no such custom existed particularly if non-user was not accidental or due to natural causes.

Customary rights may even exist over the land of another (eg rights of entry for recreation or taking water, rights of way), and are in the nature of easements ('quasi-easements').

1.8 Legislation

Introduction

The modern importance attached to legislation and the overriding effect of Parliament's will manifested through statute has not always existed, though statutes (in one form or another) have existed for many centuries. Ancient statutes did not follow the modern form nor did they always enjoy the respect and obedience given to modern legislation by the judiciary.

Parliament initially played a minor role in law-making though it gradually developed functions of ratification of royal decrees and initiator of royal legislation (by presenting grievances to the Crown). In the modern law, statute law fulfils a number of important functions, since it not only expresses the will of the democratically elected Parliament (insofar as their will is clearly expressed in statute) but carries out social, legal and administrative reforms. With the generally conservative approach of the judiciary and the constraints of the doctrine of precedent, major legal reform is usually left to Parliament: see, for example, *Lim Poh Choo* v *Camden & Islington Area Health Authority* [1980] AC 174 (HL) where the House declined to initiate major reforms of the law governing damages for personal injury:

> '... so radical a reform can be made neither by judge nor by modification of rules of court. It raises issues of social, economic and financial policy not amenable to judicial reform, which will almost certainly prove to be controversial and can only be resolved by the legislature after full consideration of factors which cannot be brought into clear focus, or be weighed and assessed, in the course of the forensic process ... it is this limitation, inherent in the forensic process, which sets bounds to the scope of judicial law reform ...' (Lord Scarman)

The 'limitation' referred to is that the court is always confined to the issues raised and argued by the litigants and is very rarely in a position to consider the full implications of a major change in the law. Parliament is, however, in such a position and is further able to make use of reports of the Law Commission (a permanent body set up to consider issues of law reform) or a Royal Commission specially set up to consider a particular area of the law.

Modern legislation

Since 1973 there have been two major sources of legislation binding within the English legal system: the traditional parliamentary legislation was joined by that of the European Communities on the coming into force of the European Communities Act 1972. European law is dealt with in detail in Chapters 17 and 18.

The modern authority of statute law is clear and is quite able to alter and abolish sections of the common law: subject to the restraints of the democratic system, laws may also be enacted contrary to morality or religion. Further, international law is only made part of English law by statutory incorporation: *Attorney-General for Canada* v *Attorney-General for Ontario* [1937] AC 326 at 347–348.

With the exception of private member's bills most legislation is initiated by the government. The initial impetus may be that of the government seeking to implement its own party policy, or from the Law Commission (or Royal Commission) pointing out defects in the existing law and making recommendations for reform. Government bills are usually dealt with by the government ministry or department most concerned and their proposals form the basis of instructions sent to parliamentary counsel who draft the bills. The drafting of a bill involves consultation between counsel (who is a qualified barrister) and the relevant ministry (or even the Cabinet if it is sufficiently important).

Prior to its introduction into Parliament, the final draft of the relevant bill is approved by the department whose concern it is. It is also attended by counsel who drafted it, and who will draft any subsequent amendments made during its passage. The basic stages in the passage of a bill are:

1. Introduction of the Bill
2. First reading
3. Second reading
4. Committee stage
5. Report stage
6. Third reading
7. Royal Assent.

Form and functions of modern legislation

Form

In brief, there are a number of forms of legislation. The most important form is, of course, an Act of Parliament which is enacted in accordance with the unlimited legislative power of Parliament subject to compliance with European Community law. It is now well established that no court may impugn an Act or go behind it in order to see if there were irregularities of procedure: *British Railways Board* v *Pickin* [1974] AC 765.

The most commonly used version of an Act is the Queen's Printer's Copy though various editions are published (not least by Old Bailey Press), with or without commentaries, and as appendices to practitioners' works.

Functions

Reform and revision of law. This function of legislation (viz reform of 'lawyers' law') is not a function in which Parliament generally initiates, except where it has other implications. The initiative for legal reform usually comes from the Law Commission or specially appointed Royal Commissions, usually on ministerial recommendation. A separate Criminal Law Revision Committee deals with reform of the criminal law.

Social legislation. This form of legislation deals with wider and often more fundamental issues than simple revision of the substantive law. It often involves a wholesale abolition of existing principles and the creation of a new system or structure of rules: for example, major reforms of taxation, such as the creation of capital transfer tax to replace estate duty in the Finance Act 1975 (consolidated in the Capital Transfer Tax Act 1984). Capital Transfer Tax is now called inheritance tax and the 1984 Act has been renamed accordingly. While some minor revisions of the law (and some major, such as the new approach to tax planning – *Furniss* v *Dawson* [1984] 2 WLR 226 (HL)) are carried out by the courts, particularly the House of Lords, social reform is almost wholly outside the scope of the activities of the judiciary. Indeed, it is not normally in a position to take such steps and the judges are not democratically acceptable as instigators of social reform.

Consolidation. It often happens that when Parliament enacts a statute on a particular topic (eg the parts of the Finance Act 1975 dealing with capital transfer tax), the new law requires amendment which is dealt with by subsequent statutes – and additions and deletions are made as the effects and problems of the new law become apparent with time. A consolidating statute is one which brings together all the statutory provisions on a given topic and, together with any consequential amendments, puts them into one statute. An example is the Taxation of Chargeable Gains Act 1992 which consolidates the many statutory provisions relating to the taxation of chargeable gains.

Codification. In areas of the law which are well developed and the principles of which are well worked out in a body of case law and statute, statutes are sometimes enacted which bring together all the rules (both common law and statutory) and present them in a single statutory code. From thenceforth, the new statute is the starting point in that area of the law and case law will, in time, build up around the codified provisions. Examples are the Criminal Law Act 1977 (conspiracy), the Criminal Attempts Act 1981 and the Police and Criminal Evidence Act 1984.

The operation of statutes

Geographical operation

There is a presumption that an Act of Parliament is operative throughout the United Kingdom but nowhere else unless a contrary intention appears in the Act, though often law reform statutes extend only to England and Wales since Scotland and Northern Ireland have separate systems of law.

Temporal operation

A statute comes into force on the day it receives the Royal Assent unless some other date is specified in the Act itself: Interpretation Act 1978. Very often Acts now provide that they are to come into force on 'a day to be appointed' usually by a Minister or by Order in Council (ie by Statutory Instrument).

Often sections of an Act are brought into operation at different times: for example the Children Act 1989, various sections of which were brought into force on different dates and which was not fully in force until 14 October 1991.

There is a presumption against retrospective operation except for certain financial and revenue statutes: *R* v *Fisher* [1969] 1 All ER 100 and *Wilson* v *Dagnall* [1972] 1 QB 509.

Obsolescence

A statute never becomes ineffective due to the passage of time and, if it is desired that it should no longer be in force, it must be repealed, unless it was stated to be for a fixed period, or for a particular purpose, long since gone. Repeal must be by statute, and can be either express or implied, implied repeal of an earlier statute being the result of an enactment of a later inconsistent statute. Since 1965 the Law Commission has been systematically reviewing the statute book and repealing obsolete statutes in regular Statute Law Repeal Acts. As a result, generally only effective legislation remains in force.

Subordinate legislation

Despite the ever increasing volume of primary legislation, the complexities of governing modern society necessitates the delegation of legislative functions to inferior bodies, such as Ministers and local authorities. Clearly Parliament simply does not have the time or resources to enact in the form of primary legislation, which can be fully debated and scrutinised by both Houses, every single piece of legislation that is needed. The result is subordinate (or delegated) legislation: that is, legislation produced by an inferior body which nevertheless has the force of law.

Subordinate legislation may be classified: according to purpose; or according to procedure.

Classification according to purpose

Regulations for the purpose of bringing a statute into operation. Some statutory instruments are designed to bring into force the whole or part of an Act of Parliament which for some reason it is not desired to put into effect immediately upon Royal Assent. There may be more than one of these Commencement Orders per Act and there is in general no requirement as to the time after Royal Assent in which such an order must be brought in.

Regulations for the purpose of amending statutory provisions. For example the European Communities Act 1972 s2(2) delegates power to give effect to Community obligations. Orders in Council and Ministerial regulations made under these delegated powers have the effect of Acts of Parliament and may be made even where they conflict with Acts of Parliament.

Regulations which add to, explain, or give effect to general statutory provisions.

Regulations for the purpose of clothing a statute. The general principles of a piece of legislation may be expounded in the 'framework' statute, but it is left to the subordinate authority to clothe that statute, by means of delegated legislation, with the detail necessary to give it effect.

Classification according to procedure
This is the way of implementing the law-making power. The main kinds of delegated legislation are:

Orders in Council. These are the oldest and most dignified form of delegated legislation, and are made by the Queen 'by and with the advice of Her Majesty's Privy Council'. Only those Orders in Council made under statutory authority may be classified as delegated legislation, and they must be distinguished from those Orders in Council made under the Royal Prerogative.

Ministerial Regulations. Ministers of the Crown may be empowered to make regulations and issue directions, rules and orders relating to matters within their departmental jurisdiction.

Local authority and other bye-laws. These comprise rules made by local authorities and other statutory undertakers, for the regulation, administration or management of the district or service administered by the authority or undertaking concerned.

Miscellaneous categories. These include local authority orders (for example compulsory purchase orders), and measures taken by the General Synod of the Church of England.

1.9 Case law

Law reporting, in one form or another, has been an integral feature of the English legal system since the thirteenth century. The earliest reports may simply have been notes of cases collected on scraps of parchment, passed around by members of the profession for their own use. At some stage, reporting became popular enough to be performed on a wider (though unofficial) basis and the Year Books, the great series of medieval reports, began late in the reign of Edward I.

The Year Books ceased in 1535, and were ultimately superseded by the so-called innominate reports, which initially did not differ in style from the Year Books. With the appearance of reporters and commentators such as Plowden and Coke later in the sixteenth century, reporting underwent a revolution and a new thoroughness and attention to detail became apparent, in addition to the provision of learned comment.

The late seventeenth and eighteenth centuries saw a decline in the standard of reporting which was not overcome until the appearance of Burrow's Reports in the late eighteenth century. Gradually, there was an increase in professional and judicial supervision of reporting, and haphazard methods of reporting were replaced by periodical series of reports. Eventually, in 1865 the Incorporated Council of Law reporting was set up and the official Law Reports began, which continue to be produced now in the following series:

AC	Appeal Cases
QB	Queen's Bench Division
Ch	Chancery Division
Fam	Family Division

Until the new Family Division was set up, there was a series of Probate Reports (P), dealing with the reports of cases in the Probate, Admiralty and Divorce Division.

In addition to the official series (which contain the summarised arguments of counsel, and are checked by the judges responsible for the judgments), the Incorporated Council also produces the Weekly Law Reports (WLR) which appeared in 1953 to replace Weekly Notes (WN). Volumes 2 and 3 WLR reproduce all the cases to be printed in the official series and Volume 1 contains cases not reported in the official series which are considered of interest.

Various other series of reports also exist, the main commercial series of general reports being the All England Law Reports (All ER). Other major series include:

Cr App R	Criminal Appeal Reports
CMLR	Common Market Law Reports
ECR	European Court Reports (the official reports of the European Court of Justice)
RTR	Road Traffic Reports
STC	Simon's Tax Cases
Lloyd's Rep	Lloyd's List Reports (commercial law)

Case notes may also be found in the major journals, such as the Solicitors' Journal (SJ), or New Law Journal (NLJ). Current Law contains a brief summary of most cases on a monthly basis (as well as noting recent articles), whether reported or not. The Times and other newspapers also publish abbreviated reports which are sometimes cited in court.

Unreported cases may be cited to the court, transcripts being obtainable (depending on the court) from the official shorthand writers. In the case of Court of Appeal decisions, transcripts are available in the Supreme Court library. The computerised system LEXIS makes available, inter alia, a comprehensive collection of English and other cases. However, the House of Lords has warned against the bolstering up of cases by the use of unreported Court of Appeal authority: see *Roberts Petroleum Ltd* v *Bernard Kenny Ltd* [1983] 2 AC 192 discussed in Chapter 3, section 3.1.

Case law is of great importance as a source of law because of the potential for judicial law reform: see, for example, *Woolwich Building Society* v *Inland Revenue Commissioners* [1992] 3 WLR 366 (HL). The issue of judicial law reform is explored in detail in Chapter 3.

1.10 European law

The European Community and European Union

The United Kingdom acceded to the European Economic Community (as it then was) on 1 January 1973 and from that date European Community law has been an important source of English law. If a national law of a member state conflicts with Community law, the latter prevails: see *Costa* v *ENEL* [1964] CMLR 425. The framework of the European Union and the implications of Community law are explored in detail in Chapters 17 and 18.

The European Convention on Human Rights

English law has also been affected by the United Kingdom's membership of the European Convention on Human Rights. The influence of human rights jurisprudence as a source of law will increase dramatically when the Human Rights Act 1998 is brought into force (probably during the year 2000), because the Act incorporates the bulk of the Convention into English law, enabling judges to apply its provisions directly to English cases instead of indirectly. The historical influence of the European Convention and the likely impact of the Human Rights Act 1998 are explored in detail in Chapter 19.

2

Interpretation of Legislation and Law Reform

Interpretation of legislation

2.1 Introduction

2.2 The canons of interpretation

2.3 Other principles of construction

2.4 Aids to interpretation and construction

2.5 The influence of the European Convention on Human Rights and the likely impact of the Human Rights Act 1998

2.6 Judges as law reformers

Law reform

2.7 Law reform bodies

2.8 Examples of reform

2.9 A Ministry of Justice?

Interpretation of legislation

2.1 Introduction

There is nothing unusual in the process of interpretation: it is the ordinary function of the courts to interpret statutory provisions (viz give meaning to the provisions) and apply them. Problems occur when statutory words are unclear, or at least are not instantly susceptible of a clear interpretation, and the court must resolve uncertainties and, occasionally, resolve ambiguities in the language used. This latter process can be distinguished from the everyday interpretation of statutes and is sometimes called statutory construction so as to distinguish it from the more ordinary function. In the great majority of cases, litigation does not involve problems of construction: usually the argument turns on the application of clear provisions to the disputed facts of the case.

The problem of uncertainty arises generally because it is unclear whether the particular statutory provisions are meant to cover the factual situation before the court. This can be a particular problem when a situation arises which the draftsman clearly did not envisage, not necessarily because the drafting was badly done, but perhaps because the situation could not have been foreseen (especially if the statute is quite an old one) and is quite novel. After all, draftsmen cannot be expected to foresee and be able to cope with every possible eventuality: what they must do is draft provisions within their terms of reference and try to ensure that the principles are sufficiently clear to enable the courts to deal with new situations as they arise.

Ambiguity is a problem which tends to occur less frequently than uncertainty and is the problem of a particular word or phrase, used in a statute, which gives rise to two or more meanings. Since many statutes create new 'legal situations' (ie venture into areas not previously covered by statute), all of these competing meanings may be quite plausible – the problem is rarely dealt with simply by stating that one possible construction is so 'absurd' that it can be discarded. An example of ambiguity is provided by *Fisher* v *Bell* [1961] 1 QB 394, where the question arose whether a display of 'flick-knives' was included in the phrase 'offer for sale' in the Restriction of Offensive Weapons Act 1957. A strict contractual analysis of the display indicated that it was merely an invitation to treat and not an 'offer for sale', and so the court held, finding the shopkeeper not guilty of an offence under the Act.

Sometimes a provision is so badly drafted that it is almost impossible to construe sensibly – such as the ill-fated s16(2)(a) of the Theft Act 1968 (*R* v *Royle* [1971] 3 All ER 1359 – 'a judicial nightmare', per Edmund Davies LJ at p1363) which was ultimately replaced by an entire Act, the Theft Act 1978. Fortunately, such occurrences are rare.

As should already be quite clear, the function of the courts in interpreting and construing statutes is a vital one, since it is the courts which must 'give life' to the provisions by considering and applying them. To a certain extent (much greater in cases of uncertainty and ambiguity) the court is responsible for the development of the law created by a particular statute. In cases of clear and easily applicable provisions, the possibility of judicial discretion is much less, but in cases of construction, a court may have the 'last word' in the meaning and scope of a statute – at least, until Parliament intervenes. The judicial function was put quite strongly by Lord Reid in *Black-Clawson International Ltd* v *Papierwerke Waldhof-Aschaffenburg AG* [1975] AC 591:

> 'We are seeking the meaning of the words which Parliament used. We are seeking not what Parliament meant but the true meaning of what they said.'

This appears to focus on the fact that the courts are not concerned with the abstract notion of parliamentary intention but with the words by which Parliament seeks to make its intention manifest. Lord Wilberforce in the same case contrasted the different functions of Parliament and the courts:

> 'Legislation in England is passed by Parliament and put in the form of written words. This legislation is given legal effect ... by virtue of judicial decision, and it is the function of the courts to say what the application of the words used to particular cases or individuals is to be.'

He noted that the frequently repeated statement 'that it is the function of the courts to ascertain the intention of Parliament' can, if too 'unreflectingly' repeated, lead to 'neglect of the important element of judicial construction' which is not confined to a 'mechanical analysis' of words, but should be related to matters such as:

> 'Intelligibility to the citizen, constitutional propriety, considerations of history, comity of nations, reasonable and non-retroactive effect and, no doubt, in some contexts, to social needs.'

See also the purposive approach to statutory construction explained in *Pepper* v *Hart* [1993] 1 All ER 42 (HL); see section 2.2 below.

It is traditionally said that the approach of the judiciary can be classified by reference to the three canons (or rules) of statutory interpretation, the literal, golden and mischief rules. In addition to these three main rules, there are a number of other rules of construction, as well as presumptions of construction. However, as will be seen, none of these so-called rules are truly rules because much depends on the approach of the particular judge.

2.2 The canons of interpretation

The literal rule

The literal rule of interpretation is that the intention of Parliament is to be found by giving the words their ordinary and literal meaning. The general rule was stated by Lord Esher MR in *R* v *Judge of the City of London Court* [1892] 1 QB 273:

> 'If the words of an Act are clear, you must follow them even though they lead to a manifest absurdity. The court has nothing to do with the question whether the legislative has committed an absurdity.'

Thus, on this approach, the court does not consider the result of the application of the rule, which may or may not be sensible. Examples of applications of this rule where the results are at least questionable include *Inland Revenue Commissioners* v *Hinchy* [1960] AC 748 where the House of Lords held that a penal provision that a person delivering an incorrect tax return should forfeit 'treble the tax which he ought to be charged under this Act' (ie the Income Tax Act 1952, s25(3)(a)) meant that the penalty was three times the whole amount payable for the relevant year. Parliament showed that it had intended only three times the amount unpaid by changing the law shortly afterwards. See also *Fisher* v *Bell*, above, where 'offer for sale' was construed strictly in accordance with standard contract law. Was this, in fact, the 'plain meaning', or was that simply a non-technical meaning of 'display to encourage sale' – which is what the Act of 1957 appears to have been attempting to prevent?

The literal rule was the product of the nineteenth century and reached its most extreme expressions during that time. The extreme nineteenth-century view was typified by a dictum of Lord Halsbury in *Hilder* v *Dexter* [1902] AC 474:

> 'In construing a statute I believe the worst person to construe it is the person who is responsible for its drafting. He is very much disposed to confuse what he intended to do with the effect of the language which in fact has been employed.'

Compare the dictum of Lord Reid in *Black-Clawson*, quoted above.

The inflexibility of the literal approach when applied with full rigour can be seen in relation to the judicial attitude to 'omissions': that is, the willingness to give sense to a statute by reading in additional words in order to further the intention of Parliament. In *Seaford Court Estates Ltd* v *Asher* [1949] 2 KB 481 Lord Denning said:

> 'if the makers of the Act had themselves come across this ruck in the texture of it, how would they have straightened it out? He [the judge] must then do as they would have done. A judge must not alter the material of which it is woven, but he can and should iron out the creases.'

Another classic example is *Magor and St Mellons* v *Newport Corporation* [1952] AC 189; [1951] 2 All ER 839. Under the Local Government Act 1933, compensation was payable to two district councils which had their boundaries reduced by the expansion in the boundaries of Newport Corporation. However, the two councils were ultimately amalgamated into one and Newport Corporation argued that no compensation was payable since it was only payable to surviving councils and, in fact, they were not surviving, having been abolished to form one new one. The Corporation succeeded. However, in the Court of Appeal, Denning LJ dissented on the basis that the obvious intention was to provide compensation and said he had:

> '... no patience with an ultra-legalistic interpretation which would deprive them of their rights altogether ... we sit here to find out the intention of Parliament ... and carry it out, and we do this better by filling in the gaps and making sense of the enactment than by opening it up to destructive analysis.'

In the House of Lords, Lord Simonds was very critical of this approach:

> 'The duty of the court is to interpret the words that the legislature has used. Those words may be ambiguous, but, even if they are, the power and duty of the court to travel outside them on a voyage of discovery are strictly limited ... [and of Denning LJ's dictum said] it appears to me to be a naked usurpation of the legislative function under the thin disguise of interpretation and it is less justifiable when it is guesswork with what material the legislature would, if it had discovered the gap, have filled it in. If a gap is disclosed, the remedy lies in an amending Act.'

However, it is not always the case that the courts will take such a strict approach: in many constructions there is an element of filling gaps, since the words must be interpreted and a gloss put on them in order that they might be made to operate in practice. For example, in *Nothman* v *Barnet London Borough Council* [1979] 1 All ER 142 (HL); [1978] 1 WLR 220 (CA) the court had to construe para 10 of Schedule 1 of the Trade Union and Labour Relations Act 1974 which limited the right not to be unfairly dismissed and excluded it in cases, inter alia, where an employee at the date of dismissal had reached 'the normal retiring age ... or, if a man, attained the age of sixty five, or, if a woman, attained the age of sixty'.

In the Court of Appeal Lord Denning dealt with the problem in his usual robust manner:

> '... Whenever the strict interpretation of a statute gives rise to an absurd or unjust situation, the judges can and should use their good sense to remedy it (by reading words in, if necessary) so as to do what Parliament would have done had they had the situation in mind.'

The House of Lords split three to two over the construction of those words, the majority holding that para 10 specified two limits, one for when there was a 'normal retiring age' and one when there was not. The minority held that the limits were cumulative and that the plain meaning was that the earlier should apply. The objection of the majority to this approach was that it involved: 'tacking on to the end of it the words "whichever is the earlier" ' (Lord Salmon at p146).

Equally, it could be said of the majority that their approach required the insertion of the words 'where there is no normal retiring age'. Curiously enough, with the exception of Lord Russell, both majority and minority considered they were applying the 'literal meaning': 'I think that the words are clear and free from ambiguity' (Lord Diplock, dissenting).

All the Law Lords expressed strong disapproval of Lord Denning's comments in the Court of Appeal, on the ground that Lord Denning was crossing the line between interpretation and judicial legislation. The constitutional objections to judicial creativity in this field surfaced again in *Duport Steels Ltd* v *Sirs* [1980] 1 WLR 142 (HL). Lord Denning's approach to statutory construction in this case drew strong condemnation from the Law Lords on the ground that he was trying to advance a policy in conflict with the plain words of an Act of Parliament simply because he found the parliamentary policy 'unjust'. Lord Diplock emphasised the constitutional doctrine of the separation of powers as justification for confining the judiciary to the interpretation and application of statute law:

> 'Where the meaning of the statutory words is plain and unambiguous it is not for judges to invent fancied ambiguities as an excuse for failing to give effect to its plain meaning because they themselves consider that the consequences of doing so would be inexpedient, or even unjust or immoral.'

Lord Scarman agreed, saying:

> '... in the field of statute law the judge must be obedient to the will of Parliament as

expressed in its enactments ... Unpalatable statute law may not be disregarded or rejected merely because it is unpalatable.'

Hence the literal rule is a constitutional virtue in safeguarding the sovereignty of Parliament, the separation of powers, the rule of law and, indeed, the independence and impartiality of the judges themselves. However, as will be seen, it is difficult to maintain such constitutional purity in the face of judicial determination to apply the law as humanely and fairly so far as it is possible to do so.

The golden rule

This so-called golden rule is said to apply in cases where the plain meaning of the words produce a 'manifest absurdity'. In *Grey* v *Pearson* (1857) 6 HL Cas 61, Parke B (later Lord Wensleydale) said:

> '... the grammatical and ordinary sense of the words is to be adhered to, unless that would lead to some absurdity, or some repugnance or inconsistency with the rest of the instrument, in which case the grammatical and ordinary sense of the words may be modified, so as to avoid the absurdity and inconsistency but no farther.'

In *River Wear Commissioners* v *Adamson* (1877) 2 App Cas 743, Lord Blackburn said:

> 'I believe it is not disputed that what Lord Wensleydale used to call the golden rule is right, viz that we are to take the whole statute together and construe it all together, giving the words their ordinary significance, unless when so applied they produce an inconsistency, or an absurdity or inconvenience so great as to convince the court that the intention could not have been to use them in their ordinary signification, and to justify the court in putting on them some other significance, which, though less proper, is one which the court thinks the words will bear.'

An example of the application of this rule (and they are comparatively rare) is *R* v *Allen* (1872) LR 1 CCR 367: the word 'marry' in s57 of the Offences Against the Person Act 1861 (bigamy) was construed so as to give effect to the least absurd result, namely, 'go through a ceremony of marriage' – the alternative 'contract a valid marriage' would be impossible, since it is not possible to contract a valid marriage when one is already validly married. However, the rule is not entirely clear in its extent (quite apart from problems of application, see below), for on one reading it closely resembles the literal rule:

> 'The golden rule is that the words of a statute must prima facie be given their ordinary meaning.' (Viscount Simon in *Nokes* v *Doncaster Amalgamated Collieries* [1940] AC 1014)

The usual meaning is that of Parke B, quoted above. Even in that case, there must be a manifest absurdity before the court will depart from an otherwise plain meaning – and cases such as *IRC* v *Hinchy*, *Fisher* v *Bell* and *Magor and St Mellons* v *Newport* indicate that odd 'literal' constructions do not automatically lead to use of the golden rule.

The mischief rule and modern purposive construction

The 'mischief' rule is a departure from the other two rules in that it concentrates, not solely on the words of the statute, but on the purpose for which Parliament enacted the statute. It is derived from *Heydon's Case* (1584) 3 Co Rep 74 (Court of Exchequer), where the court 'resolved' that four matters are to be had regard to:

> '1st What was the Common Law before the making of the Act.
> 2nd What was the mischief and defect for which the Common Law did not provide.
> 3rd What remedy the Parliament hath resolved and appointed to cure the disease of the Commonwealth.
> And,
> 4th The true reason of the remedy; and then the office of all the Judges is always to make such construction as shall suppress the mischief, and advance the remedy.'

The narrow application of this rule occurs where the literal rule cannot be applied due to ambiguities. An example of this occurred in the case of *Kruhlak* v *Kruhlak* [1958] 2 QB 32, where it was decided that a 'single woman' for the purpose of affiliation proceedings was a woman with no husband to support her and that did not necessarily mean an unmarried woman (ie the mischief was a woman with an illegitimate baby and no means of support).

In *Universal Corporation* v *Five Ways Properties* [1979] 1 All ER 552 (CA) Buckley LJ said that:

> '... that doctrine [viz the mischief rule] ... does not entitle the court to disregard the plain and natural meaning of wide general terms in a statute. If the language is equivocal and requires construction, then the doctrine is a proper one to refer to; but if the language is quite plain then the duty of the court is to give effect to what Parliament has said.'

See also the dictum of Viscount Simons in the *Hanover* case, below, for a potentially wider approach.

In the *Black-Clawson* case, Lord Diplock noted that the original meaning of this canon of construction was that only the statute itself could be looked at to ascertain the mischief. Now, however, certain documents extraneous to the statute can be used 'with caution'. In that case, the HL held that use could be made of the report of the Law Commission (or equivalent) to discover what the mischief was (and for no other use) for which the statute was enacted. As Lord Reid pointed out:

> '... the mischief which this Act [Foreign Judgments (Reciprocal Enforcement) Act 1933, s8] was intended to remedy may have been common knowledge 40 years ago. I do not think that it is today. But it so happens that a committee ... made a full investigation of the matter and reported some months before the Act was passed.'

The advantage of this approach is that, at least, it requires the court to consider the purpose of the statute and to construe the words in that context: see *NWL Ltd* v *Woods* [1979] 1 WLR 1294 (HL).

In *Attorney-General* v *Jones* [1990] 1 WLR 859 the Court of Appeal was called upon to consider the meaning of s42 of the Supreme Court Act 1981. Lord

Donaldson MR concluded that the section is ambiguous and that it followed 'that it is both permissible and necessary to have regard to its purpose, to the mischief at which it is directed'. Again, in *Southern Water Authority* v *Nature Conservancy Council* [1992] 3 All ER 481 the question arose as to whether, for the purposes of s28 of the Wildlife and Countryside Act 1981, a water authority was an 'occupier' of land by reason of carrying out ditching operations on it. After noting that the Act itself demonstrated that 'occupier' had no fixed meaning, Lord Mustill said: 'We must therefore consider what kinds of occupier must have been intended to fall within the prohibition with which we are here concerned.' His conclusion ('that the section was never intended to apply to persons such as the ... water authority') was reinforced by consideration of other provisions of the Act and their effect.

There is a growing tendency, perhaps encouraged by Europe, towards a purposive construction of statutes which do not deal with penal or revenue matters and this principle is not limited to statutes passed after the principle had been authoritatively declared by the courts: *R* v *Registrar-General, ex parte Smith* [1991] 2 WLR 782. Indeed, in *Pepper* v *Hart* [1993] 1 All ER 42 Lord Griffiths felt able to say:

> 'The days have long passed when the courts adopted a strict constructionist view of interpretation which required them to adopt the literal meaning of the language. The courts now adopt a purposive approach which seeks to give effect to the true purpose of legislation and are prepared to look at much extraneous material that bears on the background against which the legislation was enacted.'

See further section 2.4, below.

2.3 Other principles of construction

In common with most rules and principles governing the interpretation of statutes, the following principles are not of mandatory application and much depends on the particular problem before the court, as well as the preferences of that court.

The statute should be read as a whole

This is obviously an important principle since words often take on a particular, more precise, meaning when they are placed in the context of other words. Since the courts profess to be giving effect to the intention of Parliament, to read statutory words out of context could scarcely be justified. As Cross writes, 'it is difficult to believe that the notion of construction in complete isolation was ever taken wholly seriously' though there are isolated examples of attempts to do such, even in the twentieth century: see Lord Greene's criticism of the trial judge in *Re Bidie* [1948] 2 All ER 995.

In *Attorney-General* v *Prince Ernest Augustus of Hanover* [1957] AC 436 (HL) it was held that:

'... the Act (enacted in Queen Anne's reign) must be construed as it would have been construed immediately after it became law.' (Lord Normand)

Viscount Simonds made what were then somewhat 'revolutionary' remarks concerning 'context':

'... words, and particularly general words, cannot be read in isolation, their colour and context are derived from their context ... I use 'context' in its widest sense, which I have already indicated as including not only other enacting provisions of the same statute but its preamble, the existing state of the law, other statutes in pari materia, and the mischief which I can, by those and other legitimate means, discern the statute was intended to remedy.'

This passage was cited by Lord Upjohn in *DPP* v *Schildkamp* [1971] AC 1, 23. Its importance lies in the fact that it recognises that a reasonable result often cannot be achieved by a 'purely semantic process' (Cross), by simply trying to construe the actual words and only looking to the object of a statute when the words lead to doubt.

Ejusdem generis

This simply means that when a series of words is used, a series of particular words followed or preceded by general words, such as 'and other such' or 'including', the general words must be construed with reference to the particular words. The particular words (there must be at least two to make a 'series': *Allen* v *Emmerson* [1944] KB 362) are said to make a genus, that is, a category or 'family' of objects. To include a particular matter or situation within the general words, they must be shown to be ejusdem generis ('of the same type') with the particular words.

In *Powell* v *Kempton Park Racecourse* [1899] AC 143 (HL) the court had to decide whether a racecourse was comprised in the definition of 'house, office, room ... or other place' within the Betting Act 1853. It was held not to be ejusdem generis with those places, ie 'other place' was confined to indoor places.

Presumptions

Presumptions, when they are used, merely presume that a given approach is to be taken (eg penal statutes are strictly construed), but such a presumption always gives way to contrary intention (express or implied). Common presumptions include:

1. Penal statutes are construed strictly in favour of the accused. For example, in *R* v *Highbury Corner Magistrates' Court, ex parte Di Matteo* [1991] 1 WLR 1374, Watkins LJ said:

   '... the words used in s43 [of the Powers of Criminal Courts Act 1973] should be given their natural and ordinary meaning, unless on a reading of the section there are two possible interpretations, in which case, this being a penal provision, the interpretation most favourable to the defendant should be adopted.'

In *Wychavon District Council* v *National Rivers Authority* [1993] 2 All ER 440 Watkins LJ said that it was a well-known truism that:

'... where ... a word appears ... in a penal section and ... it is capable of bearing more than one meaning, the meaning most favourable to the subject must be adopted.'

2. Criminal offences usually require fault (that is, mens rea: *Sweet* v *Parsley* [1970] AC 132).
3. Statutes are not intended to derogate from common law rights.
4. Statutes are not intended to have retrospective effect.
5. Parliament, when enacting statutory duties in apparently absolute terms, is to be presumed not to have intended that those terms should apply so as to reward serious crime committed in the past; likewise, Parliament must be presumed not to have intended to promote serious crime in the future: *R* v *Registrar-General, ex parte Smith* [1991] 2 WLR 782.
6. United Kingdom legislation does not apply to foreign persons outside the United Kingdom where acts are performed outside the United Kingdom: *Arab Bank plc* v *Mercantile Holdings Ltd* [1994] 2 All ER 74.

The principle that an ambiguity in a statute should not be construed in a manner which derogates from common law rights does not constrain the courts to invent an ambiguity or to construe an ambiguity in a way which does not make good sense: per Lord Templeman in *Waltham Forest London Borough Council* v *Thomas* [1992] 3 WLR 131.

In *Pepper* v *Hart* [1993] 1 All ER 42 Lord Mackay of Clashfern LC suggested that any ambiguity in a taxing statute should be resolved in favour of the taxpayer. However, the majority approach, which favours a purposive approach to the interpretation of statutes, and the use of external aids such as Hansard to discover Parliament's 'true' intention, may mean that the use of presumptions will become less common in future years.

Conflicting provisions

It was sometimes suggested that where there is a conflict between two sections in the same Act, the last of them must prevail. This is not the case. In such circumstances, if the provisions cannot be reconciled, the court must determine which is the leading provision and which the subordinate and which must give way to the other: *R* v *Moore* [1995] 4 All ER 843 (court gave 'rectifying construction' to conflicting provisions of the Powers of Criminal Courts Act 1973).

Subordinate legislation

Where this is doubt, subordinate legislation is to be construed so as not to be ultra vires the enabling Act: *Raymond* v *Honey* [1983] 1 AC 1.

Reconciliation with European Community law

Primary or subordinate legislation enacted to give effect to the United Kingdom's obligations under Community law must be interpreted as far as possible so as to achieve the intended results, even though this may involve a departure from a literal application of the words which the legislature has chosen to use: per Lord Diplock in *Garland* v *British Rail Engineering Ltd* [1983] 2 AC 751. See also per Lord Dillon LJ in *Morris Angel and Son Ltd* v *Hollande* [1993] 3 All ER 569 (CA). See further Chapter 18.

When United Kingdom judges are required to interpret European Community law itself they must follow the same principles of interpretation as the European Court of Justice, ie because EC law is expressed in generalised terms of principle, and is full of gaps and lacunae, judges must fill in those gaps according to the spirit of Community law. This is known as the European 'teleological' approach: per Lord Denning MR in *Bulmer (HP) Ltd* v *J Bollinger SA* [1974] 3 WLR 202 (CA). It will be seen that United Kingdom judges have adopted a more purposive approach to the construction of purely domestic law (section 2.4 below), but it should be noted that this approach falls well short of the kind of judicial creativity employed for the interpretation of European Community law.

2.4 Aids to interpretation and construction

Internal aids

These are matters appearing within the Queen's Printer's Copy of the Act, and can, with a few exceptions, be used to construe the individual provisions of that Act: that is, the court may read the statute as a whole, in order to understand the provisions from their context. Indeed, it is often the case that a statute will contain a specific section defining certain key words used throughout all, or part, of the statute.

The matters to which the court may have regard in construing statutory provisions are:

1. *The long title* – the formal description of the Act, placed at its beginning (in *R* v *Secretary of State for Foreign and Commonwealth Affairs, ex parte Rees-Mogg* [1994] 1 All ER 457 Lloyd LJ said 'the days are long since past when courts declined to regard the long title as an aid to construction').
2. *The short title* – the shorter title used for reference.
3. *Schedules* – these are fully part of the statutory provisions, in any case, and have the same legal force as the individual sections themselves.
4. *Preambles* – in older legislation preambles were often included, being (sometimes) lengthy expositions of the purpose of the enactment. They are rarely used in modern legislation, but may be used to construe the statute: see *Prince Ernest Augustus of Hanover*'s case, above.

Marginal notes may not be used to interpret an Act since these are simply summaries of particular sections and are not part of the statute: *Re Woking Urban District Council* [1914] 1 Ch 300, 322. However, regard may be had to them for an indication of the mischief with which the Act is dealing: *R v Kelt* [1977] 1 WLR 1365. Further, the traditional view was that *punctuation* should be disregarded, but it seems that this is no longer the position unless to take account of it would so alter the sense as to be contrary to the plain intention of the statute: *Hanlon v The Law Society* [1981] AC 124.

Statutory history

In some cases the historical development of particular statutory provisions may be used to construe the modern version, particularly if there is a change in the words used. In *Stoke-on-Trent City Council v B & Q (Retail) Ltd* [1984] 2 All ER 332, the House of Lords made use of the statutory predecessors of the Local Government Act 1972 s222 in order to decide whether the council had authority (usually vested in the Attorney-General) to use an injunction (a civil law remedy) to prevent a breach of the criminal law – in this case, the legislation prohibiting Sunday trading. The addition to the current Act of words not in the predecessor section were held to grant that authority to local councils. See also *Armah v Government of Ghana* [1968] AC 192.

External aids

These are matters lying outside the actual statute itself, some of which may be used as an aid to construction. Examples include the Interpretation Act 1978, dictionaries, reports from law reform bodies and reports of parliamentary debates in Hansard. Each will be considered in turn.

The Interpretation Act 1978
This contains some basic rules, eg that male includes female, singular includes plural unless otherwise stated in the statute, and that an Act comes into force as soon as it receives Royal Assent unless the date for its operation is expressly postponed by the Act in question.

Dictionaries
These would seem to be useful, especially if the court is seeking to discover the ordinary, 'literal' meaning of a word. However, much depends on the individual tribunal, and there are instances of dictionaries being used and others where their use is rejected. In *R v Callender* [1992] 3 All ER 51 the Court of Appeal sought assistance from the Shorter Oxford English Dictionary in establishing the meaning of 'employment' in the context of s16 of the Theft Act 1968: see also *R v McFarlane* [1994] 2 WLR 494 (reference was made to Oxford dictionaries when deciding that 'clipper' was a prostitute for purposes of s30(1) of the Sexual Offences Act 1956).

Law Commission (or Royal Commission) reports

Reports of committees, such as the Law Commission, are not generally admissible, but they are admissible in order to discover the 'mischief' which a particular statute was enacted to remedy, though it had once been thought that such reports were even inadmissible on this point: *Assam Railways and Trading Co Ltd* v *IRC* [1935] AC 445. However, in the *Black-Clawson* case (above) the House of Lords held that such reports could be used to ascertain the mischief – but no further. The reason is quite clear, and was noted as early as 1898 by Lord Halsbury in *Eastman Photographic Materials Co Ltd* v *Comptroller General of Patents* [1898] AC 571 at 575:

> 'I think no more accurate source of information as to what the evil or defect which the Act ... now under consideration was intended to remedy could be imagined than the Report of that Commission which had led to the particular enactment.'

See also dicta of Lord Denning MR in *Letang* v *Cooper* [1965] 1 QB 197, to similar effect.

Reports of Parliamentary debates – Hansard

For many years it could be said that the use of these was absolutely prohibited: see Lord Wilberforce in *Black-Clawson*. His Lordship gave two reasons why this was so. The first is a practical objection: 'the courts would merely have to interpret ... two documents instead of one'. The second is a constitutional objection, concerning the division in function between Parliament and the courts: 'it would be a degradation of that process if the courts were to be merely a reflecting mirror of what some other interpretation agency might say'.

However, in *Pepper* v *Hart* [1993] 1 All ER 42 the House of Lords (Lord Mackay of Clashfern LC dissenting) concluded that the time had come to relax, in certain circumstances, the rule prohibiting courts from referring to parliamentary material as an aid to statutory construction. The relaxation applies (in the words of Lord Browne-Wilkinson):

> 'where: (a) legislation is ambiguous or obscure, or leads to an absurdity; (b) the material relied on consists of one or more statements by a minister or other promoter of the Bill together if necessary with such other parliamentary material as is necessary to understand such statements and their effect; (c) the statements relied on are clear'.

The case which gave rise to this decision concerned the interpretation of s63 of the Finance Act 1976. There was no doubt that the section was ambiguous and that statements made by the responsible minister during the Bill's passage through Parliament were clear. Accordingly, their Lordships were able to take account of the minister's statements, as recorded in Hansard in deciding upon the section's meaning.

An example of a court (the House of Lords) exercising its new but restricted ability to refer to statements made by a minister in Parliament and recorded in Hansard is *Scher* v *Policyholders Protection Board (No 2)* [1993] 4 All ER 840 where the House of Lords was called upon to construe certain provisions of the

Policyholders Protection Act 1975. The House consented to receive, in accordance with *Pepper* v *Hart*, extracts from the parliamentary records of debates during the committee and report stages of the passage of the Policyholders Protection Bill through the House of Lords (see also *Chief Adjudication Officer* v *Foster* [1993] 2 WLR 292). However, in *R* v *Secretary of State for Foreign and Commonwealth Affairs, ex parte Rees-Mogg* [1994] 1 All ER 457 the court refused to look at Hansard because, inter alia, the statutory provision in question was not ambiguous.

Lord Browne-Wilkinson's three conditions for the use of Hansard do not apply to the interpretation of United Kingdom primary or delegated legislation which implements international or European Union law, where a broader, purposive approach and a more generous use of Hansard is permitted: *Three Rivers District Council* v *Bank of England (No 2)* [1996] 2 All ER 363 (QBD, Commercial Court).

Whilst many commentators welcomed *Pepper* v *Hart* as a sensible step for ascertaining legislative intentions, some have criticised it:

'Reference to Hansard necessarily sets an interpretation within the immediate contemporary understanding of the government of the day ... It risks imposing a literalism in interpretation ... on the basis of an interchange, possibly in a nearly empty chamber late at night, indicative only of what [the government] would like the law to be.' (David Robertson, *Judicial Discretion in the House of Lords* (1998), pp171–172, 183, Clarendon Press, Oxford)

2.5 The influence of the European Convention on Human Rights and the likely impact of the Human Rights Act 1998

The Human Rights Act 1998 will bring about fundamental changes in statutory interpretation when it is brought into effect. Section 3 of the 1998 Act provides that 'So far as it is possible to do so, primary legislation and subordinate legislation must be read and given effect in a way which is compatible with the Convention rights' (ie the European Convention on Human Rights). This applies to existing or future legislation. It is unlikely that s3 will be interpreted as overturning all the existing principles of statutory construction, but there is little doubt that it will encourage judges to take a much more purposive approach based on the morality of legislation and the spirit of the Convention. For details of the Act see Chapter 19, and see further Marshall 'Interpretating Interpretation in the Human Rights Act' [1998] PL 167 and Klug 'The Human Rights Act 1998, *Pepper* v *Hart* and All That' [1999] PL 246.

2.6 Judges as law reformers

It has been seen that the process of statutory interpretation offers opportunities (albeit limited ones) for judges to develop legal principles and reform aspects of law.

In Chapter 3 judicial law reform will be considered in the context of the doctrine of precedent – but again the conclusion will be that the scope for such reform is inevitably limited for constitutional reasons, not least the sovereignty of Parliament. The main engine for law reform is the legislature and in practice this means the governing party, influenced by its political ideology, public opinion, pressure groups and the like. It is also influenced by the work of non-political law reform bodies, on which judges, lawyers and academics play important roles. The rest of this chapter is concerned with the work of these law reform bodies.

Law reform

2.7 Law reform bodies

Standing committees

In 1959 the Home Secretary set up the Criminal Law Revision Committee to examine such aspects of criminal law as the Home Secretary may from time to time refer to it. The first important reference was the law of larceny and similar offences which resulted in the Theft Act 1968. Subsequently, the Lord Chancellor established the Statute Law Commission, the Law Reform Committee and the Commission on Private International Law.

The Law Commission was set up by the Law Commission Act 1965 for the purpose of promoting the reform of the law. The Commission consists of a chairman (a High Court judge) and four others, all of whom must be persons appearing to the Lord Chancellor to be suitably qualified by the holding of judicial office, by experience as a person having a general qualification (within the meaning of s71(3) of the Courts and Legal Services Act 1990), or as a teacher of law in a university.

In their twenty-fifth annual report (1990) the Commission observed that the ultimate proof of the value of their work comes only when Parliament decides to give legislative effect to their recommendations. In practice this means that they must find favour with the government, and that either a Bill must be included in the government's legislative programme, or that a Private Member who is successful in the ballot for Private Members' Bills decides to introduce a Bill giving effect to the recommendations in one of the Commission's reports.

In its twenty-eighth annual report, published in April 1994, the Commission complained that only four of its reports had been implemented since 1990 and that more than thirty, many of them uncontroversial, were awaiting legislative attention. This was despite efforts by the Law Commission to improve its communications with MPs and raise its profile with the general public. Indeed, its efforts appeared to backfire when the tabloid press and some MPs criticised its 1992 Report (No 207) on reform of family property law for 'subverting family values'. It seems likely that the role of the Law Commission will be confined by political pressures to making only technical improvements in branches of the law. See further Cretney 'The Law Commission: True Dawns and False Dawns' (1996) 59 MLR 631.

Ad hoc committees

Over the last 100 years many changes in law have been based on the reports of Royal Commissions or official committees. They are made up of a wide cross-section of people who are often experts or are concerned in the matters in question. These committees are impartial and non-political. However, the members are not sitting full time and so they are slow and not suitable for matters requiring long-term continuing examination. The committee makes recommendations which must be considered by the Minister concerned and if he is satisfied proposals are put before Parliament.

2.8 Examples of reform

Law Commission

Examples of reports implemented, in whole or in part, include *Family Law: Review of Child Law: Guardianship and Custody* (Law Com No 172) – Children Act 1989; *Law of Contract: Minors' Contracts* (Law Com No 134) – Minors' Contracts Act 1987; *Deeds and Escrows* (Law Com No 163), *Transfer of Land: Formalities for Contracts for Sale etc of Land* (Law Com No 164); and *Transfer of Land: The Rule in Bain v Fothergill* (Law Com No 166) – Law of Property (Miscellaneous Provisions) Act 1989; *Corroboration of Evidence in Criminal Trials* (Law Com No 202) – ss32 and 33 Criminal Justice and Public Order Act 1994; *Rape within Marriage* (Law Com No 205) – s142 Criminal Justice and Public Order Act 1994; and *Statute Law Revision: 13th Report* (Law Com No 179) – Statute Law (Repeals) Act 1989 (which continues the long tradition of repealing specified enactments which are no longer of practical utility).

Royal Commissions

An example of extensive reform can be seen in the changes in the law resulting from the Royal Commission on Criminal Procedure (1981) Cmnd 8092 and recommendations on several aspects of the criminal process. Its recommendations have largely been implemented in two Acts:

1. The Police and Criminal Evidence Act 1984 dealing with police powers in the investigation of offences.
2. The Prosecution of Offences Act 1985 dealing with the prosecution of offences.

Another notable example in recent years is the work of the Royal Commission on Criminal Justice (1993) Cmnd 2263. The Commission investigated the causes of miscarriages of justice in the criminal justice system and its eventual findings and proposals have led to many reforms of the law of evidence, criminal procedure and the appeal system, notably the setting up of the Criminal Cases Review Commission.

During 1999 a Royal Commission will examine the second stage in the reform of the House of Lords, ie what should replace the traditional chamber following the first stage of reform (the abolition of the voting rights of the majority of hereditary peers).

2.9 A Ministry of Justice?

Outside the United Kingdom this is very common. The basic concept is that all the 'legal' functions of government, including responsibility for the police, prisons, courts, judiciary and prosecutions, should be entrusted to a single government department under the control of an elected minister who is directly accountable to the legislature. In 1998 50 Labour MPs signed a Commons motion urging the creation of such a Ministry of Justice, on the grounds that it would increase efficient administration of justice and provide a more powerful and responsive engine for law reform. However, the government (and the main opposition party, the Conservatives) are unconvinced of the need for such reform, and many backbench MPs also oppose reform on the ground that the independence of the legal system might be at risk if the functions outlined above are put under the control of a single political minister, particularly if he is not a lawyer.

In the United Kingdom the duties of a Ministry of Justice are divided as follows:

1. The Lord Chancellor is responsible for the courts and legal aid.
2. The Home Secretary is responsible for police, probation service and prisons.
3. The Attorney-General is responsible for the Crown Prosecution Service and giving the government legal advice.
4. The Director of Public Prosecutions is responsible for criminal prosecutions.
5. The two main branches of the legal profession make their own arrangements for the education and training and discipline of lawyers. However, the Lord Chancellor may obtain greater powers to regulate such matters under proposals contained in the Access to Justice Bill 1999.

The Lord Chancellor is accountable only to the House of Lords but there is a minister of state in the Lord Chancellor's Department who is accountable to the House of Commons. The presence of the junior minister has weakened the argument that the Department is not sufficiently accountable to the Commons.

The creation of the Law Commission in 1965 also lessened the pressures for a Ministry of Justice to facilitate law reform. However, an uncomfortable division of functions remains and the role of the Lord Chancellor is likely to be a continuing source of contention and debate, especially within the context of a reformed House of Lords.

For an historical account of the movement towards a Justice Department for the United Kingdom: see Hall and Martin 'A Ministry of Justice' [1998] NLJ 830.

3

The Doctrine of Precedent

3.1 Introduction

3.2 Stare decisis: meaning

3.3 Principal elements of stare decisis

3.4 The operation of precedent within the hierarchy of the courts

3.5 The European Court of Justice (ECJ)

3.6 The European Court of Human Rights (ECHR)

3.7 The House of Lords

3.8 The Court of Appeal

3.9 The High Court

3.10 Other courts

3.11 Reform proposals

3.1 Introduction

It is an important aspect of the English legal system that most of the major rules and principles of the common law have been developed (often by accident) and further elaborated in the daily work of the courts in resolving the disputes brought to them. Unlike most major continental jurisdictions (including Scotland), which are based upon the 'civil law' system of the Romans, statute and codified law have not played such an important part in the development of English law although the vast growth of legislation over the last century or so has altered this balance very significantly.

Traditionally it is said that judges do not make law, but only declare what the law is, by considering and applying rules laid down in previous cases, which themselves were based on the rules of earlier cases and so on. However, this 'declaratory' theory of law is simplistic in the following aspects:

1. It overlooks the fact that the judges must of necessity extend and modify existing

rules in so far as the established rules must be applied to new cases, to new situations. In the words of Lord Radcliffe:

> 'Judicial law is always a reinterpretation of principles in the light of new combinations of facts ... true, judges do not reverse principles, once well established, but they do modify them, extend them, restrict them or even deny their applicability to the combination in hand.' (*Not in Feather Beds*, 1968.)

2. It overlooks the creative function of the more 'dynamic' lawmakers amongst the judiciary (more apparent at certain periods of history than others) who develop existing rules into a new form which it is possible to categorise as 'new law'. For example, the 'distillation' of the principle in *Hughes* v *Metropolitan Railway* (1877) 2 App Cas 439 by Denning J in *Central London Property Trust Ltd* v *High Trees House Ltd* [1947] KB 130 to 'create' a new form of equitable forbearance (promissory estoppel). The classic statement of the heart of the modern tort of negligence, the duty of care, by Lord Atkin in *Donoghue* v *Stevenson* [1932] AC 562 was a departure from precedent and a generalisation of more limited rules.

Nevertheless, it remains true that the judicial process of applying and developing the law is largely a conservative one and radical change is left to Parliament.

Precedent, in the sense of treating like cases alike and following established rules of law and practice, has been present in the English legal system for many centuries, as is clear from the continued interest in law reporting from the thirteenth century onwards. However, the medieval view of decided cases was not that of the twentieth century, which sees the decision in the case itself as binding. The medieval attitude was that decisions were examples of the application of rules of law, several examples demonstrating an established custom which would be very persuasive in a medieval court.

The modern doctrine only emerged in the nineteenth century with the establishing of an official system of reliable law reporting which, of course, is indispensible to the operation of the doctrine. Formerly, any report of a case made by a barrister was regarded as reliable, as this was usually a precondition to the citation of a report in court. Now, however, a report by a solicitor or a person having a Supreme Court qualification (within the meaning of s71 of the Courts and Legal Services Act 1990) has the same authority as if it had been made by a barrister: s115 of the 1990 Act.

Although there is no rule that an unreported decision may not be put before the court in a subsequent case, almost invariably precedents will be contained in law reports. Indeed, in *Roberts Petroleum Ltd* v *Bernard Kenny Ltd* [1983] 2 WLR 305, Lord Diplock opined that the House of Lords should not allow the citing before it of transcripts of unreported judgments of the Court of Appeal unless they contained a statement of some principle of law the substance of which could not be found in any law report. The *Practice Statement (Judgments)* [1998] 2 All ER 667 confirms the procedural practice followed by the Court of Appeal (Civil Division) and High Court in this area, namely that leave to cite unreported cases will not usually be granted unless counsel are able to assure the court that the transcript in question contains a relevant statement of legal principle not found in reported authority and that the authority is not cited because of the phraseology used or as an illustration of the application of an established legal principle. For a critique, see Bennion 'Citation of Unreported Cases: A Challenge' [1998] NLJ 1520.

It is surprising to note that there is no official control over which cases are and are not reported. It is arguable that this is an unhappy state of affairs given the obvious importance of law reports to the doctrine of precedent in the English legal system.

In addition to the generally conservative views of judges, the doctrine is upheld for a number of reasons.

Fairness

It is based on a principle of 'fairness', that is treating like cases alike. This is also convenient in that it is obviously wasteful of effort to reconsider every like case and consider what the applicable principles should be. Precedent allows a judge to have a ready-made solution to hand, with the possibility of distinguishing previous decisions if they are significantly different. Most cases do not involve disputes as to the principles to be applied at all, since these are usually clear, but rather disputes as to the facts and the application of the rules to those facts.

Certainty

In theory, with the large number of points of law which have already been decided, it should be a relatively simple matter to discover the relevant principles applying in the particular case. Of course, the many variations in facts and circumstances mean that in some cases, the relevant principles are unclear (or their application is uncertain). However, the great majority of cases do not involve disputes as to the law, only as to the facts and the application of those rules.

Flexibility

The fact that the decisions are decisions of judges, and not statutory provisions, means that they can be subsequently overruled or distinguished (see below) where they are incorrect, cease to be applicable or are simply not applicable to the instant case.

Predictability

Predictability relates to the certainty argument. With the large number of reported decisions it should, in theory at least, be relatively easy to predict on the basis of those decisions the relevant rules applicable and the result of the present case. This enables legal advisers to give to their clients more precise and accurate advice as to what are their chances of success in bringing or defending a particular claim. Consequently, the settlement of claims and disputes, saving time and money for all concerned, becomes more likely.

A fairly typical example of the judicial attitude is shown by Russell LJ's speech in *Gallie v Lee* [1969] 2 Ch 17 (CA):

> 'I am a firm believer in a system by which citizens and their advisers can have as much certainty as possible in the ordering of their affairs ... an abandonment of the principle that this court follows its own decisions on the law would I think lead to greater uncertainty and tend to produce more litigation ...'

3.2 Stare decisis: meaning

The doctrine of binding precedent or 'stare decisis', stated briefly, is that any previous decision of a court, depending upon its position in the hierarchy of courts, is binding on a subsequent judge who is dealing with a case which is not reasonably distinguishable from that previous decision.

The doctrine arises out of the rule that it is not the function of a judge to make new law but only to decide cases in accordance with the law as it exists. Thus in effect it is part of the doctrine of the separation of powers.

It is the statement of law made by the judge in his judgment which may (or may not) be binding. Such statements may be either 'ratio decidendi' or 'obiter dicta'.

3.3 Principal elements of stare decisis

Ratio decidendi

It is ironic that the ratio, the heart of the doctrine, is so difficult to define since it is the ratio alone which is binding on future courts (within the court hierarchy). The status of the ratio is well illustrated by a dictum of Lord Reid's in *Nash (Inspector of Taxes) v Tamplin & Sons Brewery (Brighton) Ltd* [1952] AC 231:

> 'It matters not how difficult it is to find the ratio decidendi of a previous case, that ratio must be found. It matters not how difficult it is to reconcile that ratio when found with statutory provisions or general principles, that ratio must be applied to any later case which is not reasonably distinguishable.'

Two points can be made about the ratio decidendi:

1. Only pronouncements of law can be ratio.
2. Only those reasons (or reason) which are necessary to reach the decision in the particular case can be ratio.

The combination of the findings of fact and the items in these two points are responsible for the judgment in the case. As the American jurist Wambaugh put it:

'When a case turns on only one point the proposition or doctrine of the case, the reason for the decision, the ratio, must be the general rule without which the case must have been decided otherwise ...'

A L Goodhart regards the ratio as the legal principle to be derived from the judge's decision on the basis of the facts regarded by the judge as material. However, Goodhart's test does not really help decide which facts are regarded by a court as material.

One major difficulty which occasionally arises is the inability of later courts, or lawyers, to discover the ratio of a particular case. In these circumstances, the various attempts at defining 'ratio' may be of some help, but often it is in the difficult cases that these attempts break down – particularly if, as sometimes happens, in a multiple-judge court, each judge gives a different reason for his decision (or one judge gives separate reasons for his decision). A striking example is the House of Lords' decision in *Boys* v *Chaplin* [1971] AC 356 where there were *five* separate lines of reasoning (though a majority agreement on some points, and on the ultimate result).

A further problem is when it is impossible to discover the legal basis for the decision of the court on the facts: for example, the case of *Elder, Dempster & Co Ltd* v *Paterson, Zochonis & Co Ltd* [1924] AC 522 (HL). In *Scruttons Ltd* v *Midland Silicones Ltd* [1962] 2 WLR 186 (HL) Lord Reid said of the *Elder, Dempster* case:

'It can hardly be denied that the ratio decidendi of the *Elder, Dempster* decision is very obscure ... when I look for such a principle I cannot find it, and the extensive and able arguments of counsel ... have failed to discover it.'

In such a case, the only binding element of the judgment is the decision itself and it only binds in cases which are not reasonably distinguishable. However, in the *Midland Silicones* case Lord Reid held that the *Elder, Dempster* case was distinguishable in several respects. Further it will only be principles of law which are binding. Therefore words which are construed in a certain way in one contract need not have the same effect in future contracts: see *Ashville Investments* v *Elmer Contractors* [1988] 3 WLR 867.

Obiter dicta

These are legal reasons or pronouncements which are not necessary for the decision in the case, and hence are not ratio and not binding. They are therefore said to be obiter – 'by the way'. In *Behrens* v *Bertram Mills* [1957] 1 All ER 58, Devlin J said:

'If a judge gives two reasons, both are equally binding. But he may make an obiter observation – it is equally possible for it to be an additional reason, but he may not wish to make it part of the ratio, for example, because he is not sufficiently convinced of its cogency to give it the full authority of precedent.'

Although an obiter dictum (plural – 'dicta') is not binding on subsequent courts, some may be influential or 'persuasive' in later cases in helping make up a judge's mind on a novel or difficult point (see 'persuasive authority', below). If such dicta are used in a later case they may become binding if they are made part of a later ratio decidendi. Well-known examples of influential obiter dicta are the 'neighbour principle' of Lord Atkin in *Donoghue* v *Stevenson* [1932] AC 562 (HL) and the extension of this to negligent misstatements in *Hedley Byrne* v *Heller & Partners Ltd* [1963] 3 WLR 101 (HL).

Persuasive authority

These are decisions and dicta which are not binding but may strongly influence future decisions which use them as support – this is particularly so if such dicta are part of the judgments of respected judges. Such authority includes:

1. Obiter dicta – see above.
2. Recommendations of the Privy Council – these are paticularly influential, since the Judicial Committee is usually made up of Law Lords.
3. Decisions of courts of Commonwealth jurisdictions.
4. Decisions of Scottish or Irish courts, even though they are not part of the English legal system.
5. Decisions of courts inferior to that hearing the case.

Distinguishing

It is inherent in the doctrine of 'treat like cases alike' that where a case is sufficiently dissimilar then the previous rule need not be followed – the two cases may be distinguished. It is often said that a previous case can only be distinguished if it is 'reasonable' to do so, eg if the material facts are dissimilar. Of course, what is reasonably distinguishable depends on the particular cases and the particular court – some judges being more inclined to 'distinguish' disliked authorities than others. If the notion is carried to extreme lengths then judges would be able to avoid the unpleasant consequences of applying disliked rationes by distinguishing them on inadequate grounds. While distinguishing is an important factor in maintaining fairness and flexibility in stare decisis, if carried to such lengths it would undermine the system.

Overruling and reversing

Overruling

A court of competent jurisdiction within the hierarchy of the courts may declare that the decision in a previous case is no longer good law: for example because that previous court did not correctly interpret the law or because the later court considers that the rule of law contained in the previous ratio is no longer supportable or desirable. An example of the former is the overruling of *Horsler* v *Zorro* [1975] Ch 302 by the House of Lords in *Johnson* v *Agnew* [1979] 2 WLR 487, and an example of the latter is the House of Lords' decision in *Miliangos* v *George Frank (Textiles) Ltd* [1975] 3 WLR 758 which overruled previous authority that judgments could not be given in foreign currency. Cases may also be overruled by statute.

It should be remembered that only courts of competent jurisdiction may overrule previous precedents. For example, the House of Lords may overrule the decisions of any court in the legal system, including its own: see, for example, *Murphy* v *Brentwood District Council* [1990] 3 WLR 414 where the House of Lords overruled its own decision in *Anns* v *Merton London Borough* [1977] 2 All ER 492. The Court of Appeal (Civil Division) may neither overrule a decision of the House of Lords nor its own previous decisions. This is so even if the reason for the earlier decision is now questionable or clearly wrong. In the *Miliangos* case (above), the Court of Appeal had sought to alter the foreign currency rule itself by following its own earlier decision in *Schorsch Meier GmbH* v *Hennin* [1975] QB 416, which had refused to follow earlier House of Lords' authority (*Re United Railways of Havana and Regla Warehouses* [1961] AC 1007) affirming the currency rule. The House of Lords agreed that the rule should be changed, but that it was not the function of the Court of Appeal to disregard House of Lords' authority:

> 'Courts which are bound by the rule of precedent are not free to disregard an otherwise binding precedent on the ground that the reason which led to the formulation of the rule embodied in such precedent seems to the court to have lost cogency ...' (Lord Simon)

However, whilst the Court of Appeal cannot overrule a decision of the House of Lords, or one of its own previous decisions, it is permitted to 'depart' from (ie not follow) such a decision in limited circumstances: see further section 3.8 below.

The effect of overruling a previous authority is that authority is treated as 'bad law' and is no longer binding either on subsequent courts, or the court itself which is overruling it. In effect, this gives overruling 'retrospective' effect since it affects not only future cases, but the present one also – even though that case arose before the precedent was overruled. Indeed, this can seem unfair to parties who may have relied on that precedent only to find it overruled on appeal. This is one reason why courts are reluctant to overrule well-established precedent and accounts, in part, for the fact that the House of Lords rarely overrules its previous decisions.

Reversing

This is simply an overturning, on appeal, of the decision of the court below that hearing the appeal. The appeal court will then substitute its own decision.

Per incuriam statements

A decision which is reached per incuriam is one reached through 'want of care'. A Court of Appeal decision reached per incuriam is not binding on subsequent Courts of Appeal: *Young* v *Bristol Aeroplane Co Ltd* [1944] KB 718 (CA). Similarly, the

High Court is not bound by one of its own previous decisions reached per incuriam: *Younghusband* v *Luftig* [1949] 2 All ER 72.

Per incuriam does not signify mere carelessness on the part of the court, or the fact the case was badly argued or judgment badly reasoned. It is confined to the narrow grounds of failure to consider binding authority or statute. In *Morelle Ltd* v *Wakeling* [1955] 2 QB 379 (CA) Lord Evershed MR stated that:

> '... the only cases in which decisions should be held to have been given per incuriam are those of decisions given in ignorance or forgetfulness of some inconsistent statutory provision or of some authority binding on the court concerned: so that in such cases some part of the decision or some step in the reasoning on which it is based is found, on that account, to be demonstrably wrong.'

In *Secretary of State for Trade and Industry* v *Desai* (1991) The Times 5 December Scott LJ said that to come within the category of per incuriam it must be shown not only that the decision involved some manifest slip or error but also that to leave the decision standing would be likely, inter alia, to produce serious inconvenience in the administration of justice or significant injustice to citizens.

However, this rule does not appear to permit the Court of Appeal to ignore decisions of the House of Lords. In *Cassell* v *Broome* [1972] AC 1027 Lord Denning MR held the House of Lords' decision in *Rookes* v *Barnard* [1964] AC 1129 to be per incuriam on the basis that it ignored previous House of Lords' decisions. He was rebuked sternly by the House of Lords who considered that the Court of Appeal 'really only meant' that it 'did not agree' with the earlier decision.

> 'Even if this is not so, it is not open to the Court of Appeal to give gratuitous advice to judges of first instance to ignore decisions of the House of Lords.' (Lord Hailsham)

Similarly, it had been assumed that the High Court could not use the per incuriam principle in order to depart from a decision of the House of Lords or Court of Appeal, but, rather surprisingly, the principle was invoked by the High Court recently in order to depart from a decision of the Court of Appeal: *Hughes* v *Kingston-upon-Hull City Council* (1998) The Times 9 December, which is considered in Chapter 8, section 8.6.

3.4 The operation of precedent within the hierarchy of the courts

It is a fundamental to the doctrine of precedent that it operates within the system of the courts and the authority of a decision and a court's ability to overrule a previous decision depends on its position within that hierarchy. Each court will be considered in turn.

3.5 The European Court of Justice (ECJ)

Except as to questions of the interpretation of European law (referred under art 234 of the EC Treaty) the ECJ has no authority within the English legal system. Where it has authority its decisions are binding on the courts of member states, but not binding on itself.

3.6 The European Court of Human Rights (ECHR)

The decisions of the ECHR are not binding on United Kingdom courts, though they have been treated as persuasive in order to resolve ambiguities in English law and this will probably continue to be the case when the Human Rights Act 1998 is implemented. Section 2 of the 1998 Act requires a court determining a question relating to a Convention right to 'take account' of the opinions and decisions of the ECHR. Hence, whilst these decisions will not be strictly binding, they will become highly persuasive whenever provisions of the 1998 Act are being applied.

3.7 The House of Lords

As the final court of appeal in the English legal system, the decisions of the HL are binding on all courts beneath it in the hierarchy. The HL for the greater part of the twentieth century also regarded itself as bound by its own decisions, following *London Street Tramways Co v London County Council* [1898] AC 375:

> 'I do not deny that cases of individual hardship may arise ... but what is that occasional interference with what is perhaps abstract justice, as compared with the inconvenience ... of having each question subject to being re-argued.' (Lord Halsbury)

However, in 1966 the HL changed its opinion and issued a *Practice Statement* [1966] 1 WLR 1234:

> 'Their Lordships regard the use of precedent as an indispensable foundation upon which to decide what is the law and its application to individual cases. It provides at least some degree of certainty upon which individuals can rely in the conduct of the affairs, as well as a basis for orderly development of legal rules.
>
> Their Lordships nevertheless recognise that too rigid adherence to precedent may lead to injustice in a particular case and also unduly restrict the proper development of the law. They propose, therefore, to modify their present practice and, while treating former decisions of this House as normally binding, to depart from a previous decision when it appears right to do so.
>
> In this connection they will bear in mind the danger of disturbing retrospectively the basis on which contracts, settlements of property and fiscal arrangements have been entered into and also the special need for certainty as to the criminal law.
>
> This announcement is not intended to affect the use of precedent elsewhere than in this House.'

The 1966 *Practice Statement* was considered by Lord Bridge of Harwich when the House of Lords overruled in *R v Shivpuri* [1986] 2 WLR 988 their own recent decision in *Anderton v Ryan* [1985] 2 All ER 335. He felt that the *Statement* was 'an effective abandonment of [the House's] pretension to infallibility' and, where there was an error, it was better that it should be speedily corrected. Lord Hailsham was prepared to distinguish *R v Shivpuri* from *Anderton v Ryan* but the clear statement that the earlier case has been overruled is a welcome sign of a seeking to achieve as much clarity in the law as possible rather than relying upon fine and perhaps misleading distinctions.

The *Practice Statement* did not alter the fundamental attitude of the HL to precedent, but allowed the House more flexibility in changing its mind. However, as can be seen, the HL also emphasised the need for certainty, and the power which the *Practice Statement* acknowledged has been used very sparingly. In *Miliangos v George Frank (Textiles) Ltd* [1975] 3 WLR 758 the Law Lords said that the 1966 *Statement* could be utilised in civil law if a better rule can be stated, provided that no procedural difficulties arise from the change in the law.

It is perhaps the undesirability of causing uncertainty which has often led the HL to decline to overrule established authority and to say that such matters are best left to Parliament. A good example of this is *Jones v Secretary of State* [1972] 2 WLR 210 where seven law lords considered the earlier decision of *Re Dowling* [1967] AC 725, and though four considered it to have been wrongly decided they refused to overrule it. Little guidance was forthcoming as to when the HL would overrule previous precedents. Lord Reid said that a change would be considered in old authority 'where some broad issue is involved', but that 'it should only be in rare cases that we should reconsider questions of construction of statutes and other documents'.

Lord Wilberforce stated his fears concerning too willing an approach to reconsider statutory construction on the basis that litigants would take a chance and appeal in the hope of persuading the House to reconsider. Lord Simon suggested that inconvenience in the construction of statutes caused by judicial interpretation should more appropriately be left to the consideration of Parliament. Lord Pearson was concerned that the advantage of finality should not be lightly thrown away 'by too ready use of the recently declared liberty to depart from previous decisions'.

Nevertheless, where a court is faced with conflicting decisions of the House of Lords as to the construction of a statute, the later decision should be followed, certainly where the court believes that the earlier HL decision would have been reversed if the HL in the earlier case had been aware of the principle enunciated in the later HL decision: *Moodie v Inland Revenue Commissioners* [1993] 1 WLR 266, itself a decision of the House of Lords.

The House of Lords is also prepared to adopt an 'activist' approach so as to modernise the common law where there is an overpowering need to do so, even if it means overruling precedents which have stood for many years, in both civil law

(*British Rail* v *Herrington* [1972] 1 All ER 749 on occupiers' liability to child trespassers) and the criminal law.

In *R* v *R (Rape: Marital Exemption)* [1991] 4 All ER 481 (HL) the House held that the common law rule that a husband could not be guilty of raping his wife because marriage implied the wife's consent to sexual intercourse was obsolete. Such a retrospective change to the criminal law does not infringe the European Convention on Human Rights because it is a progressive and foreseeable evolution of the common law through judicial law-making: *CR* v *UK* (1995) The Times 5 December (ECHR).

The Law Lords have shown greater hesitation in effecting change in other areas, where the need for change may still be highly contentious. In these areas the 'leave it to Parliament' argument has prevailed: examples are the reduction of what would otherwise be murder to manslaughter in a particular class of case: *R* v *Clegg* [1995] 1 All ER 334 (HL); and the abolition of the presumption of doli incapax in the area of children's liability for crimes: *C* v *DPP* [1995] 2 All ER 43 (HL). In the latter case the 'leave it to Parliament' approach led quite swiftly to statutory abolition of the presumption of doli incapax: s34 Crime and Disorder Act 1998. In *C* v *DPP*, above, Lord Lowry gave the following guidance on the propriety of judicial law-making:

> '... (i) if the solution is doubtful, the judges should beware of imposing their own remedy;
> (ii) caution should prevail if Parliament has rejected opportunities of clearing up a known difficulty or has legislated while leaving the difficulty untouched;
> (iii) disputed matters of social policy are less suitable areas for judicial intervention than purely legal problems;
> (iv) fundamental legal doctrines should not be lightly set aside;
> (v) judges should not make a change unless they can achieve finality and certainty.'

The issue of judicial law-making has continued to trouble the Law Lords in recent cases. In *Westdeutsche Landesbank Girozentrale* v *Islington London Borough Council* [1996] 2 All ER 961 (HL) the Law Lords were divided three to two on the question whether the rules of equity should be judicially developed so as to permit an award of compound interest on a judgment for repayment of money had and received. The majority were against such development, taking the view that Parliament had twice legislated on the matter and that therefore it must be left to Parliament to amend that legislation in order to provide the remedy in question. The two dissenting Law Lords (Lords Goff and Woolf) were prepared to develop the law of restitution to provide the remedy in order to meet the 'moral justice' of the case. Lord Goff made the following observations on the creative role of judges:

> '... it is the great advantage of a supreme court that, not only does it have the great benefit of assistance from the judgments of the courts below, but also it has a greater freedom to mould, and remould, the authorities to ensure that practical justice is done within a framework of principle. The present case provides an excellent example of a case in which this House should take full advantage of that freedom ...
> ... It would be strange indeed if the courts lacked jurisdiction in such a case to ensure that justice could be fully achieved by means of an award of compound interest, where it

is appropriate to make such an award, despite the fact that the jurisdiction to award such interest is itself said to rest upon the demands of justice. I am glad not to be forced to hold that English law is so inadequate as to be incapable of achieving such a result. In my opinion the jurisdiction should now be made available, as justice requires, in cases of restitution, to ensure that full justice can be done. The seed is there, but the growth has hitherto been confined within a small area. That growth should now be permitted to spread naturally elsewhere within this newly recognised branch of the law. No genetic engineering is required, only that the warm sun of judicial creativity should exercise its benign influence rather than remain hidden behind the dark clouds of legal history.'

In another recent case the Law Lords were again divided three to two on the issue of judicial law reform, but this time Lord Goff found himself in the majority favouring such reform. In *Kleinwort Benson Ltd* v *Lincoln City Council and Other Appeals* [1998] 4 All ER 513 (HL) the Law Lords held (Lords Browne-Wilkinson and Lloyd dissenting) that the common law rule precluding recovery of money paid under a mistake of law should no longer be maintained. Since such judicial development is retrospective in effect the decision enables those who entered transactions in reliance on the overruled decisions to re-open them, ie the decision effectively allows the six-year limitation period to run afresh – a bold piece of judicial law reform! The majority were convinced, however, that the need to meet the 'moral justice' of the case must prevail over any problems the change of law might cause in the commercial world. The minority, whilst agreeing on the need for the change, preferred to leave the whole issue of reform of restitution law and limitation periods to Parliament. For a critique: see Bennion 'A Naked Usurpation?' [1999] NLJ 421.

3.8 The Court of Appeal

For the purposes of the doctrine of precedent a 'full court' (of five or more judges) has the same authority as that of a three-judge court or even a two-judge court since they are all sittings of equal status: *Langley* v *North West Water Authority* [1991] 3 All ER 610.

In general, both divisions of the CA are bound by the decisions of the HL and by their own previous decisions. To this general rule there are some exceptions.

The Civil Division

Three exceptions were established in *Young* v *Bristol Aeroplane Co Ltd* [1944] KB 718:

1. Where there are conflicting CA decisions, the CA may choose which one to follow.
2. The CA may disregard one of its own previous decisions if it cannot be reconciled with a decision of the HL. If such a decision was later in time than

the HL decision and had overlooked the HL decision it would be covered by the per incuriam exception, below. If it had not overlooked the HL decision but had chosen not to follow it (eg because it thought the HL decision was reasonably distinguishable) it is for the CA to decide at its discretion whether the apparently conflicting CA precedent should be followed – clearly if the HL precedent was not reasonably distinguishable the CA *must* disregard the conflicting CA precedent.

If the HL decision was later in time than the conflicting CA decision then the CA may choose to follow the prior CA decision if it believes that the HL decision involved only a general consideration of the issues raised by the earlier CA decision and has not substantially undermined its authority. If, however, this is not the case it would appear that the CA must treat the conflicting CA precedent as impliedly overruled by the later HL decision: *R* v *Secretary of State for the Home Department, ex parte Al-Mehdawi* [1989] 1 All ER 777 (CA).

3. It may disregard a decision of the CA reached per incuriam, ie without due care, for example as a result of overlooking a relevant binding authority: *Rakhit* v *Carty* [1990] 2 All ER 202, *Rickards* v *Rickards* [1989] 3 WLR 748 and see further *Per incuriam statements* at section 3.3 above.

Note that the 1966 *Practice Statement* gives no power to the Court of Appeal: *Davis* v *Johnson* [1978] 2 WLR 553 (HL). In this case, in the Court of Appeal, Lord Denning MR had suggested that the 1966 *Practice Statement* could be adopted by the Court of Appeal (Civil Division) so as to enable the judges to reform the law in a sensible and humane manner. However, when the case went to the House of Lords the Law Lords were strongly critical of Lord Denning's attempts to confer on the Court of Appeal a wider discretion than that given by *Young* v *Bristol Aeroplane Co Ltd*. Lord Diplock observed that it is the House of Lords, as the appellate court of last resort, which is best placed to reform the law judicially. Further, to extend the 1966 *Practice Statement* to the Court of Appeal would greatly undermine certainty and predictability of law-making.

Criminal Division

The rules laid down in *Young* v *Bristol Aeroplane Co Ltd*, above, have been used as guidelines by the Criminal Division, which also applies the doctrine of stare decisis less strictly than the Civil Division in cases where the liberty of the subject may be affected by previous decisions in which the law has either been misapplied or misunderstood: *R* v *Taylor* [1950] 2 KB 368, *R* v *Gould* [1968] 2 WLR 643 and *R* v *Newsome; R* v *Browne* [1970] 2 QB 711.

Both divisions – a summary of the rules of precedent

In *Limb* v *Union Jack Removals Ltd* [1998] 2 All ER 513 at 522–523 Brooke LJ summarised some of the aspects of the doctrine of precedent in so far as it relates to both divisions of the Court of Appeal. He suggested that the following five principles can be derived from the authorities:

1. Where the court has considered a statute or a rule having the force of a statute its decision stands on the same footing as any other decision on a point of law.
2. A decision of a two-judge Court of Appeal on a substantive appeal (as opposed to an application for leave) has the same authority as a decision of a three-judge or a five-judge Court of Appeal.
3. The doctrine of per incuriam applies only where another division of the court has reached a decision in ignorance or forgetfulness of a decision binding upon it or of an inconsistent statutory provision, and in either case it must be shown that if the court had had this material in mind it *must* have reached a contrary decision.
4. The doctrine does not extend to a case where, if different arguments had been placed before the court or if different material had been placed before it, it *might* have reached a different conclusion.
5. Any departure from a previous decision of the court is in principle undesirable and should only be considered if the previous decision is manifestly wrong. Even then it will be necessary to take account of whether the decision purports to be one of general application and whether there is any other way of remedying the error, for example by encouraging an appeal to the House of Lords.

3.9 The High Court

As a court of first instance

The divisions of the High Court sitting as trial courts are bound by decisions of the courts superior to them, but are not binding on themselves. An example of a refusal by a High Court judge to follow a decision of another High Court judge, both sitting at first instance is the case of *Re Jeffrey S Levitt Ltd* [1992] 2 All ER 509. Although Ferris J had made his decision after full argument, Vinelott J felt compelled to reach a different conclusion, not least because a House of Lords speech and certain statutory provisions had not been drawn to Ferris J's attention, and subsequent decisions, one of the Court of Appeal, supported his (Vinelott J's) view of the matter. However, judges still tend to follow the decisions of their fellow puisne judges on the basis of judicial comity (mutual co-operation) and certainty. In *Colchester Estates* v *Carlton Industries* [1984] 2 All ER 601 Nourse J in the Chancery Division was faced with two conflicting first instance decisions (*Swallow Securities* v *Brand* (1983) 45 P & CR 328 and *Hamilton* v *Martell Securities* [1984] 1 All ER 665).

He said that, since the second decision was not given in ignorance of the first, the general rule was that a first instance judge should follow the second judgment of the two conflicting cases, in the interests of certainty.

Where a judge of first instance is confronted by conflicting decisions of the Court of Appeal, in the later of which the earlier had been fully considered, he is bound to follow the later decision: *Miliangos* v *George Frank (Textiles) Ltd* [1975] 3 All ER 801.

It had been thought that the High Court could not invoke the per incuriam rule as justification for departing from a House of Lords or Court of Appeal decision, but the rule was used for this purpose in *Hughes* v *Kingston-upon-Hull City Council* (1998) The Times 9 December: see further Chapter 8, section 8.6.

As an appeal or review court: Divisional Courts

Usually Divisional Courts of the High Court have treated the rules of *Young* v *Bristol Aeroplane Co Ltd*, above, as equally applicable to them, and for this purpose a full court of five judges has the same authority as one composed of three or even two judges: *Younghusband* v *Luftig* [1949] 2 All ER 72.

In *R* v *Governor of Brockhill Prison, ex parte Evans* [1997] 1 All ER 439 the Divisional Court departed from several of its own previous decisions concerning judicial review of prison governors. Lord Bingham CJ emphasised that the Divisional Court should not depart from its own decisions unless satisfied that they are clearly wrong, especially where public officials such as prison governors have founded their practice on those decisions. See also *R* v *Greater Manchester Coroner, ex parte Tal* [1984] 3 WLR 643.

3.10 Other courts

The inferior courts are bound by the decisions of those above (ie the superior courts). The position of the Crown Court, as a superior court, is unclear – though it may be that a High Court judge sitting in the Crown Court is in the same position as a puisne judge sitting in the High Court at first instance.

3.11 Reform proposals

Though the doctrine of precedent exists for a number of reasons, including certainty and predictability, it is not entirely clear that it does not go too far and lead to rigidity and inflexibility, particularly given the reluctance of the House of Lords and the general inability of the Court of Appeal (Civil Division) to overrule their own decisions. The 'leave it to Parliament' view in the House of Lords does not necessarily mean that Parliament will deal with the matter immediately, quickly, or even at all.

The following matters could be said to mitigate the harshness of the doctrine:

1 Appeals.
2 Parliamentary reform.
3 Distinguishing – must generally be 'reasonable', though see Lord Reid in *Jones* v *Secretary of State* (above).
4 *Young* v *Bristol Aeroplane* exceptions – of limited application.

Should the Court of Appeal be permitted to depart from its own previous decisions (see above)? Would this necessarily mitigate some of the rigours of the doctrine – or would there be similar reluctance to overrule as the House of Lords has shown?

It has been suggested that the courts could adopt the practice of 'prospective overruling', under which the effect of a change in the law would take place only from a future date and would not affect those who have reasonably relied on the overruled decision, such as the parties in the case which is resulting in the decision to overrule. This practice is followed in the superior courts of the United States of America. In Europe the European Court of Justice adopts a modified version of prospective overruling by giving the benefit of the change in the law to the party in the case who persuaded the court to make the change. Both kinds of prospective overruling offend the principle that like cases should be treated alike and have been opposed on this ground by some senior judges, including Lord Mackay, the former Lord Chancellor. However, other senior judges have expressed support for the concept of prospective overruling: for example Lord Browne-Wilkinson in *Prudential Assurance Co* v *London Residuary Body* [1992] 3 All ER 504 at 512b.

It has also been suggested that a codification of the law would solve, or at least alleviate, some of the problems which are created by the operation of the doctrine of precedent (eg too much case law and other sources of authority; inflexibility, etc). However, this would depend on what type of codification was selected. Broadly speaking, there are two main types of codification:

1. The type predominant in English legislation such as the Theft Act 1968 and the Sale of Goods Act 1979 (this Act really consolidates the original Act of 1893, which had codified the then existing case law, with case and statute law which occured in the interim), that is, an amalgamation and reform of all the law relating to a given topic and putting it in the form of a single statute. This does not affect the basic operation of stare decisis, but merely creates a new starting point from which new case law will build up (in interpreting the statute) – with some reference, perhaps, to the pre-codification of the law.
2. The type predominant in civil law jurisdictions on the Continent (such as France or West Germany) where the code is absolute and there is no doctrine of stare decisis at all. Cases are not binding authority and the practice of the courts does

not become a source of law until the point is established by the agreement of many different judgments.

It will be noted that the two main types of codification are quite different in their operation. The effect of the first type on the present system would not be fundamental, since the doctrine of precedent would still remain, with all its attendant problems (and advantages). The only positive advantage would be that the source of law on a given topic would now be concentrated in one place and that some of the previous problems would be ironed out – it would prevent the accretion of too much case law. However, case law on the interpretation of the new codified statute would soon appear. The effect of the second type, on the other hand, would be radical since it would involve an abolition of the doctrine of stare decisis and the development of new techniques for the interpretation of the new code. It is true that some of the problems with the present system would be dealt with (eg the existence of too much authority) but new problems would be created. It would have to be decided, for example, how the code would be constructed: should it be detailed, dealing with every conceivable situation or should it merely lay down more general guidelines and directions for the courts to follow? The sort of problems that this type of codification might engender are as follows:

1. If the code is a detailed code (of the 'absolute' second type), then this will entail the need for a better system of law reform and revision, since it will be no longer be possible for judges to develop the law on a case-by-case basis. Certainty would be achieved, but at the cost of rigidity and slowing down of the development of legal principles.
2. If the code is more general, laying down fairly broad guidelines and rules but leaving a certain amount to judicial discretion, this would permit more flexibility to cover novel situations, but perhaps only in return for too much discretion and consequential uncertainty (of course, much depends on the issue of the desirability of certainty in the law).
3. Uncertainty as to the interpretation of the new code and its relation to the old law.
4. The need to develop new techniques for the interpretation of the code.
5. The time and cost needed to codify the law.

Part II: The Personnel of the Legal System

4

The Judiciary and the Magistracy

The judiciary

4.1 Introduction – the concept of a career judiciary

4.2 Judicial offices and statistics

4.3 Appointment of judges

4.4 Training of judges

4.5 Removal and retirement

4.6 Immunity, independence and impartiality

4.7 Functions of a judge

The magistracy

4.8 Lay magistrates (Justices of the Peace)

4.9 Stipendiary magistrates

The judiciary

4.1 Introduction – the concept of a career judiciary

Unlike some countries the English legal system does not have a career-structured judiciary, that is certain lawyers chosen at the beginning of their career to be judges and who work their way up the profession. All English judges, from the ranks of Lords of Appeal in Ordinary to county court judges, are at present usually chosen from the ranks of practising lawyers, mainly barristers but with a steadily increasing number of solicitors.

By contrast in France, for example, judges are 'career judges' in the sense that they do not practise as advocates prior to appointment as judges. There is only one form of training, at a national Judges' College (the École Nationale de la Magistrature). Entrance is for postgraduate law students through competitive exams and interviews. Training at the college lasts for two years, during which the trainee judge receives a salary (in other countries training can last for up to six years!). Training involves courses on criminology, penology, procedural law, evidence, how to handle witnesses, psychology, ethnic awareness and so on. Exams are held in each subject. On graduating from the College the typical young French judge will start as an examining judge (a juge d'instruction) in criminal law in a small town, deciding whether there is sufficient evidence to prosecute and supervising the collection of evidence by the police. He/she will then preside over trials, possibly starting as a juvenile court judge. During tenure he/she must undergo compulsory continuous education involving refresher courses, often lasting at least a week for each course. Promotion is decided on the basis of experience, interests and wishes and according to vacancies. Promotion is determined by relevant central government civil servants.

In the English legal system there have been such substantial improvements in the training of judges that some have argued we are moving closer to the establishment of a judicial training college and a career-structured judiciary. However, in 1996 Henry LJ, the head of the Judicial Studies Board responsible for the training of judges, said that such developments did not represent the first steps towards the creation of such a college but rather were part of a gradualist approach designed to satisfy an independent-minded and critical clientele. For the training of judges see section 4.4 below.

4.2 Judicial offices and statistics

Lord Chancellor

The Lord Chancellor is the only judge appointed on an openly 'political' basis since, by convention, he is a member of the Cabinet. He is appointed by the Crown on the advice of the Prime Minister. Where there is a change of government there will be a change of Lord Chancellor. For example, Lord Irvine was appointed to replace Lord MacKay following the election of the Labour government on 1 May 1997.

The Lord Chancellor holds the highest judicial office and is: Speaker of the House of Lords; the government's principal spokesman on matters of law; a minister of the Crown; and (usually) a Cabinet minister.

The Lord Chancellor recommends most judicial appointments to the Crown. The Lord Chancellor is ex officio head of the Chancery Division of the High Court and president of the Court of Appeal (although he/she rarely sits in either); he/she presides (when present) over judicial sittings in the House of Lords. No 'formal' qualifications are required but he/she is invariably a lawyer of considerable experience and standing and may previously have served the government as a law officer (Attorney-General or Solicitor-General).

Lord Chief Justice

This appointment is made by the Crown on the recommendation of the Prime Minister after consultation with the Lord Chancellor. In the absence of the Lord Chancellor, the Lord Chief Justice is president of the High Court; he/she is also president of the Queen's Bench Division and presides over the Criminal Division of the Court of Appeal. In practice, he/she sits in the appellate courts, normally the Court of Appeal or the Queen's Bench Divisional Court.

Master of the Rolls

This appointment is again made by the Crown on the advice of the Prime Minister. He/she presides in the Civil Division of the Court of Appeal, a key position. Although the House of Lords is the final appellate court, the number of civil appeals heard by the House in an average year is about 50 while it is over 1,500 in the Civil Division of the Court of Appeal.

President of the Family Division

He/she is appointed by the Crown on the advice of the Prime Minister. He/she is responsible for the management and organisation of the Family Division of the High Court and presides as a judge in that Division. He/she is an ex officio member of the Court of Appeal.

Vice-Chancellor

He/she is appointed by the Crown on the advice of the Prime Minister. He/she organises the business of the Chancery Division of the High Court and sits as a judge in that Division. He/she is an ex officio member of the Court of Appeal.

Lords of Appeal in Ordinary

They are appointed by the Crown on the advice of the Prime Minister.

They must have held 'high judicial office', as defined by s25 of the Appellate Jurisdiction Act 1876 (eg a judge of the High Court or the Court of Appeal), for not less than two years, or for not less that 15 years have been:

> '(a) person who has a Supreme Court qualification, within the meaning of s71 of the Courts and Legal Services Act 1990;
> (b) an advocate in Scotland, or a solicitor entitled to appear in the Court of Session and the High Court of Judiciary; or
> (c) a practising member of the Bar of Northern Ireland.' (Section 71(2), Sch 10, para 1, Courts and Legal Services Act 1990.)

The maximum number of servicing Law Lords is set at 12. They hold office during good behaviour, but may be removed on the address of both Houses of

Parliament. Although full members of the House of Lords they do not usually take part in political debate.

Lords Justices of Appeal

They are appointed by the Crown on the advice of the Prime Minister.

They must have a ten-year High Court qualification within the meaning of s71 of the Courts and Legal Services Act 1990; or be a judge of the High Court.

The maximum number of Lord Justices is set at 38. They sit in the Court of Appeal, either division, but usually the court is organised so that at least one appeal judge has experience of the branch of law involved in the case before the court.

High Court judges

They are appointed by the Crown on the advice of the Lord Chancellor.

Often referred to as 'puisne' judges – inferior or subordinate – their correct title is 'Justices of the High Court'. They must have a ten-year High Court qualification, within the meaning of s71 of the Courts and Legal Services Act 1990, or be a circuit judge who has held that office for at least two years.

Until the passage of the 1990 Act appointments were restricted to practising barristers (usually Queen's Counsel) of at least ten years' experience of advocacy or barristers who had become circuit judges. The 1990 Act permitted solicitor circuit judges to be considered for appointment and also provided for the extension of rights of advocacy in the High Court to solicitors. Eventually this should lead to more solicitor judges being appointed to the High Court bench. Lord Mackay, the then Lord Chancellor, also used his delegated powers under the 1990 Act to lift the ban on employed government lawyers working for the government legal service and Crown Prosecution Service from becoming judges after retirement (1994).

On appointment High Court judges receive a knighthood. The maximum number of High Court judges is 96. In addition to serving as a judge in one of the three divisions of the High Court (Queen's Bench Division, Chancery Division and Family Division), a High Court judge hears the more serious offences tried on indictment in the Crown Courts, eg murder cases.

Circuit judges

They are appointed by the Crown on the advice of the Lord Chancellor. The position of circuit judge was introduced by the Courts Act 1971. All county court judges, who until then were exclusively concerned with civil work, became circuit judges and, additionally, were assigned to the Crown Court. Circuit judges now, therefore, undertake a mixture of civil and criminal work as do their High Court counterparts.

By virtue of the Courts and Legal Services Act 1990, Sch 10, para 31, no person is qualified to be appointed a circuit judge unless he/she has a ten-year Crown Court or ten-year county court qualification within the meaning of s71 of the 1990 Act; or he/she is a recorder; or he/she has held a full-time appointment for at least three years in one of the offices listed in Part IA of Sch 2 to the 1971 Act, which include coroners, taxing masters of the Supreme Court, stipendiary magistrates and district judges.

Section 52 of the Criminal Justice and Public Order Act 1994 provides that, in certain circumstances (eg an appeal against conviction otherwise than before a High Court judge), circuit judges are able to act as judges of the Court of Appeal (Criminal Division).

Recorders

They are appointed by the Crown on the advice of the Lord Chancellor. They serve as part-time judges of the Crown Court. They must have a ten-year Crown Court or county court qualification under s71 of the Courts and Legal Services Act 1990. The appointment is often regarded as an 'apprenticeship' since a recorder who demonstrates judicial ability may be appointed as a circuit judge or High Court judge.

District judges

They are appointed by the Crown on the advice of the Lord Chancellor. They hear the less serious cases in the county courts. Section 74(1) and (2) of the 1990 Act provided that the offices of registrar, assistant registrar and deputy registrar for each county court district and district registrar, assistant district registrar and deputy district registrar for each district registry of the High Court, became the offices of district judge, assistant judge and deputy district judge respectively. The office of registrar of the principal registry of the Family Division of the High Court became the office of district judge of the principal registry of the Family Division.

Judicial statistics

As at February 1998 the number of women judges was as follows:

Lords of Appeal in Ordinary	0
Lords Justices of Appeal	1
High Court judges	7
Circuit judges	30 (out of 547)
Recorders	69 (out of 862)
District judges	38 (out of 337)

As at May 1997 the number of ethnic minority judges was as follows:

Lords of Appeal in Ordinary	0
Lords Justices of Appeal	0
High Court judges	0
Circuit judges	5
Recorders	12
District judges	2

Source: Lord Chancellor's Department.

4.3 Appointment of judges

Traditionally the decision-making process by which judges have been appointed was shrouded in secrecy. It was not until 1986 that the Lord Chancellor's Department published information about this process. At that time there were no advertisements for vacancies on the bench and no objective job descriptions for particular judicial posts. Applications could be made for the positions of circuit judge, but appointment to the High Court bench was by invitation only. There were no formal interviews for vacancies; instead officials in the Lord Chancellor's Department took 'soundings' from serving judges and senior practising lawyers and then compiled files on potential candidates. The subject of a file had no opportunity to check the accuracy of the information in it and no opportunity to challenge recommendations that may have been made by those consulted by the Department. Indeed, the sources of recommendations were kept strictly confidential. No reasons were given for particular decisions, but it was believed that Lord Chancellors took into account very subjective criteria such as a candidate's 'standing' and 'temperament'.

Not surprisingly these arrangements were blamed for producing an 'unrepresentative' judiciary. Judges seemed to share the same characteristics: a public school education, followed by Oxford or Cambridge; white; male; middle-aged and establishment-minded. The taking of soundings as a method of appointment was said to perpetuate an 'old boy network' in which white males recommended other white males from the same background or who belonged to the same social clubs. Criteria such as 'standing' and 'temperament' were said by critics to be 'built-in head winds' which obstructed the advancement of women and ethnic minorities.

In response to these criticisms, and because of disquiet over the low representation of women and ethnic minorities among the judiciary, reforms in the methods of judicial appointments have been introduced in recent years. In the autumn of 1994 advertisements were published for positions as circuit and district judges. They contained 'job descriptions' directly related to the skills required for a trial judge rather than the old criteria of 'standing' and 'sound temperament'. Matters such as legal knowledge, intellectual ability, integrity, fairness, humanity, courtesy and communication skills were stressed. Short-listed applicants are now interviewed by a panel including a serving judge, a lay person and an official of the Lord Chancellor's Department. Recommendations are then made to the Lord Chancellor. The advertisements contain a pledge that appointments will be made regardless of gender, race, religion or sexual orientation.

A similar system of advertisements and interviews was instituted for High Court vacancies in February 1998. However, Lord Irvine, the Lord Chancellor, has made it clear that he makes his final decision on all appointments not solely on the advice from the interview panels but also on the results of confidential consultations about prospective candidates. But he has stated that such consultations will not take the form of traditional 'soundings' but will be systematic and objective, focusing on the real strengths and weaknesses of individual candidates. Such information-gathering will evaluate an individual's talents, experience and professional merits, based on the assessments of judges and practitioners with direct knowledge of those qualities. Lord Irvine has also tried to make the system as open and accountable as possible by instructing that any adverse allegations made about a candidate must be disclosed to that candidate, who should then be given an opportunity to rebut them. The source of an allegation will also be disclosed.

Like his predecessor (Lord Mackay) Lord Irvine has rejected 'quick fix solutions' aimed at tackling the low representation of women and ethnic minorities among the judiciary. Use of positive discrimination, fast track methods of promotion and quotas have thus been rejected, mainly because they would undermine the fundamental principle that the best qualified candidates must be appointed regardless of gender or race. Instead Lord Irvine has encouraged more applications for judicial positions from female and ethnic minority lawyers. The Lord Chancellor's Department is also developing schemes to make the judicial system more sympathetic and responsive to the needs of women and minorities, eg by enabling prospective applicants to spend time 'shadowing' a judge so as to obtain knowledge of, and confidence in, the discharge of judicial functions. This and other proposals were made by Lord Irvine in a series of speeches during 1998 in which he reiterated his intention to modernise the appointments system so as to promote fairness and equality of opportunity. He will be making annual reports to Parliament on judicial appointments; the first to be published will be in the year 2000, covering the period 1998–1999.

Whilst there has been support for these changes, critics continue to argue that more radical reforms are required to deal with an apparently growing crisis of public confidence in the judiciary. Proposals include:

1. Appointing candidates as stipendiary magistrates for three to four weeks as a period of probation which, if successfully completed, would be followed by promotion to assistant recorders.
2. Creating a system of permanent part-time judges in the High Court and on circuit (which might prove attractive for women in combining a judicial career with the responsibility of bringing up a family).

3. Introducing psychological tests for candidates to assess character and detect undesirable prejudices.
4. Widening the pool of candidates to include pure academic lawyers (there is a good proportion of women and ethnic minorities among the teachers of law). The traditional view that only advocates make good judges is being increasingly challenged: being a player in the game is not necessarily a prerequisite for being a good referee!
5. Establishing a Judicial Appointments Board, composed of lay persons with some experience of the justice system, to advise the Lord Chancellor on senior judicial appointments. The Board would be under a duty to provide reasons for its advice.

So far Lord Irvine has rejected all of the above, although the establishment of a Judicial Appointments Board is a long-term objective of the Labour government.

For a useful analysis: see further Drewry 'Judicial Appointments' [1998] PL 1.

4.4 Training of judges

Traditionally judges had no training in judicial functions prior to appointment to the bench. It was assumed that practise as an advocate was sufficient experience to take on such functions. However, the view was challenged by Lord Bridge's *Report on Legal Education and Training* (1978) and the result was the establishment of the Judicial Studies Board in 1979 as part of the Lord Chancellor's Department.

At first the Board operated on a part-time basis with very limited resources, but as the value of its work came to be appreciated more government funds were provided and it underwent considerable expansion in the mid-1980s and again in 1996, when it was given an independent budget and separated from the Lord Chancellor's Department. Since 1979 the Board has arranged courses and seminars for trainee assistant recorders and new circuit judges. Refresher seminars are organised for circuit judges and recorders and newly appointed Queen's Bench Division judges are invited to attend. Seminars are arranged for judges of all levels on specific matters.

In 1991 an advisory committee on cases concerning members of ethnic minorities was established. Arising out of the committee's work, there is a training programme aimed first at educating judges (and magistrates) on basic cultural differences of the main ethnic minority communities and then at identifying the areas that most commonly cause offence. The programme also involves sessions in racial awareness as part of the compulsory training and refresher courses for judges and magistrates.

In 1996 the Board announced more spending for 'equal treatment' training designed to cover gender awareness, and sensitivity to unrepresented parties, witnesses, jurors, victims and their families, children and persons under physical and mental disability.

In 1998 the Board was granted a special budget of £1,050,000 by the Lord Chancellor's Department to spend on case management training in preparation for the civil procedure reforms stemming from the implementation of Lord Woolf's report *Access to Justice* (1996) – the implementation date being 26 April 1999. Lord Irvine, the Lord Chancellor, has also appointed 30 civil judges to oversee this training.

Lord Irvine also announced that £4.5 million would be spent on a comprehensive training programme for judges (also magistrates and tribunal members) so as to prepare them for the obligations that the Human Rights Act 1998 will place on them when it is brought into force (probably during the year 2000). His Department will also provide judges with access (either through textbooks or information technology) to the judgments of the European Court of Human Rights.

4.5 Removal and retirement

Judges of the High Court and above, with the exception of the Lord Chancellor, hold office during good behaviour subject to a power of removal by the Monarch on an address presented by both Houses of Parliament. This provision derives from the Act of Settlement 1701, and is now contained in the Supreme Court Act 1981.

Judges below High Court level (eg circuit judges and recorders) may be removed from office by the Lord Chancellor on the grounds of incapacity or misbehaviour.

Discipline is administered by the Lord Chancellor usually through private letters of reprimand, though sometimes the Lord Chancellor has issued public rebukes to judges who have made insensitive comments etc.

Resignation from the bench is unusual; in February 1998 Harman J resigned from the High Court bench following severe criticism from the Court of Appeal concerning his dilatory and negligent conduct in delivering judgment in a civil case.

It has sometimes been suggested that an independent 'judicial conduct tribunal' should be set up to supervise judicial standards and to advise the Lord Chancellor on questions of discipline and removal.

The general retirement age for all judges, other than the Lord Chancellor, is 70: s26 Judicial Pensions and Retirement Act 1993. The Lord Chancellor may serve beyond the age of 75. The Lord Chancellor has power under the 1993 Act to extend the service of circuit judges and recorders, a year at a time, up to the age of 75 if he considers it desirable in the public interest.

4.6 Immunity, independence and impartiality

Immunity is an extension of the principle of an independent judiciary. A judge may not be sued in a civil action for anything done or said while acting in his judicial capacity: see *Sirros* v *Moore* [1974] 3 WLR 459.

The immunity varies with the status of the judge:

1. Judge of superior court – no action lies against him for anything he says or does in exercise of his judicial office even if he is malicious or acts in bad faith.
2. Judge of inferior court – the same immunity as above but only when acting within his jurisdiction.

Neither the Lord Chancellor nor any of the designated judges is liable in damages for anything done or omitted in the discharge or purported discharge of any of their functions under Part II of the Courts and Legal Services Act 1990: s69(1).

The independence of the judiciary is a key feature and one which runs parallel with immunity. The independence of the judiciary means that the judges are not controlled by the legislature or the executive. They do not take part in politics and cannot become Members of Parliament at the same time (although some were MPs before being appointed as judges). In the House of Lords the Law Lords do not, by convention, take part in political controversy or take part in party politics, although they do take part in debates on topics connected with the law. The Lord Chancellor, again by convention, keeps his political activities completely separate from his judicial responsibilities.

The impartiality of a judge is essential to the fair administration of justice. For this purpose the appearance of impartiality is as important as actual impartiality.

One particular concern about serving judges has been whether they were members of the Freemasons Society (an ancient, exclusively male secret organisation dedicated to protecting the interests of members). In 1998 Jack Straw, the Home Secretary, encouraged the establishment of a voluntary register so that judges (and magistrates) could declare membership of this body. Compulsory disclosure was strongly resisted by the judiciary on the ground that it would be a step towards politicisation of judges. In response to a preliminary questionnaire from the Lord Chancellor's Department, 247 judges (out of approximately 5,000) declared themselves to be Freemasons, whilst 64 refused to make any declaration.

A judge is automatically disqualified from sitting as a judge if he has a direct financial interest in the outcome of the case or is so closely connected to one of the parties in the case as to share their interest in the outcome. This is known as actual bias and is comparatively rare. It is more usual for complaints to be made of apparent bias in the form of some kind of non-financial interest in the case and in order for a complainant to have the decision set aside on the ground of bias he/she must establish not merely a reasonable suspicion of bias but a real danger of bias: *R v Gough* [1993] 2 WLR 883 (HL).

Although cases of actual bias are rare they do cause considerable damage to the perception of an independent and impartial judiciary. Hence there was grave concern when it was discovered that a Law Lord had heard an appeal on a matter in which he had a direct personal interest. In November 1998 Lord Hoffmann, with four other Law Lords, heard an appeal against a decision that General Pinochet enjoyed sovereign immunity as a former head of state from extradition to Spain, which wanted to try him for acts committed whilst he was head of state in Chile. Amnesty International was granted leave to participate in the appeal hearing before the Law Lords. Lawyers for Amnesty argued that there could be no sovereign immunity from extradition in cases where the allegations involved such grave crimes as authorising murder, torture and similar violations of fundamental human rights. By a majority of three to two the Law Lords accepted this argument and allowed the appeal. Lord Hoffmann was one of the majority.

Subsequently it emerged that Lord Hoffmann was a director and chairperson of a charitable organisation which had been incorporated to carry out the charitable work of Amnesty International. Lord Hoffmann had not declared this relationship during the appeal hearing. Lawyers for General Pinochet then lodged a petition asking the House of Lords to set aside the ruling on the ground of bias. Five Law Lords who had not sat during the earlier appeal were convened to hear this application. Unanimously they agreed that Lord Hoffmann had been disqualified as a matter of law automatically by reason of his relationship with Amnesty International. The earlier ruling was therefore set aside and a rehearing ordered: *Re Pinochet Ugarte* [1999] NLJ Rep 88.

This was an unprecedented event and dealt a severe blow to the prestige of the most senior judges in the English legal system. The circumstances caused such concern that Lord Irvine, the Lord Chancellor, wrote to Lord Browne-Wilkinson, the senior of the twelve Law Lords, proposing that in future a judge must disclose any matter giving rise to the appearance of a conflict of interest concerning a case in which he/she is about to adjudicate or hear an appeal. Critics have argued that this may not be enough to restore public confidence in the judicial system and that much closer scrutiny will be needed, possibly on the lines of the American system, where challenges to judges' interests and public 'vetting' of applicants to the bench are routine. Whilst judges should not be required to avoid outside interests it is essential that such interests should be declared to enable parties to decide whether to object to a particular judge hearing their case.

4.7 Functions of a judge

These may be summarised as follows:

1. Supervisory – conduct of the trial.
2. Sole arbiter of any legal issue
3. In civil cases the judge alone decides fact and law, but certain actions (eg libel and slander) may be tried with a jury: s69 of the Supreme Court Act 1981. In jury cases the judge must leave fact-finding to the jury.
4. In civil cases the judge decides quantum of damages unless this decision falls to be made by the jury, eg in defamation cases. However, even in these cases judicial guidance can be given to the jury in the matter of assessing damages.

5. To interpret, clarify and give effect to the law.
6. In criminal cases, the role of summing up to a jury.
7. In criminal cases, passing sentence.
8. In exceptional cases, to reform the law. Whilst in theory judges cannot create new rules of law, in practice this must inevitably happen either through the development of judicial precedents or through the process of statutory interpretation. In rare cases where there is no authority to guide them, judges may feel compelled to create new principles of law: see, for example, in civil law, *R* v *Human Fertilisation and Embryology Authority, ex parte Blood* [1997] 2 All ER 687 (CA); and, in criminal law, *Shaw* v *Director of Public Prosecutions* [1962] AC 220 (HL).

Finally, it should be noted that in addition to the purely judicial functions outlined above a judge may be called upon to exercise quasi-judicial functions involving a mixture of fact-finding, administration and policy formulation, eg when chairing a Royal Commission or a tribunal of inquiry.

The magistracy

4.8 Lay magistrates (Justices of the Peace)

The relevant statute is the Justices of the Peace Act 1997, which consolidates earlier legislation.

Appointment of lay magistrates

Lay magistrates are appointed by the Lord Chancellor on behalf of the Crown from people who have been put forward by local party political organisations, or by leading members of the community or by voluntary organisations, and those put forward are in general people of standing, generally with a record of good service to the community. Indeed, individuals may put themselves forward for consideration. The Lord Chancellor is assisted by local advisory committees (about 94) and he attempts to maintain as far as possible a balance between the sexes, political parties, social classes and races.

The greatest difficulty in attempting to obtain magistrates representative of the community as a whole is that their services are unpaid, although they may receive allowances to cover travelling expenses, subsistence and financial loss occasioned by the performance of their duties.

There are few formal qualifications. On appointment a magistrate must be over 21 and (unless there are exceptional circumstances) below 65 (50 in the case of a juvenile bench) and must normally reside within 15 miles of the boundary of the

Commission of the Peace to which he or she is appointed. There are no formal 'character' qualifications, although the following, among others, will not be accepted:

1. A person convicted of certain offences, or subject to certain court orders.
2. An undischarged bankrupt.
3. A serving member of the Monarch's forces.
4. A member of the police service or the spouse of such a member.
5. A close relative of a person who is already a magistrate on the same bench.

There are approximately 30,000 lay magistrates in England and Wales, just under half of whom are women. A few years ago ethnic minorities comprised less than 2 per cent of the lay magistracy, but recent efforts to improve recruitment have resulted in an increase to between 6 per cent and 7 per cent of new appointments. Only about 15 per cent of lay magistrates have a manual labour background and probably a majority of lay magistrates support the Conservative Party.

Lord Irvine, the Lord Chancellor, has expressed his desire for greater political and social balance among the lay magistracy:

> 'There should be a proper balance of suitable people who support the main political parties, as well as those who are politically uncommitted. Benches of magistrates should be microcosms of their communities' (letter to *The Times*, 15 October 1997).

During the summer of 1998 Lord Irvine revised the procedures for appointing lay magistrates. The reforms include the introduction of a clear job description for magistrates; the six key qualities defining the personal suitability of candidates are declared to be: good character; understanding and communication; social awareness; maturity and sound temperament; sound judgment; and commitment and reliability.

Lord Irvine urged the local advisory committees which recommend appointments to put forward suitable candidates who reflect the communities they serve in terms of gender, ethnic origin, occupation, geographical location and political persuasion.

Training of lay magistrates

A frequent criticism is that lay magistrates do not need to be legally qualified. However, all newly appointed magistrates undergo training under the supervision of the Judicial Studies Board. The objects of the training are to enable justices to understand their duties, to obtain sufficient knowledge of the law to follow normal cases, to acquire a working knowledge of the rules of evidence and to appreciate the nature and purpose of sentences. The first stage of training consists mainly in attending court as an observer, and instruction on the duties of a justice of the peace, on the practice and procedure in courts, and on the methods of punishment and of treatment. The second stage must be completed within 12 months of appointment and consists of further instruction and visits to certain penal institutions. Magistrates also undergo refresher training. Special training is given to those magistrates who deal with juvenile or family matters.

A new training programme was launched by Lord Irvine in the autumn of 1998. The new training involves 'hands on' practical experience (ie sitting in courts) and sessions in equality awareness. Experienced magistrates act as monitors on the new courses.

Removal and retirement

Magistrates are removable by the Lord Chancellor for good cause (eg conviction of a serious offence). Lay magistrates retire at 70.

Immunity

Under s108 of the Court and Legal Services Act 1990 no action lies against a Justice of the Peace (or a justice's clerk) in respect of any act or omission when acting in the execution of his duty and with respect to any matter within his jurisdiction, but an action will lie if the matter was not within his jurisdiction and it is proved that he acted in bad faith.

Functions of lay magistrates

These may be summarised as follows:

1. Issuing of warrants and summonses.
2. Granting and withholding bail.
3. Exercising summary jurisdiction.
4. Presiding over committal proceedings.
5. Matrimonial and guardianship jurisdiction (in the family proceedings court) and other limited civil jurisdiction.
6. Administrative functions (eg granting licence applications).
7. Juvenile jurisdiction. The youth court is not an independent court but is the magistrates' court sitting in a special capacity.
8. Administering oaths or taking affidavits for the purposes of an application for a grant of probate or letter of administration.

The magistrates' clerk

Lay magistrates can only sit if they have a qualified clerk. The clerk must advise the magistrates as to the law and practice, but he/she must not interfere with their decision and the decision is liable to be quashed by an order of certiorari if this is seen to happen: *R v Eccles Justices, ex parte Farrelly* (1992) The Times 17 June. The clerk, who must have a five-year magistrates' court qualification within the meaning of s71 of the Courts and Legal Services Act 1990 or then be or previously have been a justices' clerk, is a salaried official. He/she is a key figure in the magistrates' courts. It is important that the magistrates themselves must make the decisions, yet lay magistrates often need to call on the help of the clerk who brings points to their attention. The responsibilities of the magistrates' clerk also include the consideration of applications for legal aid in criminal cases.

4.9 Stipendiary magistrates

The system of stipendiary (full-time salaried) magistrates was first set up at the end of the eighteenth century to deal with the defects in the administration of justice in London. Most large conurbations now have stipendiary magistrates as well as lay magistrates, and this is necessary because of the vast quantity of work that has to be dealt with by the magistrates' courts. (There are approximately 50 metropolitan stipendiary magistrates in Greater London and about 36 provincial stipendiary magistrates.)

A stipendiary magistrate must have a seven-year general qualification within s71 of the Courts and Legal Services Act 1900. Stipendiaries are appointed by the Lord Chancellor. Their salary is determined by the Home Secretary. Retirement is at 70, although the Lord Chancellor may grant extensions up to 75 if he believes it to be in the public interest.

A stipendiary magistrate sits alone to hear cases and does not require the assistance of a magistrates' clerk. Stipendiary magistrates tend to be more efficient than lay magistrates in disposing of cases and also more independently minded when it comes to assessing evidence (it is often said that lay magistrates rely too much on the advice of their clerk and are too willing to believe police evidence). However, the cost of replacing all lay magistrates with stipendiaries would be prohibitive and is not a realistic option.

5

The Jury System

5.1 The jury in civil cases

5.2 The jury in criminal cases

5.3 Arguments for and against the jury system

5.4 Reform proposals

5.1 The jury in civil cases

Composition

A jury of eight persons may sit in county court trials and a jury of 12 in High Court trials. Issues concerning method of selection of jurors, jury deliberations and other related matters are the same as those concerning the jury in criminal cases and are dealt with in detail in section 5.2. below.

Suitability of civil juries

Civil jury trials are rare because of their cost, which has to be paid by the losing party. Hence litigants are reluctant to opt for a jury, even where one is available to them, because of the risk of escalating costs. The availability of a civil jury has also been limited by statute.

Section 69(1) of the Supreme Court Act 1981 provides that the right to claim a jury in a civil case is limited to fraud, defamation, malicious prosecution and false imprisonment, but that the claim may be denied if the court is of the opinion that the trial requires prolonged examination of documents. Section 69(3) provides that jury trial may nevertheless be ordered if the judge thinks fit, eg because of public interest considerations. Hence, in all other cases a party may request a civil jury which may be ordered as a matter of judicial discretion, though for this purpose the similarity of some other tort to any of the torts listed in s69(1) is not a factor to be taken into account when exercising this discretion: see *Racz* v *Home Office* [1994] 2 WLR 23 (HL).

Judges have become reluctant to order a civil jury, particularly in personal injury cases, on the ground that lay people are not suitable for deciding complex issues of law and evidence or for assessing compensation on a rational basis: see *Ward* v *James* [1966] 1 QB 273 and *H* v *Ministry of Defence* [1991] 2 WLR 1192.

Assessing compensation

Where a civil jury sits in a case it has the function of determining liability and the task of assessing compensation if finding in favour of the claimant. In recent years concern was expressed over an apparent tendency by juries to award very large sums of compensation, particularly against newspapers in defamation cases and against the police in false imprisonment and malicious prosecution trials. As a result a right of appeal against such awards has been provided by statute. Section 8 of the Courts and Legal Services Act 1990 provides that the Court of Appeal may set aside an award of damages by a jury which the Court regards as excessive (or inadequate) and may substitute such sum as appears to the court to be proper. This power has been interpreted so as to be exercised consistently with art 10 of the European Convention on Human Rights, which declares the need to safeguard freedom of expression: *Rantzen* v *Mirror Group Newspapers* [1993] 3 WLR 953 (the Court of Appeal reduced a jury's award of libel damages from £250,000 to £110,000 on the ground that the former sum was excessive and inhibited press freedom).

However, the issue of irrational compensation awards by juries continued to trouble judges. In *Ward* v *James*, above, it had been held that trial judges should not give any specific guidance to juries on appropriate sums in particular cases. As a result trial judges were deterred from offering any guidance to juries on how to assess adequate and reasonable compensation. A change of practice occurred in *John* v *Mirror Group Newspapers Ltd* [1996] 2 All ER 35. In this case the Court of Appeal, in reducing a compensation award for defamation, said that trial judges would be able in future to provide guidance to defamation juries in the way they assessed damages. Sir Thomas Bingham MR (as he then was) said that, without such guidance, the jury 'were in the position of sheep loosed on an unfenced common, with no shepherd'. He added that giving guidance to a jury would not undermine its constitutional position but rather buttress its constitutional role by rendering jury proceedings more rational and so more acceptable to public opinion. The principle laid down in *John* v *Mirror Group Newspapers Ltd* has since been extended to trials involving the assessment of compensatory and exemplary damages for false imprisonment, malicious prosecution and consequential torts: see *Thompson* v *Commissioner of Police of the Metropolis* [1997] 2 All ER 762.

Finally, it should be noted that the Defamation Act 1996 has abolished trial by jury for defamation claims of £10,000 or less.

5.2 The jury in criminal cases

Introduction

Trial by jury is now used only in a trial on indictment in the Crown Court. It is generally considered that the far greater expense involved in holding a jury trial (as compared to a summary trial in the magistrates' court) is justifiable only for serious offences. For the classification of offences into indictable offences, offences triable either way (where the accused has the right to insist on a jury trial) and summary offences, see Chapter 13, section 13.10.

Composition

A jury of 12 sits in the Crown Court to determine the guilt or innocence of the accused. The empanelment of the jury involves each juror swearing an oath to give a true verdict (ie an honest verdict) according to the evidence. In theory a jury should provide a trial by one's peers (ie equals), who should be unbiased and representative of the local community. However, the law regarding composition of juries and the practices followed in selecting jurors have been criticised for producing unrepresentative and possibly prejudiced jurors.

Qualifications for jury service

Every person between the ages of 18 and 70 is qualified for jury service provided:

1. that person is registered as a parliamentary or local government elector; and
2. has been ordinarily resident within the United Kingdom for any period of at least five years since attaining the age of 13; and
3. is not ineligible for or disqualified from jury service.

Disqualifications: Juries Act 1974, Sch 1, Pt II, as amended by the Juries (Disqualifications) Act 1984, disqualifies any person who within the United Kingdom:

1. Has been sentenced to imprisonment for life (or to be detained during pleasure) or to a term of five years or more, custody for life or youth custody for a term of five years or more.
2. Has had passed on him a sentence of imprisonment or custody of any duration during the last ten years (even if not actually served, eg because suspended) or any order for community service during the last ten years, or has been placed on probation during the last five years.
3. Is on bail in criminal proceedings (inserted by s40 of the Criminal Justice and Public Order Act 1994).

Certain people are rendered ineligible by the Act: those concerned with the administration of justice, judges, magistrates, police officers, lawyers, the clergy and the mentally ill: Sch 1, Pt 1 of the 1974 Act, as amended.

There is a further category of persons who, though eligible, may claim to be excused as of right: doctors, nurses, MPs and members of the armed forces. This category recognises that certain people may have more pressing duties than jury service: ss8 and 9 and Sch 1, Pt III of the 1974 Act.

Jurors aged between 65 and 70 are excused if they do not wish to sit upon the jury. Additionally, s42 of the Criminal Justice and Public Order Act 1994 extends excusal to include a practising member of a religious society or order the tenets or beliefs of which are incompatible with jury service.

Section 9B of the Juries Act 1974, as inserted by s41 of the Criminal Justice and Public Order Act 1994, provides that where it appears that, on account of physical disability, there is doubt as to a person's capacity to act effectively as a juror, the person may be brought before the judge. It is for the judge to determine whether or not the person should act as a juror; but he must affirm the summons under the 1974 Act unless he is of the opinion that the person will not, on account of his disability, be capable of acting effectively as a juror, in which case he must discharge the summons. In *Re Osman* [1995] 1 WLR 1327 it was held that a profoundly deaf juror should be discharged because he could not follow the proceedings without an interpreter, and it would not be appropriate to permit the interpreter to retire with a jury.

The court now has a discretion to defer jury service if the person summoned shows good reason. This means that they will not have to sit on a jury at the time for which they are summoned but may put it off to a later date. Such a step may be taken by people with previously booked holidays: s120 Criminal Justice Act 1988.

In April 1996 a new procedure for giving information to the jury was introduced. Everyone called for jury service will be shown a 17-minute video about the functions of a juror. There will also be information in the video about eligibility requirements and courtroom procedures.

Empanelling the jury: challenges

Traditionally the defence had a right to make a number of 'peremptory' challenges (ie challenges without giving reasons), but this right was abolished by s118(1) of the Criminal Justice Act 1988. Consequently both prosecution and defence may only 'challenge for cause' (ie state good reasons for a challenge), and such a challenge is heard by the trial judge either 'in camera' (ie the courtroom is cleared of jurors, members of the public and the press) or in chambers: s118(2) of the 1988 Act. A challenge for cause can be made either to the whole panel summoned or to an individual juror. A challenge for cause is only possible on three grounds under s12(4) of the 1974 Act:

1. The juror is not qualified to serve.

2. The juror is biased (ie proof of actual bias is available).
3. The juror may reasonably be suspected of bias (ie there is apparent bias). For this purpose there must be a real danger of apparent bias: see *R v Gough* [1993] 2 WLR 883 (HL).

Usually the names of jurors are announced in open court but may be withheld as a protective measure to prevent the risk of jury intimidation. Such a measure does not affect rights of challenge because the defence is entitled by s5(2) Juries Act 1974 to reasonable facilities for inspecting the panel from which the jurors are to be drawn: *R v Comerford* [1998] 1 All ER 823.

The prosecution, on behalf of the Crown, has a special right to 'stand by' a member of the jury panel, ie to exclude that juror who is then held in reserve and used only if no other members of the jury panel remain available for jury service (which is most unlikely to happen since the abolition of peremptory challenges). The circumstances in which it is proper for the prosecution to exercise its right to stand by a juror are:

1. where a jury check reveals information justifying exercise of the right to stand by and the Attorney-General personally authorises the exercise of the right to stand by; and
2. where a person who is about to be sworn as a juror is manifestly unsuitable and the defence agrees that the exercise of the right to stand by would be appropriate: *Practice Note* [1988] 3 All ER 1086.

The principle of random selection

The general principle is that eligible jurors are chosen at random by computer from local electoral registers. Any party to the proceedings is entitled to inspect the panel from which the jurors are to be drawn, but this contains only the names and addresses of jurors. In theory it is open to a party to conduct his own inquiry into the background of such persons, but since this is likely to be costly (there may be up to 150 names on the panel) only the prosecution, with its state resources, is in a position to do this. In order to prevent the prosecution from having an unfair advantage in this matter the Attorney-General has limited the prosecution's right to check on a juror's background to the following cases:

1. where national security is involved, in which case the police may check security records of jurors; and
2. where a terrorist offence is alleged, in which case the police may check only the criminal records of jurors to ensure that no disqualified jurors sit on the jury in such a case: *Practice Note* [1988] 3 All ER 1086.

The trial judge also has a discretion to order a security check on a jury during a trial but he must do so only after informing both prosecution and defence of such intention: *R v Obellim* [1997] 1 Cr App R 355.

Clearly the practice of jury-vetting undermines the principle of random selection and at one time the constitutionality of such a practice was in question: see *R v Sheffield Crown Court, ex parte Brownlow* [1980] 1 WLR 892. However, subsequently the Court of Appeal declared that jury-vetting practices were lawful and, indeed, necessary in the public interest to ensure, for example, that disqualified persons did not sit on juries: *R v Mason* [1981] QB 881.

It has been argued that the principle of random selection can lead to unsuitable juries which may contain uneducated, or anti-establishment or otherwise prejudiced people. Unlike the American system, in which potential jurors may be cross-examined by each side for weeks prior to the trial, there are no formal interviews, tests or questions to determine the suitability of juries in the English legal system. It appears that the trial judge has a discretion to allow some questioning of jurors during empanelment, but it seems that in ordinary criminal cases judges are reluctant to permit questioning of jurors to elicit bias. In *R v Andrews* (1998) The Times 15 October the defence requested that a questionnaire be put to the potential jurors to establish whether they had been affected by substantial adverse publicity concerning the accused prior to the trial. The Court of Appeal upheld the trial judge's decision to refuse this request on the ground that such questioning was of doubtful efficacy and might be counter-productive in bringing the attention of a juror to prejudicial matters. It was said that questioning of potential jurors, whether orally or by use of a questionnaire, was to be avoided save in the most exceptional circumstances, such as where it was alleged that potential jurors might have a direct interest in the case (eg by having lost money in transactions which formed the basis of the trial).

In his book *What Next in the Law* (1982) at pp70–78 Lord Denning argued that random selection can produce 'irresponsible' jurors and that prospective jurors ought to be interviewed to assess their suitability and even required to produce character references. Others have expressed concern about the under-representation of ethnic minorities on juries even in areas where there are sizeable numbers of ethnic minority households. It has been argued that it is unfair if a black defendant is faced with an all-white jury: see further Herbert 'Racism, Impartiality and Juries' [1995] NLJ 1138. However, it appears that the trial judge is not required as a matter of fairness to ensure a racially balanced jury even in cases with sensitive racial overtones: see *R v Ford* [1989] 3 WLR 762. The Royal Commission on Criminal Justice (1993) Cmnd 2263 recommended that in exceptional cases either side should be able to apply to the trial judge to ensure the selection of a jury containing up to three people from ethnic minority communities, with one or more of this group of three coming from the same ethnic minority as the accused or the victim of the crime if either side should so request. However, any move towards race quotas on juries has so far been resisted by the senior judiciary on the ground that they would seriously undermine the principle of random selection which ensures a trial by one's equals (regardless of race) rather than by one's racial group. It may be that the answer to this problem lies not in 'packing' a jury with black members but rather in ensuring that random selection is carried out in such a way as to reflect accurately the local population – eg by using driving licence numbers and/or social security numbers rather than the electoral register.

Jury deliberations – the secrecy of the jury room

When the jury is asked to retire to consider its verdict its deliberations should take place in the jury room in secrecy. It should be the trial judge's primary concern to ensure that the jury, once it has retired, is kept free from outside influence or eavesdropping: *R* v *Bean* [1991] Crim LR 843. However, by virtue of s43 of the Criminal Justice and Public Order Act 1994, s13 of the Juries Act 1974 is substituted so that if the court thinks fit it may at any time (whether before or after the jury has been directed to consider its verdict) permit the jury to separate. Clearly there is a danger that a jury might be influenced by outside events or pressures and hence the trial judge must give appropriate warnings to a jury who are to separate prior to reaching their verdict: see *R* v *Oliver* (1995) The Times 6 December. If a jury is not allowed to separate and the trial is adjourned overnight the jury is accommodated at a local hotel and in such a case must not continue its deliberations at that hotel: *R* v *Young* [1995] 2 WLR 430.

It is quite wrong, once a jury has retired to the jury room to consider its verdict and has subsequently sent a note to the judge during their deliberations, for a judge to give directions to the jury through the medium of a court clerk. Any judge receiving a note from the jury relating to the defendant should inform counsel and disclose the terms of the note, reconvene the court without the jury and invite submissions as to the matter, and then recall the jury so as to give any necessary directions: *R* v *Green* [1992] Crim LR 292.

The secrecy of the jury's deliberations has been placed on a statutory basis by s8 of the Contempt of Court Act 1981. By virtue of s8(1), disclosure of the deliberations of a jury, even if obtained indirectly, is a contempt of court: *Attorney-General* v *Associated Newspapers Ltd* [1994] 2 WLR 277. Even academic research into the jury system is affected by s8 of the 1981 Act.

The verdict

The trial judge will instruct the jury to try to reach a unanimous verdict, but if the jury cannot agree after a reasonable period of deliberation the judge may then direct them on a majority verdict: s17 Juries Act 1974. He may accept a majority verdict as follows:

1. In a case where there are not less than 11 jurors, ten agree.
2. In a case where there are ten jurors, nine agree.

(It may be that during a trial the original jury of 12 is reduced in number where, for example, some members are discharged because of illness; the trial judge has discretion to allow the trial to continue in such circumstances. The numbers on a criminal jury must not fall below nine. A jury of nine must be unanimous.)

The court should only accept a majority verdict of guilty if the foreman of the jury states in open court the numbers who agreed on and dissented from the verdict: s17(3) Juries Act 1974. This requirement is mandatory but the discharge of a jury is not a bar to the rectification of a verdict so as to comply with s17(3): *R v Maloney (Peter James)* (1996) The Times 25 March (CA).

The general principle is that the jury's verdict is sovereign and unchallengeable on appeal. The Court of Appeal has shown great reluctance to investigate allegations of impropriety in jury proceedings, presumably because of concern that exposing jury deliberations to scrutiny might shake public confidence in the entire jury system: see *R v Thompson* [1962] 1 All ER 65. In *R v Miah; R v Akhbar* (1996) The Times 18 December the rule was reaffirmed that the Court of Appeal will not receive evidence of discussions which take place in the jury room. It is different if the discussions take place elsewhere: *R v Young*, above. The sovereignty of the jury also explains why a jury gives no reasons for its verdict. By contrast in America jurors are frequently interviewed by the media as to their reasons for reaching particular decisions: see further Prichard 'A Reform for Jury Trial?' [1998] NLJ 475.

Each juror swears an oath to give a true verdict according to the evidence but concern has sometimes been expressed when a jury delivers what appears to be a 'perverse' verdict, ie one not justified by the weight of the evidence in the case. It may be that in some cases juries have acquitted defendants as a result of unconscionable motives, such as anti-police or anti-establishment feeling. However, in other cases the motives may have been more honourable, eg to show disapproval of a harsh law. It has been argued that the surprising acquittal in *R v Ponting* [1985] Crim LR 318 was due to jury repugnance over the law concerning official secrets. It may be that in such cases the 'perverse' verdict can be defended as a means by which the jury enforces public morality and demonstrates the conscience of society: per Lord Devlin 'The Jury's Sovereignty' [1991] LQR 398–404.

Section 54 of the Criminal Procedure and Investigations Act 1996 gives the High Court power to set aside an acquittal and to order a retrial if it is in the interests of justice to do so in any case where the acquittal has been 'tainted' by a subsequent conviction for an offence involving interference with or intimidation of witnesses or jurors in the case in question.

By virtue of s51 of the Criminal Justice and Public Order Act 1994 it is an offence to intimidate or threaten to harm (physically or financially) any person assisting in the investigation of an offence, any witness or potential witness or any juror or potential juror. This offence is in addition to any offence subsisting at common law.

5.3 Arguments for and against the jury system

For

1. The jury, since it is randomly selected from a wide selection of the population, is best able to reflect the views of society and when a person's liberty is at stake it is a matter of principle that he should be tried by his peers.
2. Fact-finding is a matter of common sense and does not require specialised legal training and the 12 opinions of the jury are better than the single opinion of the judge since it is more likely to prevent individual biases governing the course of the fact-finding.
3. The jury is less 'prosecution-minded' than many judges and magistrates, being an 'organ of the disestablishment'. It can be totally independent because it is unaccountable.
4. The jury is particularly suited to judge questions of defamation (civil jury) since the test which is applied is that of 'right-thinking people generally': see *Sim* v *Stretch* [1936] 2 All ER 1237.
5. The jury is generally regarded by the public as the 'bulwark of individual liberties'. Justice must be seen to be done: per Lord Denning MR in *Ward* v *James* [1966] 1 QB 273.
6. Juries are a barometer of public feeling on the state of the law, eg by deliberately acquitting against the weight of the evidence to express disapproval of a 'bad' or 'unpopular' law.

Against

1. The jury is uneducated in the law and is often unable to weigh evidence correctly and appreciate the significance of certain matters. Complex fraud cases are particularly likely to cause problems for the lay jury. The Roskill Report (1986) recommended the replacement of the jury in such cases by a judge sitting with expert assessors.
2. The present law of evidence in criminal cases is much distorted by the need to accommodate the biases and inexperience of the jury and to keep from them matters which would unduly prejudice them against the accused, but which are not actually relevant to the weighing of evidence in the case (eg informing them of the accused's criminal record which may be totally irrelevant to the present case).
3. The jury may be too easily swayed by good oratory from counsel.
4. The jury can be dominated by two or three strong-minded individuals.
5. It is perhaps not possible to guarantee that there has been absolutely no tampering with the jury.
6. Juries may bring in perverse verdicts (ie against the weight of the evidence) as

the result of irresponsible decision-making. A perverse verdict is contrary to the jurors' oaths.

5.4 Reform proposals

For recent proposals aimed at a reclassification of criminal offences: see Chapter 13, section 13.11, *Reform proposals*. The proposals will, if implemented, considerably reduce the availability of jury trial in criminal cases.

In February 1998 the Labour government invited discussion of its proposals for changes to trial by jury in serious fraud cases. It announced four options, namely:

1. abolition of the jury and its replacement with a special tribunal composed of a trained judge and two specialist members who would have expertise in commercial affairs (the Roskill Report's recommendation); or
2. abolition of the jury and its replacement with a trained single judge or panel of trained judges, sitting with or without lay commercial advisers; or
3. retaining jury trial but restricting the role of the jury to issues of dishonesty, with a single trial judge making all other decisions; or
4. replacing the traditional jury with a special jury selected by qualifications or tests or who could demonstrate specialist knowledge (eg City of London accountants).

For a critical discussion of these proposals: see Rhodes 'Juries in Fraud Trials' [1998] NLJ 239.

6

The Legal Profession

6.1 Introduction: the divided legal profession

6.2 Solicitors

6.3 Barristers

6.4 The Crown Prosecution Service

6.5 Reform of the legal profession

6.1 Introduction: the divided legal profession

Unlike the position in most systems of law, the English legal profession is not a single profession exercising various functions, but a divided profession comprising barristers and solicitors. This division is a historical one stretching back into the twelfth and thirteenth centuries when, as a result of the growing complexities of the developing system of justice, claimants began to employ agents and experienced representatives to plead their cases before the courts. In modern times the divided profession has been justified on the ground that there is a continuing need for specialisation of function.

Practising barristers have been regarded as specialists in advocacy; it has been argued that the specialised nature of court proceedings requires a practical knowledge of the adversary system and an intimate awareness of the rules of evidence and procedure. Comparisons were often drawn with the medical profession; solicitors were regarded as 'general practitioners' dealing with routine problems, but referring a client to a specialist (a barrister) if his or her claim needed to be conducted in a court ('the operating theatre'). Lord Donaldson, a former Master of the Rolls, once expressed the view that it would be as impractical to merge solicitors and barristers as it would be to merge the professions of doctor, dentist and veterinary surgeon:

'No-one suggests that those professions should be fused because the divisions between them represent natural demarcation lines in terms of the public's needs. The same is true of the law': letter to *The Times*, 30 July 1996.

However, this contention can be disputed on the ground that there is no evidence of specialist training in the legal profession comparable to that found in the medical profession. Until 1969 barristers received no training at all in the art of advocacy, and until 1989 the practical training element of the Bar examinations consisted of a very short period of elementary exercises in pleading and drafting for which there were no formal examinations. Since 1989 the Bar examinations have laid more emphasis on formal appraisals of practising skills but they have still been criticised for giving inadequate tuition. The Royal Commission on Criminal Justice (1993) Cmnd 2263 recommended that practising barristers needed compulsory continuing education in areas such as forensic science and psychology. The 'apprenticeship' which a young barrister must serve as a 'pupil' to a senior barrister before being allowed to practise has also been criticised for being an inadequate training period.

Hence, it is not surprising that the basis for the divided profession has been attacked as fallacious, particularly when it was used to justify a monopoly of advocacy rights enjoyed by barristers in the higher courts. Steps were taken to break this monopoly under the Courts and Legal Services Act 1990, but, as will be seen, they did not lead to a significant change in the traditional discharge of lawyers' functions. The Access to Justice Bill 1999 proposes much more radical reforms (see section 6.5 below) which some have argued will inevitably lead to a fused profession. This would mean common legal training with graduates joining firms of lawyers, with each firm developing a specialist department of advocates if it so wishes, as, for example, in Canada, where the specialist advocates have retained the title of 'barristers'. Alternatively, there might be common legal training but a continuing division of practitioners so as to allow a distinct corps of higher court advocates, as happens in New Zealand and some Australian states.

Fusion, or significant moves towards it, would, it has been argued, provide a more rational and cost-effective basis for a modern legal profession. In theory a client would be paying one lawyer instead of two (or more) for all the work on his or her case, including advocacy in court if required. However, opponents of fusion and of moves towards it have argued that large city firms would employ the best advocates, thereby reducing client choice and the geographical spread of legal advice (at present any solicitor in England and Wales has right of access to any barrister in independent practice). It has also been argued that an independent Bar is a valuable safeguard of the constitution: a barrister is expected to put his or her duty to the court above any loyalty he or she may feel to his or her client. An employed lawyer who appears as an advocate for his or her employer might be faced with a conflict of interest; if the employed lawyer is a Crown prosecutor and his or her employer is the state the potential conflict of interest could have serious implications for citizens' rights.

Hence, opponents of fusion and of extended rights of advocacy (which they see as inevitably leading to fusion) have fought a long campaign in defence of the traditional system. These opponents mainly comprise the Bar and the senior judiciary; during the 1980s the campaign against the proposed reforms eventually contained in the Courts and Legal Services Act 1990 was known as 'Bar Wars' and a similar campaign is currently under way against the proposals in the Access to Justice Bill 1999: see further section 6.5 below.

6.2 Solicitors

There are approximately 70,000 solicitors in independent practice working for firms ranging from big city partnerships of up to 200 or more to small rural partnerships of six or less, including some one-man/one-woman practices. In addition, a number of solicitors work as employed legal advisers in various fields, such as local government, commerce, the government legal service and the Crown Prosecution Service.

Qualification

The road to becoming a solicitor depends upon whether one is a law graduate, a non-law graduate or a mature student for whom work experience may be a substitute for a degree.

A 'qualifying' law degree is one which has covered the seven 'foundations of legal knowledge' (contract law, law of tort, criminal law, constitutional and administrative law, land law, trusts and European Union law) and a course on the English legal system. The precise content of such a degree and the manner in which it is taught is left to the law schools. The holder of a qualifying law degree is then entitled to attend the one-year full-time Legal Practice Course at the Law Society's College of Law (or other approved institution). This is followed by a two-year training contract with a law firm during which time a 'professional skills course' must be taken. This is followed by admission to the roll. If after admission a solicitor wishes to practise advocacy in the higher courts, he/she must follow a six-year route to qualification in higher advocacy rights, and they must undertake education for the rest of their careers. Indeed, since November 1998 Continuing Professional Development has been a requirement for all practising solicitors.

Non-law graduates must take a conversion course in the seven 'foundations of legal knowledge' and the English legal system. This course is known as the Common Professional Examination (CPE) and may be taken in one year by full-time students or over two years by part-time and mature students. It must be taken at an approved institution, though distance-learning courses are available from such institutions. Successful completion of the CPE enables the graduate to proceed to the Legal Practice Course and then along the same route as law graduates.

Functions

A solicitor in independent practice working for a law firm operates like a businessman with an office to run and substantial correspondence. He or she deals with the preparatory stages of litigation (interviewing witnesses etc) and has direct contact with his or her clients. However, the bulk of a solicitor's work is non-litigious and includes conveyancing, drafting wills, the supervision of settlements, administration of estates, matrimonial problems and matters arising from employment, immigration and company law. The majority of solicitors will handle a cross-section of work but there is a trend towards specialisation, especially in London.

Rights of advocacy (rights of audience)

Solicitors in independent practice

Traditionally, such solicitors had very restricted opportunities to appear as advocates in the courts. They have long had rights of audience in the magistrates' courts, county courts and before certain tribunals. They have also been allowed to appear in certain types of non-jury cases in the Crown Courts, eg in proceedings on appeal from the magistrates' court or in committals for sentence from the magistrates' court. The opportunity to obtain greater rights of advocacy came with the passage of the Courts and Legal Services Act 1990. Under ss27–33 of the 1990 Act rights of audience were extended to those persons who could satisfy criteria established by their professional governing bodies, provided that those criteria have been approved by a panel comprising the Lord Chancellor and four senior judges (the Lord Chief Justice, the Master of the Rolls, the President of the Family Division and the Vice-Chancellor).

The solicitors' governing body, the Law Society, eventually made rules which were approved by the judges' panel enabling solicitors in independent practice of at least three years' experience to apply for a higher courts' qualification upon successful completion of training courses and tests in advocacy, evidence and procedure (courses and tests being run by and set by the Law Society). Applicants also need to show experience of advocacy – at least two years' experience in the magistrates' courts and county courts.

A holder of the higher courts' (criminal proceedings) qualification has rights of audience in the Crown Court and in other courts in all criminal proceedings. A holder of the higher courts' (civil proceedings) qualification may appear in the High Court and in other courts in all civil proceedings. The holder of the higher courts' (all proceedings) qualification may appear in all courts in all proceedings.

By May 1998 only 624 solicitors out of approximately 70,000 had qualified as higher court advocates and many of the 624 were exempted from the training courses because they had previously been barristers or had judicial experience. This failure to dent the Bar's domination of advocacy rights may be due to a number of factors; for example, the need to obtain at least two years' experience of lower court advocacy is an almost impossible requirement to demand of typical City solicitors; also the cost of qualifying (estimated at over £2,300) makes it difficult for smaller firms to sponsor their solicitors for higher courts' qualifications. Alternatively, it may simply be that there is not great demand for rights of audience among solicitors, the majority of whom may be content to leave advocacy to the Bar.

Employed solicitors
Whilst the Law Society and the Crown Prosecution Service campaigned for the above rules and criteria to apply also to employed solicitors, the judges' panel refused to endorse them, and instead further reviews were ordered concerning the position of employed lawyers. In June 1995 the Lord Chancellor's Advisory Committee on Legal Education and Conduct recommended (by a majority of nine to eight) that employed lawyers should continue to be denied the right to apply for advocacy certificates under the system established by the Courts and Legal Services Act 1990.

However, following fresh representations by the Law Society and the Crown Prosecution Service, the judges' panel approved new rules in February 1997 which amounted to a very limited relaxation of the restrictions applying to employed solicitors wishing to exercise advocacy rights in the higher courts.

Under the approval employed solicitors, like solicitors in private practice, will have to apply individually to the Law Society for rights of audience in the higher courts. Employed solicitors will need to have practical experience and to have passed relevant tests following a training course. However, the approval states that employed solicitors will not be able to appear as advocates on their own in the following situations:

1. for the prosecution in criminal proceedings which have been committed for trial to the Crown Court;
2. in civil proceedings in the higher courts in any hearing which is intended to dispose in whole, or in part of, the merits of the case; and
3. for local authorities in care proceedings.

The Bar welcomed the restriction on criminal proceedings as being necessary to prevent the establishment of a state prosecution service, while the Law Society emphasised that there were new opportunities for employed solicitors, eg by being involved in Crown Court and High Court cases as juniors led by solicitor-advocates or barristers and by acting on their own in Plea and Directions Hearings and other preliminary criminal proceedings. Employed solicitors will also be able to conduct guilty pleas. Nevertheless, the new rules were seen as a blow to employed solicitors, particularly those employed by the Crown Prosecution Service. The Law Society said that it would continue its campaign to have rights of audience in jury trials extended to employed solicitors. It may be that this campaign will eventually be successful: see the proposals in the Access to Justice Bill 1999, section 6.5 below.

Regulation and discipline
Solicitors are officers of the Supreme Court and were originally regulated and

disciplined by the judges. However, this function is now exercised partly by the Law Society and partly by the courts.

The Law Society was constituted by Royal Charter in 1845 and has always been a voluntary organisation: about 85 per cent of solicitors are members. Under the Solicitors Act 1974 it makes training regulations, provides club facilities and maintains the roll of solicitors (under the formal supervision of the Master of the Rolls). A solicitor found in serious breach of professional rules may be 'struck off' the roll, ie suspended from the ability to practise. Solicitors are accountable to the Law Society for such matters as the handling of clients' money and insurance cover for claims arising from their work. Discipline is administered in serious cases by the Solicitors' Disciplinary Tribunal, comprising solicitors and lay members. Appeal lies to the High Court or, in certain cases, to the Master of the Rolls. The Tribunal makes an annual report to the Lord Chancellor.

Less serious complaints by clients against solicitors can be made to the Office for the Supervision of Solicitors (Ofsol), established in 1996 to replace the much criticised Solicitors' Complaints Bureau. Although Ofsol is a Law Society institution it operates on new procedures designed to speed up the handling of complaints and to improve communications between all those involved in a complaint.

The solicitors' profession is also supervised by the Legal Services Ombudsman, an institution set up by ss21–26 of the Courts and Legal Services Act 1990. The Ombudsman's general function is to investigate the way in which a complaint has been dealt with by, inter alia, the Law Society. However, the Ombudsman may not investigate, inter alia, any issue which is being or has been determined by, inter alia, the Solicitors' Disciplinary Tribunal.

Relationship with clients

As far as a solicitor's relationship with his client is concerned, a solicitor owes both contractual and tortious duties of care, arising from his retainer by his client – which also (depending upon its scope) gives him his authority to act for that client. There is limited immunity from a suit for damages for breach of that duty of care, but only so far as the solicitor is carrying out litigation work which would have been carried on by a barrister had one been engaged: see *Saif Ali* v *Sydney Mitchell & Co* [1978] 3 All ER 1033 (HL).

A solicitor also owes a fiduciary duty, derived from the equitable notion of fraud, to his client which requires him to act in good faith in all his dealings with and on behalf of his client. For example, in the making of gifts by a client to his solicitor there is a presumption of undue influence. A solicitor must show in such circumstances (in order to rebut such a presumption) that such a gift was not made by reason of such influence; that is, that the solicitor was not taking advantage of his client's weaker position.

The confidential relationship of solicitor and client which arises out of the solicitor's fiduciary duty has other important consequences, notably the fact that all communications between them are 'privileged' and cannot be required to be disclosed in evidence without the client's consent: *Wheeler* v *Le Marchant* (1881) 17 Ch D 675. The reason for this privilege is to allow the client to be free to obtain legal advice without fear of disclosure.

Liability to third parties

A solicitor can be sued in contract or tort by third parties. In the former his liability is usually governed by the law of agency. He can therefore be indemnified by his client for acts within the scope of his authority. Where he acts without his client's authority he can be sued for breach of warranty of authority: *Yonge* v *Toynbee* [1910] 1 KB 215. A solicitor's liability in tort is governed by the usual principles applicable under the law of torts. Under the rapidly developing tort of negligence, particularly in respect of negligence causing economic loss (purely financial loss), a solicitor may be liable to beneficiaries for loss caused by faulty drafting of a client's will, even though the beneficiary is not in a contractual relationship with that solicitor: *Ross* v *Caunters* [1979] 2 All ER 580.

6.3 Barristers

There are approximately 8,500 barristers in independent practice, ie self-employed, working from sets of chambers (on average 20 members to a set in London and 15 to a set in the provinces). A set of chambers shares secretarial facilities and the services of a 'practice manager' (formerly known as a barristers' clerk), who negotiates fees with solicitors and distributes work among the barristers. Each barrister must pay rent for his 'tenancy' in chambers, plus contributions to overheads such as the salary of the practice manager (who may alternatively be paid commission on fees earned by the barristers).

In addition, a number of barristers work as employed legal advisers in various fields, such as local government, commerce, the government legal service and the Crown Prosecution Service.

Qualification

A barrister can only practise if he has been 'called to the Bar' of one of the four Inns of Court (Inner Temple, Middle Temple, Gray's Inn and Lincoln's Inn). These are very old institutions dating back to the fourteenth century.

In order to be called to the Bar and to practise in England and Wales, a prospective applicant must complete the following three stages:

The academic stage
This involves either passing a qualifying law degree course with a minimum of

Second Class Honours (Upper Division) or passing the conversion course known as the Common Professional Examination (one year for full-time students, two years for part-time and mature students). The Common Professional Examination is available to non-law graduates. For the definition of a qualifying law degree: see section 6.2, above.

The vocational stage
After joining one of the Inns those intending to practise in England and Wales must take the one-year full-time Bar Vocational Course (BVC) at the Inns of Court School of Law in London or at one of six other institutions validated to run the BVC. Since some of these institutions are many miles from London, where the Inns of Court are situated, trainee barristers are no longer required to eat a number of dinners at their Inns as a prerequisite to call to the Bar.

Instead a new system of 'qualifying units' was introduced from October 1997, which, together with the Bar exams, must be completed in order for a student to be called to the Bar. The new units involve various activities at the Inns of Court, such as residential weekends, one-day lecture programmes, lecture evenings combined with buffet suppers, and formal dinners involving activities such as lectures and debates. Students will be able to choose units which most suit their particular needs, eg if long distances are involved in travelling to their Inn they might prefer a residential weekend to a single formal dinner.

The new rules are designed to bring Bar traditions up to date and to be less onerous for those students studying for the Bar at institutions based several hundred miles from London.

The practical stage
After being called to the Bar, the pupil barrister embarks on a one-year period of apprenticeship known as 'pupillage' which is supervised by a pupil master. The first six months are spent in chambers as a non-practising pupil and, on satisfactory completion of this period, the pupil is issued with a practising certificate. He/she may then accept work ('briefs') and appear in court and, at the end of another six months (possibly spent in a different set of chambers), a final certificate is issued.

In the past, the average pupil received no income during pupillage, but things are now very different. Apart from scholarships and low interest loans, as from October 1991 there has been a minimum of 450 awards of at least £6,000 per annum each made available by chambers. Chambers may choose to provide substantially larger awards, or to fund more than the minimum number of pupils. Some of the top sets are in fact providing awards which equate to the rates of pay offered to those entering other professions. Of course, pupils may also receive income from practice during their pupillage.

Continuing education

During 1997 the Bar Council established an Advocacy Studies Board to promote training in advocacy and to raise standards. The Council also announced that newly qualified barristers involved in jury trial work will be required to undergo compulsory training in advocacy, and that eventually such training will be extended to cover more experienced barristers involved in such work. The reforms are part of the profession's first compulsory programme to improve standards, reflecting public concern at inconsistent standards of advocacy, particularly in criminal trials. Particular problems of advocacy which needed correction were prolixity, lack of preparation and over-aggressive techniques. The programme will end the assumption that advocacy skills cannot be taught but can only be learnt 'on the job'. The programme requires completion of 42 hours of training in advocacy, including refresher courses on changes in the law.

Queen's Counsel

Queen's Counsel (QCs) or 'silks' (because of their silk gowns) are the senior practitioners of the Bar and they constitute about 10 per cent of its practising membership. After ten years' practice as a junior (all barristers who are not silks are known as 'juniors') a barrister may apply to the Lord Chancellor to 'take silk' (ie to be appointed QC) and on doing so changes his/her practice considerably: the heavy load of a junior in drafting pleadings and paperwork is lost and greater fees may be charged. There is also an increase in status, and judges will (naturally enough) tend to respect the arguments of silks to a greater extent than juniors. Indeed, almost all puisne judges are appointed from the ranks of the silks.

The rule that a QC could not appear in court without a junior was abolished in 1977, though it is still the usual practice – the junior bearing the greater part of the preliminary work (particularly the paperwork). In consequence of this, the client whose case is difficult enough to merit engaging a QC to argue it in court often will have to pay both the QC's fees and those of his/her junior.

Appointment to the office of Queen's Counsel is approved by the Queen on the recommendation of the Lord Chancellor. There has been much criticism of the appointments system, not least because of its secrecy and, allegedly, its dependence on patronage. A working party (chairman Michael Kalisher QC) appointed by the Bar Council to consider the appointment of Queen's Counsel submitted its report in June 1994. It did not recommend any structural change in the selection system, but it suggested ways in which it could be improved. For example, there should be formal published criteria for the grant of silk: appointments should be based solely on merit with no positive discrimination in favour of women or ethnic minorities.

The Queen also appoints Queen's Counsel honoris causa, an honour for lawyers – including solicitors – who have made a distinguished contribution in the legal field otherwise than as practising advocates, for example as academics.

Functions

The basic work of a practising barrister (or 'counsel' as he or she is also known) is advocacy and litigation, though there is a certain amount of paperwork to do in even the most litigious practices – typically settling pleadings and giving written opinions on difficult legal points and advising, for example, as to the strength of a client's case. More specialist practices (particularly trusts, property, tax, company, landlord and tenant, wills and conveyancing) tend to involve more paperwork, some practitioners devoting nearly all their time to advising and drafting and spending very little time in court. Barristers are not all of a type: some, as noted, specialise in certain cases (including tax, commercial, shipping, building contracts), and some have 'general' practices doing a mixture of common law work, crime and matrimonial.

Rights of advocacy (rights of audience)

Upon call to the Bar and completion of pupillage a person who is entitled to practise at the independent Bar and who has secured a tenancy in chambers has rights of advocacy in every court, from the highest to the lowest, in the English legal system. The rights extend to tribunals in cases where legal representation is permitted by a tribunal. These rights of audience were confirmed by the Court and Legal Services Act 1990. Employed barristers (including those working for the Crown Prosecution Service) are not entitled to exercise such rights of audience and were not permitted to apply for higher courts qualifications under the procedures introduced by the 1990 Act. However, this may change under proposals contained in the Access to Justice Bill 1999 (see section 6.5 below).

An advocate (whether a barrister or solicitor) owes a duty not only to the client, but also to the court, which in fact overrides the duty to the client. The advocate must draw the court's attention to all the relevant authorities, even if harmful to that advocate's case. The advocate must not conceal the facts or set up a defence where his or her client had made a confession of guilt to that advocate. It is also the special duty of prosecuting counsel to assist the court and not to press for conviction. The nature of these obligations makes it difficult, it is said, for them to be performed by an employed advocate who may be under pressure from his or her employer to win the case. There is said to be particular danger if the employer is the state: independent prosecution barristers have frequently complained about pressure from the Crown Prosecution Service (CPS) opposing their views of the case. If CPS barristers prosecute would the case always be settled according to the CPS perspective and, if so, would it affect the quality of justice? Or is independence (and the integrity it rests on) a state of mind rather than a method of practice or payment? See further section 6.5 below.

Regulation and discipline

The Inns of Court are governed by the benchers, who are judges and senior members of the Bar appointed by other benchers. They exercise disciplinary powers over barristers and students through the Council of the Inns of Court, which appoints disciplinary tribunals for this purpose. Decisions of such tribunals are subject to appeal to 'visitors' to the Inns of Court, who are usually senior judges. In the most serious cases of professional misconduct a barrister can be 'disbarred' by his Inn, ie suspended from the ability to practise.

The General Council of the Bar is responsible for the professional standards of the Bar in accordance with a code laid down under the supervision of the judges. It is responsible for the receipt or initiation and investigation of complaints against barristers and for the prosecution of disciplinary charges before disciplinary tribunals.

The barristers' profession is also subject to the jurisdiction of the Legal Services Ombudsman, though the Ombudsman may not investigate, inter alia, any issue which is being or has been determined by a disciplinary tribunal of the Council of the Inns of Court.

During the 1990s the General Council of the Bar carried out a standards review and, in 1996, established the Bar Compensation Bureau to hear complaints concerning 'poor and shoddy' services. During 1999 barristers' chambers will be 'kite-marked' (ie accredited by an approved outside organisation) for good service in such matters as management of cases, how fees are charged and how well barristers communicate with clients. The Bar Council hope that kite-marking will help stamp out disreputable practices such as double-booking of cases and the problem of late-returned briefs, which cause a barrister to pull out of a trial at the last minute.

Relationships with clients

Traditionally a client cannot approach a barrister directly – the client must go through a solicitor, who chooses a barrister, negotiates a fee with the practice manager of that barrister's chamber and arranges conferences between the client and the barrister when it is necessary for the two to meet and speak directly. However, in recent years the rules prohibiting the public's access to barristers have been significantly relaxed by the Bar Council. Professional bodies, such as those representing accountants and architects, were permitted to instruct barristers directly. Then, in November 1997, a pilot scheme was launched enabling citizens' advice bureaux, law centres and Shelter (the housing charity) to have direct access to barristers. The Bar Council has also announced that during 1999 it will be licensing bodies such as trade unions, charities and health authorities to instruct barristers directly. It may be that the Bar Council will eventually scrap all restrictions on access to barristers and if it does so one of the last restrictive practices of the legal profession will be dismantled.

Traditionally there is no contract between a barrister and the client, although s61(1) of the Courts and Legal Services Act 1990 abolished any rule of law which prevented a barrister from entering a contract for his or her services. However, the Bar Council retains the right to regulate the matter and many relationships in this field remain non-contractual; payment of fees may be a matter of professional etiquette, though the Law Society has stated that solicitors are responsible for seeing that barristers are paid for work done on their briefs.

Barristers (like all advocates) cannot be sued for professional negligence in so far as advocacy in court and connected pre-trial work is concerned, mainly on grounds of public policy (to prevent constant re-litigation and protect advocates from unfair pressures): see *Rondel* v *Worsley* [1969] 1 AC 191 and *Saif Ali* v *Sydney Mitchell and Co* [1978] 3 All ER 1033.

The cab-rank rule

One of the most important rules of conduct (sometimes referred to as rules of professional etiquette) is the cab-rank principle: that is, a barrister in independent practice, in any field in which he professes to practise and irrespective of whether his client is paying privately or is legally aided or otherwise publicly funded, must:

1. accept any brief to appear before a court in which he professes to practise;
2. accept any instructions; and
3. act for any person on whose behalf he is briefed or instructed.

A barrister must do this irrespective of the party on whose behalf he is briefed or instructed, the nature of the case, and any brief or opinion which he may have formed as to the character, reputation, cause, conduct, guilt or innocence of that person. It is a serious breach of the Code of Conduct for counsel to return a brief without the consent of his professional client.

The cab-rank rule does not apply to solicitor-advocates under the rules of conduct made by the Law Society under the Courts and Legal Services Act 1990.

6.4 The Crown Prosecution Service

Introduction

Traditionally the functions of investigating crime and prosecuting offenders belonged to the police. However, critics argued that the prosecuting function involved questions of law, evidence and public policy for which the police were not professionally trained. A high proportion of cases (approximately 40 per cent) collapsed at trial due to insufficient evidence and the cause was said to be the lack of a professional prosecutors system. Further, it was argued as a matter of principle that the investigative and prosecuting functions should be exercised by separate institutions in order that independent minds could be applied to the results of police investigations.

As a result of the pressure for reform the Crown Prosecution Service (CPS), consisting of salaried lawyers appointed and employed on civil service criteria, was established by the Prosecution of Offences Act 1985. The CPS employs about 2,000 lawyers (two-thirds solicitors and one-third barristers) as well as lay staff.

Constitution

The Director of Public Prosecutions (DPP) was made head of the Crown Prosecution Service. The post of DPP had been existence for over a hundred years prior to the 1985 Act and hence the basic duties of the DPP continued in regard to prosecution, with the additional responsibilities of management of the CPS under the 1985 Act. It is the DPP's duty to commence and conduct a prosecution whenever it appears to be of importance or difficulty or which for any other reason requires the DPP's intervention. Further, the DPP always has the power to intervene in or take over any prosecution which has already been commenced. The 1985 Act established the offices of Chief Crown Prosecutor and Crown Prosecutor, who are responsible for the conduct of most prosecutions, and who work under the direction of the DPP. (For the manner in which the discretion to prosecute is exercised see Chapter 13, section 13.3.)

The DPP is accountable to Parliament through the Attorney-General, the chief law officer of the Crown, who is a member of the government and an elected MP. The DPP is required to make an annual report to the Attorney-General on the work of the CPS. The CPS is responsible for the prosecution of all criminal cases resulting from police investigations in England and Wales, with the exception of certain minor offences (such as some traffic offences).

Reorganisation

The relationship between the CPS and the police had been uneasy from the start. First, many police officers resented the transfer of their prosecuting functions to an independent agency, regarding it as a slur on their reputation for impartiality and professionalism. Second, there were severe administrative problems of co-ordination between 43 police force areas and 13 CPS area offices. This caused communication difficulties and lost paperwork which impeded the operation of the CPS. Morale among Crown Prosecutors fell as a result of overwork, staff shortages and denial of advocacy rights in jury trials in the Crown Courts, the latter remaining with the independent Bar. The loss of public confidence in the CPS led to a governmental review of its operational performance. The review was conducted by Sir Iain Glidewell, a former Court of Appeal judge. In June 1998 the Glidewell Report (Cmnd 3960; summary Cmnd 3972) recommended a decentralisation of the CPS so as to create a localised criminal justice system and to bring about closer working relationships between CPS lawyers and the police. The government accepted the Report and, as a result, from April 1999 there will be 42 CPS areas corresponding to police force areas (there are 43 police force areas but for CPS purposes the Metropolitan Police and City of London Police, which are two separate forces, will count as one force).

It is intended that the Chief Crown Prosecutors who will head the 42 areas shall enjoy a much higher public profile, substantial autonomy and an independent budget. It was believed that the previous system concentrated too much power in a centralised bureaucracy and that the new arrangements will command greater public confidence. During the summer of 1998 Dame Barbara Mills announced her early retirement from the post of DPP. She was replaced by David Calvert-Smith QC, who was put in charge of implementing the Glidewell Report. A new post of Chief Executive has been created to relieve the DPP of much of the managerial and administrative work involved in running the CPS. The new Chief Executive will be in charge of a slimmed down national headquarters in the hope of ending the cumbersome bureaucracy that bedevilled the operation of the CPS since its creation.

Rights of advocacy (rights of audience)

In magistrates' courts CPS lawyers (solicitors or barristers) conduct the daily lists of prosecutions which were previously presented by the police or local authority prosecuting solicitors. Section 53 of the Crime and Disorder Act 1998 authorises lay staff employed by the CPS to present straightforward guilty plea cases in magistrates' courts.

As employed lawyers CPS solicitors and barristers were initially denied advocacy rights in the higher courts following the setting up of the CPS. This became a source of discontent among CPS lawyers who regarded advocacy work as more attractive than much of the routine desk work which they had to handle in preparing prosecutions. They also felt that, having worked in detail on a particular prosecution, they were as able as a barrister from the independent Bar to present that prosecution in a Crown Court jury trial. The DPP, on behalf of the CPS, campaigned for such advocacy rights, arguing that granting them would boost morale among CPS lawyers and help with recruitment. The Law Society also campaigned on behalf of the employed solicitors working for the CPS. Eventually in February 1997 the judges' panel approved Law Society rules permitting a limited extension of rights of audience in the higher courts for employed solicitors, but this extension did not go so far as to cover jury trials: see section 6.2, *Rights of advocacy*. However, it appears that full advocacy rights will be granted to all CPS lawyers as a result of the radical reforms proposed in the Access to Justice Bill 1999: see section 6.5. below.

6.5 Reform of the legal profession

Legal education: the ACLEC Report (April 1996)

The first full-scale scrutiny of legal education since 1971 was undertaken by the Lord Chancellor's Advisory Committee on Legal Education and Conduct (ACLEC) during the period 1992–1996. Its Report, published on 25 April 1996, contains proposals which some will see as paving the way to eventual fusion. No action has so far been taken to implement its recommendations, but the debate about them will undoubtedly continue after the Access to Justice Bill 1999 is passed, because the changes proposed by that Bill (considered below) has important implications for the way future lawyers are educated and trained.

ACLEC's main object was to ensure that law students are not forced into making premature choices over which specialist branch of the legal profession they ought to join. For this purpose ACLEC recommends that graduates should be trained together to obtain a new interim qualification called the Licentiate in Professional Legal Studies. The new course would involve 18 weeks of specialist study to obtain the practical knowledge and skills needed by lawyers. On-the-job training in law firms and chambers could be taken before or after the new course. Formal training contracts and pupillage would continue, so that once the student had decided on one branch of the profession he/she would be faced with a period of six months' training in either a law firm or chambers (ACLEC is hoping to persuade the Law Society to cut the time of solicitors' training contracts for this purpose). ACLEC states that the Licentiate would obtain wide recognition and serve as a springboard to entry to other professions for those students wishing to practise otherwise than as pure lawyers.

Rights of advocacy (rights of audience): the proposals in the Access to Justice Bill 1999

In December 1998 the government published a White Paper, *Modernising Justice* (Cm 4155) proposing, inter alia, radical changes to rights of audience, which will be implemented after the Access to Justice Bill 1999 becomes law (probably by the autumn of 1999). The Bill proposes an extension of existing rights of audience so that all lawyers, upon qualification, obtain rights of advocacy in all courts, right up to and including the House of Lords. This will, of course, end the traditional monopoly of advocacy rights of barristers in the Court of Appeal and House of Lords and end their near monopoly in the High Court and Crown Courts. For the first time a wider range of lawyers, including Crown Prosecution Service lawyers and other employed lawyers, will have rights of audience – most notably in jury trials in the Crown Courts (thereby posing a serious threat to the existing incomes of independent practitioners at the Bar), subject to their meeting any additional training requirements imposed by their respective professional bodies (eg pupillage, completion of advocacy training courses) and to their compliance with revised rules of conduct (new rules will be needed for employed lawyers who wish to practise as advocates).

One of the most controversial aspects of the reforms is the proposal that all rules and requirements concerning advocacy will no longer be subject to the approval of the panel of senior judges established under the Courts and Legal Services Act 1990. Instead the Lord Chancellor alone will have power to approve or veto the new rules and restrictions, although he will be obliged to consult the senior judiciary on such matters and his decisions will be subject to parliamentary approval.

Lord Irvine, the Lord Chancellor, has said that the purpose of the reforms is to end the bureaucratic system established by the 1990 Act concerning the granting of rights of audience. The 1990 Act, he said, had failed in its objectives of widening such rights and ending anti-competitive restrictive practices. He has declared that he will strike down and replace any rule proposed by a professional body which unduly limits rights of audience or which is anti-competitive. In a House of Lords debate on the Bill he said:

> 'I cannot accept the notion that an employed lawyer faces unresolved conflicts of interests, has lower ethical standards or cannot be trusted ... we wish to ensure that advocates are chosen because they have the skills to do the job, not because they belong to one part of the profession or another.'

The Law Society and the Crown Prosecution Service have welcomed the proposals for providing greater client choice of legal services and a 'level playing field' for all lawyers. The Bar Council has strongly criticised the proposals for amounting to 'fusion of the legal profession by the back door' and risking the reduction in the number of independent practitioners at the Bar by 50 per cent.

In January 1999 a House of Lords select committee expressed concern on the ground that the reforms would give the Lord Chancellor too much individual power over who may appear in court and that this would be constitutionally objectionable (infringing the separation of powers and the traditional role of judges in such matters). In response Lord Irvine promised that the Bill would be amended so as to emphasise the preservation of an independent legal profession and that a statement of purpose to this effect in the Bill would govern the exercise of his powers in regard to determining rights of audience. The result may be that the Lord Chancellor will only be able to intervene if a professional body is acting 'unreasonably' over the granting of rights of audience. Further, the exercise of the Lord Chancellor's powers on this question may be subject to the affirmative resolution procedure in Parliament, which gives MPs and peers a more powerful check on those powers.

For a critical discussion of the reform proposals: see Zander 'Will the Reforms Serve the Public Interest?' [1998] NLJ 969; Zander 'More Louis XIV than Cardinal Wolsey' [1998] NLJ 1084; Lord Ackner 'More Power to the Executive?' [1998] NLJ 1512; and Gibbons 'Those Same Old Arguments' [1998] NLJ 1546.

The Advisory Committee on Legal Education and Conduct (ACLEC)

There is a controversial proposal in the Access to Justice Bill 1999 to abolish ACLEC (and possibly replace it with a smaller legal services consultative panel). ACLEC was established by ss19 and 20 of, and Sch 2, to the Courts and Legal Services Act 1990. ACLEC is independent of the government. It consists of a chairman and 16 other members. The chairman must be a Lord of Appeal in Ordinary or a judge of the Supreme Court.

ACLEC has a central role in arrangements for deciding who should have rights of audience before the courts or the right to conduct litigation, and who should be allowed to prepare applications for the grant of probate. The Committee helps shape applications for authorisation to grant those rights from professional and other bodies, and offers advice on the applications to the Lord Chancellor and the four designated judges. It replaced a non-statutory Advisory Committee set up in 1971. ACLEC has the general duty of assisting in the maintenance and development of standards in the education, training and conduct of those offering legal services. It does so by performing functions relating to general education and training (including continuing education and training), training in advocacy and training in the conduct of litigation; it may also consider what form of practical training is necessary in other areas concerned with the provision of legal services and it must have regard to the efficient provision of legal services for persons with special needs. The proposal to abolish ACLEC in its present form has fuelled the concern that the Lord Chancellor will be obtaining too much power over the legal profession when the Access to Justice Bill 1999 is implemented.

Part III: Methods of Adjudication and the Financing of Legal Services

7

Courts, Tribunals and Alternative Dispute Resolution

7.1 Divisions of the courts

7.2 The main English courts

7.3 Tribunals and inquiries

7.4 Arbitration

7.5 Alternative dispute resolution (ADR)

7.6 Diagrams of the main English court structure

7.1 Divisions of the courts

The two fundamental divisions of the court are superior and inferior courts and courts of record and courts not of record.

Superior and inferior courts

Superior courts have unlimited jurisdiction, and include the House of Lords, the Privy Council, the Supreme Court and the Crown Court.

Inferior courts have jurisdiction limited either by value or geographically or both (eg county courts, magistrates' courts).

Courts of record and courts not of record

This is a historical division, based upon whether the court kept official records of its proceedings or not. This no longer applies.

Civil and criminal

English law and procedure are divided into two categories, civil and criminal, and a case must be one or the other. Some courts have jurisdiction over both civil and criminal cases (eg the House of Lords, the Court of Appeal and magistrates' courts).

Courts of common law and equity

Until the Judicature Act 1873 the common law was administered solely by the courts of common law and the rules of equity by the Court of Chancery, the two being quite separate – having different procedures, being based on different principles, and offering different remedies. However, ss24–25 of the 1873 Act 'fused' the administration of law and equity. The jurisdiction of both the superior common law courts and the Court of Chancery was transferred to the High Court and judges are now required to apply both sets of rules, where relevant. Thus the modern Chancery Division of the High Court, though it is assigned some specialist matters once dealt with exclusively by the old Court of Chancery, no longer is the sole administrator of equity. Where the rules of common law and equity are in conflict, those of equity prevail.

7.2 The main English courts

The purpose of this section is to give a basic outline of each of the main English courts in the present court structure.

For the European Court of Justice see Chapter 17, section 17.2, and for the European Court of Human Rights see Chapter 19, section 19.3.

The House of Lords

Originally Parliament was a court which exercised certain judicial functions but by Tudor times this jurisdiction came to be exercised exclusively by the House of Lords. Until the Appellate Jurisdiction Act 1876 which created Lords of Appeal in Ordinary, appointed from eminent judges and lawyers, to hear appeals, any peer could hear appeals and vote on the decision, and often the only lawyer present was the Lord Chancellor. One result of this was that House of Lords decisions before 1876 carried very little legal authority, except in cases where the judges were invited to advise the House of the law.

Appeals are heard by at least three, and usually five (and exceptionally, seven), judges who must be drawn from the Lords of Appeal in Ordinary, the Lord Chancellor and any other peer who has held 'high judicial office', which is defined by the 1876 Act. In practice only the Lords of Appeal ('law lords') normally sit, although some Lord Chancellors do so. The law lords are usually appointed from Lord Justices of Appeal, although there are usually two who were Scottish judges because the House of Lords is also the final appeal court for Scotland. Their maximum number is twelve.

Appeals are heard generally in a committee room and their lordships do not wear robes. Strictly the lords do not give 'judgments' but instead give 'opinions' stating the reasons for their vote whether to allow or dismiss the appeal. If the House is equally divided the appeal is dismissed, and while normally this situation does not arise because an uneven number sits, it can occur – such as when a law lord dies before giving judgment and the House is otherwise equally divided: see *Kennedy* v *Spratt* [1972] AC 83 (Lord Upjohn died).

The House of Lords has very little original jurisdiction. The trial of one of its members 'by his peers' was abolished in 1948 and impeachment (prosecution of political offenders) is obsolete. The only remaining matters of original jurisdiction are breaches of privilege and disputed claims to peerages.

The jurisdiction of the House is almost entirely appellate, hearing appeals from (mainly):

1. The Court of Appeal (with the leave of either the Court of Appeal or the Appeals Committee of the Lords).
2. The High Court ('leap frog' procedure, with leave of the House of Lords, on a point of law of general public importance).
3. A Divisional Court of the Queen's Bench Division in a criminal cause or matter, with the leave of that court or the House.

Note that the House of Lords is not part of the Supreme Court, even though it is the highest appellate court. This is due to the fact that when the Supreme Court was formed it was intended to abolish the Lords. This was only reversed by the 1876 Act.

Finally, the Judicial Committee of the House of Lords will not be affected by the planned reform of the House during 1999, when the voting rights of most hereditary peers are due to be abolished. All Law Lords are life peers and will continue to operate in their traditional manner. However, long-term reform of the upper House may revive the debate as to whether the Court of Appeal should become the final appellate court on domestic matters for England and Wales (as well as for Scotland and Northern Ireland).

The Court of Appeal

This is the highest of the three courts which constitute the Supreme Court of England and Wales, the others being the High Court and the Crown Court. The Lord Chancellor is president of the Supreme Court.

The Court of Appeal is composed of (1) ex officio judges who are the Lord Chancellor, the Lord Chief Justice (the president of the criminal division), the Master of the Rolls (the president of the civil division), the president of the Family Division, Lords of Appeal in Ordinary and former Lord Chancellors, and the Vice-Chancellor, and (2) the Lords Justices of Appeal. See also Chapter 4, section 4.2 *Circuit judges*. In practice only the Master of the Rolls and the Lord Chief Justice of the ex officio judges sit in the civil and criminal divisions respectively. High Court judges may also sit with Lords Justices, and frequently do so in the criminal division. The normal number is three, but when a difficult and important point of law is in issue, the court may consist of five. Interlocutory appeals may now be heard by a single judge sitting in chambers (in private). Further, appeals from county courts are now usually heard by two judges, though three should sit if a difficult point arises. The administrative work of the divisions is supervised by two registrars.

The Court of Appeal is a creature of statute and its powers are those conferred by the relevant Acts of Parliament. The civil appeal system is considered in Chapter 11 and the criminal appeal system in Chapter 16.

The High Court

This was established by the Judicature Acts 1873 and 1875, which abolished the old courts – Court of King's Bench, Court of Common Pleas, Court of Exchequer, Court of Chancery, the Courts of Admiralty, Probate and Divorce and Matrimonial Causes and others – and transferred their jurisdiction to the High Court. The High Court originally contained five divisions:

1. Queen's Bench Division
2. Common Pleas Division
3. Exchequer Division
4. Chancery Division
5. Probate, Divorce and Admiralty Division.

However, in 1880 the Exchequer and Common Pleas Divisions were abolished and their business transferred to the Queen's Bench Division. In the Administration of Justice Act 1970 the remaining three divisions were reorganised by the creation of a new Family Division in place of the Probate, Divorce and Admiralty Division. The admiralty work was transferred to the Queen's Bench Division, contentious probate work to the Chancery Division and the Chancery Division's jurisdiction over wards of court transferred to the new division. The great majority of puisne judges sit in the Queen's Bench Division. High Court judges are called puisne (pronounced 'puny') judges (from the law French for 'junior' or 'inferior').

Before the Courts Act 1971 the High Court sat solely in the Law Courts in the Strand, although High Court judges also tried civil cases on assize. That Act abolished the assizes and instead provided that the High Court could sit at other locations.

The High Court has both civil and criminal jurisdiction, original and appellate. Although all three divisions have equal competence, in practice they have separate jurisdiction laid down partly by the rules and partly by statutory provisions. There are no financial or geographical limitations to the High Court jurisdiction (except that its jurisdiction is confined to England and Wales, since Scotland and Northern Ireland have their own laws and legal systems).

The Queen's Bench Division of the High Court
The head of this division is the Lord Chief Justice. Its original civil jurisdiction includes tort and most contract actions; it also deals with commercial and admiralty actions. It has a lesser civil appellate jurisdiction, its Divisional Court hearing appeals by way of case stated from magistrates' courts (except in matrimonial matters) and from the Crown Court. It also hears appeals from district judges. More important is its criminal appellate function, as most of the appeals by case stated from magistrates' and the Crown Court are in criminal matters. The division exercises the supervisory jurisdiction of the old Court of King's Bench by means of the prerogative orders granted by the Divisional Court.

Judges of this division also spend part of their time trying serious criminal matters in first tier Crown Courts and hearing Queen's Bench Division actions in the same locations.

There are two specialist courts of the Queen's Bench Division with specialist judges assigned to them: the Commercial Court and the Admiralty Court. These two 'courts' have similar procedures which differ from those in general operation in the division: they deal more efficiently with the specialist nature of the subject matter.

The Chancery Division of the High Court
The head of this division is the Lord Chancellor, who in practice never sits; so the effective head is the Vice-Chancellor, who is now also an ex-officio judge of the Court of Appeal. Most chancery actions are heard in London, but chancery actions are also tried at certain centres in the major cities. This division tries most matters concerned with land and is given jurisdiction over contentious probate, bankruptcy, revenue matters, trusts, company matters and winding up, and patent and trade mark actions (which are heard in the Patents Court).

The Chancery Division divisional court has appellate jurisdiction in relation to bankruptcy appeals from the county courts and land registration. Income tax appeals from the Special Commissioners of Inland Revenue are heard by a single judge.

The Family Division of the High Court
The head of this division is the President of the Family Division. Its jurisdiction includes all defended matrimonial causes, declarations of legitimacy and of validity of a marriage, proceedings for a decree of presumption of death, wardship, adoption, guardianship and certain matrimonial property matters. It deals with all proceedings under the Child Support Act 1991. The divisional court of the division hears appeals from magistrates' courts and county courts in adoption, guardianship proceedings and appeals by way of case stated in matrimonial proceedings in magistrates' courts.

The Crown Court

History
Before 1972 the courts where trials on indictment took place were the 61 Assize Courts and the 173 Quarter Sessions together with the Central Criminal Court, commonly known as 'the Old Bailey', and the Crown Courts of Liverpool and Manchester. Both Assizes and Quarter Sessions had a local jurisdiction, so that in general they could only try crimes committed within their locality and also the methods of court administration varied from area to area.

The present structure
The Courts Act 1971 abolished Assizes (both criminal and civil sides) and Quarter Sessions. All serious crime is tried on indictment in the Crown Court (which is a single court sitting in many locations composed of many judges).

There are four types of judge in the Crown Court:

1. High Court judges
2. Circuit judges
3. Recorders
4. Assistant recorders/deputy circuit judges.

The High Court judges are usually those attached to the Queen's Bench Division. Circuit judges are full-time judges who sit in both the Crown Court and county courts, and recorders are part-time judges, appointed for a limited period. When the Crown Court is hearing an appeal from a magistrates' court, lay justices of the peace sit with a single circuit judge. Deputy circuit judges and assistant recorders are ad hoc appointments for a very short period, though used to a great extent. Assistant recorders are persons who have a ten-year Crown Court or county court qualification within s71 of the Courts and Legal Services Act 1990.

The Crown Court has exclusive jurisdiction over all criminal trials on indictment for offences wherever committed. Procedure is governed by Crown Court Rules, which are delegated legislation made by the Crown Court Rules Committee under s84 of the Supreme Court Act 1981. The Crown Court is part of the Supreme Court and is a superior court of record, but it is under the supervisory jurisdiction of the High Court as expressed by the issue of prerogative orders, and a circuit judge is not a High Court judge.

England and Wales are divided into six administrative regions called circuits, with at least two presiding judges. Crown Court cases are allocated according to the composition of the court: that is, High Court judge, circuit judge or recorder, or a court which includes justices of the peace. Allocation is made by the Lord Chief Justice with the concurrence of the Lord Chancellor.

County courts

Although there were county courts in earlier times, the present-day county courts were established by statute in 1846 and have only civil jurisdiction. Although they deal with many relatively minor claims they are important as they offer a comprehensive, speedy and relatively cheap procedure and deal with the bulk of civil litigation.

There are about 280 county courts in England and Wales. Some of these are specially designated divorce county courts which deal with undefended divorces and related matters and this jurisdiction is not geographically limited.

The county courts are grouped for administrative purposes into the same circuits as Crown Courts. They are staffed by circuit judges, most county courts having at least one judge virtually permanently attached to that court. The administrative business is the concern of the district judge who has a seven-year general qualification within s71 of the Courts and Legal Services Act 1990.

The district judge also deals with procedural matters and tries minor cases ('small claims'). Appeal from the district judge is to the circuit judge and from there to the Court of Appeal.

Magistrates' courts

Magistrates' courts are composed of justices of the peace or, in the big cities, a stipendiary (professional salaried) magistrate. A stipendiary magistrate must have a seven-year general qualification within s71 of the Courts and Legal Services Act 1990. For trying an information summarily there must be at least two and not more than seven justices of the peace (in practice there are usually three) or one stipendiary. A single lay justice may hear committal proceedings for cases which are going for trial at the Crown Court.

Magistrates' courts have a very wide and varied jurisdiction, only part of it being criminal, but their jurisdiction is limited geographically and is confined to minor matters.

The criminal jurisdiction has two aspects, trial and committal proceedings. Certain offences can only be tried summarily (ie in a magistrates' court), and certain other offences may be tried either on indictment or summarily. Where a case is to be tried on indictment in the Crown Court then the other aspect of the jurisdiction arises. Before a case can be tried at the Crown Court it must have been sent there by a magistrates' court.

Magistrates also issue summonses and warrants which start the whole criminal process and grant bail.

There are special magistrates' courts, known as youth courts, which deal with people under the age of 17 who commit offences. A youth court is composed of at least three lay justices from a special panel, consisting of at least one man and one woman. The youth court must not sit in any place where an adult court has been sitting within the last hour and, unlike adult courts, the proceedings are not in public.

The magistrates' courts also have a very varied civil jurisdiction. Probably the most important is over family proceedings (in family proceedings courts) under which the court can grant maintenance and custody and make a non-cohabitation order, but complex cases under the Children Act 1989 should be transferred to the nearest county court. Magistrates' courts can also deal with adoption proceedings, and are responsible for the recovery of a large number of debts such as council tax, gas, electricity and water charges, income tax and national insurance contributions. They also grant and revoke several kinds of licences, especially licences to sell alcohol. Appeals on family matters go to the Divisional Court of the Family Division.

Magistrates can award compensation (maximum £5,000 for any one offence) for personal injury, loss or damage.

7.3 Tribunals and inquiries

The word 'tribunal' is defined by the Oxford Dictionary as a 'judgment seat ... A court of justice; a judicial assembly'. It is thus possible, if confusing, for an ordinary court of law to be referred to as a tribunal. The word now tends to be used in a different context from the normal court system to mean a panel to resolve disputes between, for example, the citizen and an officer of a government agency or between individuals in an area of law in which the government has legislated the conduct of their relations. These tribunals may be conveniently called 'administrative tribunals'.

In the Social Security Appeals Tribunal the applicant is usually appealing against the decision of an adjudication officer who is an employee of the Department of Social Security. The officer may have decided that the applicant is not entitled to statutory sick pay and the applicant is informed with the adjudication officer's decision that there is a right of appeal. This is conducted by the independent tribunal, usually composed of three persons, of whom the chairman has a five-year general qualification within s71 of the Courts and Legal Services Act 1990.

Although the location and general appearance of the tribunal may make it seem as if it is an offshoot of the civil service department from which the appeal is being made, it is stressed to the appellant that the tribunal is, in fact, totally independent. Appeals from the decisions of immigration officers would be in the same category of a tribunal which deals with matters where the individual is challenging the decision of the state.

A different type of administrative tribunal is the industrial tribunal where the applicant will often be appealing against his employer's decision to dismiss him and will allege that this is unfair. The tribunal in this instance will consist of a chairman having a seven-year general qualification within s71 of the 1990 Act, usually full-time, and two 'wingmen', one representing the interests of employers and the other being drawn from a trade union. Appeal lies to the Employment Appeal Tribunal.

Tribunals are generally governed by the Tribunals and Inquiries Act 1992 and by the basic characteristics of openness, fairness and impartiality. By virtue of the Franks Report 1957 (Cmnd 218) tribunals have proliferated and it is generally thought that their expertise and their expedited process makes them not only invaluable to the already overburdened courts but that they perform a useful function in themselves. Unfortunately legal aid is not often available in tribunals but there is more opportunity for representation of a party by a non-lawyer, and many individuals have the benefit of advice and assistance from, for example, trade unions.

The second sort of tribunal can be referred to as a 'domestic tribunal' in that it deals with the internal matters of professional associations. Some of these are created by statute (eg General Medical Council's disciplinary committee), others are voluntary (eg Bar Council).

Tribunals of inquiry are often set up to enquire into matters of urgent importance. This is done by Parliament.

A number of statutes empower Ministers to hold local inquiries, for example on planning schemes. These are held by an inspector who reports to the Minister who has to make the final decisions.

Control of tribunals has increased over recent years. The Council on Tribunals reviews the operations of the various tribunals and the High Court can supervise their working by means of the prerogative orders even though there is often no statutory right of appeal. Such supervision takes the form of reviewing the legality of the tribunals' acts (eg for want of natural justice), not by way of rehearing on the merits.

7.4 Arbitration

The jurisdiction of arbitrators usually arises out of contracts, but some statutes provide for disputes to be referred to arbitration. Arbitration is used widely in shipping, commerce and the building and engineering professions.

Any provision in a contract which purports to oust the jurisdiction of the courts is void but it is usual for a contract (or sometimes a lease) to provide that a dispute be referred first to arbitration. If one party commences court proceedings without arbitration the other may, if he has taken no step in those proceedings, apply to the court to stay the proceedings until after arbitration and this order is usually granted. On the other hand, if all parties agree, the High Court may exercise the arbitrator's powers.

The governing statute must be decided according to the ordinary rules of English law (unless otherwise provided). The contract provides how the arbitrator is to be appointed, and it is common to provide that if the parties cannot agree on an arbitrator that some body or person such as the president of the Law Society shall appoint an arbitrator.

Under s69 Arbitration Act 1996 there is a right of appeal on a point of law to the High Court if the parties consent, or with the leave of the court. Appeal lies to the Court of Appeal, but only with leave on an important point of law.

There is a trend towards arbitration in the commercial world. It is usually a quicker and therefore less costly method of settling disputes. It is also possible to arrange the hearing for a time convenient to both parties. Although the parties must pay the arbitrator's fees (often quite high), arbitration may be preferred because it is a private form of dispute settlement which can be cost-effective in that the decision (known as an award) can be reached more quickly than by using the court system.

7.5 Alternative dispute resolution (ADR)

In 1990 the London Common Law and Commercial Bar Association recommended that there should be a pilot scheme in the county court and their report to this effect was adopted by the Bar Council. Alternative dispute resolution (ADR) would involve the use of lawyers to try to resolve disputes at an early stage by using conciliation and giving the parties an impartial view of the likely outcome of any trial. Decisions would not be binding, but if the procedure was successful much money would be saved and judges would be freed to deal with more difficult cases.

Subsequently, a Bar Council committee, chaired by Beldam LJ, proposed pilot schemes in county courts and the High Court to evaluate the potential of ADR in different kinds of proceedings. The legal rights of the parties would be unaffected by any mediation process and mediators would help the parties to find solutions rather then attempt to suggest or impose them. Mediators would be lawyers with at least seven years' experience and they would be given training in mediation techniques. Similar proposals have been made by the National Consumer Council.

On 8 December 1993 the then Lord Chancellor, Lord Mackay of Clashfern, urged people to resolve disputes without using the formal courts system, commending informal, accessible procedures such as those found in the small claims arbitration procedures. Ombudsman schemes had, he added, recently been gaining the confidence and imagination of the public. A characteristic that all ombudsman schemes have in common is their potential to adjudicate between disputing parties without the trappings or expense of going to court, he explained. Early settlement by informal means in most (but not all) instances was 'far more satisfactory for the parties than pursuing their disputes through the courts – however user-friendly and cost-effective court procedures might be'.

In a *Practice Statement* [1994] 1 All ER 34 Cresswell J, while emphasising the primary role of the Commercial Court as a forum for deciding commercial cases, said the judges of the court wished to encourage parties to consider the use of ADR, such as mediation and conciliation, as a possible additional means of resolving issues or disputes. The judges would not act as mediators or be involved in any ADR process but would in appropriate cases invite parties to consider whether their cases, or certain issues in their cases, could be resolved by means of ADR. By way of example only, ADR might be tried where the costs of litigation were likely to be wholly disproportionate to the amount at stake. The clerk to the Commercial Court would keep a list of individuals and bodies that offered mediation, conciliation and other ADR services. The list would also include individuals and bodies offering arbitration services.

In a *Practice Note* [1996] 3 All ER 383 the Commercial Court formally encourages the use of alternative dispute resolution (ADR) in the Commercial Court and summarises the advantages of ADR in a commercial context as follows:

1. it significantly helps to save litigants the ever-mounting cost of bringing their cases to trial;
2. it saves them the delay of litigation in reaching finality in their disputes;
3. it enables them to achieve settlement of their disputes while preserving their existing commercial relationships and market reputation;
4. it provides them with a wider range of settlement solutions than those offered by litigation; and
5. it is likely to make a substantial contribution to the more efficient use of judicial resources.

The pre-trial check list (*Practice Note* [1995] 1 All ER 385) deals specifically with ADR and asks:

1. Have you (the solicitor) or counsel discussed with your client(s) the possibility of attempting to resolve this dispute (or particular issues) by ADR?
2. Might some form of ADR procedure assist to resolve or narrow the issues in this case?
3. Have your or your client(s) explored with the other parties the possibility of resolving this dispute (or particular issues) by ADR?

Family mediation

Tony Wells, the director of development for the Council for Family Proceedings, has said:

> 'The essential feature of mediation in family disputes is that parties are assisted to work out their own solution to their dispute. The task of the mediator is to enable the parties to do this work. The mediator sees the parties together without their legal advisers. The mediator does not offer advice or suggest solutions. He or she will clarify any proposals made and also the objections to them, as well as what might make a proposal acceptable. The work will focus on what the parties want for the future – not what has happened in the past.'

Training programmes for mediators are run by the Family Mediators' Association. Lawyers selected for training (other mediators are, for example, workers or counsellors) are expected to have had at least five years' experience as family lawyers. The National Association of Family and Conciliation Services is the biggest provider of out-of-court mediation and it has estimated that, where there was a clear outcome, in 38 per cent of cases disputed issues were completely resolved.

The Green Paper *Looking to the Future: Mediation and the Ground for Divorce*, published 6 December 1993, contained proposals for the reform of divorce, based largely on recommendations made by the Law Commission. At the heart of the proposed reform is the use of mediators to help resolve issues between the parties with minimal conflict. The proposals are part of the Family Law Act 1996, but it is expected to take several years before the relevant provisions can be brought into force.

7.6 Diagrams of the main English court structure

The civil courts

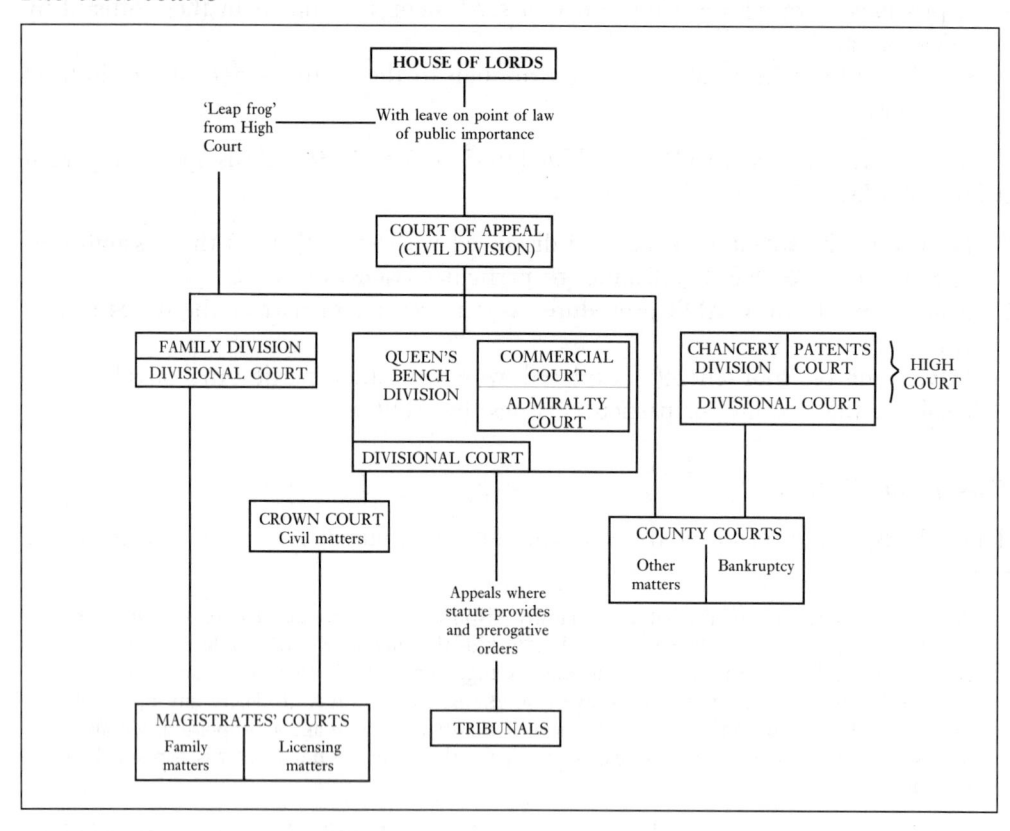

```
                        HOUSE OF LORDS
        'Leap frog'    With leave on point of law
        from High      of public importance
        Court
                    COURT OF APPEAL
                    (CIVIL DIVISION)

  FAMILY DIVISION    QUEEN'S    COMMERCIAL     CHANCERY    PATENTS  ⎫
  DIVISIONAL COURT   BENCH      COURT          DIVISION    COURT    ⎬ HIGH
                     DIVISION   ADMIRALTY                           ⎭ COURT
                                COURT          DIVISIONAL COURT
                     DIVISIONAL COURT

        CROWN COURT                    COUNTY COURTS
        Civil matters                  Other        Bankruptcy
                                       matters
                    Appeals where
                    statute provides
                    and prerogative
                    orders

  MAGISTRATES' COURTS         TRIBUNALS
  Family     Licensing
  matters    matters
```

Diagrams of the main English court structure 117

The criminal courts

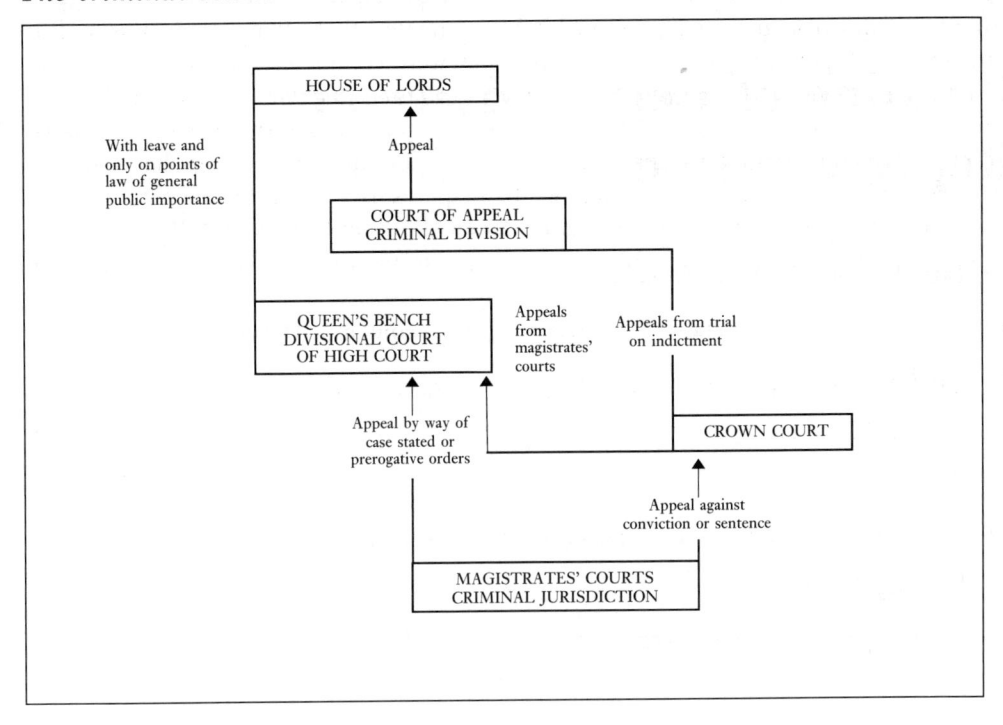

```
                        HOUSE OF LORDS
                              ▲
   With leave and           Appeal
   only on points of
   law of general
   public importance   COURT OF APPEAL
                       CRIMINAL DIVISION


                                Appeals      Appeals from trial
                    QUEEN'S BENCH  from         on indictment
                    DIVISIONAL COURT magistrates'
                    OF HIGH COURT    courts
                                                         CROWN COURT
                                                              ▲
                       Appeal by way of
                       case stated or           Appeal against
                       prerogative orders       conviction or sentence

                              MAGISTRATES' COURTS
                              CRIMINAL JURISDICTION
```

8

Funding of Legal Advice and Representation

8.1 Introduction: the legal aid scheme

8.2 Legal advice and assistance: the green form scheme and ABWOR

8.3 Civil legal aid

8.4 Criminal legal aid

8.5 Costs

8.6 Alternative methods of funding: legal expenses insurance and conditional fees

8.7 Free legal services

8.8 Reform proposals: the Access to Justice Bill 1999

8.1 Introduction: the legal aid scheme

A national scheme for the provision of legal aid, that is funding for legal advice and representation, was founded in 1949. The scheme is now administered by the Legal Aid Board which was set up by s3 of the Legal Aid Act 1988.

The Board has a legal aid fund out of which payments are made and into which contributions are received and the balance of the cost of the scheme is covered by money provided by Parliament. All members of the legal profession are under a duty not to involve the fund in unnecessary expenditure. The Board has between 11 and 17 members and includes two solicitors and two barristers. The Lord Chancellor appoints the Board and one of its members to be Chairman.

For the purposes of administration, the Board operates in 13 areas, each area consisting of:

1. An area secretary.
2. An area office – to deal with applications for legal aid and the control of certificates and green forms.
3. An area committee comprising practising solicitors and barristers – to deal with appeals.

4. A criminal legal aid committee – to deal with appeals from magistrates' courts' refusals of criminal legal aid.

The scheme has three aspects, each considered below, in relation to which the rules and procedure are very different. These three aspects are: legal advice and assistance; civil legal aid; and criminal legal aid.

Additionally, it is to be noted that if someone is not sure whether he qualifies for legal aid or not, he may always ask a solicitor for a 'fixed fee interview' which costs a maximum of £50. This will provide up to half an hour's advice and most solicitors who do legal aid work will provide this service, some for less than the maximum fee of £50, and a few for no fee ('pro bono' work).

8.2 Legal advice and assistance: the green form scheme and ABWOR

The green form scheme

This scheme was first introduced by the Legal Advice and Assistance Act 1972 and is now contained in Pt III of the Legal Aid Act 1988.

Services provided under the scheme include written or oral advice from a legal representative, usually a solicitor (or counsel), on any questions of English law and on any steps which it may be appropriate for the applicant to take. This, therefore, will include the giving of general advice, writing letters, negotiating. The scheme does not cover:

1. the making of wills;
2. the conveyancing of property;
3. divorce (though ancillary matters such as maintenance and custody of children are covered);
4. defamation;
5. cases going to tribunals and arbitrations;
6. cases going to European courts.

The name 'green form scheme' comes from the method of applying: application is made at a solicitor's office by filling in a green form. This contains questions concerning the applicant's income and capital as legal advice and assistance is available only to applicants whose resources are within the limits specified in regulations pursuant to s9 of the Legal Aid Act 1988. It is for the solicitor to calculate whether the applicant qualifies: this is a necessary part of this aspect of the legal aid scheme as it ensures that the green form scheme of legal advice is given quickly and that administration costs are kept low. From January 2000 only firms awarded franchises and contracts by the Legal Aid Board to do green form work will be able to offer advice under this part of the legal aid scheme. Franchise awards are conditional on meeting approved quality standards.

The relevant figures

An applicant who is receiving income support, income-based jobseekers' allowance, family credit or disability working allowance is eligible for free legal advice and assistance unless he is out of scope on capital (see below).

If the applicant is not in receipt of the above state benefits his disposable income must be taken into account. The applicant qualifies for legal advice and assistance if:

1. his/her disposable income is £83.00 or less a week; and
2. his/her disposable capital is £1,000 or less (assuming no dependants).

(*Note*: All figures given in this chapter apply as from 12 April 1999. There will be a further uprating in April 2000).

In calculating disposable income and capital, allowances are made for dependants. As a general rule the following are not counted in assessing disposable capital: the value of the house the applicant lives in, household furniture and effects, clothing and tools of his trade.

Contribution system

None. The applicant is ineligible if weekly disposable income exceeds £83 or if capital exceeds £1,000 (assuming no dependants).

Limitation

The scope of the scheme is limited by the Legal Aid Act 1988 in that advice and assistance may only be given immediately by a solicitor to the extent that he considers that the cost of giving it will not exceed a total of two hours' worth of work, or three hours in matrimonial cases involving the preparation of a petition. If the advice or assistance will cost more, the solicitor must obtain approval from the legal aid office before giving it.

The aim of the scheme, therefore, to give immediate initial advice, is limited to a relatively small amount of advice and assistance. Delay is involved in obtaining any greater amount of advice or assistance. Generally the scheme makes only advice available, not representation.

Assistance by way of representation (ABWOR)

This covers a solicitor's costs for preparation and representation in most civil cases in magistrates' courts (eg separation, maintenance and defended adoption proceedings). Application is made on the green form and another form. The income conditions are the same as for legal advice and assistance (although the limit here is £178 per week) and a person with no dependants may qualify for ABWOR provided his/her savings do not exceed £3,000.

Contribution system for ABWOR

No contribution is required if disposable income is less than £75 per week. If weekly disposable income is between £75 and £178 a weekly contribution of one-third of the excess income over £75 is required. A person automatically qualifies on income free of contribution if on income support, income-based jobseekers allowance, family credit or disability working allowance. A person automatically qualifies on capital if on income support or income-based jobseekers allowance. Allowances are made for dependants. Disposable capital is assessed in the same way as for the green form scheme, above.

A person requiring representation that is not covered by the ABWOR scheme must seek funding for it through civil legal aid or criminal legal aid.

8.3 Civil legal aid

Scope

In a civil case, legal aid may be obtained to pay for all work leading up to and including the court proceedings and for representation by a solicitor and, if necessary, a barrister. The position is mainly governed by Pt IV of the Legal Aid Act 1988. Legal aid is available for proceedings in all the main courts.

However legal aid is not available for:

1. Undefended matrimonial proceedings.
2. Judicial and administrative tribunals.
3. Arbitrations.
4. Proceedings before a coroner's court.
5. Proceedings involving libel or slander, although legal aid may be granted to pursue a claim for malicious falsehood: see *Joyce* v *Sengupta* [1993] 1 WLR 337.

Further, as from February 1999 only about 200 franchised solicitors' firms will be allowed to handle medical negligence claims funded by civil legal aid. (The franchises are awarded under the Legal Aid Board's Quality Assurance Scheme.)

Financial requirements

The first condition of eligibility is that the applicant is within the financial requirements.

In order to qualify for free legal aid the applicant must have a disposable income of less than £2,680 per year and (unless the applicant is receiving income support or income-based jobseekers allowance) a disposable capital of less than £3,000 (assuming no dependants). Contributions will be required if the applicant has a disposable income of between £2,680 per year and £7,940 per year (£8,751 per year in personal injury cases) and/or if the applicant has a disposable capital of between

£3,000 and £6,750 (£8,560 for personal injury cases). Ineligibility starts at more than £7,940 per year (£8,751 in personal injury cases) and at more than £6,750 in capital (£8,560 for personal injury cases). These figures assume no dependants.

'Disposable income' is calculated as follows:

1. Applicant's income for the following twelve months is assessed.
2. Income tax, national insurance, superannuation, pension contributions, employment expenses, rent, water rates, council tax and mortgage payments are deducted.
3. Allowances for family and dependants are deducted.

What is left is the applicant's disposable income.

'Disposable capital' is calculated in a similar way as for the green form scheme, above, but there are some differences. In particular, no allowance is made for dependants, but there is an allowance (a 'capital disregard') for pensioners (men and women over 60 for this purpose) related to disposable incomes, excluding net income from capital.

Contribution system

Contribution from capital is required of the excess over £3,000. It comprises an on-going monthly contribution from income of 1/36th of excess over £2,680 for the life of the legal aid certificate. The assessments are carried out by officials from the Legal Aid Board.

The merits test

The second condition of eligibility is that the applicant has reasonable grounds for taking, defending or being a party to the proceedings and that it is reasonable to grant legal aid in all the circumstances. This question is decided (often with the help of a written opinion of counsel) by the appropriate legal aid office; there is a right of appeal to the area committee.

8.4 Criminal legal aid

Scope

The provision of legal aid for those charged with a criminal offence is governed by Pt V of the Legal Aid Act 1988. It applies to criminal proceedings before any of the following courts:

1. House of Lords;
2. Court of Appeal (Criminal Division);
3. the Crown Court; and the
4. magistrates' court.

Application for legal aid by a defendant in criminal proceedings is made to the magistrates in the magistrates' court which is dealing initially with the defendant's case. In practice it is the magistrates' clerk who will determine the application. There has long been concern at discrepancies in awards of legal aid by different magistrates' courts in similar types of cases. There is a suspicion that some magistrates' clerks may be as much influenced by a desire to protect the public purse as by the merits of particular applications. However, rights of review and appeal are available: see *The merits tests*, below.

It should be noted that a person being questioned by the police about an offence has a right to free legal advice under the duty solicitor scheme and there is often a duty solicitor available at magistrates' courts or on call to give free advice and representation on a first appearance. Both services are available without a means test.

Financial requirements

The free legal aid income and capital limits are £51 per week and £3,000 respectively; there are no upper limits. Contributions from capital are the excess over £3,000 and a defendant may be required to pay such contribution as appears reasonable in the light of his/her commitments and resources. Weekly contributions from income are £1 for every £3 or part of £3 by which disposable income exceeds £51. No contribution is payable if the disposable income is less than £52 per week, or if the applicant is in receipt of income support, income-based jobseekers' allowance, family credit or disability working allowance. In calculating disposable income and capital, allowances are made for dependants.

The merits test

Apart from financial considerations, it is laid down by s21(2) of the Legal Aid Act 1988 that legal aid must be granted where it is desirable in the interests of justice. The criteria to be followed by the court are the criteria set out in ss22(2) of the Legal Aid Act 1988 which are as follows:

1. The offence is such that if proved it is likely that the court would impose a sentence which would deprive the accused of his liberty or lead to loss of his livelihood or serious damage to his reputation.
2. The determination of the case may involve consideration of a substantial question of law.
3. The accused may be unable to understand the proceedings or to state his own case because of his inadequate knowledge of English, mental illness or other mental or physical disability.
4. The nature of the defence is such as to involve the tracing and interviewing of witnesses or expert cross-examination of a witness for the prosecution.

5. It is in the interest of someone other than the accused that the accused be represented.

Where criminal legal aid is refused on the ground that it is not in the interests of justice, in some serious cases the Legal Aid Board may be able to review the decision. For less serious offences or where the court has refused criminal legal aid on financial grounds, another application may be made to the magistrates' court, or if the matter goes to the Crown Court, to that court.

8.5 Costs

Green form and ABWOR

In the case of legal advice and assistance, if the solicitor's costs are less than the amount of any contribution the balance will be refunded. Where money or property is recovered or preserved, as a general rule the solicitor must use this to pay his account if the account is for more than the amount of any contribution. The same rules apply to assistance by way of representation (ABWOR).

Civil legal aid

With civil legal aid, if the case costs less than the assisted person's actual contribution he will receive a refund. If this does not apply and the assisted person wins his case, the amount that he will have to pay depends on whether (1) the other side is ordered to pay his costs and in fact does so; and/or (2) he is awarded any money or recovers or preserves any property as a result of the proceedings.

Where (1) applies, the assisted person will receive back some, if not the whole, of any contribution. However, if the other side does not pay the assisted person's costs in full, they may be deducted from any moneys ordered by the court to be paid to him, and actually paid, as much as may be needed to cover those costs. This is known as the 'statutory charge' and it also applies to any property recovered or preserved in the case. For this purpose, 'Property has been recovered or preserved if it has been in issue in the proceedings: recovered by the claimant if it has been the subject of a successful claim, preserved to the respondent if the claim fails': per Lord Simon of Glaisdale in *Hanlon* v *The Law Society* [1981] AC 124.

However, maintenance and the first £2,500 of any money or property recovered in matrimonial proceedings are exempt from the statutory charge. The Legal Aid Board also has discretion to defer enforcing the statutory charge on a matrimonial home recovered or preserved in matrimonial proceedings.

If the assisted person loses the case, the most he will normally have to pay is his maximum contribution. However, the court may also order him to pay part or all of his opponent's costs, depending on his (the assisted person's) means and his conduct in connection with the dispute. In certain circumstances the costs of a successful unassisted person may be payable out of the legal aid fund: see, eg, *R v Greenwich London Borough Council, ex parte Lovelace (No 2)* [1992] 1 All ER 679 and *Hanning v Maitland (No 2)* [1970] 1 QB 580.

Criminal legal aid

As to criminal legal aid, at the end of the case the court will decide what should happen to any contributions which have not yet fallen due: they could be ordered to be paid or they could be cancelled. If the contributions paid are more than the actual costs, the difference will be refunded. If the assisted person is acquitted, or successfully appeals against his conviction, the court should normally order the repayment of any contribution and remit any unpaid instalments due under the order, unless there are circumstances which make such a course of action inappropriate.

8.6 Alternative methods of funding: legal expenses insurance and conditional fees

Legal expenses insurance

Legal expenses insurance schemes are today generally available either freestanding or as 'add-ons' to household and motor insurance cover. About 7 per cent of the population have freestanding legal expenses insurance and that figure rises to about 27 per cent when add-on policies are included. However, this is still very low compared to insurance cover taken out by households in many European legal systems. It seems that people in this country are deterred by the costs involved or, perhaps, are unaware of the availability of such cover. It may also be that insurance companies are fixing premiums at too high a level. Insurance companies are also unwilling to offer cover for 'high risk' areas (criminal cases, family law disputes, etc) so that only a limited amount of unmet need can be filled by legal expenses insurance. The Law Society has also stated that insurance should be seen as a supplement to the legal aid scheme and not a substitute for it. Insurance cover plays an important supplementary role to conditional fees.

Conditional fees

Section 58 of the Courts and Legal Services Act 1990 gave the Lord Chancellor power to make rules allowing lawyers to operate a conditional fee system under which the lawyer may agree to accept a case on the basis that if he loses he will not be paid a fee ('no win, no fee').

This principle of payment has operated for many years in Scotland where lawyers are said to take cases 'on spec', ie on a speculative basis. In America there is a different system of 'contingency fees' under which a lawyer may bargain for a percentage of the compensation award if he/she wins the case for the client. (In the American legal system each side pays their own costs). In English common law both conditional and contingency fees are unlawful and unenforceable for being contrary to public policy on the ground that, by giving the lawyer a financial stake in the outcome of litigation they may encourage unnecessary litigation ('ambulance-chasing'!) or unethical tactics in attempting to win a case. Codes of practice for barristers and solicitors have forbidden such methods of payment: *Swain v The Law Society* [1983] 1 AC 598. It follows that only conditional fees expressly authorised under s58 of the Courts and Legal Services Act 1990 are lawful in the English legal system: *Hughes v Kingston-upon-Hull City Council* (1998) The Times 9 December. In this case the High Court took the unusual step of not following a decision of the Court of Appeal (*Thai Trading Co (A Firm) v Taylor* [1998] 3 All ER 65, because the High Court discovered that the Court of Appeal had overlooked *Swain v The Law Society*, above, a House of Lords decision.

In September 1995 Lord Mackay, the then Lord Chancellor, introduced the first system of conditional fees under s58 of the 1990 Act. It was provided that such fees could only be charged in personal injury cases, insolvency cases and human rights cases. The scheme provided that a lawyer who won a case under a conditional fee could charge an 'uplift' on his normal fee. The uplift could be up to double his normal fee. The conditional fee scheme was clearly designed as a supplement to the legal aid scheme, being aimed at middle-income groups who fell outside the financial eligibility criteria for legal aid but who were deterred from pursuing or defending claims by the very high costs of litigation.

The system proved popular and successful, particularly in straightforward personal injury claims such as road accident cases where lawyers were usually confident of a win and therefore willing to take a case upon a conditional fee. In July 1998 Lord Irvine used his power under s58 of the 1990 Act to extend the conditional fee regime to all non-family civil cases. It was not extended to cover criminal cases. The new regime, like the old one, permits a lawyer to accept a case on the basis that if he/she loses, he/she will not be paid a fee and that if the lawyer wins he/she may charge up to double his/her normal fee (the 'success element' or 'uplift').

However, the system of conditional fees is not without problems. In the English legal system a winning litigant can usually expect to recover from the losing side his/her costs under the rule that 'costs follow the event'. Hence, a losing party who has financed his/her action under a conditional fee will still have costs to pay, and thus the risk of losing and facing a large costs bill may continue to deter a party from litigating if he/she falls outside the legal aid scheme. Further, even the winning party may find that he/she has something still to pay, since an award of costs does not at present cover the 'success element' in the conditional fee. If the winning party is a plaintiff this amount may have to come out of his/her compensation award and because the success element of the conditional fee could involve a 100 per cent uplift this could be a comparatively large deduction from the compensation award. Hence, this problem may also deter claimants from using a conditional fee as a source of funding the claim.

When the first scheme of conditional fees was introduced in September 1995 the Law Society negotiated with insurance companies to provide costs cover at a special low premium (about £95 for road accident cases and £150 for other cases), and although this cover went some way to solving the costs of conditional fees, it did not provide a complete solution because: the insurance covered only ordinary legal costs and not the 'success element' or 'uplift' charged by the winning party's lawyer; the insurance premium itself was not recoverable from the losing party as part of the award of costs; and insurance cover was either not available or the premium was too high for cases that were regarded as highly unpredictable and potentially very costly, such as medical negligence cases.

Following the extension of the conditional fee system in July 1998, Lord Irvine LC promised to introduce legislation so as to enable an award of costs against a losing party to cover both the success element of the winning party's conditional fee and insurance premium that the winning party had to incur. Further, Lord Irvine said that his Department would work on making changes to the legal insurance market so as to encourage insurers to provide cover for the success element of conditional fees, particularly in areas traditionally regarded as unpredictable/ expensive.

A proposal to extend the English system of conditional fees to family law disputes over property and other family assets has been dropped from the Access to Justice Bill 1999 (there was a fear that the proposal, if implemented, would undermine the policy of encouraging divorcing couples to settle their disputes amicably through mediation rather than hostile litigation).

8.7 Free legal services

To help overcome apparent unmet legal need several sources of free legal advice have grown up. Although, in general, they can be of limited assistance, the following institutions have the useful function of putting those in need of help 'on the right track', that is, providing initial basic advice and, if appropriate, informing them of the legal aid scheme and sending them to a solicitor willing to undertake such work. The following are the main sources of free legal advice.

Law centres
Law centres specialise in those areas of work which may not be well served by private practice. These include housing, welfare rights, immigration, health, family, disability rights, employment, and education. On the other hand, law centres do not undertake commercial work, conveyancing, probate, divorce, adult crime or large personal injury claims.

Law centres should employ at least one solicitor with three years' post-qualification experience, but they also employ barristers and non-lawyers. Subject to certain conditions, a solicitor employed by a member of the Law Centres Federation may give advice to and otherwise act for members of the public. Law centres operate mainly in poorer urban areas. At one time during the 1980s and early 1990s law centres faced acute funding problems and were often dependent on local authority grants and money from charities. Some law centres were forced to close through lack of funding. However, the future for law centres looks brighter as a result of the proposed overhaul of the legal aid scheme, under which law centres will be offered greater opportunities to participate in a Community Legal Service: see further section 8.8 below.

Legal advice centres

These only provide legal advice and cannot undertake litigation. Because they are staffed by volunteers they cost very much less to run than the law centres. The majority of these centres are staffed by lawyers on a rota basis but there is no uniform pattern. Many university law faculties now run advice centres where second and third year students get practical experience of legal problems. When a client needs to start proceedings he is referred to a local solicitor.

Citizens' advice bureaux

Set up in 1939 to give emergency service during the war, the National Association of Citizens' Advice Bureaux, a registered charity, now has over 1,400 main bureaux and other outlets, including one at the Royal Courts of Justice (which is now funded by the Lord Chancellor's Department). Most central funding comes from the Department of Trade and Industry, while local bureaux rely mainly on local authority support. Donations also come from the private sector and charitable trusts. Anyone may turn to a local bureau for advice and information on every subject from social security to taxation, debt counselling to consumer rights. The great majority of advisers are trained volunteers and many bureaux have honorary legal advisers – solicitors or barristers who attend regular sessions in a voluntary capacity. A greater role for citizens' advice bureaux is proposed under the government's plans for a Community Legal Service: see section 8.8 below.

Free Representation Units (FRU)

Set up by students in London in 1972, in 1993 the original unit represented over 2,000 clients, particularly in tribunals where there is usually no legal aid. Over half of these cases were in industrial tribunals and the next largest number were before social security tribunals. The unit now has a full-time administrator and a full-time solicitor who carries out all preparatory work, but it relies on volunteers, mainly students, pupils and junior barristers, to represent the clients.

In July 1993 FRU launched, with the whole-hearted support of the Bar Council, a Chambers Scheme directed at all barristers in London and the South East. The Scheme aims to meet the rapidly increasing demand for FRU's services and to enlist also the help of experienced barristers who would commit themselves to appearing in a specified number of cases every year.

Birmingham also has a Free Representation Unit and there are similar schemes in the Northern and the Wales and Chester Circuits.

In the summer of 1996 the Bar established a Pro Bono Unit, run on a charitable basis, under which a register of barristers is kept. Those on the register are prepared to offer up to three days of their time to deserving cases in any field of law where the applicant would otherwise be unable to afford legal advice or representation, provided the case does not require the assistance of a solicitor (unless the referring solicitor, or another solicitor, volunteers to assist).

8.8 Reform proposals: the Access to Justice Bill 1999

In the autumn of 1997 Lord Irvine, the Lord Chancellor, had proposed the replacement of civil legal aid (apart from family and social welfare cases) with an expanded conditional fee scheme. However, following strong opposition to this plan from lawyers' groups and backbench Labour MPs, Lord Irvine modified his proposals. Although the expansion of conditional fees went ahead in July 1998 Lord Irvine said he would defer the withdrawal of civil legal aid pending an assessment of how the system was working. Furthermore, he said, conditional fees would only replace civil legal aid in the following areas if he decided to go ahead with such withdrawal:

1. personal injury claims (other than for medical negligence);
2. inheritance disputes;
3. disputes concerning the administration of a trust;
4. certain types of company law claims;
5. partnership disputes;
6. disputes before the Lands Tribunal;
7. neighbour boundary disputes; and
8. cases pursued in the course of a business.

In March 1998 Lord Irvine issued a consultation paper setting out the above ideas and other ideas for reform of legal aid: *Access to Justice with Conditional Fees*. In December 1998 he published a White Paper setting out the government's finalised proposals for reform, to be implemented by the Access to Justice Bill, expected to become law by the autumn of 1999. The detailed reasons for the proposals are set out in the White Paper: *Modernising Justice* (Cm 4155).

The government proposes that the legal aid scheme (currently costing £1.6 billion per year) should be dismantled. In certain areas (listed above) civil legal aid will be replaced purely by conditional fees, eg road accident cases where conditional fees have proved a popular and workable replacement for legal aid. In the remaining area not covered by conditional fees (ie all criminal cases, and most family and social welfare cases) legal aid will be replaced by a quality-controlled system provided by specialist lawyers working under contract.

It is proposed that the new system will consist of a Community Legal Service for the remaining civil disputes (target date: year 2000) and a Criminal Defence Service for all criminal cases (target date: year 2003). Contracts under each system will be awarded only to those lawyers and advice centres (eg law centres and citizens' advice bureaux) who are willing to accept strictly controlled budgets and agreed standards; lawyers will no longer be paid according to the amount of work they handle, hence ending the apparent abuse of the current system under which there is no incentive to handle cases quickly or work efficiently – the scandal of unscrupulous lawyers 'milking' the legal aid fund by claiming an unreasonable number of hours per case will end.

The Legal Aid Board will be renamed the Legal Services Commission and will monitor the allocation of contracts on the basis of local needs. The new Commission will also be responsible for assessing the need for state-funded help in individual civil cases and for this purpose there are to be stiffer tests designed to identify the true wealth of a particular applicant and to determine the suitability of the case for state funded help. Under the proposed 'Funding Assessment' for civil cases the Commission would ask such questions as:

1. Would a prudent person spend his or her own money to bring or defend the action? If the answer is no, then only wider public interest reasons would justify state funding (eg for a test case that could establish liability for harm caused by a dangerous drug).
2. Is the case more suited to mediation than to adjudication?.
3. Could the action be funded in another way – eg by a conditional fee?

In criminal cases there will be automatic state-funded assistance for all those facing criminal charges. However, in each case the new Commission will assess the true need for such assistance so that, upon a conviction, a wealthy defendant will be expected to pay for his trial costs.

The White Paper summarises the reasons for these radical reform proposals as being the need to give more people access to justice and to obtain the best value for taxpayers' money spent on legal services and the courts. The proposals were also designed to encourage more use of mediation and non-legally qualified advice workers in civil cases. The White Paper admits that in criminal cases the award of work to specialist panels of lawyers may lead in the long term to the employment of state-salaried lawyers ('public defenders') in certain geographical areas and areas of work such as youth courts.

It remains to be seen whether all the proposals will be implemented in their existing form – amendments to the Access to Justice Bill seem certain during its passage through Parliament as MPs and peers voice the concerns expressed by the legal profession. The Law Society has warned that a system of block contracts will seriously reduce public choice; it estimates that the number of solicitors' offices offering legal aid at present could be reduced from around 10,000 to about 3,000, thereby destroying local access to justice in many areas. The Bar Council criticised the plan for block contracts as risking a 'sausage-machine mentality' to processing justice and also expressed concern over the moves towards a USA-style public defender system on the ground that it would reduce public choice.

In the House of Lords concern was expressed over the Lord Chancellor's sweeping powers to give directions to the new Legal Services Commission on the operation of the proposed Community Legal Service and Criminal Defence Service. There was a fear that a Lord Chancellor might use these powers to give priority to financial stringency rather than a citizen's right of access to justice. In response to this particular concern Lord Irvine LC conceded amendments to the Bill effectively curbing these powers through a set of governing principles that include an emphasis on access to justice and expeditious settlement of disputes. He also agreed that provisions on how money will be allocated for the new legal services should be laid before Parliament in draft and subject to affirmative resolution.

See further Zander 'The Government's Plans on Legal Aid and Conditional Fees' (1998) 61 MLR 538 and Lord Ackner 'Conditional Fee Agreements' [1998] NLJ 477.

Part IV:
Civil Proceedings

9

Civil Procedure in the High Court

Procedure prior to 26 April 1999

9.1 Jurisdiction: High Court or county court?

9.2 Issue and service of the writ

9.3 Acknowledgement of service

9.4 Exchange of pleadings

9.5 Discovery

9.6 The summons for directions (O.25)

9.7 Interlocutory applications

9.8 Bringing proceedings to an end before trial

9.9 The trial

9.10 Judgment, interest and costs

9.11 Enforcement of judgments

9.12 A new approach to civil litigation

Reform: the Woolf Report, *Access to Justice* (1996)

9.13 Recommendations of the Woolf Report

9.14 Reactions to the Woolf Report

Procedure from 26 April 1999

9.15 Introduction

9.16 Jurisdiction

9.17 Pre-action protocols

9.18 Judges as trial managers

9.19 Issue and service of proceedings

9.20 The defence's response

9.21 The allocation stage

9.22 Disclosure

9.23 Interlocutory applications

9.24 The listing questionnaire stage

9.25 Bringing proceedings to an end before trial

9.26 Sanctions

9.27 The trial

9.28 Judgment, interest and costs

9.29 Miscellaneous changes in terminology

9.30 Effect on precedents

Procedure prior to 26 April 1999

9.1 Jurisdiction: High Court or county court?

Civil actions in England and Wales could generally be commenced in either the High Court or County Court, depending in some cases on the value of the subject matter of a claim or the amount of damages being claimed. The complexity and importance of the legal and/or factual issues could also be relevant to determining which court should hear the action. While the choice of court was the plaintiff's (the person who was bringing the action), the action could be transferred up to the High Court or down to the county court either on the court's own motion or on a successful application for transfer by either party. If the plaintiff's choice of court was inappropriate to the action he/she could be penalised in terms of costs. Although the court could also strike out an action commenced in the wrong court it generally would not do so if the choice of court had been the result of some genuine mistake in procedure on the part of the plaintiff or his/her advisers: see *Restick* v *Crickmore* [1994] 1 WLR 420 (CA).

For the limits on county court jurisdiction: see Chapter 10, section 10.1.

9.2 Issue and service of the writ

For the sake of brevity the first part of this chapter considers only the procedure regulating an action commenced by writ in the Queen's Bench Division of the High Court prior to 26 April 1999. Such an action would often be concerned with a claim in contract or in tort, the latter frequently being concerned with a claim for damages resulting from personal injuries. The procedural rules were set out in the *Supreme Court Practice*, popularly known to practitioners as the *White Book*. Rules were set out as Orders and were cited thus: RSC O.1 r1 (Rules of the Supreme Court O.1 r1).

The writ was issued when the court stamped the completed form with the court seal. The information contained in the writ had to include:

1. The names of the parties and their status (plaintiff, defendant, a firm, etc).
2. The division of the High Court.
3. A statement of claim endorsed on the writ or a concise statement of the nature of the claim and remedy sought.
4. Any claim for interest and costs.
5. The name and address of the plaintiff or his solicitor for service.

The writ was issued by the court, but the plaintiff had to serve it on (that is, deliver it to) the defendant. A writ had to be served, together with a form of acknowledgement of service, within four months of the writ being issued. After four months had elapsed the plaintiff had to apply for a renewal of the writ if it still had not been served. It could be served personally, but more usually it would be posted, in which case seven days from posting was allowed before service was deemed to have occurred.

Where service of the writ – or any document – was not practicable, the court could allow 'substituted service' (O.65 r4). This was service in some other manner so that the writ came to the defendant's notice, for example by post to some person with whom the defendant was likely to communicate.

Service of the writ by fax was not permitted, although other documents in the action could be served by this method: *Hastie and Jenkerson* v *McMahon* [1991] 1 All ER 255 (CA).

9.3 Acknowledgement of service

If a defendant wished to dispute the claim then he had to acknowledge service and state his intention to defend. He had 14 days from service in which to do so if he resided in England and Wales.

Failure to acknowledge service and state an intention to defend allowed the plaintiff to apply for judgment in default under O.13. This involved filing an affidavit with the court verifying that the writ was properly served. The defendant could only have the judgment set aside if he could show it was irregularly obtained or that there was some defence on the merits.

(A similar procedure for obtaining judgment in default was available to the plaintiff if the defendant, having acknowledged service and stated an intention to defend, did not serve a defence within 14 days of service of the statement of claim: O.19.)

9.4 Exchange of pleadings

Pleadings were formal, written documents, which each party served on the opponent, and which contained the allegations of fact on which each party relied as supporting his case. The principle behind pleadings was that each party was entitled to know what the other's case was and it was desirable that the parties should know what they were 'fighting' about, since this saved time and costs and could lead to a settlement.

In *Practice Note* [1995] 1 All ER 385 it was stressed that RSC O.18 r7 (facts, not evidence, to be pleaded) would be strictly enforced. In advance of trial, parties should use their best endeavours to agree which were the issues or the main issues, and it was their duty so far as possible to reduce or eliminate the expert issues.

The main forms of pleading were:

Statement of claim

This was the first document after the writ and was the plaintiff's outline of his claim against the defendant. It had to be either endorsed on the back of the writ or served separately within 14 days of the defendant's acknowledgement of service. It was a concise statement of all the material facts which were alleged to constitute the plaintiff's cause of action. The statement of claim had to end with a 'prayer for relief', namely a claim for the relevant remedies.

Defence

This was the defendant's opportunity to deal with the plaintiff's allegations and to present the issues from his point of view. The document had to be served by the defendant on the plaintiff within 14 days of the service of the statement of claim. The defence had to deal with each of the plaintiff's allegations separately and the defendant could admit; deny ('traverse'); not admit (does not deny, but requires the plaintiff to prove his allegation); confess and avoid (admit the facts but establish other facts which nullify the legal effect claimed by the plaintiff); or object in point of law.

If the defendant did not deal with an allegation in his defence he was taken to have admitted it, though occasionally a defendant would use a 'general traverse' which was a general denial of any of the plaintiff's allegations which he had not already dealt with.

Counterclaim

Though the defendant had been sued by the plaintiff, the defendant could himself have a claim against the plaintiff which need not be connected with the main proceedings. Accordingly, the defendant could raise his claim and plead it in the same document as his defence if it could be tried without inconvenience at the same time as the main proceedings. The counterclaim put the defendant in the position of plaintiff, with regard to that claim, vis-à-vis the plaintiff in the main proceedings.

Reply

If no further pleadings were served after the defence, then the plaintiff was treated as having 'joined issue', with the defendant on all matters raised in the defence (that is, contested them). However, the plaintiff could serve a reply if he wished to add anything after he had seen the defence: for example admit portions of the defence or rebut allegations. However, he could not raise fresh claims against the defendant; this could only be done by amending his statement of claim with the leave of the court. After the reply no further pleadings could be served without the leave of the court (if there was a counterclaim by the defendant which the plaintiff wished to defend, the plaintiff could serve that defence in the same document as the reply).

Particulars

If any allegations in any pleadings (either plaintiff's or defendant's) was too vague or too general then the other party could request further and better particulars of the allegation and if the request was refused they could apply for an order for the particulars sought. This was in pursuance of the principle that each party was entitled to reasonable notice of the other's case and should not be taken by surprise at trial.

Amendment of pleadings

In the ordinary course of litigation an amendment to pleadings, eg to add another ground to a defence, ought to be allowed for the purpose of determining the issues between the parties provided the amendment would not cause injustice to the other party.

In relation to the amendment of a statement of claim, in *Beoco Ltd* v *Alfa Laval Co Ltd* [1994] 4 All ER 464 the Court of Appeal said that the guiding principle was that all amendments should be allowed at any stage in the proceedings to enable all issues between the parties to be determined, provided the amendment did not result in prejudice or injustice to the other party which could not properly be compensated in costs. In the absence of any special reasons, where a plaintiff made a late amendment which substantially altered the case the defendant had to meet and without which the action would fail, the defendant was entitled to the costs of the action down to the date of amendment.

9.5 Discovery

Within 14 days from the close of pleadings the parties had to exchange lists of relevant documents in their possession, custody or control. This process was known as 'discovery'. In most actions begun by writ discovery of documents was automatic, ie it took place without a court order. Any dispute over whether a document must be disclosed could be referred to the court, which could, if necessary, make an order for discovery (or for further discovery) against any party who failed to comply voluntarily: O.24.

9.6 The summons for directions (O.25)

This was an essential step in the action and had to be taken out by the plaintiff within one month from close of pleadings and after discovery. The summons requested the court to arrange a hearing before a High Court master so that all outstanding pre-trial issues be dealt with in a sort of 'stocktaking' manner. The master could also give directions on all matters relating to the trial itself: that is, place and mode of trial, method of giving evidence especially matters such as plans, documents, models, photographs, and so on. The master also fixed the period in which the plaintiff must set down the action for trial.

9.7 Interlocutory applications

There were a large number of procedural steps – some compulsory, some optional – available at the interlocutory stage, which was the time between joinder of issue and trial. Among the most important interlocutory steps were the following:

Exchange of witness statements (O.38)

As the modern approach to the conduct of litigation requires the earliest possible identification of both the real issues and the relative strengths of the parties, the exchange of witness statements prior to trial under RSC O.38 r2A was an important and appropriate innovation, the normal rule being for simultaneous exchange. This was said to be part of the 'cards on the table' philosophy: *Mercer v Chief Constable of Lancashire* [1991] 2 All ER 504. The exchange had to take place within 14 weeks of close of pleadings.

Extensions of time

The time limits given above in relation to all the various procedural steps could be extended with leave of the court if a party applied for an extension and could show good reason for it.

Joinder of parties and actions

Sometimes it was necessary after issue and service of the writ and defence for further parties or causes of action to be added to ('joinder') those already pleaded. Again such joinder could be ordered by the court upon application by either party.

Injunctions (O.29 r1)

It was often the case that the damage that the plaintiff was seeking to prevent would have been done by the time the matter came to trial, some two years or more later. An interlocutory injunction prevented this. For example, if a newspaper was planning to publish a defamatory story, an interlocutory injunction would prevent publication.

Applications were made – frequently ex parte (ie in the absence of the other side) – by summons to a Queen's Bench judge in chambers. The principles which applied in many cases can be found in the decision of the House of Lords in *American Cyanamid Co v Ethicon Ltd* [1975] AC 396. If an injunction was ordered ex parte, it would stay in force until there could be an inter partes hearing.

A particular type of injunction was the Mareva injunction (named after *Mareva Compania Naviera SA v International Bulk Carriers SA* [1975] 2 Lloyd's Rep 509). It was sometimes the case that a defendant, fearing judgment, would seek to dissipate his assets, perhaps by removing them from the jurisdiction. A Mareva injunction 'froze' assets and prevented their disposal until the issues were decided. To make a successful application, a plaintiff had to show he had a good arguable case and that there was a real risk of dissipation which would frustrate any judgment.

An equally drastic measure was the Anton Piller order (after *Anton Piller KG v Manufacturing Processes Ltd* [1976] Ch 55). This allowed the plaintiff's agents to enter the defendant's premises and seize specified documents or property. This was most often used in intellectual property cases (eg copyright) and there had to be a real danger that the property would be destroyed. Failure to comply with the order placed the defendant in contempt of court.

9.8 Bringing proceedings to an end before trial

There were numerous ways in which proceedings could be brought to an end before trial. Among the most important were:

Settlement

A great proportion of all civil actions were settled by agreement of the parties at some stage between the commencement of proceedings and trial, though it was not unknown for cases to settle during trial. Indeed, it is fair to say that the English legal system is designed to achieve settlement rather than litigate disputes. It should be remembered that it is the task of counsel to achieve the best result for his client (within limits), and this frequently means reaching settlement, rather than 'fighting' in court. It is clearly advantageous in very many cases to settle since the saving of costs can be considerable, and if a plaintiff's claim is strong there is often little point in pursuing matters. Consequently, a great deal of time was spent 'behind the scenes' making various offers, and counter-offers, to settle in an effort to reach some form of compromise. If settlement was reached, notice was given to the court and in certain cases the court had to approve the settlement. It would then draw up an order (which had the force of any court order) which had been agreed beforehand by the parties.

Summary judgment under O.14

This was a useful procedure whereby the plaintiff could apply for summary judgment at an early stage in proceedings if the defendant had stated an intention to defend but had no real defence to the claim (or part of the claim). The master could award judgment to the plaintiff if he considered that there was no triable defence.

Otherwise the master could give the defendant leave to defend either unconditionally (ie there was a triable defence) or conditionally (if he suspected the good faith of the defendant or thought the defence might be a sham). The condition would be that the defendant must pay a sum of money into court as security for the plaintiff's costs.

If the claim was for liquidated damages (ie a specified sum of money) judgment would be given for that sum together with interest and costs. If the claim was for unliquidated damages (ie to be assessed by the court), judgment would be given as to liability only, with damages to be assessed at a separate hearing.

Payment into court (O.22)

This course was often adopted by a defendant who largely admitted liability but disputed the amount claimed. This was done by paying into court the sum which was considered by the defendant to be due, and by serving due notice on the plaintiff. If the plaintiff, who had to acknowledge receipt in three days, decided to accept the money (which he had to do within 21 days and at least before the trial began) the action came to an end. If the plaintiff left the money in and was ultimately awarded a lesser sum than the sum paid in (even by as little as one penny) then he had to pay the parties' costs from the date of the payment into court. In *Roache* v *News Group Newspapers Ltd* (1992) The Times 23 November a plaintiff in a libel action had been awarded the same sum as the defendants had paid into court. The Court of Appeal decided that, for the purposes of costs, it was the defendants who had been in substance the successful parties. Accordingly, the plaintiff was ordered to pay the defendants' costs after the date of their payment into court.

The judge could not be told of the payment in until all questions of liability and quantum of damages had been settled, otherwise his view of the case might be prejudiced.

Payment into court could be of great tactical advantage to the defendant since by paying in a realistic sum he could put pressure on the plaintiff to accept it in settlement.

Dismissal for want of prosecution

The defendant could apply to strike out the plaintiff's action if the plaintiff had been guilty of unreasonable delay in proceeding with the various steps required to bring the action to trial. For this purpose delay was unreasonable and a ground for striking out if it was intentional and 'contumelious' (ie a stubborn refusal to proceed), or where the delay was inordinate, inexcusable and prejudicial to the defence: see *Birkett* v *James* [1977] 3 WLR 39 (HL), *Roebuck* v *Mungovin* [1994] 2 WLR 290 (HL) and *Shtun* v *Zalejska* [1996] 3 All ER 411 (CA).

9.9 The trial

Although the judge could decide which party should begin and even, in a non-jury action, to dispense with opening speeches, traditionally the plaintiff began. His/her counsel would open the case by stating the facts on which he relied as disclosed in his pleadings. He then called his witnesses and each was examined-in-chief by the plaintiff's counsel, cross-examined by the defence counsel and re-examined by the plaintiff's counsel. At the close of his evidence his counsel could make submissions on the relevant law, citing authorities, including those relevant authorities which supported his opponent's case and which he had to attempt to distinguish.

Defence counsel would then call his witnesses who were similarly examined-in-chief, cross-examined by the plaintiff and re-examined. He then made his legal submissions and his closing speech.

If the defence called evidence the plaintiff's counsel had the right to make a closing speech in reply and could exceptionally call evidence in rebuttal.

The judge then gave judgment, which he could reserve (ie give at a later date) on the issues of liability and damages.

9.10 Judgment, interest and costs

Judgment for the plaintiff would involve the award of an appropriate remedy, usually, damages (money compensation), though sometimes injunctions would be granted to restrain the defendant from doing something or ordering him to do something. Interest could be awarded on damages from the date the right of action arose to the date of judgment.

Since 1989, in personal injury cases, the court increasingly approved 'structured settlements' whereby successful plaintiffs received whatever proportion of their damages they wished by means of a series of future annual payments, the defendants discharging their obligations by the purchase of an annuity. For plaintiffs this meant an assured (and an increasing) income for life and a saving on tax and costs; for defendants, a lower overall cost. Costs would be awarded as part of the judgment.

Judgment for the defendant would comprise a costs award only. Costs were a matter for the court's discretion. The court had the power to disallow the whole of any 'wasted costs' or order the legal representative concerned to pay the wasted costs.

'Wasted costs' meant any costs incurred by a party as a result of any improper, unreasonable or negligent act or omission on the part of any legal or other representative or any employee of such a representative; or which, in the light of any such act or omission occurring after they were incurred, the court considered it was unreasonable to expect that party to pay.

In *Ridehalgh* v *Horsefield* [1994] 3 WLR 462 the Court of Appeal laid down guidelines in relation to wasted costs orders so as to safeguard the traditional immunity of an advocate. See also *Tolstoy-Miloslavsky* v *Lord Aldington* [1996] 2 All ER 556 (CA).

Detailed provision as to costs and their taxation (assessment by the taxing master, in the absence of agreement between the parties) was to be found in O.62. There were only two bases of taxation, 'standard' and 'indemnity'. Standard allowed a reasonable amount in respect of all costs reasonably incurred', with any doubts resolved in favour of the paying party. Indemnity allowed all costs 'except in so far as they are of an unreasonable amount or have been unreasonably incurred'. In this case, any doubts which the taxing officer might have were resolved in favour of the receiving party.

9.11 Enforcement of judgments

High court judgments are usually enforced by writs of execution which are directed to the sheriffs of the relevant counties. Other methods of execution are available depending on whether the judgment is a money or other judgment. For example, a charging order can be placed on the debtor's land as security for the debt or a garnishee order can be made against the debtor's bank account so that debts owed to the debtor can be assigned to the judgment creditor.

9.12 A new approach to civil litigation

The 'cards on the table' approach

Traditionally civil litigation was conducted on strictly adversarial lines; the opposing parties were treated like combatants on a battlefield, with the court acting as facilitator of proceedings and the trial judge acting as neutral umpire. The burden was on the parties themselves to take the steps required of them under the rules of practice and there was much scope for delaying tactics if those suited one side. Disputes could drag on for years and the civil courts could become clogged with actions, causing further delays and hardship to parties. It was eventually accepted that radical reform was required, possibly involving an entire change of philosophy as to the conduct of civil litigation. Judges began to talk of the need for a 'cards on the table' approach to litigation and new practice directions were issued encouraging judges to be more pro-active in encouraging prompt compliance with time limits etc.

On 24 January 1995 Lord Taylor of Gosforth CJ gave practice guidelines (*Practice Note* [1995] 1 All ER 385) applying to all lists in the Queen's Bench and Chancery Divisions, except where other directions specifically applied. His Lordship said that the paramount importance of reducing the cost and delay of civil litigation made it necessary for judges sitting at first instance to assert greater control over the preparation for and conduct of hearings than had hitherto been customary. Failure by practitioners to conduct cases economically would be visited by appropriate orders for costs, including wasted costs orders. The court would accordingly exercise its discretion to limit: discovery; the length of oral submissions; the time allowed for the examination and cross-examination of witnesses; the issues on which it wishes to be addressed; and reading aloud from documents and authorities. Other specific points included:

1. In cases estimated to last for more than ten days a pre-trial review should be applied for or in default could be appointed by the court. It should when practicable be conducted by the trial judge between eight and four weeks before the date of trial and should be attended by the advocates who were to represent the parties at trial.
2. Unless the court otherwise ordered, there had to be lodged with the listing officer (or equivalent) on behalf of each party (with copies to the other parties) no later than two months before the date of trial a completed pre-trial checklist in the form annexed to the practice direction. The checklist covered setting down, pleadings, evidence, documents, pre-trial review, length of trial and alternative dispute resolution.

3. No less than three clear days before the hearing of the action or application each party should lodge with the court (with copies to other parties) a skeleton argument concisely summarising that party's submissions in relation to each of the issues, and citing the main authorities relied upon.
4. The opening speech should be succinct. At its conclusion other parties could be invited briefly to amplify their skeleton arguments. In a heavy case the court could in conjunction with final speeches require written submissions, including the findings of fact for which each party contended.

This *Practice Note* paved the way for the more radical reforms that were about to be proposed by Lord Woolf, who had been appointed to advise on the reform of civil procedure. (The Woolf Report is considered below.)

Fees

In November 1998 the Lord Chancellor's Department announced proposals for substantial increases in civil court fees and a new payment system which will require parties to 'pay as they go', ie to pay for each stage of a civil action, with the costs obviously mounting if a party chooses to go on. The aim of the proposals is to make the civil courts almost self-financing and hence ease the burden on taxpayers, as well as encouraging early settlement of cases. The proposals have been criticised on the ground that they will deter many lower income households from pursuing reasonable claims for justice.

Reform: The Woolf Report, *Access to Justice* (1996)

9.13 Recommendations of the Woolf Report

Lord Woolf summed up his proposals as providing 'a new landscape for civil justice for the twenty-first century'.

In summary the most significant of the recommendations were as follows:

1. Retention of the formal separation between the High Court and county court and retention of the separate status of High Court judge, circuit judge and district judge.
2. A new framework for the High Court and county courts involving the creation of three or four new 'civil trial centres' in the regions with each centre headed by a senior civil judge to create a better working relationship between the judiciary and court administrators. There should also be new specialist courts at the High Court and in the regions reserved for medical negligence cases. Housing cases should be handled by specialist judges in local county courts.
3. High Court and county court jurisdiction to become a single jurisdiction with one set of procedural rules to replace those in the existing White and Green

books. This would create 'open one-door entry' for litigants, ie litigants will be able to start a case in any court and a 'procedural judge' at that court will then take responsibility for allocating the case to the appropriate part of the system.
4. The new system should consist of three tracks to which cases will be allocated according to their value and complexity:
    a) a 'fast track' for non-complex claims in which a hearing will be held in the county court within 30 weeks of the issue of proceedings (compared to an average of 80 weeks at present). The hearing should be a fixed three-hour hearing, subject to an absolute maximum of one day if extended beyond the three hours by the judge conducting the hearing. Much of the preliminary work should be done on paper rather than through oral submissions. No oral evidence from expert witnesses should be allowed. Legal aid should be available for fast track claims. Costs will be capped at £2,500.
    b) a 'small claims track' for non-complex claims. The small claims track should involve county court adjudication methods by district judges without legal aid.
    c) a 'multi-track' with claims being allocated according to their individual complexity. Estimates of costs in each case should be either published by the court or agreed by the litigants and approved by the court. Teams of judges should be involved in making allocation decisions on the multi-track, whereas a single procedural judge (a district judge) should allocate cases on the fast track or small claims track. For the more complex cases on the multi-track there should be a case management conference before a single procedural judge (eg a High Court master if the case is in London) followed by a pre-trial review before the trial judge. The trial judge should be a High Court judge for complex cases regardless of the amount claimed. Non-complex cases should be heard by circuit or district judges under a special streamlined 'no-frills' procedure with fixed budgets.
5. Judges to be formally trained as case and trial managers so that they can become properly involved in the administration of the courts and provide 'hands on' management of cases by dictating the pace of hearings, enforcing strict time limits, taking responsibility for the calling of witnesses (especially expert witnesses) so as to ensure equality ('a level playing field') for litigants. Judges should become familiar with information technology facilities such as laptop computers and video-conference facilities. Law clerks or research assistants could be appointed from the ranks of recently qualified barristers or solicitors to assist judges working on case management.
6. It is expected that the court will appoint its own expert witness, with his or her costs being borne equally by each side, either instead of or additional to the experts to be called by each side. Meetings of experts should be ordered by the court so as to produce a single opinion if possible (or each side should agree on the use of a single expert). Agreement on expert evidence is especially relevant to fast track cases where no oral evidence from experts will be possible.

7. Oral evidence to be limited, with more emphasis on written submissions and pre-trial reading of documents by the judge. However, in his interim Report (1995) Lord Woolf emphasised that he was not proposing the abolition of the oral tradition: 'The approach ... is to preserve the best features of the present adversary system, while giving a more interventionist management role to the court.'
8. Judges to have a greater power to strike out unworthy actions or to settle cases or parts of cases summarily (allowing only the 'core' of the dispute to go to trial). There should also be greater powers to impose sanctions (eg striking out whole or part of the claim, or ordering costs to be paid immediately, or imposing a higher rate of interest for costs) in cases where lawyers fail to meet the required deadlines. There should be a new discretionary power to allocate the burden of costs at the end of a case by reference to the conduct of the parties.
9. Greater control of pre-trial pleadings (to be known as 'statements of case') and of discovery (to be known as disclosure) so as to avoid verbosity and to produce precise statements of facts. There should be new 'pre-action protocols' setting out what information the parties should give one another about their cases and on what timescale.
10. Encouragement of early settlements through a 'plaintiff's offer' under which the plaintiff could suggest a sum lower than his or her actual claim at which he/she would be prepared to settle. If the defendant refuses to accept the offer and then loses the case the defendant would be penalised either in costs or in extra interest on the damages. Tough penalties are proposed in the form of interest rates of up to 25 per cent on top of the normal interest to be imposed on those unreasonably refusing settlement offers.
11. Encouragement of alternative dispute resolution (ADR) with emphasis on arbitration, mediation and ombudsmen to facilitate out-of-court settlements. For this purpose information for litigants should be improved either through advice agencies at court or electronic information kiosks. Legal aid should be provided for ADR methods.
12. There should be provision for some courts to sit in the evenings or at weekends, with mobile hearings being operated in remote rural areas.
13. The establishment of a Civil Justice Council as a general supervisory body for implementing the civil justice reforms proposed in the Final Report.

Lord Woolf summarised the advantages of the proposed reforms as follows:

1. they would end the present system of 'trial by combat' which had encouraged unreasonable behaviour by litigants;
2. they would create a simpler, more accessible, more flexible system;
3. cases would be handled in a manner proportionate to their value and complexity;
4. there would be greater certainty over the costs and duration of proceedings; and

5. the new system would ensure a 'level playing field' for litigants preventing wealthier litigants (eg insurance companies) from playing with the system to their advantage.

9.14 Reactions to the Woolf Report

The general reaction to the Woolf Report was favourable; it was welcomed by consumer groups, the legal profession, the judiciary, the government and opposition parties. Indeed the Conservative government responded quickly in 1996 to introduce legislation designed to implement the first stage of the Woolf reforms. The Civil Procedure Act 1997 established a rule-making authority to produce the single set of procedural rules for the High Court and county courts. The Act also established a Civil Justice Council to supervise the implementation of the civil procedure reforms. However, Lord Mackay, the former Lord Chancellor, and Lord Irvine, his successor, warned that the training of judges as trial managers and the computerisation of the courts could take several years to complete.

The most notable criticism of the Woolf Report came from Professor Michael Zander (who retires from the London School of Economics in the summer of 1999). Writing in *The Times* (6 August 1996) Professor Zander expressed the view that most litigants want a fair hearing and will not feel that justice has been done by a short, sharp trial with restricted oral evidence and an interventionist judge chivvying the parties to a resolution of their dispute. He also argued that judges as trial managers will involve unnecessary bureaucratic costs in many cases which would normally have been settled out of court anyway, as well as resulting in longer and more complex trials for those cases that do go to court. (Zander relied on empirical evidence of the effects of judicial case management in other jurisdictions, eg the United States, for his conclusions.)

Nevertheless, the substance of the Woolf Report is to be implemented as from 26 April 1999. The new Civil Procedure Rules (CPR) were made in the autumn of 1998 and new Practice Directions are being issued to supplement them.

Procedure from 26 April 1999

9.15 Introduction

From 26 April 1999 ('Big Bang Day') a unified code of procedural rules for the Court of Appeal (Civil Division), the High Court and the county court are introduced, save for specialist jurisdictions. The opportunity has been taken to reduce the complexity of the rules and make them more 'user-friendly' to lay persons by the use of English and simple expressions rather than traditional legal

150   Civil Procedure in the High Court

Latin. The new code is contained in the Civil Procedure Rules 1998 (CPR), which replace the traditional White and Green Books. Practice Directions have been and will be made to supplement the CPR. In addition, the Civil Procedure Act 1997 amended some of the law so as to prepare for the changes and also established the Civil Justice Council.

The Civil Justice Council

The Civil Procedure Act 1997 provides that the Council is to be an advisory body to the Lord Chancellor and the judiciary advising on developments in the civil justice system and making proposals for research. Its objectives are to ensure that the new civil justice system is accessible, fair and efficient. The Council will meet four times a year to review progress. Its members are appointed by the Lord Chancellor and include, among others:

1. barristers;
2. solicitors;
3. persons with experience in, and knowledge of, consumer affairs;
4. persons with experience in, and knowledge of, the lay advice sector; and
5. persons able to represent the interests of particular kinds of litigant (for example, businesses or employees).

9.16 Jurisdiction

(For previous rules see section 9.1, above, and Chapter 10, section 10.1.)

As from April 26 1999 there is a three-track system based on the value and complexity of the claim:

1. Most cases worth less than £5,000 will be dealt with by a district judge on the 'small claims track' (see further Chapter 10, section 10.11).
2. Cases worth £5,000 and above up to £15,000 will be dealt with under a fixed timetable on the 'fast track': cases should usually be heard within 30 weeks of allocation, with limits on procedure, disclosure, evidence and the length of the trial, and scales of fixed costs based on and in proportion to the value of the claim.
3. Cases worth £15,000 and above, or any other case which is unusually complex or raises special problems, will be dealt with on the 'multi-track', closely supervised by a judge and tailored to each case. This will involve case management conferences and pre-trial hearings.

9.17 Pre-action protocols

These protocols are an essential part of the new civil justice system. So far they have been established only for clinical negligence and personal injury cases (on the fast track). The protocols require each party to complete various steps in the conduct of the case *before* proceedings are issued, for example sending a letter of claim in *detailed* form, exchanging witness statements and conducting negotiations (a process known as 'front-loading information'). The defendant has up to three months to respond to the pre-action letter of claim. If possible the parties are expected to agree on the use of a single medical expert at the trial. The protocols are designed to set standards for better communications between the parties and to facilitate earlier settlements or, failing such settlements, more efficient case management. Judges are encouraged to enforce the protocols strictly by penalising those who breach them. For sanctions see section 9.26, below.

9.18 Judges as trial managers

Judges have been given special training in case management techniques by the Judicial Studies Board so as to control civil litigation in accordance with the 'overriding objective' set out in Pt 1 of the CPR 1998, namely, to ensure that cases are conducted justly and with expedition and proportionality. For this purpose the judge should:

1. ensure that the parties are on an equal footing;
2. save expense;
3. deal with a case in ways which are proportionate:
   a) to the amount of money involved;
   b) to the importance of the case;
   c) to the complexity of the issues; and
   d) to each party's financial position;
4. ensure that the case is dealt with expeditiously and fairly;
5. allot to it an appropriate share of the court's resources while taking into account the need to allot resources to other cases; and
6. ensure that the parties, as well as the court, give effect to the overriding objective.

In order to achieve the overriding objective the judge should in each case:

1. identify the issues at an early stage;
2. decide promptly which issues need full investigation and trial;
3. dispose summarily of those that do not require such treatment;
4. encourage parties to use alternative dispute resolution where appropriate;
5. encourage parties to cooperate with each other in the conduct of the case;

6. help the parties to settle the whole or part of the case;
7. decide the order in which the issues are to be resolved;
8. fix timetables or otherwise control the progress of the case;
9. consider whether the likely benefits of taking a particular step will justify the cost of taking it;
10. deal with as many aspects of the case as is practicable on the same occasion;
11. deal with a case without the parties' attendance at court if this is possible;
12. make appropriate use of technology; and
13. give directions to ensure that the trial of a case proceeds quickly and efficiently.

9.19 Issue and service of proceedings

(For previous rules see section 9.2, above, and Chapter 10, section 10.3.)

Assuming any applicable pre-action protocols have been complied with, proceedings may be commenced by the claimant (previously known as the plaintiff) issuing a claim form (previously known as the writ). Notes are provided to assist the average litigant in filling in the claim form. These notes explain the three-track system and tell the claimant to indicate in the heading of the claim form whether he/she wants the claim to be commenced in the county court or High Court. Most claims worth less than £15,000, as well as personal injury claims below £50,000, must be issued in the county court.

As before, the particulars of the claim and the remedy sought can be set out on the claim form itself or in a separate document served with the claim form or within 14 days of service of the claim form. 'Pleadings' will become known as 'statements of case' from 26 April 1999. The claimant's statement of case must be concise, of substance and specific. Points of law, as well as of fact, may be relied on. The statement of case must be verified by a statement of truth, ie sworn to be true. Hence the statement of case becomes a kind of affidavit punishable by contempt (not perjury) if the maker made a statement dishonestly and untruthfully.

The rules about methods of service of the claim form are similar to the previous rules and, as before, service must take place within four months of the issue of the claim form. The new rules permit modern methods of service such as e mail and fax (overruling on this point *Hastie and Jenkerson* v *McMahon* [1991] 1 All ER 255). The court has power to authorise 'alternative methods' of service (previously known as substituted service) but, if a method is unusual, the obligation will be on the claimant to prove that the method used was likely to have brought proceedings to the defendant's attention. In practice claimants will leave it to the court (either High Court or county court) to effect service by first class post. The court will then notify the claimant as to when the claim form is deemed to have been served. If a party wishes to effect service himself/herself he/she can do so but must notify the court in writing of such intention.

9.20 The defence's response

(For previous rules see sections 9.3 and 9.4, above, and Chapter 10, section 10.4.)
The defendant may either:

1. admit the claim and make an offer to pay; or
2. file a defence to the whole or part of the claim; or
3. file an acknowledgement of service within 14 days of service of the particulars of claim and then file a defence within 28 days of service of the particulars of claim.

A defence statement of case must be verified by a statement of truth. The right to make a counterclaim and reply are available as before but will be known as 'Part 20 claims' because they are regulated by Pt 20 of the CPR 1998.

Judgment in default applies as before except that under the new system the claimant will be allowed to give an estimated figure in a claim for unspecified (unliquidated) damages. Unless a defence is served judgment will be given for that estimate (or for a specified/liquidated claim) without a further assessment hearing.

9.21 The allocation stage

After the defence has been filed the court will serve an allocation questionnaire on each party so as to enable a district judge of the county court to allocate the claim to the appropriate track, unless the judge considers that the claim or defence should be struck out or summary judgment granted. Allocation will depend on the financial value of the claim, its complexity, the importance of the action and other relevant factors. Either party can also make a written request for a one month stay of proceedings so as to attempt a settlement through alternative dispute resolution.

Following the allocation decision the district judge should give the parties appropriate directions as to how to proceed (for example on disclosure of documents), together with a timetable leading to a trial date or 'window' for trial. In fast track cases directions will be similar to previous automatic directions, with a window for trial given not later than 30 weeks ahead. In multi-track cases directions similar to those for fast track cases will be given unless the case is complex, in which event the judge must arrange for a case management conference and/or a pre-trial review. The trial date or trial window will still probably be fixed at the allocation stage. In small claims standard directions will apply (see further Chapter 10, section 10.12).

9.22 Disclosure

(For previous rules see section 9.5, above.)
Part 31 of the CPR 1998 replaces the previous concept of 'discovery of documents' with a new process simply called 'disclosure'. Parties will no longer be

under an automatic obligation to disclose documents. An obligation to disclose will arise only if ordered by the court, which has power to dispense with disclosure altogether. Unless otherwise ordered disclosure will be limited in fast track and multi-track cases to 'standard disclosure', ie the only documents that will need to be disclosed will be:

1. those relied on by a party;
2. those which adversely affect a party's own case or another party's case;
3. those which support another party's case; and
4. those required to be disclosed by any relevant Practice Direction.

Disclosure must be in accordance with the overriding objective: see section 9.18, above. Hence, interlocutory applications for general or specific disclosure which are in the nature of a 'fishing expedition' for evidence are unlikely to be successful. Staged or phased disclosure may be ordered where appropriate.

9.23 Interlocutory applications

(For previous rules see section 9.7, above, and Chapter 10, section 10.6.)

After allocation the case will proceed through its interlocutory stages to the fixed trial date or trial window. As before there are opportunities to make interlocutory applications, for example for disclosure, and for 'requests for information', ie for further details of a statement of case (previously known as requests for further and better particulars).

9.24 The listing questionnaire stage

(For previous rules see section 9.6.)

This stage effectively replaces the summons for directions in fast track and multi-track cases. The listing questionnaire will be sent to the parties shortly before the hearing date or trial window (probably about 20 weeks from the date of allocation). The parties are given 14 days to complete and return their copies of the questionnaire to the court. Failure to return the questionnaire may result in the claim or defence being struck out. When the court considers the listing questionnaire it will make any final directions and confirm or fix the trial date (the previous obligation on the plaintiff to set down the case for trial disappears under the new system).

9.25 Bringing proceedings to an end before trial

(For previous rules see section 9.8, above, and Chapter 10, section 10.7.)

Settlement

The opportunities to settle a case remain as before.

Summary judgment

RSC O.14 is replaced by Pt 24 of the CPR 1998.

Under the new procedure either claimant or defendant may apply for summary judgment and the test is whether the claimant has a real prospect of succeeding or the defendant has a real prospect of defending.

Payment into court and 'without prejudice offers'

'Without prejudice offers' and payments into court can be made under Pt 36 of the CPR 1998 not later than 21 days before trial, and with similar costs consequences. Without prejudice proposals (but not payments into court) can, under the new rules, be made before proceedings are issued (at least 21 days before issue of proceedings). The new rules also allow the claimant to make a settlement offer which will carry similar costs consequences for the defendant if it is refused and then not beaten by the court's award (the court has power to award the claimant interest at the rate of 10 per cent above base rate from the latest date that the offer could have been accepted). The changes are designed to put the parties on a more equal footing so far as tactics are concerned. Without prejudice offers must be kept open for 21 days and then may be withdrawn without the court's permission. Payments into court can only be withdrawn with the court's permission.

Striking out

Judges will have greater powers to strike out claims or defences for 'abuse of process' or failure to comply with rules or directions.

9.26 Sanctions

Under Pt 3 of the CPR 1998 the sanctions available to a judge are made known to the parties so as to try to dissuade breach of the rules. Sanctions may be imposed for failure to comply with the CPR 1998, or Practice Directions, or pre-action protocols. Sanctions include striking out, refusals to grant extensions of time and refusals to allow documents not disclosed to be relied on. See further section 9.28, below, concerning costs.

9.27 The trial

(For previous rules see section 9.9, above, and Chapter 10, section 10.8.)

Fast track cases will normally be limited to one day's duration, with limits on experts giving oral evidence. Jointly instructed experts should become the usual practice. The court will have discretion to appoint a single expert if the parties cannot agree.

Multi-track cases will be heard in much the same way as under the previous system except that in complex cases much of the groundwork will have been performed at a pre-trial case management conference conducted by the trial judge.

9.28 Judgment, interest and costs

(For previous rules see section 9.10.)

The process of delivering the judgment remains unchanged. Penal interest rates can be set to punish misconduct during the action. In regard to costs, orders for costs and wasted costs orders can be made to punish breach of the rules of procedure, though wasted costs orders are likely to become sanctions of last resort as other penalties will usually be more appropriate and proportionate to the particular breach.

Fast track cases will eventually (not immediately) have fixed costs covering the costs of the trial and preparation for it. Costs will be fixed according to the amount claimed – there will be no discretion to vary the fixed costs. If counsel is used there will be a fixed fee for counsel and also a fee for the solicitor's attendance – fees will no longer be assessed according to how long a lawyer has spent on the case, hence the incentive for lawyers to deal with cases quickly. Costs of experts additional to a court appointed expert will not be recoverable from the opponent. Other miscellaneous costs will be assessed at the end of the trial by the trial judge (parties will be expected to give the judge breakdowns of such costs).

Costs in multi-track cases will be assessed at the end of the hearing and based on estimates given by the parties at the allocation and listing stages. The expression 'taxation of costs' is replaced by the description 'detailed assessment' and the taxation master becomes known as the 'costs judge'.

In general in both fast track and multi-track cases the previous rule that 'costs follow the event' (ie the loser pays) will be modified so as to allow the court to pay closer attention to the degree of success and to the conduct of all parties.

9.29 Miscellaneous changes in terminology

The rules of procedure have been rewritten in 'plain English' and some of the more significant changes in terminology are as follows:

- 'writ' becomes 'claim form'
- 'affidavit' becomes 'statement of truth'
- 'pleading' becomes 'statement of case'
- 'plaintiff' becomes 'claimant'
- 'subpoena' becomes 'witness summons'
- 'minor/infant' becomes 'child'
- 'guardian ad litem' becomes 'litigation friend'
- 'ex parte' becomes 'without notice'
- 'inter partes' becomes 'with notice'
- 'leave' becomes 'permission'
- 'in camera' becomes 'in private'
- 'liquidated sum' becomes 'specified sum of money'
- 'unliquidated sum' becomes 'unspecified sum of money'
- 'Mareva injunction' becomes 'freezing injunction'
- 'Anton Piller order' becomes 'search order'

9.30 Effect on precedents

Many of the precedents on the civil procedure prior to 26 April 1999 become of historic interest only because, from 26 April 1999, the judges in exercising their powers will have first recourse to the overriding objective set out in Pt 1 of the CPR 1998.

10

Civil Procedure in the County Court

Procedure prior to 26 April 1999

10.1 Jurisdiction: High Court or county court?

10.2 Bringing proceedings

10.3 Issue of proceedings (actions) and service

10.4 Pleadings

10.5 Automatic directions

10.6 Interlocutory applications

10.7 Bringing proceedings to an end before trial

10.8 The trial

10.9 Enforcement of judgments

10.10 Small claims procedure

Procedure from 26 April 1999

Small claims

10.11 Jurisdiction and allocation

10.12 Pre-trial procedure

10.13 The trial

10.14 Costs

10.15 Effect on precedents

Procedure prior to 26 April 1999

The governing statute was the County Courts Act 1984.
　　The procedural rules were set out in the County Court Rules (the Green Book).

10.1 Jurisdiction: High Court or county court?

The jurisdiction of the county court was unlimited in proceedings for contract, tort and recovery of land and it was further provided that in cases of concurrent jurisdiction between the High Court and county court:

1. An action of which the value was less than £25,000 had to be tried in a county court unless:
   a) a county court considered that it ought to transfer the action to the High Court for trial and the High Court considered that it ought to try the action;
   b) it was commenced in the High Court and the High Court, having regard to the said criteria, considered that it ought to try the action.
2. An action of which the value was £50,000 or more had to be tried in the High Court unless:
   a) it was commenced in a county court and the county court did not consider that the action ought to be transferred to the High Court for trial; or
   b) the High Court considered that it ought to transfer the case to a county court for trial.
3. The High Court and the county courts, when considering whether to exercise their powers of transfer, had to have regard to the following criteria:
   a) the financial substance of the action, including the value of any counterclaim;
   b) whether the action was otherwise important and in particular, whether it raised questions of importance to persons who were not parties or questions of general public interest;
   c) the complexity of the facts, legal issues, remedies or procedures involved; and
   d) whether transfer was likely to result in a more speedy trial of the action, but no transfer could be made on the ground of sub-para (d) alone.

Further particular points in relation to county court jurisdiction were:

1. claims for damages in respect of personal injuries had to be commenced in a county court, unless the value of the action was £50,000 or more;
2. county courts did not normally have jurisdiction to hear and determine any action for libel or slander;
3. Where a plaintiff had a cause of action for more than the county court limit, he could abandon the excess and so give the county court jurisdiction;
4. It was not lawful for a plaintiff to divide a cause of action for the purpose of bringing two or more actions in one or more of the county courts;
5. A county court did not have power to order mandamus, certiorari or prohibition (the prerogative orders used in public law).

The above jurisdictional rules applied to county court hearings before a circuit judge. The jurisdiction of the district judge (who is the county court equivalent of a High Court master) was defined and limited as follows:

1. General jurisdiction to hear actions in matters not exceeding £5,000 and all other proceedings with the consent of the parties and leave of the judge.
2. Interlocutory proceedings.
3. Taxing officer for costs.
4. Jurisdiction conferred specifically by rule or statute.

10.2 Bringing proceedings

In the county court, proceedings mainly comprised actions.

Actions

These were approximately equivalent to actions in the High Court which were begun by writ and in the county court were begun by summons. They fell into three main categories: default, fixed date and rent actions.

Default actions

These were used to recover debts, liquidated *and* unliquidated damages. The plaint note gave the defendant notice that judgment in default could be entered against him if he did not either pay the claim (plus costs) or file a defence/counterclaim within 14 days. 'Plaint' refers to the type of entry made in the court records; parties applying for relief were given plaint notes.

Fixed date actions

These were used for any relief other than damages or money payments (eg recovery of land or equitable remedies). The plaint note gave the defendant notice of the 'return day': that is, the date of the pre-trial review or, in the case of possession actions, the date of the hearing itself.

Rent actions

Though arrears of rent are regarded as a debt (and therefore one might have supposed the use of a default action), they were recoverable by means of a modified form of fixed date action using a special form of summons which made no provision for the service of a defence. The defendant had to either turn up on the return day or pay the sum required; if this was not done judgment would be entered against him.

10.3 Issue of proceedings (actions) and service

Unlike the issue of process in the High Court, where it was the responsibility of the plaintiff or his agents to serve proceedings, in the county court it was the responsibility of the court office itself:

Stage 1: the plaintiff took to the court office: a request for the issue of a summons, naming the parties and stating the nature of the claim; two copies of the particulars of claim (like the High Court statement of claim); and the plaint fee.

Stage 2: the court office prepared and issued the summons and delivered a plaint note to the plaintiff.

Stage 3: service on the defendant, usually by the court or by the plaintiff personally. Service was usually by post, either to the address given in the request for summons or to the defendant's residence or place of business. In the case of default actions the court also served a blank form of admission, defence or counterclaim.

10.4 Pleadings

The principles governing the drafting of pleadings were the same as in the case of the High Court and the function and appearance of the pleadings of both courts almost identical, save that in the county court, the plaintiff's claim was called the particulars of claim. In general, the County Court Rules (CCR) as to pleadings were by no means as detailed nor as thorough as those in the Rules of the Supreme Court (RSC).

Unlike in the High Court procedure, pleadings in the county court were filed at the Court Office and copies were sent by the court to the necessary party.

10.5 Automatic directions

Automatic directions applied in almost all county court cases. This meant that, at the close of pleadings, a timetable of routine directions had to be followed, without the need for court orders. For example exchange of witness statements had to take place within ten weeks. The date for the trial had to be fixed within six months and the action would be struck out after 15 months if the date for trial had still not been fixed by then.

10.6 Interlocutory applications

There were fewer interlocutory matters than in the High Court, though the applications were generally similar in type: applications were usually made by giving notice to the other party, though some could be made 'ex parte' (without notice to the other party). If, for example, it was necessary to arrange a pre-trial review (the equivalent to the High Court summons for directions) one could be applied for, though usually it was unnecessary as everything was usually covered by the automatic directions. Other applications included ones for striking out, discovery, and interlocutory injunctions.

10.7 Bringing proceedings to an end before trial

These were the same as, or similar to, the methods available in a High Court action begun by writ: see Chapter 9, section 9.8. A county court summary judgment was normally applied for after the delivery of the defence rather than before, as was normally the case in the High Court.

10.8 The trial

The manner of trial in the county court was very similar to that in the High Court: see Chapter 9, section 9.9. The county court judge had power to indicate the order of speeches and could dispense with opening speeches. A special method of trial was reserved for small claims (below).

10.9 Enforcement of judgments

A judgment or order of a county court for the payment of a sum of money which it was sought to enforce wholly or partially by execution against goods:

1. must be enforced only in the High Court where the sum which it is sought to enforce is £5,000 or more;
2. must be enforced only in a county court where the sum which it is sought to enforce is less than £600 (as from 26 April 1999); and
3. in any other case can be enforced in either the High Court or a county court.

In general the methods of enforcement available in the county court are much the same as in the High Court, though it is generally believed that the High Court sheriffs are more efficient in obtaining execution than the county court bailiffs.

10.10 Small claims procedure

The term 'small claims' was used to mean money claims which were not valued at more than £3,000. Money claims were commenced by default summons and there were two aspects to small claims procedure:

1. If no defence or counter-claim had been filed the plaintiff could obtain judgment in default. The amount of the claim was assessed by the district judge.

2. If a defence was filed, then the claim was automatically referred to arbitration by the district judge.

Arbitration of small claims

The use of arbitration was meant to encourage the litigant in person in small claims by utilising a procedure which was far more informal than the usual procedure; hearings were in chambers (private) unless the district judge referred the matter to a full trial in open court because of its complexity. The strict procedural rules of trial and rules of evidence were relaxed. The decision of a district judge in such an arbitration could be set aside only if he made an error of law or misconducted the proceedings. The general terms of reference for the conduct of arbitration included:

1. Any hearing had to be informal and the strict rules of evidence should not apply.
2. At the hearing the arbitrator could adopt any method of procedure which he considered to be convenient and to afford a fair and equal opportunity to each party to present their case.

The object of this procedure was to discourage the use of legal representatives in small claims cases by removing one of the main incentives for having representation – the complex rules of procedure and evidence. This procedure was particularly suited to consumer disputes (eg complaints of simple breaches of contract in supplying faulty household equipment) where the legal points were not too complex. The procedure was also suitable for housing disputes, especially as the district judge had power to award the remedies of specific performance and/or injunction: *Joyce* v *Liverpool City Council* [1995] 3 All ER 110 (CA).

Another consequence of the referral to arbitration were the costs rules; solicitors' charges on an arbitration were not allowed except for:

1. The cost of commencing proceedings.
2. The cost of enforcing the district judge's award.
3. Costs occasioned by the unreasonable conduct of the other party.

This was the so-called 'no costs' rule.

In any case an application could be made to rescind the reference to arbitration in order for legal representation to be obtained and the costs of the proceedings recovered: under the 'no costs rule' it was clearly envisaged that legal expertise was required solely for commencing proceedings and enforcing awards. The grounds on one or more of which a district judge had to be satisfied in order to rescind a reference to arbitration were:

1. There existed difficult questions of law or exceptionally complex issues of fact.
2. There was a fraud charge in issue.
3. The parties agreed to rescinding the reference.
4. It would be unreasonable to proceed to arbitration having regard to the subject-

matter of the claim, the parties' circumstances or the interests of other persons likely to be affected by the award.

Examples of (4) might be personal injury claims, where the issues were too complex for the average litigant in person (*Pepper* v *Healey* [1982] RTR 411 CA: reference rescinded in road accident case because the defendant would be represented at insurer's expense), or test cases, where there was more than the litigant's own claim at stake. However, employers' liability claims involving amounts of below £3,000 could not in general be regarded as a class of case unsuited to arbitration and it was a clear misuse of process to intentionally overstate a claim in order to avoid the automatic reference to arbitration: *Afzal* v *Ford Motor Co Ltd* [1994] 4 All ER 720.

The district judge could rescind of his own motion but, if a party requested it, a hearing took place at which the district judge reviewed his decision.

Whilst the small claims procedure was generally perceived as being popular with litigants (and it will be expanded from April 26 1999) there were problems, particularly in obtaining enforcement of judgment as the procedure offered no enforcement machinery.

Procedure from 26 April 1999

See generally Chapter 9, sections 9.15–9.30.

The rest of this Chapter is concerned with the new procedure for dealing with claims on the 'small claims track'.

Small claims

10.11 Jurisdiction and allocation

As from 26 April 1999 the small claims jurisdiction is increased from £3,000 to £5,000. However, the new small claims jurisdiction does not apply to all claims under £5,000. Personal injury claims for general damages, claims for possession of land, housing disrepair claims and harassment claims may be dealt with by the small claims procedure only if they fall below £1,000; if any such claim is above £1,000 (and below £15,000) it will usually be dealt with under the fast track system. In exceptional cases, eg where the facts or law or evidence are complex, or where there are allegations of dishonesty, the claim may be allocated to the multi-track. It is for the court to assess the true financial value of a claim, ie the claimant's assessment is not decisive. The decision in *Afzal* v *Ford Motor Co Ltd* [1994] 4 All ER 720 probably becomes of historic interest only as from 26 April 1999.

Indeed, the term 'small claim' is a misleading one as from 26 April 1999 because every claim, large or small, will be commenced by the same procedure and no claim will enter the so-called small claims track until allocated to that track by the district judge. The previous system of automatic reference is discontinued as from 26 April

1999. Allocation takes place after a defence has been filed to the claimant's claim form or statement of case.

10.12. Pre-trial procedure

Standard directions apply on such matters as filing of documents: each party must supply the court and the other parties with copies of all documents (including experts' reports) to be relied on not less than 14 days before the hearing. The rules in Pt 31 of the CPR 1998 on Disclosure do not apply to the small claims track. Pre-trial reviews are likely to be rare.

10.13 The trial

No more than one day will usually be allowed for the trial. There is a significant departure from the previous approach of informal arbitration. Proceedings must take place in public and be recorded. The court is no longer required to proceed in a way which will give each party an equal opportunity to have his/her case presented, or to explain legal terms or expressions to the parties. The court can adopt any procedure it considers fair, eg by an inquisitorial questioning of witnesses before the parties do so, and by imposing limits on cross-examination. Hence, there will be a dramatic shift away from the previously popular but inadequately controlled arbitration procedures to a more focused regime. The claim can be disposed of in the absence of the parties if both sides consent. The court can grant any remedy which can be granted in fast track and multi-track cases. There is no appeal available except to a circuit judge on the grounds of a serious irregularity affecting the proceedings or a mistake of law.

10.14 Costs

The costs rules remain largely as before. The so-called 'no costs' rule is still applicable, although costs can be awarded to penalise a party for unreasonable conduct and to enforce an award. There is no advantage to a defendant to pay money into court since recoverable costs are in general limited to the costs stated on the summons.

10.15 Effect on precedents

Many of the precedents on the civil procedure prior to 26 April 1999 become of historic interest only because, from 26 April 1999, the judges in exercising their powers will have first recourse to the overriding objective set out in Pt 1 of the Civil Procedure Rules 1998.

11

Civil Appeals

11.1 Introduction

11.2 Appeals from orders of masters, registrars, High Court judges, circuit judges and district judges

11.3 Appeals to the Court of Appeal (Civil Division)

11.4 Appeals to the House of Lords

11.1 Introduction

In the modern civil justice system rights of appeal are statutory only and derive from the Supreme Court Act 1981 and rules and directions made under it. The number of civil appeals has risen steadily over recent years: 1,853 appeals were set down for hearing in 1995 (*Judicial Statistics 1996*, Stationery Office). Delays in hearing civil appeals have caused great concern in recent years: an average appeal has taken 14 months to come on for hearing, whilst some appeals have taken over five years. As a result a review of the Court of Appeal (Civil Division) was undertaken by Sir Jeffrey Bowman and his report (spring 1998) contains important recommendations for reducing the number of cases going to the Court of Appeal and for improving practice and procedures in the civil appeal system. In addition radical reforms of the leave requirement and its procedure are being implemented from 1 January 1999.

11.2 Appeals from orders of masters, registrars, High Court judges, circuit judges and district judges

These appeals are from courts of first instance. From 1 January 1999 leave will be required for all such appeals except appeals against: committal orders; refusals to grant habeas corpus; and secure accommodation orders made pursuant to s25 of the Children Act 1989: *Practice Note (Court of Appeal: Procedure)* [1999] 1 All ER 186. The purpose of the new comprehensive leave requirement is to clarify the position as to the need for leave and to reduce the number of inappropriate appeals.

The court of first instance should as a matter of routine decide whether or not to grant leave to appeal. The general rule in deciding this question is that leave should be granted unless an appeal would have no realistic prospect of success. Leave may also be given in exceptional circumstances even though the case has no real prospect of success if there is an issue which, in the public interest, should be examined by the Court of Appeal. Examples are where a case raises questions of great public interest or questions of general policy, or where authority binding on the Court of Appeal may call for reconsideration.

If the court of first instance is in doubt whether an appeal would have a real prospect of success or involves a point of general principle the safe course is to refuse leave to appeal, since it is always open to the Court of Appeal to grant leave.

Where there has already been one unsuccessful appeal to a court against the decision being challenged, for example from a district judge to a circuit judge or from a master to a High Court judge, and application is for leave for a further appeal to the Court of Appeal, a more restrictive approach to the test for leave to appeal should be adopted. Leave should be granted only if the case raises an important point of principle or practice or the case is one which for some other reason should be considered by the Court of Appeal.

Orders of masters or registrars of the High Court are usually heard by a High Court judge in chambers by way of a rehearing. The judge is not bound by any previous exercise of discretion by the master or registrar: see *Evans* v *Bartlam* [1937] AC 473 (HL). Decisions of High Court judges, whether in chambers or in open court, are challengeable in the Court of Appeal (Civil Division) unless expressly declared to be unappealable by statute: *Re Racal Communications Ltd* [1981] AC 374 (HL). In rare cases a 'leapfrog appeal' is available from the High Court to the House of Lords: see section 11.4, below.

In the county court appeals lie from the district judge to the circuit judge not by way of rehearing but on the basis of legal submissions only. Decisions of circuit judges are challengeable in the Court of Appeal (Civil Division). There are no 'leapfrog' appeals from the county court to the House of Lords.

In general appeals heard by the Court of Appeal (Civil Division) are by way of a rehearing, though on the basis of transcripts of the evidence given in the court below rather than receiving all the evidence itself. The Court of Appeal (Civil Division) can take into account fresh evidence which has come to light since the earlier hearing.

11.3 Appeals to the Court of Appeal (Civil Division)

Civil Appeals Office

The Civil Appeals Office is responsible for the administration of civil appeals. It is headed by the Registrar of Civil Appeals whose function is to deal expeditiously with all incidental applications which are necessary pending an appeal. The Registrar deals with these matters in chambers and an appeal lies from his decision to a single Lord Justice of Appeal and thence, with leave, to the Court of Appeal (Civil Division). Incidental applications may also be referred by the Registrar to a single judge of the Court of Appeal (Civil Division) in chambers, who in turn has power to refer such an application to the Court of Appeal (Civil Division). Appropriate applications can be made directly to a single Lord Justice or to the Court of Appeal (Civil Division).

Procedure

The appellant prepares a notice of appeal setting out the grounds of appeal and specifying the order for which he applies. The notice must be served on all parties to the action within four weeks of the judgment in the court below (this time can be extended with leave of the Registrar of Civil Appeals or the Court of Appeal) and within seven days the appellant must set down the appeal for hearing.

A respondent to an appeal may serve a notice contending that the order of the court below should be affirmed or varied on other grounds or he may cross-appeal that the decision (or part of it) is wrong. Otherwise the respondent (being the 'winner' in the court below) cannot appeal.

Skeleton arguments have become compulsory for legally represented parties in setting out the case for and against appeal. The purpose of a party's skeleton argument is to identify and summarise the principal points involved and to draw attention to the relevant legal authorities. It assists the judge to prepare for the hearing, thereby ensuring that the oral argument for the appeal can focus on the central issues in dispute between the parties. This reduces the time spent in court, and limits the costs for litigants and the legal system.

By advancing these objectives it can be said that the skeleton argument has been one of the most significant improvements in civil procedure in recent years. Under the procedural reforms introduced from 1 January 1999 (*Practice Note* [1999] 1 All ER 186) skeleton arguments are also required from represented applicants seeking leave to appeal so that the Court of Appeal can deal more efficiently with applications for leave to appeal. Two copies of the skeleton argument must accompany the bundle of documents which the applicant's solicitors lodge with the Civil Appeals Office for the application. If the application is listed for oral hearing at which both parties have the opportunity to attend, then the respondent's skeleton must be lodged and served within 14 days of receipt of the applicant's bundle.

Where leave to appeal is granted the appellant (and any respondent who has lodged a skeleton argument in response to the leave application) may use the same skeleton arguments for the purposes of the appeal or they may prepare fresh skeleton arguments for the purposes of the appeal. The appellant's solicitors must include with the appeal four copies of their skeleton argument and also include a copy of that skeleton argument with the set of bundles served on the respondent (at the same time as the appeal bundles are lodged with the Civil Appeals Office). The respondent's solicitors must lodge with the Civil Appeals Office four copies of their skeleton argument within 21 days of the date on which the appellant's bundle was served on them or, if earlier, not later than 14 days before the appeal hearing.

Since the date by which an appellant must file a bundle of documents is typically many months before the hearing, it follows that under the new procedure there is an obligation to prepare and file skeleton arguments at a much earlier stage of the appeal proceedings (previously the normal rule had been that a party could file such arguments 14 days before the fixed hearing date). It could be argued that the new procedure, by requiring the work to be done so long before the appeal hearing, will lead to a decline in the quality and focus of skeleton arguments particularly in areas of law where developments are rapid. (Revised skeleton arguments may not be lodged without the court's permission and such permission will be granted only if there is good reason for doing so.)

Appeals are heard usually by three judges or, in particularly important cases, by a 'full' court of five or more judges. Certain appeals and applications for leave to appeal can be heard by two judges. In the event of deadlock arising in the form of disagreement between the two judges, the entire case must be reargued before a reconvened Court of three judges (there cannot be an appeal to the House of Lords in such a case without a reconvened hearing).

Powers of the Court of Appeal

The Court of Appeal has full power to make any order which could have been made in the court below. However, the Court of Appeal is usually reluctant to upset the trial judge's finding of facts because he saw and heard the witnesses and was in a better position to assess their credibility. Further, the Court of Appeal is usually reluctant to interfere with a judge's exercise of his discretion where he has used it correctly, and with an award of damages unless it is out of proportion with awards in similar cases. Similarly an award of damages by a jury may be set aside only if excessive or inadequate: s8 of the Courts and Legal Services Act 1990.

A successful appellant is normally awarded the costs of both the appeal and the original trial.

In appropriate cases the Court of Appeal may order a new trial. The grounds on which this may be done include: a misdirection of the judge to the jury (in those few civil cases where it is still used); improper rejection of evidence; misconduct at the trial; and judgment obtained by fraud.

Reform proposals

The Bowman Report (1998) recommends that certain appeals which now reach the Court of Appeal (Civil Division) should be heard at a lower level, eg appeals against decisions in 'fast track' cases after the new civil justice system comes into force on 26 April 1999. Both the Report and the White Paper *Modernising Justice* (Cm 4155)

(1998) recommend that many routine appeals could be settled by a single member of the Court of Appeal. The Bowman Report goes so far as to suggest changes to the composition of the Court of Appeal, eg the appointment of specialist academic lawyers and practitioners to sit as members on appropriate occasions. All these proposals are designed to ease the burden of work on the Court of Appeal and improve the efficient operation of that court, but it may be that, if implemented, the effect may be to transfer the burden to a lower level of the judiciary and dilute the quality of judgments delivered in routine appeals.

11.4 Appeals to the House of Lords

From the Court of Appeal, approximately 5 per cent of all cases are taken further to the House of Lords. A further appeal only lies with either leave of the Court of Appeal or the Appeals Committee of the House (usually three Law Lords). Such leave will only generally be granted in cases of general public importance: the House is generally influenced also by the prospects of success in an appeal and the degree of disagreement the case may have engendered in the lower courts.

In certain cases, 'leapfrog' appeals may be made directly from the High Court to the House of Lords provided all the parties consent, the trial judge certifies a point of law of general importance, and the House grants leave: ss12 and 13 of the Administration of Justice Act 1969. There is no appeal from a refusal to grant a certificate.

Argument before the House (counsel are robed, though the Law Lords are not) usually takes place in a committee room of the House of Lords, and is usually oral – though the parties must provide a joint statement of facts and issues and lodge their cases after setting down. The House is usually very reluctant to interfere with a trial judge's exercise of discretion, save in those cases where the judge is demonstrably wrong either in the light of further evidence, change of circumstances, or in point of law. Such an exercise of discretion will not be interfered with 'merely on the ground that the members of the appellate court would have exercised the discretion differently': Lord Diplock in *Hadmor Productions Ltd v Hamilton* [1982] 1 All ER 1042 at 1046 (HL).

The House has an inherent jurisdiction to set aside a ruling, though naturally it is reluctant to reopen an appeal. It will do so in exceptional cases where a party has been subjected to an unfair procedure. Apart from such cases there is no further right of appeal from decisions of the House: *Re Pinochet Ugarte* [1999] NLJ Rep 88.

Part V:
Criminal Proceedings

12

Arrest, Search and Seizure and Interrogation

12.1   Introduction

12.2   Police powers to stop and search

12.3   Conduct of searches under s1 of the 1984 Act

12.4   Other powers to stop and search

12.5   Road checks

12.6   Powers of entry, search and seizure on premises

12.7   Entry, search and seizure without warrant

12.8   Powers of seizure

12.9   Powers of arrest

12.10 Arrestable offences

12.11 Power to arrest for arrestable offences

12.12 Power to arrest for offences which are not arrestable

12.13 Information on arrest

12.14 Voluntary attendance at police station

12.15 Procedure following arrest

12.16 Appearance before magistrates following charge

12.17 Interrogation of suspects and the right to legal advice

12.18 Searches and fingerprinting following arrest

12.19 Confessions: general

12.20 The use of the caution and the right to silence

12.21 Challenging the admissibility of evidence

12.1 Introduction

In the majority of criminal cases, the defendant's first involvement in the criminal process will be his contact with the police. It is with these first stages of the criminal process that this chapter is primarily concerned.

Police powers to stop, search, detain and arrest persons were developed piecemeal across many decades. There were wide variations between rural and metropolitan areas, and many anomalies, for example inconsistencies in the scope of powers to enter, search premises and seize evidence: see *Ghani* v *Jones* [1970] 1 QB 693. Rights to stop and search were often conferred in wide and uncertain terms, such as the much-criticised and now repealed 'sus' laws, and different conditions attached to the exercise of those rights according to the particular statutes creating them. Much has now been placed upon a more consistent footing with the introduction of the Police and Criminal Evidence Act 1984 (PACE) and the Codes of Practice issued thereunder.

The Codes of Practice, issued by the Home Secretary, aim to provide guidelines as to how the discretion given to police officers under PACE should be exercised. Unlike the statute, the Codes are written in a non-technical style that should be readily comprehensible by police constables, if not the averagely educated lay person. Four Codes (A–D) were initially introduced in January 1986, supplemented by Code E in 1988. A revised version of Codes A–D was introduced in April 1991, and the current versions, amended to incorporate the recommendations of the Royal Commission on Criminal Justice, and the changes in the law consequent upon the enactment of the Criminal Justice and Public Order Act 1994, came into effect on 10 April 1995. The Codes now cover the following:

Code A: The exercise by police officers of statutory powers of stop and search.

Code B: The searching of premises by police officers and the seizure of property found by police officers on persons or premises.

Code C: The detention, treatment and questioning of persons by police officers.

Code D: The identification of persons by police officers.

Code E: The tape-recording of interviews by police officers at police stations with suspected persons.

Under s67(8) of PACE, as originally enacted, a police officer was liable to disciplinary proceedings for a failure to comply with any provision of the Codes. This provision has, however, been repealed by s37(a) of the Criminal Justice and Public Order Act 1994, so that police forces have more discretion as to how they deal with officers who fail to follow guidelines on best practice. It is assumed that flagrant breaches of the Codes would still render an officer liable to disciplinary proceedings. Whilst a breach of the Codes may not, as such, affect the legality of an officer's action, and may not, of itself, render him liable to any criminal or civil proceedings, the Codes are admissible in evidence in civil and criminal and must be taken into account where relevant.

Although the Codes are not law in the strict sense, a trial judge can recognise non-compliance on the part of the police by excluding evidence obtained in breach of the Codes. Thus in *R* v *Saunders* [1988] Crim LR 521, where D was not shown a record of her statements made so that she could attest to their accuracy, and was not cautioned in terms that made clear her right to remain silent, the trial judge ruled the evidence inadmissible under s78. Note, however, the obiter statements of Lord Lane CJ in *R* v *Delaney* [1989] Crim LR 39, to the effect that the courts should not punish police officers for non-compliance by excluding evidence obtained in breach of the Codes. His view was that judges should only exclude evidence where it has been obtained after substantial and significant breaches that make it good sense to exclude evidence. Useful guidance is provided by the Court of Appeal in *R* v *Keenan* [1989] 3 All ER 598. D was charged with possession of an offensive weapon. Shortly before his trial defence counsel were served with copies of statements allegedly made by D to police officers in which he admitted knowledge that the weapon was in his car. D, who denied ever having made the statement, had not been invited to read and sign the statement. On appeal following conviction, the Court of Appeal held that the evidence of the statement should not have been admitted. The test to be adopted was, if the other evidence was compelling, the police would still secure a conviction, despite the exclusion of evidence obtained in breach of the Code. If the other evidence was weak, then it was right that the 'vital' evidence obtained in breach of the Code should be excluded since the safeguards designed to ensure its reliability had not been complied with.

In exercising the powers of stop, search, entry, seizure and arrest considered below, s117 of PACE makes it clear that, provided the power is not one that can only be exercised with the consent of some person, other than a police officer, the officer may use reasonable force, if necessary, in the exercise of the power.

With the enactment of the Human Rights Act 1998, the whole common law and statutory scheme of police powers will henceforth have to operate within the context of the Convention rights protected by the 1998 Act; for details of how the Act will be applied: see further Chapter 19. Of particular relevance to this chapter are arts 5 and 6, dealing as they do with liberty and security of the person, and the right to a fair trial respectively.

12.2 Police powers to stop and search

Traditionally police officers have not possessed a common law power to detain suspects for questioning, short of first exercising a power of arrest. Whilst cases such as *Donnelly* v *Jackman* [1970] 1 All ER 987 confirm that a constable can commit a trivial interference with an individual's liberty, for example tapping him on the shoulder to attract his attention, without exceeding the scope of his duty, *Rice* v *Connolly* [1966] 2 QB 414 is still authority for the proposition that a citizen is not required to stop and answer police enquiries per se. In that case D refused to answer a constable's questions concerning his activities and refused to provide him with his address. D's conviction for obstructing a police officer in the execution of his duty, contrary to s51(3) of the Police Act 1964, was allowed on the ground that D had been under no legal duty to provide the police with information. (Note that to provide deliberately misleading information could give rise to liability.) Similarly in *Kenlin* v *Gardner* [1967] 2 QB 510, where the defendants, two schoolboys going from house to house to remind fellow members of their rugby team of a fixture, were stopped by a constable who produced a warrant card in order to hold the boys for questioning. The defendants struggled and assaulted the officer. The question arose as to the availability of the defence of self-defence on a charge under s51(1) of the Police Act 1964 – assaulting an officer in the execution of his duty. The court held that the defence was available, as the constable had no power short of arrest to physically detain the boys for questioning.

In theory the 1984 Act does not invalidate any of these decisions but, as indicated below, a constable can now detain a suspect in order to conduct a search under s1, and failure to provide personal details may give rise to a power to arrest without a warrant under s25.

Part I of PACE confers general powers of stop and search, not restricted to metropolitan areas, and provides for the keeping of records of searches. Section 1(2) creates a general power in constables to search a person or a vehicle or anything that is in or on a vehicle, and to detain the person or vehicle for the search. The power may only be exercised if the police constable has reasonable grounds for suspecting that he will find stolen or prohibited articles as a result of the search: s1(3). In addition, the search may only be carried out if the person or vehicle is in any place to which at the time when the constable proposes to exercise the power the public or any section of the public has access, on payment or otherwise, as of right or by virtue of express or implied permission; or in any other place to which people have a ready access at the time when the constable proposes to exercise the power but which is not a dwelling: see s1(1).

So far as concerns searches of persons or vehicles on land adjacent to a dwelling-house, the Act provides by s1(4) and (5):

'(4) If a person is in a garden or yard occupied with and used for the purposes of a dwelling or on other land so occupied and used, a constable may not search him in the exercise of the power conferred by this section unless the constable has reasonable grounds for believing –
(a) that he does not reside in the dwelling; and
(b) that he is not in the place in question with the express or implied permission of a person who resides in the dwelling.
(5) If a vehicle is in a garden or yard occupied with and used for the purposes of a dwelling or on other land so occupied and used, a constable may not search the vehicle or

anything in or on it in the exercise of the power conferred by this section unless he has reasonable grounds for believing

(a) that the person in charge of the vehicle does not reside in the dwelling;
(b) that the vehicle is not in the place in question with the express or implied permission of a person who resides in the dwelling.'

The purpose of the search is to locate stolen goods or 'prohibited articles'. The definition of the former may be analogous to s24(2) of the Theft Act 1968, so that goods are 'stolen goods' if they are goods originally stolen, or which directly or indirectly represent or have at any time represented stolen goods, or are the proceeds of any disposal or realisation of stolen goods, or are goods obtained by blackmail or by deception. As regards 'prohibited articles', the Act provides by s1(7), (8) and (9) that an article is prohibited for the purposes of this part of PACE if it is an offensive weapon (defined as an article made or adapted for use for causing injury to persons, or intended by the person having it with him for such use by him or by some other person) or an article made or adapted for use in the course of or in connection with any one of a number of offences (burglary, theft, taking a conveyance, and obtaining by deception) or is intended by the person having it with him for such use by him or by some other person. Section 140 of the Criminal Justice Act 1988 extends the meaning of offensive weapon to include any article with a blade or point carried in a public place, except a folding pocket-knife.

If a search results in the discovery of what the constable has reasonable grounds to believe are stolen or prohibited articles, s1(6) confers upon him the power to seize such items.

The exercise of many of the powers granted to the police under PACE are subject to the precondition that there must be 'reasonable suspicion' or 'reasonable grounds to suspect' that a given state of affairs exists. This is particularly so in relation to the exercise of stop and search powers under s1 and also summary arrest under ss24 and 25: see further sections 12.11 and 12.12 below. Code A (as amended) gives some further guidance as to the interpretation of the phrase 'reasonable suspicion' in the context of stop and search powers. The Code provides:

'1.6 Whether a reasonable ground for suspicion exists will depend on the circumstances of each case, but there must be some objective basis for it. An officer will need to consider the nature of the article suspected of being carried in the context of other factors such as the time and the place, and the behaviour of the person concerned or those with him. Reasonable suspicion may exist, for example, where information has been received such as a description of an article being carried or of a suspected offender; a person is seen acting covertly or warily or attempting to hide something; or a person is carrying a certain type of article at an unusual time or in a place where a number of burglaries or thefts are known to have taken place recently. But the decision to stop and search must be based on all the facts which bear on the likelihood that an article of a certain kind will be found.
1.7 Reasonable suspicion can never be supported on the basis of personal factors alone. For example, a person's colour, age, hairstyle or manner of dress, or the fact that he is known to have a previous conviction for possession of an unlawful article, cannot be used alone or in combination with each other as the sole basis on which to search that person.

Nor may it be founded on the basis of stereotyped images of certain persons or groups as more likely to be committing offences.
1.7A Where a police officer has reasonable grounds to suspect that a person is in innocent possession of a stolen or prohibited article or other item for which he is empowered to search, the power of stop and search exists notwithstanding that there would be no power of arrest. However every effort should be made to secure the person's co-operation in the production of the article before resorting to the use of force.'

12.3 Conduct of searches under s1 of the 1984 Act

Once satisfied that the conditions of s1 are met, and that there are the required 'reasonable grounds' for exercising the stop and search power, a constable must, in carrying out the search, follow the procedure laid down by s2 and must usually make a record of it in accordance with s3. If, having stopped a person or vehicle for the purpose of search, the constable thinks it unnecessary actually to make the search, he need not do so (s2(1)), but that decision does not affect the lawfulness of his initial act in detaining that person or vehicle. If the constable wishes to search a person, or a vehicle which is 'attended' (which presumably means that there is a person in it or appearing to be in charge of it nearby), s2(2) and (3) ensure that the intended object of the search is made aware of the identity of the searcher and the reasons for the search.

PACE does not state what is to be done when the constable is unable to determine which of several persons is 'in charge' of a vehicle: presumably all should be told the matters in s2(3).

The extent of the search is governed by s2(9), which provides that neither the power conferred by s1 nor any other power to detain and search a person without first arresting him or to detain and search a vehicle without making an arrest is to be construed as authorising a constable to require a person to remove any of his clothing in public other than an outer coat, jacket or gloves; or as authorising a constable not in uniform to stop a vehicle.

The ambiguous wording of s2(9) could be taken to mean that a constable can require a person to remove *other* articles of clothing provided such removal is not made 'in public'. Thus if the constable asked the subject of the search to remove his trousers, and offered to allow him to do so in the privacy of a closed police van, or inside a nearby house, it may well be that the power exists to compel the subject to comply. Code A para 3.5 clearly contemplates that such power is implied into s2(9) in that it states:

'Where on reasonable grounds it is considered necessary to conduct a more thorough search (eg by requiring someone to take off a T-shirt or headgear), this shall be done out of public view for example, in a police van or police station if there is one nearby.'

Note that such searches may only be conducted by an officer of the same sex as the person searched and may not be made in the presence of anyone of the opposite sex unless the person being searched consents to their presence.

Provided the conditions in s1 are met, vehicles that are not 'attended' may be searched even though there is no person during the search who is in charge of the vehicle or otherwise responsible for it. In such a case, s2(6) and (7) provide that the fact that a search has taken place be brought to the attention of the vehicle's owner, driver or other person responsible for it. The notice should specify the name of the constable conducting the search, and should inform the owner that an application for compensation for any damage caused by the search may be made. The notice should be left inside the vehicle unless it is not reasonably practicable to do so without damaging the vehicle.

So as to avoid excessive delay in the carrying out of a search of persons or vehicles, s2(8) imposes a statutory (if rather vague) duty upon the police where it states that: 'The time for which a person or vehicle may be detained for the purposes of such a search is such time as is reasonably required to permit a search to be carried out either at the place where the person or vehicle was first detained or nearby.'

How much time is 'reasonably required' must of course depend upon the facts of each case, but it is to be hoped that the subsection will encourage the police to make the search quickly, rather than risking a civil action for unlawful detention for a period beyond what a court could later find to have been adequate.

12.4 Other powers to stop and search

The 1984 Act significantly tidies up a confused morass of varying general and local powers. Nonetheless, several powers peculiar to particular offences, places or persons survive the Act, and some have been added since. The most notable are:

1. To stop and search for prohibited drugs. The conditions for search remain those stated in s23 of the Misuse of Drugs Act 1971.
2. To search persons in public places for unlicensed firearms, or for firearms used or suspected of being intended for use in the course of crime. This power is still governed by s47 of the Firearms Act 1968.
3. To stop and search persons suspected of terrorist offences. The very wide rights given the police by the Prevention of Terrorism (Temporary Provisions) Act 1989 take priority over any of the requirements of the present Act.
4. Under s60 of the Criminal Justice and Public Order Act 1994, a police officer of or above the rank of superintendent may, if he reasonably believes that incidents involving serious violence may take place in any locality in his area, and it is expedient to prevent their occurrence, authorise the use of stop and search powers in the area for which he is responsible for a period of up to 24 hours. The period may be extended by a further six hours where it appears to the

officer who gave the initial authorisation that it is expedient to do so. The stop and search powers conferred by this section extend to stopping any pedestrian, or vehicle and searching him or the occupants of any such vehicle, or the vehicle itself, for offensive weapons or dangerous instruments (ie bladed or pointed), whether or not a constable has any grounds for suspecting that he might find such articles. If any such articles are found they may be seized by a constable.

These powers have been further extended by s25 of the Crime and Disorder Act 1998, which inserts a new subs(4A) into s60. Under this provision a police officer may require a person to remove any item that the police officer reasonably believes he is wearing wholly or mainly for the purpose of concealing his identity, such as a mask, hood or other garment. Items worn for these purposes can be seized and retained by a police officer.

5. Section 81 of the Criminal Justice and Public Order Act 1994 Act provides additional powers of stop and search in relation to terrorism by adding a s13A to the Prevention of Terrorism (Temporary Provisions) Act 1989.

Constables employed by certain statutory undertakers are also given a power of stop and search wider than that conferred on the police in general, and by s6 of the 1984 Act they may stop, detain and search any vehicle before it leaves a 'goods area' included in the premises of their employers. There is no need in such cases for the holding of 'reasonable grounds' for any suspicion of carriage by the vehicle of stolen or prohibited articles – the power is almost unlimited, though it applies only to searches of vehicles and not to searches of persons, so that any search of a person may be carried out only if the conditions mentioned in s1 of the Act are met. 'Goods area' is defined by s6(2) as 'any area used wholly or mainly for the storage or handling of goods'. The principal beneficiaries of the s6 power will be railway, dock, canal and other transport police forces, which are in theory not a part of the police force of the county in which they operate.

12.5 Road checks

Where a serious crime has been committed, it is of great assistance to the police to be able to establish roadside stations through which motor vehicles must pass and be checked to see whether they are carrying the suspect criminal or someone who may be a witness to the offence. The example of an armed raid upon an armoured security van springs first to mind; the police must act quickly if the villains are to be identified and caught before their trail becomes cold. To help in this case, and in a wide variety of others, s4 of the 1984 Act provides for short-term local powers of stop and search of vehicles. An officer may only authorise a road check under s4(3) if he has reasonable grounds for believing that a 'serious arrestable offence' has been committed; and has reasonable grounds to suspect that persons sought in connection with the offence are, or will be, in the locality in which vehicles would be stopped if the road check were authorised. Normally the authorisation to set up roadblocks must be given in writing by an officer of at least the rank of superintendent. An officer below that rank may authorise such a road check only if it appears to him that it is required as a matter of urgency.

The authorisation must specify the locality in which vehicles are to be stopped and the length of time for which the order remains in operation (normally not exceeding seven days). If a road block authorisation is granted, officers may conduct road checks for the purpose of ascertaining whether a vehicle is carrying: a person who has committed an offence other than a road traffic offence or a vehicles excise offence; a person who is a witness to such an offence; a person intending to commit such an offence; or a person who is unlawfully at large. Where a vehicle is stopped in a road check, the person in charge of the vehicle at the time when it is stopped is entitled to obtain a written statement of the purpose of the road check if he applies for such a statement not later than the end of the period of 12 months from the day on which the vehicle was stopped. In practice this power will not be used to permit a full search of vehicles, but to allow for a rather a cursory inspection and interrogation to determine whether any of the persons sought is driving or being carried in the vehicle.

The phrase 'serious arrestable offence', which occurs elsewhere in PACE, is defined by s116. It provides that the following arrestable offences are always serious:

1. an offence (whether at common law or under any enactment) specified in Part I of Sch 5 of PACE (see below);
2. any of the offences mentioned in paragraphs (a)-(dd) of the definition of 'drug trafficking offences' in s38(1) of the Drug Trafficking Offences Act 1986;
3. subject to point (4) below, any other arrestable offence is serious only if its commission has led to, or is intended or is likely to lead to: serious harm to the security of the state or to public order; serious interference with the administration of justice or with the investigation of offences or of a particular offence; the death of any person; serious injury to any person; substantial financial gain to any person; and serious financial loss to any person. Loss is serious for these purposes if, having regard to all the circumstances, it is serious for the person who suffers it. 'Injury' includes any disease and any impairment of a person's physical or mental condition;
4. an offence under ss2, 8, 9, 10 or 11 of the Prevention of Terrorism (Temporary Provisions) Act 1984 is always a serious arrestable offence for the purposes of s56 or 58 (see section 14.7 below), and an attempt or conspiracy to commit any such offence is also always a serious arrestable offence for those purposes.

Part I of Sch 5 lists those offences conclusively regarded as serious arrestable offences, these include: murder, rape, buggery, treason, manslaughter, kidnapping, incest with a girl under the age of 13 and so on. Part II provides details of other specific offences to be treated as serious arrestable offences, and is subject to amendment as new offences are created: see for example the offences added to Part

II by s85 of the Criminal Justice and Public Order Act 1994. Other offences will fall within the definition only if they are 'arrestable' in the meaning given by s24 of PACE, but have also caused or were intended to cause harm classified as 'serious' by s116(6). For example, theft contrary to s1 of the Theft Act 1968 is an 'arrestable' offence, but can qualify as a 'serious arrestable offence' only if it has caused or was intended to cause one of the s116(6) consequences, notably 'substantial financial gain to any person or serious financial loss to any person'. These phrases necessarily lack precision and whether or not the definitions are satisfied will be a question of fact in each case. In *R v Neil McIvor* [1987] Crim LR 409 (a Crown Court decision) the trial judge ruled that access to a solicitor under s58 should not have been denied as the theft alleged, 28 hunt dogs valued at £800, was not a serious arrestable offence as it did not involve a substantial loss to the victim. Similarly, in *R v Eric Smith* [1987] Crim LR 579, the theft of two video recorders from Woolworths plc was not regarded as involving substantial loss.

As will be seen further in this chapter the concept of 'serious arrestable offence' also has a key part to play in determining the extent of police powers to detain, isolate and interrogate arrested persons.

12.6 Powers of entry, search and seizure on premises

The powers of stop, search and seizure thus far discussed have all related to persons or vehicles in public places, whether those places be roads, pavements, or the gardens and yards provided for by s1(4) and (5). What of the police powers to enter buildings and other premises for the purpose of search or seizure? In the same way that Part I of PACE has clarified and consolidated rights to stop and search in public places, so Part II substantially amends the powers of entry and search of premises, and several anomalous lacunae have been closed in the process.

The police are now authorised to enter and search premises on the authority of a warrant issued by a Justice of the Peace if they suspect the commission of a 'serious arrestable offence' (see section 12.5 above) and the presence on those premises of evidence relevant to that suspected offence.

Specifically, s8 provides:

'(1) If on an application made by a constable a Justice of the Peace is satisfied that there are reasonable grounds for believing –
(a) that a serious arrestable offence has been committed; and
(b) that there is material on premises specified in the application which is likely to be of substantial value (whether by itself or together with other material) to the investigation of the offence; and
(c) that the material is likely to be relevant evidence; and
(d) that it does not consist of or include items subject to legal privilege, excluded material or special procedure material; and
(e) that any of the conditions specified in subsection (3) below [considered below] applies,
he may issue a warrant authorising a constable to enter and search the premises.'

The references to items 'subject to legal privilege', 'excluded material' and 'special procedure material' mean that no warrant may be issued by a magistrate which gives authority to enter and search for any of the following classes of evidence:

1. Documents subject to legal professional privilege according to the principles of the law of evidence and s10 of the Act. Such items are excluded from the right to search so as to preserve the defendant's right not to be compelled to incriminate himself by disclosure of anything he may have told to or been told by his legal advisers in connection with some legal matter, even though it is not the matter raised in the warrant.
2. Excluded material includes personal records of any person's physical or mental health or personal welfare acquired or created in confidence, and any human tissue or tissue fluid taken for the purposes of diagnosis or medical treatment and held in confidence, and also journalistic material held in confidence. The precise definitions of this phrase appear in s11, and a right of access to excluded material arises only on the order of a circuit judge made in an application by the police under Sch 1 of the Act. Thus, there is a safeguard against unjustified invasion of privacy.
3. Special procedure material includes certain journalistic material other than that in the definition of 'excluded material', together with certain business records held in confidence or subject to an obligation by statute not to disclose them. Such material can once again only be made the lawful object of police search and seizure on the authority of a circuit judge: s14.

Provided, therefore, that none of the evidence sought falls into the categories of 'legal privilege', 'excluded' or 'special procedure' material, a justice's warrant may issue to authorise the entry and search of premises. As s8(1)(e) provides, however, a warrant will not be issued unless one of the conditions in s8(3) applies. These conditions are designed to ensure that the draconian weapon of warrant operates only where it is impracticable or undesirable to gain access to evidence by request to the person who holds the right to grant access to it, perhaps because the evidence might be destroyed if the police are compelled to await an occupier's permission to enter, or cannot find out who has the right to allow them entry. The subsection provides:

> '(3) The conditions mentioned in subsection (1)(e) above are
> (a) that it is not practicable to communicate with any person entitled to grant entry to the premises;
> (b) that it is practicable to communicate with a person entitled to grant entry to the premises but it is not practicable to communicate with any person entitled to grant access to the evidence;
> (c) that entry to the premises will not be granted unless a warrant is produced;
> (d) that the purpose of a search may be frustrated or seriously prejudiced unless a constable arriving at the premises can secure immediate entry to them.

The application to a Justice of the Peace for issue of the warrant must be made in the form prescribed by s15, which is intended to ensure that there is good reason for its grant, and that it clearly specifies the suspected offence and, so far as is possible, the evidence sought. The constable applying for the warrant must: state the ground on which he makes the application; state the enactment under which the warrant would be issued; specify the premises which it is desired to enter and search; and identify, so far as is practicable, the articles or persons to be sought

Each warrant authorises entry on one occasion only: s15(5). If granted the warrant must specify: the name of the person who applies for it; the date on which it is issued; the enactment under which it is issued; the premises to be searched; and, so far as is practicable, the articles or persons to be sought: s15(6).

Once issued, the search warrant remains in force for only one month, and if it has not been executed within that period it lapses and must be returned to the court office from which it issued: s16(3) and (10). It must be executed at a 'reasonable hour' unless it appears to the constable executing it that the purpose of a search may be frustrated on an entry at a reasonable hour: s16(4). This test seems to be wholly subjective, so that the constable's honest even though unreasonable belief will be conclusive. The occupier or apparent occupier of the premises to be searched must be shown the warrant, provided with a copy of it, and given documentary evidence that the person seeking to execute it is a constable: s16(5).

Thus far, the courts appear to be taking a hard line in requiring compliance by the police with the search warrant safeguards. In *R v South Western Magistrates' Court, ex parte Cofie* [1997] 1 WLR 885 the court granted a declaration that a search warrant was unlawful on the ground that the officer applying for it had specified the building to be searched was '78, Oxford Gardens, W10', when in fact he knew that the building was divided into flats and that only the common parts of the building, and flat 78F in particular, needed to be searched. Beldam LJ confirmed that s15(6) of PACE was to be construed strictly, and that the officer had failed to specify the premises to be searched with sufficient particularity.

In *R v Chief Constable of Lancashire, ex parte Parker* [1993] 2 WLR 428 the applicants' premises were entered by police offices purporting to act under search warrants and items were seized. The officers carrying out the searches provided the occupiers with warrants comprising photocopies of the authorisations unaccompanied by the schedules that would have detailed the articles sought. The applicants sought judicial review seeking orders of certiorari to quash the warrants and a declaration to the effect that the entries and searches had been unlawful. The Divisional Court, granting the declarations sought, held that a search warrant comprised two documents, the authorisation and the schedule of articles to be seized. Subsections 15(7) and (8) of the Police and Criminal Evidence Act 1984 required that two certified copies should be made of any warrant, so that one might be given to the occupier, or left at the premises. The certification was required so that the occupier did not have to rely on the word of the police as to the warrant's validity. Showing the occupier a copy of the warrant would not suffice. As Nolan LJ observed:

'It seems to us clear beyond argument that when the Act refers to a warrant issued by a judge it means the whole of the original document seen and approved and put forth by him. ... It would be wholly contrary to the purpose of the legislation if a judge could authorise the police to replace the whole or a part of the original warrant, for the purposes of its execution, by an uncertified photocopy which he has not seen.'

Hence the original warrant had been valid, and certiorari would not be granted to quash it, but the subsequent searches were unlawful given the failure to comply with the statutory requirements concerning authentification an completeness of copies.

Provided the documents are in order, *R v Longman* [1988] Crim LR 534 suggests that the police can gain entry to premises before informing the occupants as to who they are. In that case a female officer, posing as an 'Interflora' delivery woman, gained entry and then produced her warrant card. The court declared such a procedure lawful, provided the police could show that providing information prior to entry would render the subsequent search nugatory.

If the constable finds the evidence connected with the suspected offence for which the warrant issued, he may seize it: s8(2).

12.7 Entry, search and seizure without warrant

The powers to enter and search premises thus far discussed have concerned the grant of a justices' warrant (or, if the search is for 'excluded' or 'special procedure' material, on the authority of a circuit judge), without the arrest of any suspect. It is now necessary to consider the police powers of entry and search of premises without such a warrant. These are contained in general terms in ss17 and 18. They are in addition to any other statutory powers of entry and search, and to the sole remaining such power at common law, that of entry to deal with or prevent a breach of the peace: s17(6). Under s17 a constable may enter and search any premises for the purpose of: executing a warrant of arrest issued in connection with or arising out of criminal proceedings; arresting a person for an arrestable offence; arresting a person for an offence under s1 (prohibition of uniforms in connection with political objects) of the Public Order Act 1936, any enactment contained in ss6–8 or 10 of the Criminal Law Act 1977 (offences relating to entering and remaining on property) or s4 of the Public Order Act 1986. A constable may also enter and search any premises for the purpose of: recapturing a person who is unlawfully at large and whom he is pursuing; saving life or limb; or preventing serious damage to property.

With the exception of entry in order to save life and limb, a constable can only exercise the power of entry under s17 if he has reasonable grounds for believing that the person whom he is seeking is on the premises. In relation to premises consisting of two or more separate dwellings, the power to enter and search is limited to any parts of the premises which the occupiers of any dwelling comprised in the premises use in common with the occupiers of any other such dwelling; and any such dwelling in which the constable has reasonable grounds for believing that the person whom he is seeking may be.

The power to search provided by s17 is limited in the sense that it is a power to search to the extent that is reasonably required for the purpose for which the power of entry is exercised.

The power to enter under s17(1)(b) (to arrest a person for an arrestable offence) is only exercisable by a constable who has reasonable grounds to suspect that an arrestable offence has been committed and who believes that the suspect is in the premises to be entered. It does not permit, for example, entry in order to question a suspect (unless it could be shown that this was for a purpose closely linked to those listed in s17(1)(e)). Where the power to enter under s17(1) is exercised, the occupant must be informed of the reasons for the entry if at all possible: see further *O'Loughlin* v *Chief Constable of Essex* (1997) The Times 12 December.

The need for an arrestable offence to have been committed was considered in *Chapman* v *DPP* (1989) 89 Cr App R 190. A Constable Sneller was called to assist an officer who was being assaulted by a number of youths. Sneller saw a youth he suspected of being involved in the attack run into the flat occupied by his father, the defendant. Sneller sought entry to the defendant's premises, but the defendant resisted, and was arrested for obstructing a constable in the execution of his duty. Sneller purported to be exercising his power of arrest under s24(6) of the Police and Criminal Evidence Act 1984, in relation to the defendant's son. The defendant's submission of no case to answer, in relation to the obstruction charge, was rejected by the justices, and he appealed by way of case stated, the question for the court being: 'whether the justices were right to conclude that [Sneller] at the time of the assault was exercising a statutory power of entry and so was a constable acting in the execution of his duty.' The court felt compelled to allow the appeal on the ground that the common assault on a fellow officer was not an arrestable offence, hence no power of arrest existed under s24(6), and in turn no power to enter under s17(1)(b). As Bingham LJ commented:

> 'What is ... inescapable and fatal to this conviction is that the justices have not found as a fact that Constable Sneller reasonably suspected ... any ... arrestable offence, to have been committed, or any facts amounting to an arrestable offence to have occurred. Such a reasonable suspicion is the source from which all a police constable's powers of summary arrest flow and the justices have felt unable to make the crucial finding which the prosecutor required. This was plainly not the result of oversight or inadvertence. Had the justices found that Constable Sneller reasonably suspected an arrestable offence to have been committed, it would have been incumbent on them to identify, at least in general terms, the arrestable offence which the police constable suspected and this, it is plain, the evidence adduced did not enable them to do. It is not of course to be expected that a police constable in the heat of an emergency, or while in hot pursuit of a suspected criminal, should always have in mind specific statutory provisions, or that he should mentally identify specific offences with technicality or precision. He must, in my judgment, reasonably suspect the existence of facts amounting to an arrestable offence of a kind which he has in mind. Unless he can do that he cannot comply with section 28(3) of the Act by informing the suspect of grounds which justify the arrest.'

It seems clear, following the House of Lords' decision in *D'Souza* v *DPP* [1992] 1 WLR 1073, that the power to enter without a warrant under s17(1)(d) (to recapture a person unlawfully at large) is only to be used in cases of 'hot pursuit'. In that case the appellant's mother had left a hospital where she was being detained for psychiatric assessment without leave being granted as required under s17 of the Mental Health Act 1983. Several hours later, uniformed officers arrived at the house where the appellant lived with her parents in order to take her mother back to the hospital. The appellant and her father refused the police officers entry as they did not have a warrant to enter the premises, but the officers nevertheless exercised a forced entry and were attacked by the appellant and her father, who were subsequently convicted of assaulting police officers in the execution of their duty contrary to s51(1) of the Police Act 1964. Allowing their appeals against conviction, the House of Lords held that s17(1)(d) of the 1984 Act could only be used by officers seeking to enter premises where they sought to apprehend a person who was unlawfully at large, and at the time of entering the premises the police officers were in 'hot pursuit' of the said person. Whilst a person absconding from a hospital in breach of the Mental Health Act would be a person unlawfully at large, in the present case there was no evidence that the police had entered the dwelling in question whilst in hot pursuit of the appellant's mother. It would appear from this ruling that if the officers had spotted the appellant's mother entering her house and had chased after her, they would have had the power of entry without warrant provided for by s17(1)(d). As a consequence of this decision it must be the case that the subsection cannot be relied upon by a constable who, acting upon information received that a person unlawfully at large is at a particular dwelling, then proceeds to visit and enter the premises to effect the recapture of such a person. Whether a constable is in 'hot pursuit' will inevitably be a question of fact to be determined in each case.

Further powers of entry and search are also conferred by s18, which permits a search of premises following the arrest of a suspect for an 'arrestable' offence, if the suspect arrested occupies or controls the premises to be searched. Under s18(1) a constable may enter and search any premises occupied or controlled by a person who is under arrest for an arrestable offence, if he has reasonable grounds for suspecting that there is on the premises evidence, other than items subject to legal privilege, that relates to that offence or to some other arrestable offence which is connected with or similar to that offence.

As with s17 a constable exercising the power to enter and search under s18 may seize and retain anything for which he may search under s18, but his powers of search are to be exercised only to the extent that is reasonably required for the purpose of discovering such evidence.

A search under s18 must normally be authorised in advance, in writing, by an officer of the rank of inspector or above. Under s18(5) however, a constable may conduct a search under s18(1) before taking the suspect to a police station, and without obtaining the usual authorisation if the presence of the suspect at a place other than a police station is necessary for the effective investigation of the offence

12.8 Powers of seizure

Certain powers to seize evidence have already been examined, for instance that permitting seizure of evidence specified in a search warrant under s8(2). A general power of seizure is conferred upon constables who are 'lawfully on any premises' by s19. The term 'lawfully on premises' encompasses not only lawful presence following entry to effect an arrest, or following arrest of a suspect, or on the authority of a search warrant, but also cases where the constable has been allowed into the premises by a person with the power to give him permission to enter, even though he is not there pursuant to any statutory or common law right of entry. For example, where the constable visits a suspect to question him, and the suspect invites the constable into his house. Under s19 a constable may seize anything which is on the premises if he has reasonable grounds for believing: that it has been obtained in consequence of the commission of an offence and that it is necessary to seize it in order to prevent it being concealed, lost, damaged, altered or destroyed; that it is evidence in relation to an offence which he is investigating or any other offence and that it is necessary to seize it in order to prevent the evidence being concealed, lost, altered or destroyed. Subsection (4) empowers a constable to require any information which is contained in a computer and is accessible from the premises to be produced in a form in which it can be taken away and in which it is visible and legible if he has reasonable grounds for believing that it is evidence in relation to an offence which he is investigating or any other offence, or it has been obtained in consequence of the commission of an offence, and that it is necessary to do so in order to prevent it being concealed, lost, tampered with or destroyed. Subsection 19(6) makes it clear that no power of seizure conferred on a constable under any enactment (including an enactment contained in an Act passed after PACE) is to be taken to authorise the seizure of an item which the constable exercising the power has reasonable grounds for believing to be subject to legal privilege.

Where the s19 power is invoked, and articles seized, those articles may be retained 'so long as is necessary in all the circumstances', for instance for use at the trial of an accused, or to allow a forensic examination of them or to find out who is their lawful owner, but must be released to the person from whom they were seized – unless there is reason to believe that they have been obtained in consequence of the commission of an offence – if a photograph or copy of them would be sufficient for the purpose for which retention is desired. These matters are governed by s22.

12.9 Powers of arrest

Where time permits, the arrest of a suspect will often be made on the authority of a warrant issued by a justice of the peace under s1 of the Magistrates' Courts Act 1980. Such a warrant may issue in respect of any offence known to law, and is obtained by deposing to the facts of the alleged offence on oath. In addition to its use as a means of taking a suspect into custody before any charge has been made, the warrant procedure also aids in detaining those who have absconded while on bail awaiting trial, or who have failed to appear at court to answer to a summons.

In many cases, however, there is not sufficient time to apply for a warrant, and the statutory powers to arrest without it will now be considered. The 1984 Act significantly simplifies the law in this area, though several powers of arrest without warrant remain in other legislation, for example s7(3) of the Public Order Act 1936 and s28(2) of the Children and Young Persons Act 1969. These preserved additional powers of arrest are listed in Sch 2 of the 1984 Act. The Act draws a distinction between 'arrestable offences', for which a power of arrest without warrant exists in every case, subject to certain conditions, regardless of the seriousness of the harm or damage done in the actual offence, and other offences which become arrestable without warrant only if the gravity of the harm, or risk of further harm, or of the suspect's absconding without having given a true name and address, call for immediate detention.

It should be borne in mind that, notwithstanding the statutory provisions considered below, there is still a common law power to arrest for breach of the peace. As the court in *Foulkes* v *Chief Constable of Merseyside Police* [1998] 3 All ER 705 confirmed, the power can be exercised even if a breach of the peace has not yet occurred, provided the person exercising the power reasonably believes that a breach of the peace might be about to occur. There must be a sufficiently real and present threat to the peace to justify depriving a citizen of his liberty at a time when he is not actually acting unlawfully.

12.10 Arrestable offences

By virtue of s24, a power to arrest without warrant exists where an offence of the following kinds is suspected: the offence is one for which the sentence is fixed by law (eg murder); the offence is one for which a person of 21 years of age or over (not previously convicted) may be sentenced to imprisonment for a term of five years (or might be so sentenced but for the restrictions imposed by s33 of the Magistrates' Courts Act 1980) – this would include serious assaults, theft, robbery and some burglaries; or the offence is one specifically stated as coming within the scope of the s24 powers. These offences include any offences: for which a person may be arrested under the Customs and Excise Acts, as defined in s1(1) of the Customs and Excise Management Act 1979; under the Official Secrets Act 1920 that are not arrestable offences by virtue of the term of imprisonment for which a person may be sentenced in respect of them; offences under any provision of the Official Secrets Act 1989 except s8(1), (4) or (5); under ss14 (indecent assault on a woman), 22 (causing prostitution of women) or 23 (procuration of girl under 21) of the Sexual Offences Act 1956; under ss12(1) (taking a motor vehicle or other conveyance without authority etc) or 25(1) (going equipped for stealing etc) of the Theft Act 1968; under the Football (Offences) Act 1991; under s2 of the Obscene Publications Act 1959 (publication of obscene matter); under s1 of the Protection of Children Act 1978 (indecent photographs and pseudo-photographs of children); under s166 of the Criminal Justice and Public Order Act 1994 (sale of tickets by unauthorised persons); under s19 of the Public Order Act 1986 (publishing etc material intended or likely to stir up racial hatred); under s167 of the Criminal Justice and Public Order Act 1994 (touting for car-hire services); or s60(8)(b) of the Criminal Justice and Public Order Act 1994 (failing to comply with requirement to remove a mask etc).

Without prejudice to s2 of the Criminal Attempts Act 1981, the powers of summary arrest conferred by s24 also apply to the offences of: conspiring to commit any of the offences mentioned in s24(2); attempting to commit any such offence; and inciting, aiding, abetting, counselling or procuring the commission of any such offence.

Section 26 provides that, subject to specifically provided for or preserved statutory powers of arrest without warrant (and those under s25 considered below) any power vested in a constable to arrest without a warrant shall cease to have effect. Care needs to be taken, however, in assessing the ambit of this provision. As the Court of Appeal held on *Gapper* v *Chief Constable of Avon and Somerset Constabulary* [1998] 4 All ER 248, s26 has no effect on those statutory powers of arrest vested in both police constables and private citizens not expressly repealed by PACE. The plaintiff therefore failed in his action for wrongful arrest where he contended that a police constable had no power to arrest without a warrant under s6 of the Vagrancy Act 1824, on the basis that the power had not been expressly preserved by s24 and Sch 2 of PACE. The Court of Appeal confirmed that s26 only abolished those statutory powers of arrest where the power was given to a police constable only (the power to arrest under s6 could be exercised by anyone); further, if the plaintiff's contention was correct it would have resulted in the manifest absurdity that a police constable's power to arrest under s6 had been abolished, whilst the citizen's power to arrest under s6 remained undiminished.

12.11 Power to arrest for arrestable offences

Given that the offence suspected falls within s24, to whom is a power of arrest allowed, and in what circumstances? There are differences between the powers of constables and those of private citizens. Section 24(4) and (5) detail the powers available to both:

> '(4) Any person may arrest without a warrant –
> (a) anyone who is in the act of committing an arrestable offence;
> (b) anyone whom he has reasonable grounds for suspecting to be committing such an offence.
> (5) Where an arrestable offence has been committed, any person may arrest without a warrant –
> (a) anyone who is guilty of the offence;
> (b) anyone whom he has reasonable grounds for suspecting to be guilty of it.'

It can be seen that a power to arrest arises against anyone who is in the act of committing an arrestable offence, or who is suspected on reasonable grounds to be committing such an offence, that is, someone who is still committing and has not yet completed the suspected crime, by s24(4). The power to arrest after the event given by s24(5) requires that an arrestable offence has been committed. If a private citizen arrests someone he suspected of having committed an arrestable offence, but it emerges that no arrestable offence was committed, the private citizen is liable in damages for false arrest. Such was the law prior to 1968, as enshrined in decisions such as *Walters* v *WH Smith* [1914] 1 KB 595, and it has since been confirmed in relation to s24(5) by the Court of Appeal in *R* v *Self* [1992] 1 WLR 476. Here the appellant, who was believed to have stolen a bar of chocolate, was arrested by a store detective and another member of the public. During the course of the arrest the appellant assaulted those trying to apprehend him. The appellant, who was ultimately acquitted of theft, but convicted of assault with intent to resist or prevent lawful apprehension, contrary to s38 of the Offences Against the Person Act 1861, contended that as he had been acquitted on the theft charge, neither the store detective nor any other member of the public could have been empowered to arrest him under s24(5) of the 1984 Act, since this required proof that an arrestable offence had been committed. It followed, therefore, that the detention had not been lawful, and thus he should not have been convicted under s38. Allowing the appeal, the Court confirmed that a condition precedent to the exercise of the citizen's power of arrest under s24(5) was that an arrestable offence had already been committed, and hence the contention in relation to s38 had to succeed. As Garland J observed:

> 'Subsection (5) makes it abundantly clear that the powers of arrest without a warrant where an arrestable offence has been committed require as a condition precedent an offence committed. If subsequently there is an acquittal of the alleged offence no offence has been committed. The power to arrest is confined to the person guilty of the offence or anyone who the person making the arrest has reasonable grounds for suspecting to be guilty of it ... If it is necessary to go further, one contrasts the words of subsection (5) with subsection (6), the very much wider powers given to a constable who has reasonable grounds for suspecting that an arrestable offence has been committed.'

Powers of arrest in wider terms are conferred on constables, in addition to those they possess in their capacity as citizens, by s24(4) and (5). These allow arrest even where no arrestable offence has in fact been committed. Under s24(6), if a constable has reasonable grounds for suspecting that an arrestable offence has been committed, he may arrest without a warrant anyone whom he has reasonable grounds for suspecting to be guilty of the offence. Under s24(7), a constable may arrest without a warrant anyone who is about to commit an arrestable offence and anyone whom he has reasonable grounds for suspecting to be about to commit an arrestable offence.

The 1984 Act does not contain a definition of what constitutes an arrest. However in *R v Brosch* [1988] Crim LR 743 the court held, following *Alderson v Booth* [1969] 2 All ER 271, that an arrest might be effected by any action or words indicating to D that he is under a compulsion and is no longer at liberty.

Reasonable suspicion

The provisions of the 1984 Act conferring powers of arrest, provided a constable has reasonable suspicion that certain preconditions exist, must be read on the basis that the officer himself must have the suspicion, ie it must be based upon matters present in the mind of the constable. The rationale for this approach is that Parliament has proceeded on the basis that police constables are independent executive officers, accountable in law for the way in which they exercise their powers. As Lawton LJ observed in *R v Chief Constable of Devon and Cornwall, ex parte Central Electricity Generating Board* [1982] QB 458 (p474):

> '... [chief constables] cannot give an officer under command an order to do acts which can only lawfully be done if the officer himself with reasonable cause suspects that a breach of the peace has occurred or is imminently likely to occur or an arrestable offence has been committed.'

Hence, a constable cannot be regarded as having a reasonable suspicion that a suspect has committed an offence simply because a superior officer orders him to effect an arrest of that suspect. The position was usefully summarised by Lord Steyn, in *O'Hara v Chief Constable of the Royal Ulster Constabulary* [1997] 2 WLR 1, as follows:

> '(1) In order to have a reasonable suspicion the constable need not have evidence amounting to a prima facie case. Ex hypothesi one is considering a preliminary stage of the investigation and information from an informer or a tip-off from a member of the public may be enough: *Hussien v Chong Fook Kam* [1970] AC 942, 949. (2) Hearsay information may therefore afford a constable reasonable grounds to arrest. Such information may come from other officers: *Hussien's* case, ibid. (3) The information which causes the constable to be suspicious of the individual must be in existence to the knowledge of the police officer at the time he makes the arrest. (4) The executive "discretion" to arrest or not as Lord Diplock described it in *Mohammed-Holgate v Duke* [1984] AC 437, 446, vests in the constable, who is engaged on the decision to arrest or not, and not in his superior officers.

The test to be applied, therefore, is (assuming the arresting officer does suspect that circumstances justifying the exercise of the power to arrest exist) whether or not a reasonable person would have shared the officer's opinion, given the information which was in the mind of the arresting officer: see further *Castorina* v *Chief Constable of Surrey* (1988) 138 NLJ 180. In applying the test the courts appear to be willing to grant the arresting officer a margin of appreciation, given that he may have been acting in the heat of the moment: see *G* v *Superintendent of Police, Stroud* (1985) The Times 29 November.

As a police constable is a public officer (ie an officer of the executive) the legality of his actions can be tested by the application of the so-called *Wednesbury* test: see *Associated Provincial Picture Houses Ltd* v *Wednesbury Corporation* [1948] 1 KB 223. Hence he should exercise his discretion as would a reasonable police officer, not taking into account irrelevant considerations, and not failing to take into account relevant considerations. Ultimately, it will be for the court to decide whether the test has been satisfied. Hence, in *Lyons* v *Chief Constable of West Yorkshire* (1997) (CCRTF 96/1379/C), it was held that a police officer had not acted unreasonably in exercising his power of arrest in relation to a L, notwithstanding that he had been previously informed (by a friend of L) that L had an alibi and hence could not have committed the crime under investigation. In *R* v *Chalkley* [1998] 2 All ER 155 police officers suspected the defendant of involvement in a robbery. Having obtained the necessary authorisation they decided to place a listening device in his home. In order to do so they arrested the defendant on suspicion of involvement in a number of credit card frauds so that he would be out of the house. On the basis of the evidence obtained the defendant was convicted of conspiracy to rob and appealed. One of the issues raised at the appeal was as to the legality of the arrest in relation to the credit card fraud. The Court of Appeal held that the arrest had been lawful. The Court felt that, provided the police officers had reasonable grounds to suspect that the defendant was involved in the credit card frauds, his arrest was lawful notwithstanding that his absence from his house provided the police with the opportunity to place the listening devices. Counsel for the defendant relied upon the proposition of Viscount Simon from *Christie* v *Leachinsky* [1947] 1 All ER 567 at 572, where he observed that:

> '1. If a policeman arrests without warrant on reasonable suspicion of felony, or of other crime of a sort which does not require a warrant, he must in ordinary circumstances inform the person arrested of the true ground of arrest. He is not entitled to keep the reason to himself or to give a reason which is not the true reason. In other words, a citizen is entitled to know on what charge or on suspicion of what crime he is seized.
> 2. If the citizen is not so informed, but is nevertheless seized, the policeman, apart from certain exceptions, is liable for false imprisonment.'

The court, however, rejected the notion that an ulterior motive would necessarily render an arrest unlawful. As Auld LJ observed (p176j–177g):

> 'In our view, the judge correctly held that the arrests were lawful. We acknowledge the importance of the liberty of the subject. It is a fundamental right of which he may only be deprived by the due process of law, which process includes an entitlement to be told why he is being deprived of it. However, a collateral motive for an arrest on otherwise good

and stated grounds does not necessarily make it unlawful. It depends on the motive. That is clear from the materially different facts of *Christie* v *Leachinsky* and the qualified manner in which the members of the judicial committee expressed the important principle for which the case is famous.

First, as to the facts, there, the police informed Leachinsky of a ground of arrest which was not a valid ground for it; here the suspected credit card fraud was a valid ground for the arrests. There, there was an alternative and valid ground for arrest of which the officers had not informed him; here there was no alternative ground or reason, valid or invalid, for arrest as distinct from the object of removing [the defendant from his house] for a while to enable the installation of the device.

Second, Viscount Simon, Lord Simonds and Lord du Parcq (with whom Lord Thankerton and Lord Macmillan agreed) were all of the view that there were qualifications and possible exceptions to the general principle that the police, in making an arrest, should be motivated only by matters relevant to the suspected offence and should tell the subject the true reason for it. Viscount Simon said ([1947] 1 All ER 567 at 573, [1947] AC 573 at 588): "There may well be other exceptions to the general rule in addition to those I have indicated, and the above propositions are not intended to constitute a formal or complete code, but to indicate the general principles of our law on a very important matter."

Lord Simonds and Lord du Parcq ([1947] 1 All ER 567 at 575 and 581–582, [1947] AC 573 at 592 and 603–604) allowed for the legality of arrest and detention by the police of a man on one charge on which they have reasonable grounds for suspecting his guilt, but with the real or main purpose of enabling them to investigate another, possibly more serious, offence of which they have as yet no such grounds and with a view to preventing his escape from justice. As Lord Simonds observed ([1947] 1 All ER 567 at 575, [1947] AC 573 at 593): "In all such matters a wide measure of discretion must be left to those whose duty it is to preserve the peace and bring criminals to justice." The reasoning for that well-known and respectable aid to justice, "a holding charge", seems to us equally appropriate to circumstances where, as here, the police have, and have so informed the subject(s) when arresting them, reasonable grounds for doing so, but were motivated by a desire to investigate and put a stop to further, far more serious, crime. Accordingly, we agree with the judge's ruling that the arrests were lawful.'

Note that the requirement of reasonable suspicion accords with art 5(3) of the European Convention on Human Rights which requires that a person should not be deprived of his liberty except, inter alia, where he is lawfully arrested or detained for the purpose of bringing him before the competent legal authority on reasonable suspicion of having committed an offence or when it is reasonably considered necessary to prevent his committing an offence or fleeing after having done so.

12.12 Power to arrest for offences which are not arrestable

Where the suspected offence does not fall within the definition of arrestable given by s24, a power to arrest without warrant is conferred upon constables – but not upon private citizens – where it is thought undesirable to follow the normal procedure of leaving the suspected offender at large and proceeding against him by simple summons to appear at court later. The general purpose of this power is to prevent the suspect's avoiding prosecution by giving false particulars, or by refusing to give any particulars at all, or to remove the risk of further harm to the suspect himself or to the public or to property. Section 25 provides that, provided a constable has reasonable grounds for suspecting that any offence which is not an arrestable offence has been committed or attempted, or is being committed or attempted, he may arrest the 'relevant person' if it appears to him that service of a summons is impracticable or inappropriate because any of the general arrest conditions are satisfied. For these purposes 'relevant person' is defined by s25(2) as any person the constable has reasonable grounds to suspect of having committed, having attempted to commit, being in the course of committing or attempting to commit the offence.

The general arrest conditions referred to in s25(3) are: that the name of the relevant person is unknown to, and cannot be readily ascertained by, the constable; that the constable has reasonable grounds for doubting whether a name furnished by the relevant person as his name is his real name; that the relevant person has failed to furnish a satisfactory address for service, or the constable has reasonable grounds for doubting whether an address furnished by the relevant person is a satisfactory address for service; that the constable has reasonable grounds for believing that arrest is necessary to prevent the relevant person causing physical injury to himself or any other person, suffering physical injury, causing loss of or damage to property, committing an offence against public decency, or causing an unlawful obstruction of the highway; and that the constable has reasonable grounds for believing that arrest is necessary to protect a child or other vulnerable person from the relevant person.

Under s25(4) an address is a 'satisfactory address' for service if it appears to the constable that the relevant person will be at it for a sufficiently long period for it to be possible to serve him with a summons; or that some other person specified by the relevant person will accept service of a summons for the relevant person at it. A constable is not authorised to arrest under s25(3)(d)(iv) (constable has reasonable grounds for believing arrest is necessary to prevent the relevant person committing an offence against public decency) unless members of the public going about their normal business cannot reasonably be expected to avoid the person to be arrested.

In *Edwards and Others* v *DPP* (1993) 97 Cr App R 301 two men, Fox and Sumner, were observed by police officers who believed them to be using cannabis. When challenged, the men appeared to try to dispose of certain substances. They were informed that they were being arrested for obstructing the officers in the execution of their duties under the Misuse of Drugs Act 1971. A woman named Prendergast intervened to prevent the arrest of Fox and was arrested for obstruction contrary to s51(3) Police Act 1964. Edwards intervened to prevent the arrest of Prendergast and was similarly arrested for obstruction contrary to s51(3). The defendants submitted that there was no case to answer since there was no power to arrest without warrant for obstruction under the Misuse of Drugs Act 1971. The magistrates found that in the circumstances there was a power to arrest under s25 of the 1984 Act as, on the facts now known, the arresting officer would have every reason to doubt the truth of any name he was given by the suspect, hence the arrests were lawful. On appeal by way of case stated, the Divisional Court considering the question of whether or not the arresting officer, in the circumstances of the case, had had the power to arrest Fox under s25(3)(a) and (b) and/or s25(3)(d)(i) of the 1984 Act, held that, as the power to arrest without warrant for obstruction of a police officer in the execution of his duty contrary to the Misuse of Drugs Act 1971 had been abolished by s26 of the Police and Criminal Evidence Act 1984, the only power to arrest for such obstruction would be that now arising under s25 of the 1984 Act, ie the power of summary arrest in relation to a non-arrestable offence. By simply telling Fox that he was 'nicked for obstruction', the officer had failed to give s25(1) of the 1984 Act or any of the general arrest conditions detailed in s25(3) as justification. The court confirmed that, by virtue of s28(5) of the 1984 Act, an arrest was not lawful unless the arrestee was informed of the grounds of arrest. In the instant case the court felt that there were no circumstances that precluded the giving of that information; it had obviously practicable for the officer to give reasons for the arrest, because that was precisely what he had done, although they were invalid. The arrest might have been valid if the general arrest conditions under s25 had been given as the reason for arrest, but the arrest could not be retrospectively validated. As Evans LJ observed:

> 'It may seem unrealistic that the court should be concerned after the event with the precise words that were used. ... Nevertheless, it has to be borne in mind that giving correct information as to the reasons for an arrest is a matter of the utmost constitutional significance in a case where a reason can be and is given at the time.'

12.13 Information on arrest

Section 28 of the 1984 Act codifies certain established principles of common law relating to the duty of the police to inform an arrested person of the fact of and reason for his arrest. Under s28(1) where a person is arrested, otherwise than by being informed that he is under arrest, the arrest is not lawful unless the person arrested is informed that he is under arrest as soon as is practicable after his arrest. Where a person is arrested by a constable this requirement applies regardless of whether the fact of the arrest is obvious. The arrest will not be lawful unless the person arrested is informed of the ground for the arrest at the time of, or as soon as is practicable after, the arrest. Again this applies (where a person is arrested by a constable) regardless of whether the ground for the arrest is obvious. Some latitude is allowed to arresting officers by s28(5) which provides that there is no duty to inform a person that he is under arrest, or of the ground for the arrest, if it is not reasonably practicable for him to be so informed by reason of his having escaped from arrest before the information could be given.

Note that s28 accords with the requirements of art 5(2) of the European

Convention of Human Rights which provides that everyone who is arrested should be informed promptly of the reasons for the arrest.

It would appear that even though reasons for an arrest are not given at the time of the arrest, the arrest can become lawful once those reasons are supplied. In *Lewis* v *Chief Constable of the South Wales Constabulary* [1991] 1 All ER 206 the plaintiffs had been arrested on suspicion of burglary and taken to a police station. One had been told the reason for the arrest ten minutes after it had occurred, the other some 23 minutes after arrest. They were detained for about five hours and then released. In an action for false arrest and wrongful imprisonment, they were awarded damages for unlawful detention of only ten and 23 minutes respectively. On appeal, Balcombe LJ rejected the contention of counsel for the plaintiffs to the effect that, if at the moment of initial apprehension the arrest was unlawful, the act was a nullity. His Lordship expressed the view that arrest was a situation; a matter of fact, citing *Spicer* v *Holt* [1976] 3 All ER 71. Whether a person has been arrested depended not on the legality of his arrest but on whether he has been deprived of his liberty to go where he pleased. There was no doubt that, on the facts of this case, the plaintiffs had been deprived of their liberty at the moment that they were arrested, and that that act was not a nullity. Arrest was a continuing act, and in his Lordship's view there was nothing inconsistent with the wording of s28(3) to say that from that moment when reasons were given the arrest became lawful, or the continued deprivation of liberty became lawful, or the continued custody became lawful. Hence the trial judge had been correct in the ruling that the period in respect of which the plaintiffs were entitled to damages was that between the arrest and the giving of reasons. The decision confirms the earlier case of *DPP* v *Hawkins* [1988] 1 WLR 1166.

Decisions such as *Abbassy* v *MPC* [1990] 1 WLR 385 confirm that a constable exercising his powers of arrest need not use technical language to indicate the offence for which D is being arrested. It is sufficient that the type of offence is identified, so that D may volunteer information that would render the arrest unnecessary. Where the arrest is made pursuant to s25, *DPP* v *Nicholas* [1987] Crim LR 474 suggests that a constable telling D that he is being arrested because of his failure to provide a name and address is enough.

12.14 Voluntary attendance at police station

At common law, the status of someone who was 'helping the police with their inquiries', but without having been formally arrested, was never very clear. It was repeatedly stated that a person was either under arrest or at liberty to leave the police station, and that the law did not recognise any form of detention as legal unless it was a lawful arrest. For the avoidance of doubt, and following the recommendations of the 1981 Royal Commission on Criminal Procedure, s29 of the 1984 Act now provides:

'Where for the purposes of assisting with an investigation a person attends voluntarily at a police station or at any other place where a constable is present or accompanies a constable to a police station or any such other place without having been arrested –
(a) he shall be entitled to leave at will unless he is placed under arrest;
(b) he shall be informed at once that he is under arrest if a decision is taken by a constable to prevent him from leaving at will.'

12.15 Procedure following arrest

Once a suspect has been arrested, whether with or without a warrant, he must be taken to a police station as soon as is practicable after his arrest, unless the arrest was made at such a station: s30(1). Provision is made by that section for conveying the suspect to a 'designated police station', defined by s35 as being one specified by the Chief Officer of Police for the detention of arrested persons, unless it is impracticable to do so in the short term. The suspect may be searched at the time of his arrest if there is reason to believe that he may present a danger to himself or to others, or may have upon him anything which he might use to escape from lawful custody, or which might be evidence relating to an offence: s32(1) and (2). These latter words are wide enough to allow a search for evidence of an offence other than that for which the arrest has been made. The search may also extend to premises in which the suspect was arrested, or in which he was present, immediately before his arrest, in order to discover evidence relating to the offence for which the arrest was made, if the arresting constable has reasonable grounds for believing that such evidence exists: s32(2) and (6), and see *R v Badham* [1987] Crim LR 202.

On arrival at a designated police station, the suspect will come under the supervision of a custody officer of at least the rank of sergeant, whose duties are prescribed by Part IV of the 1984 Act: *Vince v Chief Constable of Dorset Police* [1993] 1 WLR 415. In brief, an arrested person should not be kept in detention, but should be released either without charge or on bail, at the earliest reasonable opportunity. The custody officer must first decide, if the arrest has been without warrant, whether there is sufficient evidence to justify a charge against the suspect: s37(1). If insufficient evidence exists, the suspect must be released, either on bail or not, unless the officer has reasonable grounds for believing that continued detention is necessary to secure or preserve evidence relating to an offence, or to obtain evidence by questioning the suspect: s37(2). Records must be kept throughout the suspect's detention, detailing the decisions and reasons of the custody officer. If there is sufficient evidence to justify a formal charge, the suspect must be charged or released with or without bail: s37(7). Suspects who are not in a fit state to allow the custody officer to make a charge under subs(7) or to be released under that subsection, for example, through drunkenness or the influence of drugs, may be detained until they are fit: s37(9).

Once a charge has been made against the suspect and entered in the charge book, there is a presumption that the suspect will be released. He may be detained further only if he is an adult, his name or address cannot be ascertained or is reasonably suspected by the custody officer to be false, the custody officer has reasonable grounds for believing that the person arrested will fail to appear in court to answer to bail; in the case of a person arrested for an imprisonable offence the custody officer has reasonable grounds for believing that the detention of the arrested person is necessary to prevent him from committing an offence; in the case of case of a person arrested for a non-imprisonable offence the custody officer has reasonable grounds for believing that the detention of the arrested person is necessary to prevent him from causing physical injury to any other person or from causing loss of or damage to property; the custody officer has reasonable grounds for believing that the detention of the arrested person is necessary to prevent him interfering with the administration of justice or with the investigation of offences; or the custody officer has reasonable grounds for believing that continued detention is necessary for the protection of the suspect: s38(1) as amended by s28 of the Criminal Justice and Public Order Act 1994.

Whether or not a charge has been made, the continued detention of every suspect depends upon a review made at intervals by the custody officer or, in the case of a suspect not yet charged, an officer of at least the rank of inspector who has not been directly involved in the investigation of the offence for which the arrest was made: s40(1). The first review must be made not later than six hours after detention was first authorised under s37 or s38, the second review not later than nine hours after the first, and subsequent reviews at intervals of not more than nine hours: s40(3). There is power to postpone a review if it is 'not practicable' to carry it out by the stated time, for instance if the review would interrupt a period of interrogation and the review officer is satisfied it would prejudice the investigation subject of the interrogation, or if no review officer is available at the stated time: s40(4). In such a case, the review must take place as soon as is practicable: s40(5).

The purpose of the review is to decide whether the reason for which detention was first authorised still holds good, for example, that the suspect was a source of harm to himself or others, or that evidence for use against him might be destroyed if he were to be released. If it does not, the suspect must be released. In deciding whether detention remains justified, s40(12) requires the officer to consider any representations made by the suspect himself or by any solicitor acting for him and available at the time of the review, though he need not consider what the suspect may have to say if the latter is asleep, or unfit to make representations by reason of his condition or behaviour: s40(14).

Where the suspect has been arrested and is being detained without charge, s41 imposes a maximum period for which he can be detained in police custody without being brought before a court. The general maximum is 24 hours, calculated from the time of his arrival at the first police station to which he is taken after his arrest: s41(1) and (2)(d). The period is calculated from the time of arrest if he voluntarily attended at a police station and was subsequently arrested there or if he is arrested in a police area other than that in which he has been sought – for instance, the suspect who is wanted by the Metropolitan Police but who is arrested by a different police force and has not been questioned by the arresting police force with a view to discovering evidence of the offence. Other special provisions for calculating the 24-hour period are made in the cases of suspects who are removed from police detention for medical treatment in hospital, or who are arrested outside England and Wales.

Where the 24-hour period has expired and no charge has been made, the suspect must be released, with or without bail, unless detention beyond the 24 hours has been authorised by a superintendent under s42 or has been allowed by a magistrate's warrant of further detention under s43. Section 42 allows detention up to a total of 36 hours without charge on reasonable grounds for belief that it is necessary to secure or preserve evidence, and that the offence for which the investigation is continuing is a 'serious arrestable offence' and that the investigation is being conducted diligently and expeditiously. A warrant under s43 is issued on very similar grounds to the superintendent's authority under s42, and permits detention in police custody and without charge beyond 36 hours and up to a maximum total of 96 hours, in periods of not more than 36 hours at a time before further application to the court is necessary: see further s42 to s44 for details of the procedure at the hearing and the grounds for warrants of further detention.

The courts will construe the requirements relating to extension of detention as mandatory, unless the Act expressly provides for some discretion. Hence in *R v Slough Justices, ex parte Stirling* [1987] Crim LR 576, where the police arrived after 38 hours with an application to extend detention, the application was refused, on the basis that, under s43(7), it would have been reasonable for the police to apply in good time for an extension. Similarly, in *In the matter of an application for a warrant of further detention* [1988] Crim LR 296, where detainees were not given the opportunity to make representations via a solicitor before a superintendent extended detention from 24 to 36 hours, and a brief note was placed on custody record to the effect that the superintendent considered detention necessary because the detainees' might impede the course of justice if released, the justices accepted the detainees' contentions that the police had failed to comply with the mandatory requirements under s42. Detention beyond 24 hours had, therefore, been unlawful. Either the justices therefore had no jurisdiction to consider an application for further detention, or if they did they would decline to exercise it. Note that under s14 of the Prevention of Terrorism (Temporary Provisions) Act 1989 a person suspected of involvement in terrorist activities can be detained for up to five days without charge: see further *Brannigan and McBride v United Kingdom* (1993) 17 EHHR 539.

Detention without charge for such a long period of time is per se a breach of art 5(3) of the European Convention on Human Rights, but the United Kingdom has entered a derogation in respect of terrorist suspects.

12.16 Appearance before magistrates following charge

An arrested person who has been charged but who, pursuant to ss38–40 of the 1984 Act, has been detained in police custody, must be brought before a magistrates' court as soon as is practicable after charge, and not later than the first sitting of the court after he has been charged with the offence: s46(2). This will usually be on the day of the charge or the day after, but in cases where no court sitting is to be held for either of those days, detention in police custody is permitted until the next sitting, provided the clerk to the justices is informed of the fact that the suspect is in custody and awaiting appearance at the next sitting. It is then the duty of the clerk to arrange for a hearing not later than the day on which the charge was made, or, if a public holiday or weekend intervenes, the day after that holiday or weekend: s46(3)–(9). The obligation to bring the suspect before the court does not apply if he is not well enough: s46(9).

12.17 Interrogation of suspects and the right to legal advice

Whilst the common law recognised a general right in an accused person to communicate and consult privately with his solicitor outside the interview room (see the 'Judges' Rules'), there was no common law right entitling an accused person to have a solicitor present during police interviews: see further the speech of Lord Browne-Wilkinson in *R v Chief Constable of the Royal Ulster Constabulary, ex parte Begley; R v McWilliams* [1997] 4 All ER 833. Under PACE, however, persons arrested, whether by warrant or not, and held at a police station, are given rights to have someone named by them informed of the fact and place of their detention, and are to be allowed access to legal advice from a solicitor. Although these rights are not absolute, and can be denied for a period of time in certain circumstances, the intent of PACE is clearly that they should be respected and granted in all but the clearest cases calling for their denial.

So far as concerns notification to an outside person of the fact and place of arrest, s56 provides that when a person has been arrested and is being held in custody in a police station or other premises, he shall be entitled, if he so requests, to have one friend or relative or other person who is known to him or who is likely to take an interest in his welfare told, as soon as is practicable except to the extent that delay is permitted by other provisions in s56, that he has been arrested and is being detained there.

Delay will be permitted if the detainee is being held in connection with a serious arrestable offence, and an officer of at least the rank of superintendent has authorised it in writing. The basis for delaying access must be that the authorising officer has reasonable grounds for believing that telling the named person of the arrest will lead to interference with or harm to evidence connected with a serious arrestable offence or interference with or physical injury to other persons, or will lead to the alerting of other persons suspected of having committed such an offence but not yet arrested for it, or will hinder the recovery of any property obtained as a result of such an offence. Under s56(5A) an officer may also authorise delay where the serious arrestable offence is a drug-trafficking offence. In any event access can only be delayed for 36 hours.

If a delay in granting access is authorised the detained person shall be told the reason for it and the reason for the delay must be noted on his custody record. These conditions must be complied with as soon as is practicable.

The provision governing access to legal advice by a person detained following arrest is s58. In its terms it is very similar to s56. A person arrested and held in custody in a police station or other premises is entitled, if he so requests, to consult a solicitor privately at any time. Access to a solicitor can only be delayed if the person who is in police detention is being held in connection with serious arrestable offence and the delay is authorised by an officer of at least the rank of superintendent. The grounds for delaying access are set out in s58(8) – the officer authorising delay must have reasonable grounds for believing that the exercise of the right to consult privately with a solicitor will lead to interference with or harm to evidence connected with a serious arrestable offence or interference with or physical injury to other persons; will lead to the alerting of other persons suspected of having committed such an offence but not yet arrested for it; or will hinder the recovery of any property obtained as a result of such an offence. In any event access to a solicitor may only be delayed for 36 hours: s58(5).

The Criminal Justice Act 1988 extends the power to delay access where serious drug-trafficking offences are involved. Thus, a person held in custody at a police station shall be entitled to consult a solicitor at any time, if he so requests. The detainee may consult a solicitor of his own choice, but if he knows of none he should be informed by the police of the availability of the duty solicitor.

Under Codes C accurate records must be made of each interview and interrogation, and in some circumstances tape recordings of interviews will be permitted under s60. The suspect must be cautioned, and that caution must be administered as soon as the constable has grounds for believing that he has committed an offence. A further caution must be given before the arrested person is interviewed, and if the interview is interrupted for more than one hour, yet another caution is to be given before it is continued. Interviews of arrested persons can be carried out only with the agreement of the custody officer responsible for them and they must be allowed at least eight hours' continuous rest in any period of 24 hours. No form of oppressive conduct is to be used in questioning, and the suspect may make a written statement if he wishes. Code C also details the records to be kept, and provides for the conduct of identification parades and interrogation of those who are physically or mentally ill or who are under the age of 17, and provides that detainees must be informed of their right to free legal advice, and must be reminded of this right before any interview takes place.

A frequently voiced criticism of PACE and the original Code on interrogation was the absence of any explicit prohibition on interviews with suspects prior to their arrival at the police station. The revised Code C goes some way to meeting these objections by providing that interviews can only be held outside a police station in certain specified circumstances. Under para 11.1 exceptions can only be made where no decision to arrest the interviewee has been taken; or, the interchanges do not amount to the questioning of a person regarding his involvement or suspected involvement in criminal activity; or, delaying the interview would be likely to lead to endangering others or enabling other suspects to flee or hinder the return of any property. In *R v Khan* [1993] Crim LR 54 the Court of Appeal upheld the decision of the trial judge not to exclude, under s78 of PACE, evidence obtained by police asking D questions whilst they were searching his dwelling. The Court confirmed that the proper venue for any interrogation was the police station, where the safeguards provided by s58 and the Codes would apply, but was satisfied that, on the facts, the main thrust of the police questioning had related to the whereabouts of property.

In what circumstances, if any, will the courts permit the police to rely on evidence obtained during interrogations at a police station, where D has not been permitted to exercise his right to consult with a solicitor?

In *R v Samuel* [1988] 2 WLR 920 the appellant was interviewed by the police on four occasions about a robbery and two burglaries. The appellant denied any involvement. During the second interview he asked for access to a solicitor, but his request was refused on the ground of likelihood of other suspects involved in the robbery being inadvertently warned. At the fourth interview the appellant confessed to the two burglaries and he was charged with those offences at 4.30 pm. At 4.45 pm a solicitor was informed of the charges, but denied access. Shortly afterwards the appellant confessed to the robbery and the solicitor was allowed to see him one hour later. At the trial, the appellant contended that evidence of the latter confession should be excluded, but it was admitted and he was convicted of robbery. On appeal the Court of Appeal held that the conviction should be quashed as, in the circumstances, the refusal of access to a solicitor had been unjustified and the interview in question should not have taken place. The Court held that the crucial aspect of an interrogating officer's decision to exclude access to a solicitor under s58 was that, at the time of exclusion, he has reasonable grounds to believe that access *will* lead to or hinder one or more of the things set out in paras (a) to (c) of s58(8). As Hodson J observed:

> 'The use of the word "will" is clearly of great importance. There were available to the draftsman many words or phrases by which he could have described differing nuances as to the officer's state of mind, for example "might", "could", "there was a risk", "there was a substantial risk" etc. The choice of "will" must have been deliberately restrictive. Of course, anyone who says that be believes that something will happen, unless he is speaking of one of the immutable laws of nature, accepts the possibility that it will not happen, but the use of the word "will" in conjunction with belief implies in the believer a belief that it will very probably happen. ... What is it that the officer has to satisfy the court he believed? The right denied is a right "to consult a solicitor privately". The

person denied that right is in police detention. In practice, the only way that the person can make any of the matters set out in paras (a) to (c) happen is by some communication from him to the solicitor. For the matters set out in paras (a) to (c) to be made to happen the solicitor must do something. If he does something knowing that it will result in anything in paras (a) to (c) happening he will, almost inevitably, commit a serious criminal offence. Therefore, inadvertent or unwitting conduct apart, the officer must believe that a solicitor will, if allowed to consult with a detained person, thereafter commit a criminal offence. Solicitors are officers of the court. We think that the number of times that a police officer could genuinely be in that state of belief will be rare. Moreover it is our view that, to sustain such a basis for refusal, the grounds put forward would have to have reference to a specific solicitor. We do not think they could ever be successfully advanced in relation to solicitors generally ...'

It is submitted that to deny access to a specified solicitor may be tantamount to defamation, unless the police can produce evidence justifying the decision. As the above extract indicates, this will have to be evidence that the solicitor is likely to be duped by the suspect, or will help him pervert the course of justice. The former is perhaps possible. In *Re Walters* [1987] Crim LR 577 the Court accepted that access to a solicitor could be denied where there was evidence that the suspects had been using 'Delphic phrases' to communicate with each other. A solicitor could be used in such a case to convey an apparently innocent message that could alert other gang members. To suggest that a solicitor would knowingly engage in such activities would obviously be a very grave allegation indeed. *Samuel* was followed in *R v Alladice* (1988) 87 Cr App R 380.

Where the interrogating officers fail to inform D of his right to consult with a solicitor, or fail to act upon his request for such consultation, the trial judge will have to assess the extent to which the failure to follow the provisions of the Act and the Codes vitiates any subsequent interrogations.

In *R v Dunford* (1990) 91 Cr App R 150, where the Court of Appeal upheld the trial judge's decision to admit D's statement made in the absence of a solicitor on the basis that a solicitor's advice would not have added anything to the appellant's knowledge of his rights, Neill LJ expressly approved of the approach taken in *R v Walsh* (1990) 91 Cr App R 161, where it was stated that, whilst a breach of s58 would prima facie have an adverse effect on the fairness of proceedings:

'This does not mean, of course, in every case of a significant or substantial breach of s58 or the Code of practice the evidence concerned will automatically be excluded. The task of the court is not merely to consider whether there would be an adverse effect on the fairness of the proceedings, but such an adverse effect that justice requires the evidence to be excluded ... Breaches which are in themselves significant and substantial are not rendered otherwise by the good faith of the officers concerned.'

This decision, and others, suggests that the courts are willing to adopt a causation-based approach, assessing what difference access to legal advice might have had on D's conduct. Thus, in *R v Absolam* (1989) 88 Cr App R 322, the Court of Appeal allowed D's appeal against conviction where the trial judge had allowed in evidence statements made before access to a solicitor was submitted. Bingham LJ noted that the interrogating officers should have informed D of his right to consult a solicitor when it became apparent to them that an offence had been committed, even though the series of questions and answers taking place between the officers and D was not in any formal sense a conventional interview. He continued:

> '... it seems to us that if the learned judge had been persuaded that there were here significant and substantial breaches of the Code he would, in all probability, have excluded the answers given by the appellant ... he would, we think, had he taken the same view of the Code as we have, have formed the opinion that this was a case in which, as a result of a line of questioning initiated in remarkable circumstances but with no warning to the appellant of his right, the appellant would not have given the answers that he did, and that the prosecution would not have been in receipt of these admissions if the appropriate procedures had been followed.'

Complications can arise in cases such as *R v Anderson* [1993] Crim LR 448, where D does not request access to a solicitor, later changes his mind, but due to a breakdown in communications, the interviewing officer is unaware that D has made such a request. In that case the Court of Appeal upheld the trial judge's decision to permit in evidence D's confession, under s78, on the basis that there was insufficient evidence that 'but for' the failure to provide legal advice D would not have made the statement, and further because there was no evidence to suggest the police had acted in any way to make the statement unreliable. See further *R v Parris* (1989) 89 Cr App R 68 and *R v Silcott* (1991) The Times 9 December.

Note that in *R v Chief Constable of South Wales, ex parte Merrick* [1994] 1 WLR 663 the Divisional Court ruled that whilst the statutory right to consult privately with a solicitor created by s58(1) did not extend to a prisoner held in custody at a court following a refusal of bail, such a prisoner did have a common law right to consult with a legal adviser as soon as was reasonably practicable, bearing in mind the other demands on police officers responsible for the custody of prisoners being held at the court. On this basis the policy adopted at Cardiff Magistrates' Court (of not permitting interviews between prisoners and solicitors after 10.00 am, unless there were good reasons for the interview not having taken place earlier) was declared to be unlawful.

12.18 Searches and fingerprinting following arrest

The general power to search an arrested person at the time of arrest has already been considered. Once at the police station, a search may be conducted on the authority of the custody officer, and what is found may be seized in the circumstances provided for by s54(3) and (4). Under s54(4) clothes and personal effects may only be seized if the custody officer believes that the person from whom they are seized may use them: to cause physical injury to himself or any other person; to damage property; to interfere with evidence; or to assist him to escape; or if the custody officer has reasonable grounds for believing that the items may evidence relating to an offence.

In certain situations it will be necessary for the search carried out upon an arrested person to go beyond a simple inspection of his outer clothing and personal effects. As originally enacted, PACE provided the power to conduct an intimate search of a detainee, defining such a search as one that involved examination of the bodily orifices. This definition proved problematic in drugs cases where frequently a suspect was believed to be concealing prohibited substances in his mouth. Police officers had no right to carry out the necessary search without invoking the procedure required for intimate searches (see below). A possible loophole was identified by the court in *R v Hughes* [1995] Crim LR 407, where a constable conducting a search in public held D's nose and jaw causing D to expel the drugs he had been concealing in his mouth. D was subsequently convicted of possession of cannabis. The Court of Appeal, being asked to rule on whether: (a) there had been a search; (b) it had been an intimate search; (c) whether the evidence so obtained should have been excluded because the constable had failed to inform the defendant of the purpose of the search and had failed to make a formal record of it, dismissed the appeal, holding that the conduct of the police officer amounted to a search and there had, therefore, been breaches of the Codes of Practice, although they were not such as to render the evidence inadmissible on the grounds of unfairness. The search itself could not be classified as intimate as there had been no intrusion into the bodily orifices.

The problem has now been addressed by s59 of the Criminal Justice and Public Order Act 1994, which amends PACE so as to exclude searches of the mouth from the scope of intimate searches. The future relevance of *Hughes*, therefore will be as regards instances where concealed items are retrieved from a suspect's vagina or rectum without a physical examination having been carried out, although quite how this might be achieved poses an interesting anatomical question.

Section 55 of PACE provides for the carrying out of an intimate search where an officer of at least the rank of superintendent has reasonable grounds to believe that a person who has been arrested and is in police detention may have concealed on him anything which he could use to cause physical injury to himself or others, or that he might so use, while he is in police detention or in the custody of a court. Alternatively, the power can be based upon reasonable belief that such a person may have a Class A controlled drug concealed on him and was in possession of it with the appropriate criminal intent before his arrest.

An intimate search may only be carried out at a police station, hospital, doctor's surgery or other place used for medical purposes (see s55(8)), and may not be made by a person of the sex opposite to the person searched. Intimate searches for evidence of drugs offences may not be made at a police station: see s55(9). Non-intimate samples, such as hair (other than pubic hair), from a nail or under a nail, from body swabs (including mouth swabs but excluding other bodily orifices), saliva and footprints or similar impressions of the body other than a part of the hand, may be taken from an arrested person without his consent under conditions very similar to those allowing intimate searches: see s63.

Note that the power to take intimate and non-intimate sample extends to all recordable offences, and not merely serious arrestable offences. Following amendments introduced by the Criminal Evidence (Amendment) Act 1997, the range of persons from whom a non-intimate sample can be taken, notwithstanding that the appropriate consent has not been given has been extended to include persons convicted of an offence listed in Sch 1 to the 1997 Act (notably sexual offences and offences of violence) before 10 April 1985 who are still in custody for that offence, or detained under the Mental Health Act 1983. The 1997 Act also extends the power to take non-intimate samples without consent from those detained following an acquittal on grounds of insanity or a finding of unfitness to plead.

Intimate samples, meaning a sample of blood, semen or other body tissue, fluid, urine, pubic hair, dental impression, or a swab from a body orifice other than the mouth, may not be taken against the arrested person's will. An intimate sample, other than one of urine or a dental impression may be taken only by a registered medical practitioner, and a dental impression may only be taken by a registered dentist. A court may draw such inferences as seem justified from a person's refusal to consent to the taking of an intimate sample.

Once samples are taken, they can be used by the police to investigate offences other than that for which the suspect has been detained. Hence, in *R* v *Kelt* [1994] 2 All ER 780, the Court of Appeal held that it was permissible for the police to use a blood sample lawfully obtained from D in connection with a murder enquiry, in order to compare it with blood samples found on evidence relating to a separate incident of robbery. Express provision is now made for such cross-referencing of evidence by s65 of PACE, as amended.

A significant new power, resulting from the amendment to s62 of PACE by s54 of the Criminal Justice and Public Order Act 1994, will permit the taking of intimate samples from persons not in police detention, provided such action is authorised by an officer of at least the rank of superintendent and the consent of the person is given (although adverse inferences can be drawn from a failure to grant such consent). The criteria to be satisfied are that two or more non-intimate samples must have been provided by the person in question, in the course of the investigation into an offence, which have proved insufficient (for the purposes of DNA analysis). Alternatively, non-intimate samples can be taken from a person not in detention regardless of his consent if he has been charged with a recordable offence or informed that he will be reported for such an offence and either he has not had a non-intimate sample taken from him in the course of the investigation of that offence, or if he has, it has not proved suitable for analysis.

Fingerprints may normally be taken from an arrested person only with his consent, but s61 provides for them to be taken without consent, on the authority of an officer of at least the rank of superintendent if he has reasonable grounds for suspecting the involvement of the person whose fingerprints are to be taken in a criminal offence; and for believing that his fingerprints will tend to confirm or disprove his involvement.

12.19 Confessions: general

Confessions are an important form of evidence in that they will presumably tend to produce a plea of guilty at trial, and hence are the best evidence that the accused has actually committed the offence with which he is charged. A defendant may, however, make a confession for a number of reasons other than guilt. For example, he may be attempting to shield the truly guilty party; he may be one of those whose psychological condition or state of mind makes him a compulsive confessor (police investigations are beset with those who invent confessions to prominent crimes which they could not possibly have committed); he may confess because he is intimidated or induced to make a statement by promises; he may feel that, if the offence is not serious a confession, a guilty plea is preferable just to 'get things over'.

In such circumstances it is clear that confessions should be treated with care and not admitted in evidence, as they are unreliable as evidence of the truth. The police may wish to obtain evidence by questioning a suspect and they are allowed to do so by virtue of the notes for guidance issued in relation to Code C, which provide:

> '1B This Code does not affect the principle that all citizens have a duty to help police officers to prevent crime and discover offenders. This is a civic rather than a legal duty; but when a police officer is trying to discover whether, or by whom, an offence has been committed he is entitled to question any person from whom he thinks useful information can be obtained, subject to restrictions imposed by this Code. A person's declaration that he is unwilling to reply does not alter this requirement.'

This means that the police can ask anyone questions despite that person's unwillingness to answer them. It is possible that those questions may lead to a confession. Leaving aside the special requirements regarding juveniles and the mentally ill or handicapped, Code C states:

> '11.3 No police officer may try to obtain answers to questions or to elicit a statement by the use of oppression. Except as provided for in paragraph 10.5C, no police officer shall indicate, except in answer to a direct question, what action will be taken on the part of the police if the person being interviewed answers questions, makes a statement or refuses to do either. If the person asks the officer directly what action will be taken in the event of his answering questions, making a statement or refusing to do either, then the officer may inform the person what action the police propose to take in that event provided that that action is itself proper and warranted.
> 11.4 As soon as a police officer who is making inquiries of any person about an offence believes that a prosecution should be brought against him and that there is sufficient evidence to succeed, he shall ask the person if he has anything further to say. If the person indicates that he has nothing more to say the officer shall without delay cease to question him about that offence.'

The first part of this leads back to s76 of PACE. The second shows it is not intended that, where the police have decided there is sufficient evidence to succeed in a prosecution, they should press on to secure a confession. It is perhaps unfortunate that in a number of cases a confession is the only substantial piece of evidence the police have. The confession will, after all, be a valuable constituent towards the element of the defendant's mens rea. In theory, the defendant wants to confess in order to clear his conscience and to unburden himself of guilt. Arguably, this is a very powerful compulsion. The problem in the courts is that some defendants recant and seek to withdraw their confessions. In this situation it is up to the judge to decide in the absence of the jury whether or not the confession should be admitted in evidence; this is known as a 'voir dire' or a 'trial within a trial'.

12.20 The use of the caution and the right to silence

The position at common law

Historically, the position at common law has long been that a defendant is innocent until proven guilty, and that it is the task of the prosecution to convince the court of the defendant's guilt, principles reflected in the criminal process by the existence of the so-called right to silence. The phrase 'right to silence' is something of a misnomer in that every defendant can chose to remain silent if he so wishes – there is never any possibility of a suspect being physically compelled to respond to questioning by law. What the phrase actually relates to is the proposition that the courts were not permitted to draw any adverse inferences from the defendant's failure to provide an exculpatory answer when taxed with the details of the offence he is alleged to have committed. The rationale for the common law right to silence was that the suspect and interrogator would not have been on equal terms, given that the interrogator would inevitably be a police officer. Exceptions were recognised where the defendant could be regarded as being on equal terms with his accuser, for example in *Parkes* v *R* (1976) 64 Cr App R 25, where the defendant was accused by his landlady of murdering her daughter.

The right to silence was reflected in the old form of the caution to be administered by a police officer conducting an investigation into alleged offences, ie: 'You do not have to say anything unless you wish to do so, but what you say may be given in evidence.' Minor deviations were permitted provided the sense of the caution was preserved.

The pressure for change

The view expressed in some quarters was that the right to silence was open to abuse by more sophisticated and experienced criminals and was partly responsible for some allegedly guilty defendants escaping conviction. The criticisms of the right to silence rest to a large extent on the assertion that any innocent person would seek to exculpate himself at the earliest possible moment if he had nothing to hide. Such research as has been conducted suggests that relatively few suspects choose to remain silent when interrogated by the police, although the percentage exercising this right has substantially increased since the enactment of PACE.

Given the right of a detained person to consult privately with a solicitor under s58 of PACE, questions have been raised as to the extent to which it remains true to say that detainee and interrogator are not on equal terms. Lawton LJ, in *R v Chandler* [1976] 1 WLR 585, suggested that this might be the case, but went on to observe that, once a detainee had been cautioned, no adverse inferences were to be drawn from his silence. Curiously, the effect of this view suggests that the police would be better off allowing a detainee to have access to a solicitor but not to caution him, although such a practice would undoubtedly involve a breach of the Codes. Some, such as Lord Lane CJ, commenting in *R v Alladice* (above), have called for a re-assessment of the position. He stated:

> 'Paragraph 6.3 of the Code provides that a person who asks for legal advice may not be interviewed or continue to be interviewed until he has received it unless delay has been lawfully authorised. ... The result is that in many cases a detainee who would otherwise have answered proper questioning by the police will be advised to remain silent. Weeks later at his trial such a person not infrequently produces an explanation of, or a defence to, the charge the truthfulness of which the police have had no chance to check. Despite the fact that the explanation or defence could, if true, have been disclosed at the outset and despite the advantage which the defendant has gained by these tactics, no comment may be made to the jury. The jury may in some cases put two and two together, but it seems to us that the effect of s58 is such that the balance of fairness between prosecution and defence cannot be maintained unless proper comment is permitted on the defendant's silence in such circumstances. It is high time that such comment should be permitted together with the necessary alteration to the words of the caution.'

In July 1993 the Royal Commission on Criminal Justice, chaired by Lord Runciman, produced its report. A majority of its members proposed no change to the common law position on the 'right to silence' at a police station, but recommended that once the prosecution case was fully disclosed, it should be possible to draw adverse inferences from the introduction of any new defence or departure from any previously disclosed defence.

As a prelude to reform of the law in England and Wales, the law in Northern Ireland was amended, by virtue of the Criminal Evidence (Northern Ireland) Order 1988, to permit the trial judge to direct the jury (or himself where the case involved a 'Diplock' court), that adverse inferences could be drawn from the defendant's failure to give evidence.

Such inferences are permitted if D is silent and offers an explanation for his conduct for the first time at his trial which he could reasonably have been expected to produce when being questioned; the prosecution satisfies the court that there is a case to answer and D declines to give evidence; he gives no explanation in relation to certain facts such as substances found, or marks on clothing; he gives no explanation for his presence in a particular place.

The changes introduced by the Criminal Justice and Public Order Act 1994

Section 34 of the 1994 Act introduces a major change in the law by providing that, if a suspect fails to mention any fact relied on in his defence (being something that he could reasonably be expected to have mentioned) either when being questioned after cautioning by a constable, or after having been charged with an offence or officially informed that he might be prosecuted, the court or jury may draw such inferences from the failure as appear proper. Section 36 provides similarly in relation to an arrested person's failure to account for any object in his possession, or any substance or mark on his person, clothing or article in his possession when required to do so by a constable investigating an offence, and s37 applies similarly to an arrested person's failure to account for his presence at a particular location.

A consequence of this change in the law is the amendment to the police caution that has been in use for over 30 years. In place of the previous wording (see above) para 10.4 of Code C now requires the following wording:

> 'You do not have to say anything. But it may harm your defence if you do not mention when questioned something which you later rely on in court. Anything you do say may be given in evidence.'

Under the guidelines contained in Code C a caution must be given before any questions are put to a suspect for the purpose of obtaining evidence which may be given in a court in a prosecution. The defendant, therefore, need not be cautioned if questions are put for other purposes, for example, to establish his identity, his ownership of, or responsibility for, any vehicle or the need to search him in the exercise of powers of stop and search. A person must be cautioned upon arrest for an offence unless it is impracticable to do so by reason of his condition or behaviour at the time; or he has already been cautioned immediately prior to his arrest. When there is a break in questioning under caution the interviewing officer must ensure that the person being questioned is aware that he remains under caution. If there is any doubt on this matter the caution should be given again in full when the interview resumes.

In relation to the Criminal Evidence (Northern Ireland) Order 1988, the House of Lords has confirmed, in *R* v *Murray* [1994] 1 WLR 1, that it has had the effect of changing the law and practice relating to the defendant who fails to give evidence, thus permitting the jury to infer guilt from his silence where the prosecution had established a prima facie case against him. The European Court of Human Rights has in turn considered the extent to which the Order was at odds with the requirements of art 6 of the European Convention on Human Rights and, in *Murray* v *United Kingdom* (1996) 22 EHRR 29, confirmed (by 14 votes to five) that, given the sufficiency of the procedural safeguards designed to prevent oppression, the objectives of art 6 could still be achieved, in particular the drawing of reasonable inferences from the applicant's behaviour did not have the effect of shifting the burden of proof contrary to art 6(2). It should be noted, however, that whilst this ruling clarifies the position as regards the law in the Province, some questions may still remain in respect of ss34 and 35 of the 1994 Act. The European Court of Human Rights was willing to accept the restriction imposed by the Northern Ireland Order partly because, in the Diplock courts operating in Northern Ireland, reasons will be given by the trial judge for drawing adverse inferences if any, thus there will be evidence of the weight given to the accused's decision to remain silent. In England and Wales juries will not be required to embroider their verdicts with such explanations.

12.21 Challenging the admissibility of evidence

A confession made by an accused person may be given in evidence against him at the trial provided it is relevant and has not been excluded by the court in pursuance of s76. This initial requirement is laid down because a confession is essentially an out-of-court statement and would normally be excluded by the rule against hearsay, that only testimony given under oath by a witness as to what he directly heard or otherwise experienced is to be regarded as good evidence. A confession is admitted as an exception to the hearsay rule and is tendered by the prosecution as evidence of the truth of its contents because it is thought that a person would not make a statement against himself unless it were true. According to s82 the term 'confession' includes 'any statement wholly or partly adverse to the person who made it, whether made to a person in authority or not and whether made in words or otherwise.'

A statement made by the accused that serves to exculpate him may be excluded as a self-serving statement. It may, of course, be that a statement contains material of both an inculpatory and an exculpatory nature. Both elements would then have to be put before the court.

Section 76(2) contains the vital provision with regard to the exclusion of confessions. This states that:

> 'If, in any proceedings where the prosecution proposes to give in evidence a confession made by an accused person, it is represented to the court that the confession was or may have been obtained –
> (a) by oppression of the person who made it; or
> (b) in consequence of anything said or done which was likely, in the circumstances existing at the time, to render unreliable any confession which might be made by him in consequence thereof,
> the court shall not allow the confession to be given in evidence against him except in so far as the prosecution proves to the court beyond reasonable doubt that the confession (notwithstanding that it may be true) was not obtained as aforesaid.'

Thus where D alleges that the confession has been improperly obtained it is for the prosecution to prove beyond all reasonable doubt that this is not the case. Section 76(3) provides that, in any event, the court may require of its own motion that the prosecution should prove that the confession was not obtained as mentioned in s76(2). One effect of the subsection is that if there has been oppression the resulting confession so obtained can be excluded even though it is true, presumably to deter the police from using oppression. In this sense police impropriety is to be deprecated more than the obtaining of what may be a true confession. 'Oppression' is defined by s76(8) as including 'torture, inhuman or degrading treatment, and the use or threat of violence (whether or not amounting to torture)'. In *R v Fulling* [1987] 2 WLR 923 Lord Lane CJ commented:

> '"oppression" in s76(2)(a) should be given its ordinary dictionary meaning. The Oxford English Dictionary as its third definition of the word runs as follows: "Exercise of authority or power in a burdensome, harsh, or wrongful manner; unjust or cruel treatment of subjects, inferiors, etc; the imposition of unreasonable or unjust burdens." One of the quotations given under that paragraph runs as follows: "There is not a word in our language which expresses more detestable wickedness than oppression." We find it hard to envisage any circumstances in which such oppression would not entail some impropriety on the part of the interrogator.'

Fulling was applied in *R v Paris; R v Abdullahi; R v Miller* (1993) 97 Cr App R 99 (the 'Cardiff Three' case), where convictions were set aside on the basis that confessions had been obtained by means of oppression, following evidence that interrogating officers had continued to shout at one of the appellants the words they wanted him to say over 300 times, despite his denials of guilt. The court commented upon the importance of officers complying with the letter and spirit of the Codes of Practice.

Prior to the 1984 Act a confession would only be admitted if it were voluntary. This meant that it should not have been induced 'by fear of prejudice or hope of advantage exercised or held out by a person in authority'. This seems to be the general purport of s76(2)(b) although it is of wider application than the previous rule. It remains for the defendant to raise the question of the confession having been made in consequence of something said or done, and for the saying or doing to render unreliable the confession obtained in consequence. Presumably the repetition of 'in consequence' is not merely pleonastic or intended for emphasis but requires that the confession is made as a consequence as well as the unreliability being consequential.

A confession which has been excluded may not affect the admissibility in evidence of facts discovered as a result of the confession – although the facts should not be related to the confession itself – or of showing that the accused speaks, writes or expresses himself in a particular way.

At common law, following the decision in *R v Sang* [1980] AC 402, the judge's discretion to exclude evidence which had been improperly obtained was to be exercised on the basis that evidence should be admitted provided that its effect was not more prejudicial than probative. Pre-PACE authorities reveal a relaxed approach. Thus, in *R v Leatham* (1861) 8 Cox CC 489, Crompton J expressed the view that 'It matters not how you get it; if you steal it even, it would be admissible in evidence.' Similarly, in *Kuruma, Son of Kania v R* [1955] 1 All ER 236, Lord Goddard CJ expressed the view that if evidence was admissible the court would not be overly concerned with how it had been obtained. Lord Widgery CJ said much the same thing in *Jeffrey v Black* [1978] 1 All ER 555, where an unlawful search of the defendant's premises was undertaken and cannabis discovered there after he had been arrested for stealing a sandwich. He commented:

> 'I have not the least doubt that an irregularity in obtaining evidence does not render the evidence inadmissible. Whether or not the evidence is admissible depends on whether or not it is relevant to the issues in respect of which it is called.'

In Australia, Barwick CJ put the problem succinctly in *R v Ireland* (1970) 126 CLR 321:

> 'On the one hand there is the public need to bring to conviction those who commit criminal offences. On the other hand there is the public interest in the protection of the individual from unlawful and unfair treatment. Convictions obtained with the aid of unlawful and unfair treatment may be obtained at too high a price.'

In *R v Maqsud Ali; R v Ashiq Hussain* [1965] 2 All ER 464 murder suspects went voluntarily with police officers to a room where they were left alone. In their conversation incriminating remarks were made and tape-recorded by a hidden microphone. In the Court of Appeal the view was expressed that: 'The criminal does not act according to the "Queensbury rules" hence the method of the informer and of the eavesdropper is commonly used in the detection of crime.'

In *R v Murphy* [1965] NI 138 (Courts-Martial Appeal Court) the accused had been convicted having made disclosures of information useful to an enemy to police officers posing as subversives. Lord Macdermott CJ observed:

> 'Detection by deception is a form of police procedure to be directed and used sparingly and with circumspection: but as a method it is as old as the constable in plain clothes and, regrettable as the fact may be, the day has not yet come when it would be safe to say that law and order could always be enforced and the public safety protected without occasional resort to it.'

Section 78 of the 1984 Act now provides a statutory basis for the trial judge's discretion. It states:

> '(1) In any proceedings the court may refuse to allow evidence on which the prosecution proposes to rely to be given if it appears to the court that, having regard to all the circumstances in which the evidence was obtained, the admission of the evidence would have such an adverse effect on the fairness of the proceedings that the court ought not to admit it.
> (2) Nothing in this section shall prejudice any rule of law requiring a court to exclude evidence.'

This section curiously refers to the 'fairness of the proceedings', although it also speaks of the circumstances in which the evidence was obtained. It must be assumed that it is referring to the general fairness of the obtaining of the evidence, rather than the fairness of the proceedings as such.

In *R v Mason* [1988] 1 WLR 139 the Court of Appeal held that 'evidence' for the purposes of s78 included a confession notwithstanding that confessions were expressly dealt with by s76. Thus a confession that was admissible through not falling foul of s76(2) could nevertheless still be excluded on the grounds of its unfairness. Mason, who had been arrested in connection with an arson offence, was told by the police that they had glass fragments of the petrol-filled bottle used to perpetrate the offence on which they had Mason's fingerprints. In reality this was simply a trick, and the police thought it would be fair, even if deceitful, in that Mason would not have confessed if he knew that he had nothing to do with the bottle. Watkins LJ was highly critical of the tactics practised by the police, and in quashing the conviction, was clearly at pains not to be seen to be encouraging the use of such tactics.

Difficulties still exist where evidence has been obtained through the use of officers working 'under cover'. *R v Smurthwaite* [1994] Crim LR 53 suggests that if an officer is in the role of an agent provocateur, the courts are likely to exclude evidence thus obtained, but not where it is clearly D who initiates the criminal activity (eg soliciting a plain clothes policeman to carry out a contract killing). The problem for the court lies in making the distinction. The courts have confirmed that there is no defence in English law of entrapment, hence convictions have been upheld where police officers have used children to purchase '18' category films (see *London Borough of Ealing v Woolworths plc* [1995] Crim LR 58); where plain clothes officers have made test purchases of alcohol being sold in breach of liquor licence conditions (*DPP v Marshall* [1988] 3 All ER 683); and where police officers have posed as proprietors of a second-hand 'shop' to catch handlers selling off stolen goods: *R v Christou* [1992] 3 WLR 228.

What the courts will be wary of are procedures adopted by the police, eg activity that amounts to interrogation, that are not conducted in accordance with the Codes of Practice, thus undermining the reliability of evidence obtained. This problem was starkly illustrated by the decision of Ognall J to throw out the case against Colin Stagg, who had been charged with the murder of Rachel Nickell, because his 'confession' had been induced by repeated and persistent questioning by a WPC posing as Stagg's girlfriend: see *The Times* (1994) 15 September.

Where there is a reliable and permanent record of the evidence, the courts may lean more in favour admitting it. In *R v Cadette* [1995] Crim LR 229 the appellant had been involved in a plan to unlawfully import controlled drugs. Her telephone number had been found on a courier who had been intercepted at Heathrow Airport. The courier had planned to telephone the appellant upon arrival and, following her arrest, agreed to make the telephone call as planned in order to try to persuade the appellant to come to the airport. The courier gave the appellant no indication that she had been intercepted by the authorities. The telephone conversation was taped by the police and used in evidence against the appellant at her trial. On appeal she contended, unsuccessfully, that the evidence contained in the recording should have been excluded under s78 of PACE on the ground of unfairness. The court accepted that police officers, seeking to combat those involved in the commission of drugs trafficking, might have to resort to subterfuge. The court would examine the circumstances to see if police officers were resorting to subterfuge in order to circumvent the protections provided by the PACE and the relevant Codes. Unacceptable tactics would include a police officer obtaining statements by disguising his or her identity, participating in the commission of the criminal offence, or inciting the commission of the offence. In the instant case the evidence was admissible because the officers had simply given the appellant an opportunity to involve herself in the offence by allowing a pre-planned telephone conversation to take place. There was no question of the telephone conversation amounting to an 'interview'. The court was also persuaded by the reliability of the evidence (ie the fact that it was tape-recorded) and the fact that the administering of a caution at the outset of the conversation would have rendered the operation otiose.

Similarly, in *R v Khan (Sultan)* [1996] 3 WLR 162, the House of Lords rejected the appellant's assertions that evidence obtained by means of listening devices attached to private premises without the owner's consent should be excluded on the basis that the evidence had been obtained in breach of any right to privacy. Lord Nolan held that a trial judge had a residual discretion, under s78 of PACE, to exclude evidence if its admission would render the trial unfair, and in assessing this issue art 8 of the European Convention on Human Rights was relevant, but not decisive, of the matter. As he went on to observe:

> 'If evidence obtained by way of entrapment is admissible, then a fortiori there can hardly be a fundamental objection to the admission of evidence obtained in breach of privacy. In *R v Sang* itself, Lord Diplock noted that if evidence obtained by entrapment were inadmissible, this would have the effect of establishing entrapment as a defence to a criminal charge. ... By parity of reasoning, if evidence obtained by a breach of privacy were inadmissible, then privacy too would become a defence to a criminal charge where the substance of the charge consisted of acts done or words spoken in private. Such a proposition does not bear serious examination.'

When the incorporation of Convention rights such as art 8 are effected by the implementation of the Human Rights Act 1998, it will become positively unlawful for a public authority such as a chief constable (acting through his officers) to act in a manner that is incompatible with the Convention rights. Further the courts will, in future, have to interpret all provisions of PACE so as to ensure consistency, so far as this is possible, with the requirements of the Convention. It remains to be seen what impact this will have on the way in which the courts exercise their powers to admit evidence.

Prior to the enactment of the Police Act 1997 the only regulation that existed as regards planting of listening devices by the police was in the form of the Home

Office guidelines (*Covert Listening Devices and Visual Surveillance (Private Places)* (1984)), under which the chief constable of the relevant force had to be satisfied that, where devices were to be used to record conversations in places where a citizen would normally be entitled to presume privacy, such surveillance was required because the investigation concerned major organised crime, particularly violence. The guidelines assumed that such evidence would be admissible in court. The operations of the secret intelligence services as regards the use of listening devices have been governed by the Intelligence Services Act since 1994, and Part III of the 1997 Act now provides a statutory framework of regulation for such activities when carried out by police officers.

Under the 1997 Act it is envisaged that police officers will seek permission to enter and interfere with property or wireless telegraphy equipment from 'authorising officers – namely chief constables or equivalents. Under s93(2) permission for interference with property can be granted where:

'... the authorising officer believes –
(a) that it is necessary for the action specified to be taken on the ground that it is likely to be of substantial value in the prevention or detection of serious crime, and
(b) that what the action seeks to achieve cannot reasonably be achieved by other means.'

For these purposes conduct which constitutes one or more offences will be regarded as serious crime only if under s93(4):

'... (a) it involves the use of violence, results in substantial financial gain or is conduct by a large number of persons in pursuit of a common purpose, or
(b) the offence or one of the offences is an offence for which a person who has attained the age of twenty-one and has no previous convictions could reasonably be expected to be sentenced to imprisonment for a term of three years or more ...'

If it is not reasonably practicable for an authorising officer to grant permission, the powers conferred on the authorising officer by s93 may, in an urgent case, be exercised by an assistant chief constable in his force (or equivalent). An authorisation must be in writing, save in an urgent case where it may be given orally. Once granted authorisations will normally remain in effect for three months (if written), or 72 hours, if oral. An oral authorisation should be renewed in the normal fashion.

As soon as is reasonably practicable an authorising officer should give notice of having granted an authorisation to a Commissioner appointed under s91(1)(b).

Appointed by the Prime Minister, the Chief Commissioner, and other Commissioners will be persons who have held high judicial office within the meaning of the Appellate Jurisdiction Act 1876 (effectively current or former High Court judges). Each Commissioner is appointed for a term of three years (renewable) and holds office subject only to removal by a resolution passed by each House of Parliament, bankruptcy, or imprisonment for an offence.

Once provided with an authorisation notice a Commissioner is under a duty to scrutinise it as soon as is reasonably practicable. Under s103(1) a Commissioner may, if satisfied that, at the time an authorisation was given or renewed, there were no reasonable grounds for believing the matters specified in s93(2), quash the authorisation and order the destruction of any records relating to information obtained by virtue of the authorisation. Individuals are given the right to make complaints to Commissioners concerning authorisations under s102. Authorising officers are given a statutory right of appeal against a Commissioner's refusal to grant or renew an authorisation: s104(1). Appeals are determined by the Chief Commissioner. Note that under s91(10) the decisions of the Chief Commissioner or, subject to ss104 and 106, any other Commissioner (including decisions as to his jurisdiction), shall not be subject to appeal or liable to be questioned in any court. The Chief Commissioner is under a duty to make an annual report to the Prime Minister who, in turn, is under a duty to lay the report before each House of Parliament.

In an effort to provide greater safeguards for privacy and confidentiality, certain types of authorisation will require prior approval by a Commissioner. This will be the case where the person who gives the authorisation believes that any of the property specified in the authorisation is used wholly or mainly as a dwelling, as a bedroom in a hotel, or constitutes office premises, or that the action authorised by it is likely to result in any person acquiring knowledge of matters subject to legal privilege, confidential personal information, or confidential journalistic material. It should be noted, however, that s97(3) provides that: 'This section does not apply to an authorisation where the person who gives it believes that the case is one of urgency.'

Guidelines for police officers and other law enforcement agencies are to be found in the draft Code of Practice issued by the Secretary of State pursuant to s101(1), which will need to be approved by Parliament.

The extent to which the statutory framework satisfies the requirements of the European Convention as enacted in the Human Rights Act 1998 remains to be seen. The fact that chief constables will effectively have powers of self-authorisation, the relatively weak system of supervision, and the vague basis upon which authorisations are to be granted, suggests that the interference with the right to privacy enshrined in art 8 of the Convention may not be sufficiently 'prescribed by law'.

13

Criminal Procedure I: Preliminary Matters

13.1 Prosecution: introduction

13.2 The prosecutors

13.3 The decision to prosecute

13.4 Commencing a prosecution

13.5 Bail: introduction

13.6 A right to bail?

13.7 Conditions of bail

13.8 Challenges to bail decisions

13.9 Effect of failure to surrender

13.10 Classification of offences

13.11 Determining the mode of trial

13.12 Committal proceedings; sending a case for trial

13.1 Prosecution: introduction

If, following a period of investigation, it becomes clear that a 'suspect' should be charged with a criminal offence, the process of 'prosecution' begins. It is this prosecution which will eventually lead to the trial of a defendant, that is the person accused, either in the magistrates' court (summary trial) or in the Crown Court (trial on indictment).

13.2 The prosecutors

The police and the Crown Prosecution Service

By far the majority of prosecutions are initiated by the 43 police forces operating in England and Wales.

This is not surprising as clearly the police have many advantages over other prosecutors, including:

1. Wider powers of arrest than other citizens.
2. Powers, though limited, of search and seizure and detention of suspects.
3. Resources to investigate a crime and gather evidence.

Although the police remain the prime initiator of prosecutions, since the inception of the Crown Prosecution Service (CPS), the further conduct of the police's prosecutions rests with the CPS (see Chapter 6, section 6.4 for organisation of CPS).

Private prosecutions

Any individual is entitled to prosecute any other. However, as the Queen's Bench Divisional Court explained in *R v Tower Bridge Metropolitan Stipendiary Magistrate, ex parte Chaudhry* [1993] 3 WLR 1154, an individual prosecutor does not have an unfettered right to pursue his prosecution to trial. A private prosecutor has two hurdles to surmount: he has to persuade a magistrate to issue a summons, and thereafter, if he wishes to retain control of the case, he may have to persuade the Director of Public Prosecutions not to take it over and, perhaps, bring it to an end. Unless there are special circumstances, eg apparent bad faith on the part of the prosecutor, magistrates should be very slow to issue a summons at the behest of a private prosecutor against a defendant who already has to answer an information laid by the Crown in respect of the same matter.

Shops and stores regularly prosecute shoplifters with the charge of theft, usually with their 'store detective' as chief witness.

Individual citizens may bring prosecutions for any offence, but most tend to be in relation to smaller incidents in which the police have taken little interest, such as a fight in relation to which a charge of assault may be brought.

Section 6 of the Prosecution of Offences Act 1985 specifically retains the right of an individual to bring a private prosecution. In *R v Southwark Crown Court, ex parte Tawfick* (1994) The Times 1 December the Queen's Bench Divisional Court said that, by virtue of s27(2)(c) of the Courts and Legal Services Act 1990, the courts appeared to have a discretion to grant a right of audience to any person in any proceedings. It followed that the Crown Court could allow a private prosecution to be conducted in person, although it was likely that such a discretion would be exercised only occasionally.

The police are not able to bring an action on behalf of a private individual. They must refer any case to the Crown Prosecution Service. This was seen in the case of *R v Ealing Magistrates, ex parte Dickson* [1989] 2 All ER 1050 in which the police charged the defendant on the behalf of the Copyright Owners Federation. The Divisional Court held that the police had no power to perform these duties on behalf of private individuals.

13.3 The decision to prosecute

Section 127 of the Magistrates' Courts Act 1980 states that a prosecution for a summary offence must, with some exceptions, be commenced within six months of the offence being committed.

At present, with some exceptions, prosecutions for indictable offences may be brought at any time.

Discretion

In 1951, Lord Shawcross, who was then Attorney-General, made the classic statement on public interest, which has been supported by Attorneys-General ever since: 'It has never been the rule in this country – I hope it never will be – that suspected criminal offences must automatically be the subject of prosecution'.

There has been a steep rise in the number of criminal suspects who are cautioned rather than prosecuted. The Home Office has admitted, however, that this may refer to a 'net-widening' process, in that previously these people would not have appeared in the statistics at all because they would have been recorded only as 'no further action'.

The intention is that children and young people should be cautioned rather than prosecuted and this represents a less interventionist approach. The critics argue that the people who are cautioned would be those against whom the police would take 'no further action'. Thus, in fact, they are brought within the criminal net when they would otherwise be left out.

A caution may have the same consequence as a conviction but without the safeguards. The recipient is more likely to be prosecuted on a subsequent occasion.

In relation to the question of discretion it is to be remembered that there is a duty of the police to enforce the law: see *R v Metropolitan Police Commissioner, ex parte Blackburn* [1968] 2 WLR 893. The effect of this is that each case of potential prosecution must be considered, and 'discretion' must be used in relation to the facts of the particular case. Therefore, it is not open for the police to make a general decision, for example, not to bring any prosecutions for theft unless the value of the goods stolen was over a certain sum.

It should be remembered that the Crown Prosecution Service (CPS) normally decides whether to continue or discontinue a prosecution although the police will normally be consulted before the decision is made to discontinue or to change the charges. Such decisions (like refusals by the police to prosecute) are subject to judicial review, but only where it can be demonstrated that the decision was made on the basis of some unlawful policy, or because of a failure to act in accordance with established policy, or because the decision was perverse.

The Code for Crown Prosecutors is a public declaration of the principles upon which the decision to prosecute is taken. Its purpose is to promote fair and consistent decision-making.

The Code explains that there are two stages in the decision to prosecute and that the first is the evidential test. If the case does not pass this test it must not go ahead, no matter how important or serious it may be. If the case does pass the evidential test, Crown Prosecutors must decide if a prosecution also passes the public interest test, the second stage. The Crown Prosecution Service will only start or continue a prosecution when the case has passed both tests.

As to the evidential test, Crown Prosecutors must be satisfied that there is enough evidence to provide a 'realistic prospect of conviction' against each defendant on each charge. They must consider what the defence case may be and how that is likely to affect the prosecution case. A realistic prospect of conviction is an objective test. It means that a jury or bench of magistrates, properly directed in accordance with the law, is more likely than not to convict the defendant of the charge alleged. If a case fails the first test (the evidential test) there must be no prosecution even though the prosecution may be of the view that the public interest test is satisfied.

Public interest factors that can affect the decision to prosecute usually depend on the seriousness of the offence or the circumstances of the offender. Some factors may increase the need to prosecute but others may suggest that another course of action would be better. The Code lists common public interest factors, both for and against prosecution.

Factors favouring a prosecution include:

1. the likelihood of a substantial sentence being imposed on conviction;
2. use of a weapon or violence during the offence;
3. position of the victim (eg a person serving the public) and/or the position of the defendant (eg a person in position of trust or authority);
4. evidence that the offence was premeditated, carried out by a group, or that the defendant was a 'ringleader';
5. effect on the victim;
6. likelihood of the offence being repeated;
7. extent to which the offence, even though not serious, is a common occurrence in the area in which it has been committed.

Factors against a prosecution include:

1. the likelihood that only a nominal penalty will be imposed in the event of a conviction;

2. that the offence was the result of a genuine mistake or misunderstanding;
3. the lapse of time between the offence and the proceedings, except where the offence is serious, or where the delay has been caused by the defendant, or where the offence has only recently come to light, or where the complexity of the offence has necessitated a lengthy inquiry;
4. where the defendant is elderly or was suffering from a mental illness at the time of the offence, unless there is a real possibility of the offence being repeated;
5. the defendant has put right the harm or loss caused;
6. the adverse effect of certain information being made public.

Crown Prosecutors must always think very carefully about the interests of the victim, which are an important factor, when deciding, where the public interest lies. Where necessary, they should apply the Home Office guidelines as to cautioning and should look at all alternatives to prosecution when they consider the public interest. Crown Prosecutors should tell the police if they think that a caution would be more suitable than a prosecution.

Crown Prosecutors should never go ahead with more charges than are necessary just to encourage a defendant to plead guilty to a few. In the same way, they should never go ahead with a more serious charge just to encourage a defendant to plead guilty to a less serious one.

As a general rule the CPS is under no private law duty of care to those it prosecutes, unless it has assumed a special responsibility to a particular defendant: *Elguzouli-Daf* v *Commissioner of Police of the Metropolis* [1995] 1 All ER 833 (CA).

13.4 Commencing a prosecution

There are two methods of commencing a prosecution.

Laying an information

This is used in less serious offences and may be used by any type of prosecutor.

An information, which is the allegation that the person named in it has committed an offence, must be 'laid' before the magistrates' court. If an information is written, it may be laid by delivering it to the court. If the information is oral, the prosecutor must appear before the magistrate or the magistrates' clerk, and tell him what the allegation is.

On the basis of the information, a summons may be issued either by the magistrate or his clerk. Any summons is then served on the defendant by the prosecution, informing him of the allegation and requiring him to attend at the magistrates' court on a named day to answer the allegation.

Charging an accused

This is used in more serious offences and is used by the police only, following either a police or citizen's arrest.

'Charging' takes place at the police station. The procedure is simple and requires merely the writing down of the charge on a 'charge sheet' followed by the reading over of the charge to the accused by the police officer. The accused is either detained in custody or bailed (see below) to appear at a certain court on a certain date. In the meantime the charge sheet is sent to the court in question.

13.5 Bail: introduction

Once the decision to prosecute has been taken an immediate question arising is whether, pending trial of the defendant, he should be detained in custody or released on 'bail'. Bail is the release of a defendant subject to a duty to surrender to custody at an appointed place on an appointed date.

Bail may be granted either by the police (the custody officer at the police station) or by a court. Police bail is regulated by s38 of the Police and Criminal Evidence Act 1984 (as amended). Bail from the court is regulated by the Bail Act 1976 (as amended). This Chapter is mainly concerned with bail from a court, but police bail will be briefly considered.

Bail from the police

Bail may be refused if the custody officer has good reasons for believing that the accused will not appear at court; or that he may interfere with the investigation of crime; or that it is necessary to detain the accused for his own protection; or to prevent other injury, loss or damage; or that the accused might commit an offence if granted bail: s38 Police and Criminal Evidence Act 1984, as amended by s28(2) Criminal Justice and Public Order Act 1994.

Section 27 of the 1994 Act also gives the custody officer the power to grant bail subject to conditions, though some conditions can only be imposed by a court, eg requiring residence at a bail hostel, or requiring a medical examination.

The defendant may contest a custody officer's decision by applying to a magistrates' court, either for unconditional bail or for a variation of conditional bail.

Bail from the court

The majority of applications for bail are made in the magistrates' courts. The procedure, simply, is as follows:

1. The prosecution informs the magistrates whether or not it has any objections to bail. If it has, the magistrates are likely to give weight to such objections, which

usually come from the police. If the prosecution has no objections, the magistrates are unlikely to refuse bail.
2. If there are objections, the defence must indicate whether the application for bail is to be made or continued with.
3. If the application for bail is to be made, a prosecution witness, usually a police officer, must give his objections to bail under oath. The officer's objections may well be based on his own opinions and experience.
4. The defence may question the officer in order to suggest conditions of bail which might overcome his objections.
5. The defence may make a speech dealing with the objections, putting forward possible conditions of bail and emphasising factors in favour of bail.
6. The magistrates then make their decision based on all that they have heard.
7. Where the court hears full argument as to bail the clerk of the court must make a note of the argument.

13.6 A right to bail?

Section 4 of the Bail Act 1976 has the effect, in practice, of giving a 'right to bail' to a defendant. The effect of this is that the onus is put onto the prosecution to show why a defendant should not be granted bail rather than the onus being on the defendant to show why he should be granted bail.

Section 4 applies whenever a person accused of an offence appears or is brought before a magistrates' court or the Crown Court in the course of or in connection with proceedings for an offence.

There is no right to bail in the following circumstances.

1. When a station sergeant or officer not below the rank of inspector is considering bailing an arrestee from the police station.
2. The magistrates, having summarily convicted an offender, commit him to the Crown Court for sentence.
3. A defendant who has been convicted and sentenced, is appealing against conviction or sentence.

In these situations, the onus is on the defendant to show why he should be granted bail. To allay fears that murderers and rapists may be free to walk the streets, the magistrates must state their reasons for granting bail in cases of murder, manslaughter or rape or an attempt to commit the same.

Further, under s25 of the Criminal Justice and Public Order Act 1994, as amended by s56 of the Crime and Disorder Act 1998, a court (or a police custody officer) must be satisfied that there are exceptional circumstances which justify granting bail to a person charged with or convicted of murder, attempted murder, manslaughter, rape or attempted rape if that person has been previously convicted of any such offence or of culpable homicide and, in the case of a previous conviction of manslaughter or of culpable homicide, if he was then sentenced to imprisonment or (if he was then a child or young person) to long-term detention. Prior to the amendment by s56 of the 1998 Act there was a ban on bail in the specified circumstances but there was concern that such a ban might infringe the European Convention on Human Rights. In effect the amendment substitutes a strong rebuttable presumption against bail in the specified circumstances.

Even if the defendant has a right to bail, bail may be refused by the court in circumstances listed in Sch 1 to the Bail Act 1976, as amended by s26 of the 1994 Act.

Imprisonable offences

Part I of Sch 1 is applicable if the defendant is accused or convicted of at least one offence punishable with imprisonment. It states that the defendant need not be granted bail in any of the following circumstances:

1. The court is satisfied that there are substantial grounds for believing that, if released on bail, he would: fail to surrender to custody; or commit an offence while on bail; or interfere with witnesses or otherwise obstruct the course of justice, whether in relation to himself or some other person.
2. The court is satisfied that he should be kept in custody for his own protection or, if he is a child or young person, for his own welfare.
3. He is already serving a custodial sentence.
4. The court is satisfied that lack of time since the commencement of the proceedings has made it impracticable to obtain the information needed to decide properly the questions raised in (1) to (3) above.
5. He has already been bailed during the course of the proceedings, and has been arrested under s7 of the Bail Act 1976 (that is, for absconding).
6. Where a case is adjourned for inquiries or a report, it appears to the court that it would be impracticable to complete the inquiries or make the report without keeping the defendant in custody.
7. Where the offence in indictable or triable either way and the defendant was on bail in criminal proceedings at the date of the offence: s26 of the 1994 Act.

In making its decision under (1) above the court must have regard to such of the following considerations as appear to it to be relevant: that is, the nature and seriousness of the offence or default (and the probable method of dealing with the defendant for it) the character, antecedents, associations and community ties of the defendant; the defendant's record as respects the fulfilment of his obligations under previous grants of bail in criminal proceedings; and, except in the case of a defendant whose case is adjourned for inquiries or a report, the strength of the evidence of his having committed the offence or having defaulted. The court must also take into account any other considerations which appear to be relevant.

Non-imprisonable offences

Part II of Schedule 1 applies to a defendant charged with or convicted of an offence or offences, none of which are punishable with imprisonment. Such a defendant need not be granted bail in any of the following circumstances:

1. It appears to the court that, having been previously granted bail in criminal proceedings, he has failed to surrender to custody in accordance with his obligations under the grant of bail, and the court believes, in view of that failure, that the defendant, if released on bail (whether subject to conditions or not) would fail to surrender to custody.
2. The court is satisfied that he should be kept in custody for his own protection or, if he is a child or young person, for his own welfare.
3. He is already serving a custodial sentence.
4. He has already been bailed during the course of the proceedings, and has been arrested under s7 of the Bail Act 1976 (that is, for absconding).

13.7 Conditions of bail

Although a defendant may be granted unconditional bail, s3 of the Bail Act 1976, as amended, provides that bail may be granted on conditions.

The possible conditions under s3 of the 1976 Act are: provision of sureties; reporting; residence; and restrictions.

Provision of one or more sureties

A surety is someone who undertakes to pay the court a certain sum of money if the defendant fails to surrender to custody as he ought to. This undertaking is known as a 'recognisance'. A surety for an adult defendant has no responsibility for seeing that he complies with any other conditions which may be imposed; the position is different in the case of a child or young person defendant when his parent or parents stand as surety for him.

Where the defendant fails to appear at the trial, it is for the trial judge, in the exercise of his wide discretion, to decide whether it would be fair or just to estreat some or all of the recognisance: *R v Crown Court at Maidstone, ex parte Lever* [1995] 2 All ER 35. If a court is satisfied that a surety was blameless throughout it might be proper to remit the whole of the amount of the recognisance: *R v Crown Court at Reading, ex parte Bello* [1992] 3 All ER 353.

In *R v Wood Green Crown Court, ex parte Howe* [1992] 1 WLR 702 the Divisional Court decided that where a bail surety had undertaken to pay a sum which he could not afford, the court should have regard to his ability to pay and to the consequences for the surety of ordering payment of an amount which would inevitably lead to a term of imprisonment in default.

Reporting

The defendant may be required to report to a certain place (usually the local police station) at a certain time each day, week or month.

Residence

The defendant may be required to live at a stated address. This will entail his sleeping at that address each evening.

Restrictions

Many different restrictions may be put upon the defendant. For example, that he should not speak to a particular witness nor go to a particular place, or a curfew restriction requiring him to be home at a certain time each evening. Section 54(2) of the Crime and Disorder Act 1998 enables a court (but not a police custody officer) to grant bail subject to obtaining legal advice prior to the time fixed for surrender to custody.

13.8 Challenges to bail decisions

Reconsideration

Section 30 of the Criminal Justice and Public Order Act 1994 inserts s5B into the Bail Act 1976. Under s5B, where a magistrates' court has granted bail in criminal proceedings in connection with an offence triable on indictment or either way, or a constable has granted bail in criminal proceedings in connection with proceedings for such an offence, that court or the appropriate court in relation to the constable may, on application by the prosecutor for the decision to be reconsidered, vary the conditions of bail, impose conditions in respect of bail which has been granted unconditionally or withhold bail. No application for reconsideration may be made unless it is based on information which was not available to the court or constable when the decision was taken.

Appeal – by the defendant

Under the Bail Act 1976, whenever bail is refused a record must be made of the decision and the reasons for it. Upon request, a copy of the record must be given to the defendant.

Part IIA of Schedule 1 to the 1976 Act permits two fully argued applications for bail before the magistrates. After those the magistrates need not hear a further application unless the accused has a new argument to advance.

Appeal against the magistrates' decision to refuse bail or apply conditions may be made to the High Court or to the Crown Court.

Section 22 of the Criminal Justice Act 1967 provides that, subject to s25 of the 1994 Act (above), the High Court has jurisdiction to grant bail or vary the conditions of bail.

The Crown Court may grant bail once refused by the magistrates in the following circumstances:

1. If the magistrates remanded the defendant in custody and heard a fully argued bail application before deciding on the remand.
2. If the magistrates committed the defendant in custody to the Crown Court for trial or sentence.
3. If the magistrates convicted the defendant summarily, imposed a custodial sentence and refused to bail him pending determination of his appeal to the Crown Court.

Therefore, in almost all cases a defendant may make further application to either the High Court or the Crown Court or to both.

Appeal – by the prosecution

By virtue of s1 of the Bail (Amendment) Act 1993, where a magistrates' court grants bail to a person who is charged with or convicted of an offence punishable by a term of imprisonment of five years or more or an offence under s12 (taking a conveyance without authority) or s12A (aggravated vehicle taking) of the Theft Act 1968, the prosecution may appeal to a judge of the Crown Court against the granting of bail. This applies only where the prosecution is conducted by or on behalf of the Director of Public Prosecutions or by a person who falls within such class or description of person as may be prescribed by the Secretary of State.

Such an appeal may be made only if the prosecution made representations that bail should not be granted and the representations were made before it was granted. In the event of the prosecution wishing to exercise this right of appeal, oral notice of appeal has to be given to the magistrates' court at the conclusion of the proceedings in which bail was granted and before the release from custody of the person concerned.

Written notice of appeal must then be served on the magistrates' court and the person concerned within two hours of the conclusion of the proceedings. Upon receipt of oral notice of appeal the magistrates' must remand in custody the person concerned, until the appeal is determined or otherwise disposed of. Where the prosecution fails, within the period of two hours, to serve one or both of the written notices, the appeal is deemed to have been disposed of.

The hearing of an appeal must be commenced within 48 hours, excluding weekends and any public holiday (ie Christmas Day, Good Friday or a bank holiday), from the date on which oral notice of appeal was given.

13.9 Effect of failure to surrender

If a person who has been released on bail fails without reasonable cause to surrender to custody he is guilty of an offence: s6(1) of the Bail Act 1976. It is a single offence regardless of whether the bail was granted by the police or by a magistrates' court. In the case of failure to surrender to the Crown Court the offence will normally be dealt with as if it was a contempt. In the case of failure to surrender to a police station or a magistrates' court where bail has been granted by the police the offence must be dealt with as a summary offence. In the case of failure to surrender to a magistrates' court where bail has been granted by the magistrates' court the offence will be dealt with as if it was a contempt: see *Murphy* v *Director of Public Prosecutions* [1990] 2 All ER 390.

In *R* v *Wood Green Crown Court, ex parte Howe* [1992] 1 WLR 702 the Divisional Court considered whether a surety could 'seek to withdraw' when the defendant disappears or seems unlikely to appear for trial, or where the surety's circumstances change so that he can no longer pay the amount which he has undertaken to pay. Their Lordships believed that there is no power for a surety to withdraw unless the defendant is before the court and appropriate application is made by the prosecution or by him under s3(8) of the 1976 Act. Apart from this, s7(3) of that Act gives a constable power to arrest the defendant without warrant when a surety has made complaint in writing at a police station that the defendant is unlikely to surrender to custody. This course is, therefore, open to the surety, and it may mean that in practice the police will be able to produce the defendant in court if they can find and arrest him before the hearing. Nevertheless, the surety remains bound to produce him at the appointed time and place, and if the defendant does not appear the recognisance may be estreated.

No forfeiture of surety will be ordered if the defendant absconds after a surrender to the custody of the court, eg after arraignment: *R* v *Central Criminal Court, ex parte Guney* [1996] 2 All ER 705 (HL).

13.10 Classification of offences

In order to determine which mode of trial is suitable all criminal offences may be classified in the following three groups.

Indictable offences

An indictable offence is an offence for which an adult (aged 17 or over) must or may be tried on indictment, ie in the Crown Court before a judge and jury.

All common law offences are indictable. These include murder, manslaughter, rape and riot. Statutory offences are indictable if the statute which creates them indicates as such, for example by imposing a penalty to follow conviction on indictment.

Summary offences

Summary offences must be tried by summary trial (ie in the magistrates' court without a jury) and are all statutory offences. Examples include driving without due care and attention under the Road Traffic Act 1988, taking a pedal cycle without lawful authority under the Theft Act 1968, and all common assaults or batteries.

The statute which creates the offence will show that the offence is summary by specifying a penalty which may be imposed upon summary conviction without specifying a further penalty to be imposed upon conviction on indictment.

Offences triable either way

As has already been stated, although a summary offence *must* be tried summarily, an indictable offence must or *may* be triable on indictment. This shows that some offences may be tried either summarily or on indictment; these are said to be 'triable either way'.

An offence is triable either way if it meets either of the following conditions:

1. It is to be found in Sch 1 to the Magistrates' Courts Act 1980. These include most offences under the Theft Act 1968, bigamy and indecent assault.
2. It can be seen to be triable either way from the statute which creates it, such as reckless driving under the Road Traffic Act 1988.

Offences triable either way tend to be the sort of offences which are capable of varying in seriousness, depending upon the circumstances of the particular case. Whereas murder is always a serious crime no matter what the circumstances, theft, for example, may be serious or may be trivial depending, inter alia, upon the value of the goods stolen.

13.11 Determining the mode of trial

The first question to be decided concerns the mode of trial by which the defendant is to be tried. The decision may be made by one lay magistrate, although it is usual for two or three to be present.

If an offence is a summary offence or an indictable offence which *must* be tried on indictment, there is no choice as to the mode of trial. Therefore, the following procedure is applicable only when the offence charged is triable either way and is known as the 'plea before venue' stage of proceedings.

The procedure is contained in s17A of the Magistrates' Courts Act (MCA) 1980 (inserted by s49 of the Criminal Procedure and Investigations Act 1996), which came into force on 1 October 1997. After the charge is read to the accused the court will ask the accused to indicate his plea. Before taking that plea the court must inform the accused that if he indicates a guilty plea the court will proceed as if there has been a summary trial of the information, and that if the court then considers that it has insufficient powers to punish the accused it may send him to the Crown Court to be sentenced, using its powers under s38 MCA 1980, or may commit him if there are related offences which are to be committed for trial under s38A MCA 1980 (the latter power has been introduced by s51 Crime (Sentences) Act 1997).

The plea is then indicated by the accused. Under the law prior to 1 October 1997 magistrates had to make mode of trial decisions in the absence of any knowledge of the accused's intended plea. This led to many 'cracked trials', ie cases in which public money and administration was wasted because the accused reserved his plea for Crown Court trial but then at that trial pleaded guilty at the arraignment and was then given a sentence which the magistrates could have imposed. The new procedure is designed to ensure that cases which can properly be dealt with in the magistrates' court remain there, and to this end the taking of the plea will ensure that the magistrates are fully informed. Further, it provides an opportunity for the accused to enter a plea of guilty as soon as possible; this is a strong mitigating factor when it comes to sentencing: *R v Rafferty* (1998) The Times 9 April. Potentially many more cases should be retained in the magistrates' courts as a result of the new procedure, though possible problems could arise. For example, magistrates may be tempted to retain jurisdiction so as to dispose of cases swiftly in the interests of efficiency and this may result in more lenient sentences than that encouraged by official government policy. Second, there could be more adjournments in the magistrates' court in order for the defence to obtain further information in deciding what plea to indicate. For other problems: see Bavidge and Kerrigan 'Plea before Venue' [1998] NLJ 62.

If the accused indicates a plea of not guilty (or fails to plead, in which case a not guilty plea is entered on his behalf) the magistrates will proceed under ss19–23 of the Magistrates' Courts Act 1980, which are affected by the amendments brought in on 1 October 1997. The prosecution and the defence may each make submissions as to which method of trial is more suitable. The magistrates must then take account of any such submissions and the matters set out in s19(3) MCA 1980 before deciding whether the case is more suitable for summary trial than trial on indictment.

The matters set out in s19(3) should be read in conjunction with the National Mode of Trial Guidelines. These matters and guidelines may also be taken into account where there has been an indication of a guilty plea under the new procedure above because they may be relevant to the decision whether to retain jurisdiction for the purpose of sentencing the accused: *R v Warley Magistrates' Court, ex parte DPP* [1999] 1 All ER 251.

The matters set out in s19(3) are as follows:

1. the nature of the case;

2. whether the circumstances make the offence one of a serious character;
3. whether the punishment which a magistrates' court would have power to inflict for it would be adequate; and
4. any other circumstances which appear to the court to make it more suitable for the offence to be tried in one way rather than the other.

The opening general observations of the National Mode of Trial Guidelines (1995) are as follows:

1. the court should never make its decision on the grounds of convenience or expedition;
2. the court should assume that the prosecution version of the facts is correct;
3. the fact that the offences are alleged to be specimens is a relevant consideration, but the fact that the defendant will be asking for other offences to be taken into consideration, if convicted, is not a relevant consideration;
4. cases involving complex questions of fact or difficult questions of law or disclosure of sensitive material are more suitable for trial on indictment than summary trial;
5. in general, either way offences should be tried summarily unless the court considers that its sentencing powers are insufficient; and
6. the court should consider its power to commit an offender for sentence to the Crown Court if it should find that its powers of punishment are inadequate.

If the court decides that trial on indictment is the suitable mode of trial, that is a final decision, ie the accused does not have a right to insist on a summary trial. The accused will be informed of the decision and committal proceedings will follow (considered in detail in section 13.12, below).

If the court decides that summary trial is more suitable it will inform the accused, who is then asked whether he consents to summary trial or whether he wishes to be tried by jury at the Crown Court. Before making this choice, he should again be warned of the court's power under s38 MCA 1980 to commit him for sentence to the Crown Court if, after trying him summarily, the court convicts him and then considers that it has insufficient powers of punishment (for example because information emerges during the course of the trial which leads the court to conclude that the offence was more serious than previously thought). If the accused then chooses summary trial, the next stage will be the trial itself (considered in Chapter 14). If the accused elects trial by jury committal proceedings will follow (section 13.12, below).

Under s25(2) of the MCA 1980 magistrates have jurisdiction to re-open mode of trial proceedings if necessary if they have begun to try the information summarily, ie upon taking a plea of not guilty: *R v Horseferry Road Magistrates' Court, ex parte K* [1996] 3 All ER 719. It would appear in all other situations the mode of trial decision is final and cannot be re-opened.

Criminal damage offences

Offences of criminal damage contrary to s1 of the Criminal Damage Act 1971 must be tried summarily if the value of the property damaged or destroyed is £5,000 or less: s46 of the Criminal Justice and Public Order Act 1994. See further Bavidge and Kerrigan 'Plea before Venue – Part 2' [1998] NLJ 134.

Reform proposals

In the summer of 1998 the government issued a Consultation Paper entitled *Determining Mode of Trial in Either Way Cases*, which suggested four possible options for discussion:

1. maintaining the present classification and procedures for determining the venue for trial; or
2. reclassification of particular offences so as to make them triable only summarily (eg minor theft and indecent assault); or
3. abolition of a defendant's right to elect trial by jury for an offence triable either way so that the decision on the venue for trial for such an offence would be purely a matter for the magistrates; or
4. the right to elect jury trial for an offence triable either way should be retained only for first offenders, ie a defendant would lose the right of election if charged with an offence similar in nature to one for which he has been previously convicted.

Proposals 2, 3 and 4 obviously have serious implications for the traditional right to trial by jury, eg proposal 2, if implemented, would affect an estimated 22,000 defendants a year. The government is keen on reform because of its concern over costs and delays in the criminal justice system.

For critical responses to the Consultation Paper: see Editorial 'Juries Out' [1998] NLJ 1169 and Wolchover and Heaton-Armstrong 'New Labour's Attack on Trial by Jury' [1998] NLJ 1613.

13.12 Committal proceedings; sending a case for trial

Committal proceedings

These are applicable to an offence triable either way, either where the magistrates have decided the offence should be tried on indictment or where the accused has exercised his right to be tried on indictment. Committal proceedings take place in the magistrates' court and when the magistrates sit for this purpose they are known as 'examining justices'.

The examining justices are not concerned with the question of whether or not the defendant is guilty or whether or not the jury at the Crown Court will find him guilty. The question the examining justices must ask themselves is: 'Does the evidence placed before them at the committal proceedings show a "prima facie" case that the defendant has committed an indictable offence?'

It was often said that committals were a valuable safeguard for the defence in sparing the accused the ordeal of a trial on insufficient evidence, but the need for such a safeguard became less obvious after the establishment of a professional prosecution service in 1985. Committals were abolished for serious fraud trials (Criminal Justice Act 1987) and for certain types of sexual offence, mainly involving children (Criminal Justice Act 1991), where the transfer to the Crown Court was effected through paperwork prepared by the Crown Prosecution Service. As will be seen this transfer procedure has been replaced by a new 'sending for trial' procedure, which has also replaced committal proceedings in respect of purely indictable offences (below). Where committal proceedings survive (ie for most offences triable either way) they may take one of two forms.

First, under s6(1) of the Magistrates' Courts Act 1980, as amended by s47 of and Sch 1 to the Criminal Procedure and Investigations Act (CPIA) 1996, there may be committal proceedings with consideration of the evidence (a 'long-form committal'). The procedure is as follows:

1. The prosecution outlines its case and the evidence it will call.
2. The prosecution calls its evidence. Prior to the amendment by the CPIA 1996, above, witnesses could be called to give oral evidence and could be cross-examined by the defence. However, the taking of oral evidence (including depositions) at committals was ended by the 1996 Act in an attempt to improve efficiency and protect witnesses. The prosecution evidence is therefore limited to documentary evidence (written statements) and exhibits. Any issues as to the admissibility of evidence must be determined by the justices and any error as to admissibility is subject to judicial review by the High Court: *Williams* v *Bedwellty Justices* [1996] 3 All ER 737 (HL).
3. The defence may submit that there is 'no case to answer', that is the prosecution evidence has not raised a prima facie case.
4. The examining justices must decide whether there is a case to answer, that is, a prima facie case.

   If the examining justices decide that there is a case to answer, they state in open court that they are committing the defendant to Crown Court and they state on which charge or charges he is being committed. If the examining justices decide that there is no case to answer, the defendant is discharged. A discharge, however, is not an acquittal and the prosecution is free to charge the defendant afresh for the same offence at a later date, for example if it obtains stronger evidence: *R* v *Manchester City Stipendiary Magistrate, ex parte Snelson* [1977] 1 WLR 911.

Second, under s6(2) of the Magistrates' Courts Act 1980, there may be committal proceedings without consideration of the evidence where the following three requirements are met:

1. All the evidence before the court consists of written statements tendered in evidence under s102 of the MCA 1980 (ie no party objects to their production).
2. The defendant has a legal representative acting for him.
3. There is no submission from the defence that there is no case to answer.

Compliance with these requirements ensures that a 'short-form' committal will, in practice, be used only in circumstances in which if there had been committal with consideration of the evidence, the examining justices would have found that there was a case to answer.

The advantages of committal without consideration of the evidence are obvious, saving time and expenses for all concerned. It is not surprising, therefore, that most committals take this form. This is especially true given that a large majority of submissions of 'no case to answer' at committals, with consideration of the evidence, fail; this latter fact is understandable as the prosecution are unlikely to press ahead with a charge against a defendant if it is clear or even possible that its evidence will not satisfy even the low burden of 'prima facie case'.

Once a defendant has been committed for trial a number of final points must be considered by the examining justices.

Alibi warning

When a defendant intends to rely on an alibi at his trial (ie he intends to say that he was at a place other than the scene of the crime at the relevant time), then he must be warned of the effect of s11 of the Criminal Justice Act 1967, as amended by s5(7) of the Criminal Procedure and Investigations Act 1996 which provides that a defendant may not adduce evidence of an alibi at his trial on indictment as of right, but only with the leave of the judge, unless he has given notice of particulars of his alibi to the prosecution in advance of the trial so that the prosecution has had a reasonable opportunity to investigate the truthfulness of that alibi.

Bail

The examining justices must decide whether the defendant is to be committed on bail or in custody. It should be noted that the waiting period between committal proceedings and trial on indictment is likely to be many months and so this question is an important one, to be answered only upon full consideration of all relevant factors.

Legal aid

The examining justices may be asked to grant legal aid to the defendant to cover the costs of the defence at trial. They are unlikely to refuse, and where legal aid has already been granted thus far it is generally continued automatically.

Sending a case for trial

Sections 51 and 52 of, and Sch 3 to, the Crime and Disorder Act 1998 abolish committal proceedings for all purely indictable offences. The reforms also abolish transfer for trial proceedings for such offences (eg serious fraud offences and certain sexual offences against children).

Under the new procedure (called 'sending for trial') every adult charged with an indictable only offence must first appear before a magistrates' court to determine issues concerning legal aid, bail, the taking of depositions and exhibits. The magistrate must also provide the accused with a statement of the evidence against him as well as a notice setting out the offence(s) for which he is to be sent for trial and the place where he is to be tried.

The first opportunity for a defendant to assert that there is no case to answer will be at the Crown Court, which takes over from the magistrates' court all remaining case management duties. Any submission of no case to answer must be made prior to arraignment and it will be for the judge to decide whether 'the interests of justice' require oral evidence for this purpose. If oral evidence is permitted the normal rules on reporting restrictions will apply. The normal rules on pre-trial disclosure of evidence also apply to the new sending for trial procedure.

The purpose of the new procedure is to cut delays in the criminal justice system and for this purpose new, stiffer time limits will be imposed on the prosecution to ensure efficient preparation of cases. The new time limits will be fixed after consultations and pilot trials of the new sending for trial procedures.

14

Criminal Procedure II: Summary Trial

14.1 Introduction

14.2 Attendance and representation

14.3 The information

14.4 The trial procedure

14.5 Sentencing

14.1 Introduction

Summary trial will follow automatically if the defendant is charged with a summary offence and may be chosen as the mode of trial for an offence triable either way.

Summary trial takes place in a magistrates' court before either three (exceptionally two) lay magistrates or one stipendiary magistrate. The magistrates sit as both judge and jury, that is, they decide questions of fact and law (the latter with guidance from their legally qualified clerk). Approximately 98 per cent of all criminal trials take place in the magistrates' courts.

The procedure of a summary trial is governed by the Magistrates' Courts Act 1980 (MCA).

Magistrates' courts have geographical limits to their jurisdiction – and have jurisdiction to try any summary offence committed within the county. The purpose of this is to provide a bench with 'local knowledge' (eg of a stretch of road). However, magistrates' courts have jurisdiction to try offences either way, no matter where allegedly committed.

In addition the courts have jurisdiction to try a summary offence committed outside the county in the following situations:

1. A magistrates' court which tries a person for an offence (summary or triable either way) has jurisdiction to try him in addition for any other summary offence wherever committed: s2(6) MCA 1980.
2. If one defendant is being prosecuted in a magistrates' court in Xshire and it is necessary or expedient, with a view to the better administration of justice, that he

be tried jointly with or in the same place as another person, Xshire magistrate may issue a summons to bring that other person before Xshire magistrates' court.

Sections 49 and 50 of the Crime and Disorder Act 1998 provide for the introduction of case management mechanisms, namely optional pre-trial reviews and early administrative hearings so as to ensure more efficient pre-trial preparations. The relevant powers to conduct such reviews and hearings are conferred on single lay justices who are also authorised to delegate certain functions (not involving significant discretionary decisions) to justices' clerks.

For rules relating to pre-trial disclosure of evidence, see Chapter 15, section 15.4.

14.2 Attendance and representation

Attendance of the prosecution.

If the prosecution fails to attend at a summary trial the magistrates have a discretion: they may either dismiss the information or adjourn the case: s15 MCA 1980. If the case is part-heard and the prosecution fails to attend, the magistrates have the further alternative of proceeding in the absence of the prosecution.

Attendance of the defendant

The defendant need not be present at his summary trial.

1. By s12 MCA 1980 the defendant (including persons aged 16 or 17) is entitled to plead guilty by post for any summary offence for which the maximum penalty does not exceed three months imprisonment. In suitable cases, a notice explaining this option is served on the defendant with the summons. If he wishes to take advantage of this option the defendant must write to inform the clerk to the magistrates. In his letter the defendant may set out any mitigating factors he wishes the magistrates to take into account when sentencing him. The clerk will inform the prosecution of the defendant's decision so the prosecution need not attend either. On the day set for hearing, the clerk puts to the magistrates: proof that the summons was served; the prosecution's brief statement of the facts of the offence; and the defendant's guilty plea with any mitigating circumstances.

    The magistrates should then proceed to sentence. However, they may not sentence the defendant to imprisonment in his absence: s11(3) MCA 1980. If this is contemplated, the matter should be adjourned and a warrant issued for the defendant's arrest. The same course should be adopted whenever the magistrates consider the offence is in fact more serious than had been anticipated (eg if the offence is one of careless driving; this carries a fine and penalty points – the penalty points may 'tot-up' with previous ones to indicate the defendant must be disqualified from driving; this will not be done in his absence, and the matter will be adjourned, the defendant being summonsed to attend).

Section 45 of and Schedule 5 to the Criminal Justice and Public Order Act 1994 substitute a new s12 of the Magistrates' Courts Act 1980, extending the procedures applicable in magistrates' courts when the accused pleads guilty. The new s12 applies when a summons has been issued requiring a person to appear before a magistrates' court, other than a youth court, to answer an information for a summary offence, not being an offence for which he is liable to be imprisoned for more than three months, and, inter alia, a concise statement of facts has been served on him. If the accused then notifies the court in writing that he wishes to plead guilty without appearing, and he does not appear, the court may (but need not) dispose of the case in his absence, taking account of any submission which he may have made with a view to mitigation of sentence. However, s11(3) and (4) (any disqualification cannot be imposed in a person's absence) of the 1980 Act still apply and any written notice may be withdrawn.

Section 12A of the 1980 Act, as inserted by the 1994 Act provisions, applies where the accused, having given written notice, nevertheless appears. If he consents, the court may proceed as if he were absent, but he must be given the opportunity to make an oral submission in mitigation.

2. Section 11 sets out the options open to the magistrates if the defendant fails to appear but has not indicated that he wishes to plead guilty under s12.

    The magistrates have a discretion to proceed in the defendant's absence – s11(1) MCA 1980 – with a plea of not guilty being entered on his behalf. The prosecution is unlikely to have difficulty in proving its case with its unchallenged evidence. For this reason, the magistrates are unlikely to adopt this course if the offence seems at all serious. This course may not be adopted without initial proof that the defendant has in fact been served with the summons.

    Where a defendant claims he is too ill to attend trial and has medical support for the claim, justices should not refuse an application for an adjournment and proceed in the defendant's absence without first satisfying themselves that the excuse was not genuine.

3. Section 13(1) gives the magistrates power to issue a warrant for the arrest of the accused so as to secure his attendance at summary trial.

    Section 48 CPIA 1996 amends s13(2) MCA 1980 relating to the conditions for issuing a warrant for the arrest of an accused who has failed to appear at his summary trial (other than an accused who has pleaded guilty by post under s12 MCA 1980).

    Section 48 CPIA 1996 inserts new subss(2A) and (2B) into s13 MCA 1980. Under the new s13(2A) an arrest warrant may be issued if it is proved that the summons was served on the accused within a reasonable time before the trial or adjourned trial; and under the new s13(2B) an arrest warrant may be issued if:
    a) the adjournment now being made is a second and subsequent adjournment of the trial; and
    b) the accused was present at the last (or only) occasion when the trial was adjourned; and

c) on that occasion the court determined the time for the hearing at which the adjournment is now being made.

Representation

Both solicitors and barristers have a right of audience in the magistrates' courts. However, it is usual for a defendant to be represented by a solicitor or appear unrepresented (perhaps having been advised by the duty solicitor).

Where an accused is legally unrepresented, the court explains to him or her the substance of the charge in simple language. If such an accused, instead of asking a witness in support of the charge questions by way of cross-examination, makes assertions, the court puts to the witness such questions as it thinks necessary on behalf of the accused and may for this purpose question the accused in order to bring out or clear up any point arising out of such assertions.

14.3 The information

The information performs two functions:

1. It is the basis and justification for the issue of a summons ordering the defendant to appear at the magistrates' court.
2. It contains and constitutes the charge to which the defendant must plead.

It is the second function that is of relevance at the start of the summary trial.

The first stage in a summary trial is the clerk 'putting the information' to the defendant, and asking him if he pleads not guilty.

The defendant must then 'plead' to the allegations. A number of the pleas available to a defendant at a trial on indictment are not available in the magistrates' court. Put simply, the defendant must plead guilty or not guilty.

If the defendant pleads guilty, the procedure for sentencing is followed: see Chapter 15, section 15.6. If the defendant pleads not guilty, his trial begins.

14.4 The trial procedure

The procedure in a summary trial is as follows.

The prosecution has a right to an opening speech

Given the (usual) simplicity of most trials in the magistrates' courts, this speech is likely to be short. The purpose of an opening speech is to tell the magistrates of the charge, its background, and the nature and effect of the prosecution evidence. For instance, to open the prosecution's case in a charge of shoplifting (theft), the prosecutor may state the place and date of the offence, the nature of the goods stolen and their value, and a brief summary of what, for example, the store detective saw.

In some cases, the prosecution will not make an opening speech at all. It is clearly of less necessity in the magistrates' court, as the magistrates are experienced and do not need the preliminary explanations needed by the jury.

The prosecution calls its evidence

In all criminal trials it is for the prosecution to prove 'beyond reasonable doubt', that the defendant is guilty of the offence or offences with which he is charged. It is not for the defendant to prove his innocence. It is for this reason that it is for the prosecution to present its evidence first in order to establish at least a prima facie case against the defendant.

Generally, evidence is given orally by witnesses in court. If a witness is reluctant to attend, either side may obtain a 'subpoena' from the court which will order the witness to attend. If the witness in question then fails to attend, the magistrates, if satisfied that he has been served with the summons, that he is likely to be able to give material evidence and that he has been paid a reasonable sum of money to cover the costs of his attendance at court, may issue a warrant for his arrest.

The prosecution may call any number of witnesses who can give evidence that will work to establish any of the elements which it has to prove.

For obvious reasons, it is preferable that evidence is given orally in court; it enables the magistrates to evaluate a witness's credibility and what weight to attach to his evidence, and it enables the other side to cross-examine the witness in an attempt to challenge his evidence and cast doubt on his credibility. However, in certain circumstances, written statements may be read out and put in evidence without the attendance of the maker. In the magistrates' court these circumstances include:

1. Under s102 MCA 1980 a written statement is admissible in evidence if it is signed by the maker, contains a declaration that it is true to the best of the maker's knowledge and belief, has been served on all other parties, and no party objects to its being tendered in evidence. This provision is used mainly when evidence is undisputed.
2. A deposition taken under s105 MCA 1980 from a witness who is dangerously ill and unlikely to recover may be read as evidence at the trial if it is proved that the witness is now dead or so ill that there is no reasonable probability of his ever being able to attend. The other side must have been given notice of the intention to take the deposition and given the opportunity to cross-examine the witness (eg at his bed-side).

The majority of evidence, however, is likely to be given orally. The prosecution will call its witness forward and he will stand in the witness box. Before giving evidence, the witness must promise to 'tell the truth, the whole truth and nothing but the truth'. This promise is made either by swearing to do so 'on oath', holding the Bible, Koran or whatever is the relevant book in his right hand, or by 'affirming' to do so. The latter option is to be used if the witness has no religious convictions.

The adducing of a witness's evidence is a three-stage process and is described below.

Examination-in-chief

This consists of questions asked of the witness by the side which has called him, that is, by the prosecution of a prosecution witness.

The prosecution must elicit from the witness all the evidence of that witness on which it will seek to rely. In asking questions in order to elicit such evidence, 'leading questions' must not be asked. A leading question is one which suggests the answer. For example, if the prosecution wishes to elicit from its witness evidence that at a certain time it was raining, it would be leading a witness to ask, 'it was raining, wasn't it?' Questions should be as neutral as possible, for example, 'what were the weather conditions?'

Cross-examination

The defence may then cross-examine the prosecution witness. In doing so, any relevant question may be asked, including leading questions. Cross-examination has two purposes. First, the defence case must be 'put' to the prosecution witness in order to give him an opportunity to reply to it. For example, if the defendant is charged with the theft of a book belonging to Mr X, Mr X may be called by the prosecution and may give evidence-in-chief that the book belongs to him and so forth. The defence 'case' may be that the defendant was given permission to take the book by Mr X. If so, this must be 'put' to Mr X: that is, he must be asked, 'Did you give the defendant permission to take your book?' Second, questions asked in cross-examination may be used to 'discredit' the witness: that is, to show the witness up either as lying or at least as unreliable. In summary, therefore, any question is relevant if either it relates to whether the defendant committed the offence or to a fact which increases or decreases the likelihood of his having done so, or it relates to the credibility and reliability of the witness.

Re-examination

This consists of further questions by the prosecution of its own witness. It provides the prosecution with a chance to deal with any disfavourable answers given in cross-examination; however, it is important to note that new issues and evidence may not be adduced at this stage, otherwise the other side would not have an opportunity to cross-examine the witness on that further evidence. Re-examination, therefore, is for the purpose of clarification and, possibly, amplification, of the witness evidence given in chief only, and for that reason is usually a good deal shorter than examination-in-chief or cross-examination.

All prosecution witnesses are called and, in turn, go through the above procedure. When they have all been called, that is the end of the prosecution case and, generally speaking, the prosecution will have to rely on the evidence adduced and will be unable to call any further evidence at a later stage.

Submission of 'no case to answer'

At the end of the prosecution case it is open to the defence to make a submission of 'no case to answer'. As at committal proceedings, the submission may be based on either of the following circumstances:

1. There is no evidence going to prove an essential element of the offence charged.
2. The prosecution evidence is so obviously unreliable that no reasonable tribunal could safely convict on it: *Practice Note* [1962] 1 All ER 448.

If the magistrates consider there is no case to answer they will acquit the defendant at this stage. A formal acquittal means that the defendant cannot be charged again with the offence(s) in question.

The defence case

If there is a case to answer, the defence may wish to adduce evidence, but it need not do so. It is for the prosecution to prove the defendant's guilt, and, therefore, the defendant does not have to prove his innocence. Nevertheless, if the defendant has any evidence which suggests or proves that he is not guilty the defence will wish to call that evidence. The defendant may himself give evidence, if he wishes to, but cannot be compelled to do so as other witnesses can. If the defendant chooses to give evidence he is liable to be cross-examined in the same manner as any other witness, except that he cannot normally be questioned by the prosecution on his past record, if he has one.

Defence evidence will be given orally in the same way as the prosecution evidence was given with examination-in-chief, cross-examination and re-examination.

Adjournment

In *R v Kingston-upon-Thames Justices, ex parte Martin* (1993) The Times 10 December, the Divisional Court said that a magistrates' court's decision as to whether to grant an adjournment to any party depended on the following factors: the importance of the proceedings, and the likely adverse consequences on the party seeking adjournment; the risk that the applicant would be prejudiced if an adjournment were refused; the risk of prejudice to his opponent if the adjournment were granted; the convenience of the court and the interests of justice in ensuring the efficient despatch of business so as not to delay other future litigants; and the extent to which the applicant had been responsible for the circumstances leading to the requirement for an adjournment.

Closing speech

The prosecution has no right to a closing speech. The defence has a choice; it may either open its case with an opening speech or finish the trial with a closing speech. It is rare for the defence not to opt for a closing speech: an opening speech adds little to the case whereas a closing speech gives the defence the opportunity to review the evidence called in its entirety and to have the last word.

The decision

On the basis of the evidence they have heard the magistrates must decide whether to find the defendant guilty or not guilty.

Lay magistrates will normally 'retire', that is, leave the court, in order to discuss the evidence and their view. They may take advice on what is the law from their legally qualified clerk. Usually three magistrates sit and they may deliver a majority verdict of two to one. However, if an even-numbered bench sits and is equally divided on its decision, the chairman has no casting vote; in that event the magistrates must adjourn the case to be reheard by a bench of three different magistrates: *R v Redbridge Justices, ex parte Ram* [1992] 1 All ER 652.

A stipendiary magistrate always sits alone and will usually reach his decision immediately after the defence's closing speech without retiring from the court.

If the magistrates consider that the prosecution has not proved the guilt of the defendant 'beyond reasonable doubt' they will acquit him. The defendant is then free to go and may not be charged with the offence again. If they consider that the defendant's guilt is proved they will convict him of the offence charged and proceed to sentence him.

If, after having convicted the defendant, the magistrates are unsure of the correctness of their decision, under s142 MCA 1980, they may within 28 days of their decision direct that the case be reheard by a bench of different magistrates. This direction causes their conviction and any sentence passed to be nullified.

14.5 Sentencing

The procedure prior to sentencing is dealt with in Chapter 15, section 15.6. This section is concerned with the magistrates' powers of sentencing only.

The magistrates have certain limits on the maximum sentences they can impose. In particular, at present the maximum fine is £5,000 for any one offence, and the maximum period of imprisonment is six months for any one offence, or one year's imprisonment for two or more offences tried together.

An additional option is available to the magistrates in relation to offences triable either way (but not summary offences). Although magistrates should agree to try an offence triable either way if they consider their powers of sentencing will be sufficient if there is a conviction, it may be that their powers will prove to be insufficient in the light of new material which was not available at the time of their original decision. In those events, and normally only in those events, the magistrates may commit the defendant to the Crown Court for sentencing under s38 of the MCA 1980. The Crown Court may then deal with the defendant as if he had been convicted of the offence on indictment: s42 of the Powers of Criminal Courts Act 1973.

Section 51 Crime (Sentences) Act 1997 inserts a new s38A into the Magistrates' Courts Act 1980 and enables the magistrates' court to commit the defendant to the Crown Court for sentence after a guilty plea indication to an offence triable either way if there are related offences to be committed for trial.

The magistrates may also commit the defendant to the Crown Court for sentencing in the following circumstances:

1. When they have convicted the defendant of an imprisonable offence (summary or triable either way) committed during the operational period of a suspended sentence of imprisonment passed by the Crown Court.
2. When they have convicted the defendant of any offence committed during the period of a conditional discharge order made by the Crown Court.
3. When they have convicted the defendant of an offence triable either way at a time when he is still on licence having earlier been released from prison on parole.

15

Criminal Procedure III: Trial on Indictment

15.1 Introduction

15.2 Representation

15.3 The plea; plea and directions hearings; preparatory hearings; and plea bargaining

15.4 Pre-trial disclosure

15.5 The trial procedure

15.6 Sentencing

15.1 Introduction

If the magistrates have committed a defendant to the Crown Court for trial, a 'trial on indictment' will follow several months later.

In the summary trial, the magistrates themselves decide all questions in issue, whether they are questions of fact or law. However, a trial on indictment takes place before a judge and a jury; consequently there is a division in their respective functions.

The judge in a Crown Court is always a paid professional judge. The 'adversarial' method of trial is adopted in the English legal system: this means that each side presents its own case and the judge acts as a kind of 'umpire' during the course of the trial, ensuring 'fair play'. (This is to be contrasted with the 'inquisitorial' method adopted in other legal systems in which it is the role of the judge himself to question the witnesses, although English law allows a judge to call a witness, but only to achieve the ends of justice and fairness: see *R v Grafton* [1992] 4 All ER 609.) At the end of the trial, it is also the function of the judge to be the sole arbiter on all questions of law and to sentence a convicted defendant.

The role of the jury is to decide all questions of fact: the jury must decide whether they believe evidence presented to them or what weight to give to each piece of evidence. The final question they must decide is whether the defendant is guilty or not guilty, that is their 'verdict'.

In *R v Crook* [1992] 2 All ER 687 the Court of Appeal stressed that the public should be excluded from a trial only when and to the extent that it is strictly necessary. While it is not sufficient that a public hearing would cause embarrassment for some or all of those concerned, each application for the exclusion of the public should be considered on its own merits.

15.2 Representation

Generally, the offences being tried in the Crown Court are more serious than those tried in the magistrates' courts. This fact is reflected in the increased formality and strictness of procedure and application of rules of evidence evident in the Crown Court. Therefore, although the defendant may represent himself, he is well advised to be legally represented (legal aid is not difficult to obtain for this purpose).

Prosecuting counsel must act in the interests of justice. Although he must present prosecution evidence as persuasively as possible he should not try to win at all costs. In essence, the prosecution must act fairly towards the defence.

Defence counsel, however, need not act fairly to the prosecution; he is not in court as a 'minister of justice'. He owes a duty to the court not deliberately to mislead it, but apart from that he may use all proper means available to secure an acquittal.

The defence counsel's personal opinion is irrelevant and must not affect the way in which he presents the defence. If a defendant who insists on pleading not guilty tells his counsel he is guilty, his counsel may choose to withdraw from the case; if he continues representing the defendant he may not put forward a defence on behalf of the defendant he knows to be false but must confine himself to trying to establish that the prosecution has not proved guilt beyond reasonable doubt.

Until the Crown's case is completed, the decision whether to continue the proceedings is for the prosecution alone, and the judge cannot interfere with the prosecution's decision: *R v Grafton* [1992] 4 All ER 609.

15.3 The plea; plea and directions hearings; preparatory hearings; and plea bargaining

The plea

The following pleas are available:

Guilty
The effect of this is that the defendant admits the truth of all allegations made by the prosecution against him in the indictment (or in relation to the particular count in the indictment to which he is pleading guilty). A plea of guilty must be entered by the defendant himself; it may not be entered by his counsel on his behalf.

After a plea of guilty is entered, the sentencing procedure will follow (see section 15.6 below). If the defendant has pleaded guilty on one count, but not guilty on another, sentencing will be postponed until after the trial of the not guilty count.

Not guilty
The effect of this plea is to deny the offence charged and thus put the whole of the prosecution case into issue. If this plea is entered the trial procedure detailed at section 15.6 is followed. However, it is open to the prosecution to decide not to go ahead following a not guilty plea.

Guilty to a lesser offence
Under s6(1)(b) of the Criminal Law Act 1967 the defendant may offer a plea of not guilty as charged but guilty to a 'lesser' offence. An obvious example is in relation to a charge of murder where the defendant may offer a plea of not guilty to murder but guilty to manslaughter. However, a trial judge is only obliged to leave a lesser offence to the jury where it is necessary in the interests of justice to do so: *R v Maxwell* [1990] 1 All ER 801.

If the plea is accepted, then by s6(5) of CLA 1967, the defendant is acquitted of the offence charged but stands convicted of the lesser offence and sentencing will follow accordingly.

A plea of guilty to a lesser offence must be accepted by both the prosecution and the judge; if either is not willing to accept it it will be rejected and the defendant must choose between guilty or not guilty in relation to the offence charged.

Autrefois acquit and autrefois convict
These pleas are available to the defendant when he has been either acquitted or convicted of the offence charged in the indictment on a previous occasion. Obviously, it is rare that these pleas are suitable.

Plea and direction hearings; preparatory hearings

The charge against the defendant is contained in a formal document called an 'indictment'. An indictment may contain one or more 'counts', each of which charges one offence. A new procedure has been instituted for taking the plea: *Practice Direction (Crown Court: Plea and Directions Hearings)* [1995] 4 All ER 379 (Lord Taylor CJ).

The directions set out the detailed rules which establish plea and directions hearings (PDHs) in the Crown Court which will apply to all cases (other than serious fraud) relating to trial on indictment.

The PDH should be within six weeks of committal in cases where the defendant is on bail, and four weeks where the defendant is in custody. At the PDH arraignment will normally take place. If the defendant pleads guilty the judge should proceed to sentencing whenever possible. If the plea is not guilty, prosecution and defence will be expected to assist the judge in identifying the key issues, and to provide any additional information required for the proper listing of the case. The judge will then make such orders as appear necessary to secure the proper and efficient trial of the case.

The value of PDHs was limited by the lack of a judicial power to make binding rulings on the admissibility of evidence or on questions of law. Also the scope of a PDH did not permit a detailed examination of the issues, which might be desirable in complex or potentially lengthy cases.

The CPIA 1996 contains provisions aimed at curing these defects.

1. Power to make binding rulings at a PDH – s40 CPIA 1996 confers jurisdiction on the judge holding a PDH to give binding rulings on the admissibility of evidence or questions of law or both. ('Binding' in this context means binding on the parties to the case, not binding in the sense of setting a judicial precedent.) A binding ruling given at a PDH will be operative until the case is disposed of either by verdict or by withdrawal of the prosecution's case. However, there is a power under s40 to discharge or vary such a ruling if it is in the interests of justice to do so, and any judge may make the order to discharge or vary the ruling, including the judge who made the original ruling.
2. A new system of preparatory hearings – s29 CPIA 1996 confers a general power on Crown Court judges to order a preparatory hearing for complex or potentially lengthy cases if substantial benefits are likely to be obtained from holding such a hearing. This follows the position in regard to serious fraud trials, where preparatory hearings can be ordered under Criminal Justice Act 1987. The purpose of a preparatory hearing is to allow a more detailed investigation of the issues than is possible at a PDH so as to assist the trial judge in the management of the trial and to assist the jury in the comprehension of the issues. The preparatory hearing is treated as the start of the trial.

The judge holding a preparatory hearing must arrange for the arraignment of the accused at the commencement of the hearing unless arraignment has already occurred at a PDH. (Many preparatory hearings will be ordered at PDHs when the new law is brought into force.) At the preparatory hearing the judge may order the prosecution to give to the court and to the accused a detailed written statement of evidence. If this is done the judge may then require the accused to give the court and prosecution a written statement of the nature of the defence, written objections which he may have to the prosecution case statement and written points of law which he wishes to take.

The judge at a preparatory hearing can only make binding rulings for the general purposes of that hearing, since the power to make binding rulings under s40 CPIA 1996 (above) is restricted to the judge holding a PDH. However, in practice rulings on questions of law and the admissibility of evidence are likely to fall within the general purpose of the preparatory hearing, so that the judge will be able to make binding rulings on these issues, unless a PDH has already been held and s40 rulings made on them.

Appeals may be taken from any ruling of a judge at a preparatory hearing to the Court of Appeal (Criminal Division) with leave of that judge or of the Court of Appeal itself. Further appeal lies to the House of Lords.

Plea bargaining

Traditionally judges pass a lighter sentence where an accused person has pleaded guilty because a guilty plea may indicate remorse, which is a mitigating factor, and because it spares prosecution witnesses the ordeal of giving evidence, as well as saving court time and costs. This practice of giving a 'sentence discount' for a guilty plea was well known and encouraged and has been described as 'implicit bargaining' between the judge and the defence, ie the earlier the plea of guilty, the greater the discount from sentence. The practice has now been given statutory recognition by s48 of the Criminal Justice and Public Order Act 1994. It should be noted that judges must not 'punish' an accused who pleads not guilty, or who enters a very late plea of guilty, by imposing upon conviction a more severe sentence than the offence demands.

Other explicit forms of plea bargaining also exist but are subject to safeguards against abuse. An example is 'charge bargaining' or 'plea arrangement' where the defence specifies to the prosecution a number of pleas relevant to the crime in question and then makes an offer of a particular plea of guilty being one of the less serious pleas. This plea of guilty is in return for the dropping of the other possible charges. Such bargaining is possible only in the presence of the trial judge, preferably in open court. The judge must also approve any arrangement reached. Whereas in other jurisdictions either side may approach the judge to obtain his view on the likely sentence in the event of a specified plea arrangement, such 'sentence canvassing' is officially discouraged in the United Kingdom jurisdictions, where there is a greater fear of improper pressure being put on an accused to plead guilty or on the judge to be unduly lenient. In England and Wales, the following safeguards have been suggested by Lord Parker CJ in *R v Turner* [1970] 2 WLR 1093:

1. Defence counsel may give advice, including strong advice, to his client as to his plea but must emphasise that the client should plead not guilty if he has not committed the crime in question.
2. The accused must be left with complete freedom of choice as to his plea, in full knowledge and understanding of its implications.
3. There should be freedom of access between defence counsel and the judge, but any discussions must take place in the presence of prosecuting counsel. It is always preferable for such discussions to take place in open court, although

252 Criminal Procedure III: Trial on Indictment

discussions in judges' chambers are allowed provided a recording device or shorthand writer is available.
4. The judge should never indicate his willingness to impose a different sentence for a plea of guilty. He should only indicate the type or range of sentence he has in mind in the event of conviction, whether after a plea of guilty or not guilty.

The guidelines were later confirmed in a *Practice Direction* [1976] Crim LR 561.

In *R v Pitman* [1991] 1 All ER 468 at 470–471 Lord Lane CJ gave warnings about the dangers of plea bargaining, and in particular the undesirability of secret discussions and sentence canvassing. Further warnings against sentence canvassing and plea bargaining were given in *R v Preston* [1993] 4 All ER 638 at 655 (per Lord Mustill) and in *R v Thompson* (1995) The Times 6 February (CA).

In other jurisdictions, notably the United States of America, plea bargaining is less controlled and has become a routine part of the administration of justice, with trial judges 'rubber-stamping' agreements reached between prosecution and defence (though it should be noted that in the United States, unlike the United Kingdom, the prosecution has a formal role to play in influencing the sentencing decision).

15.4 Pre-trial disclosure

The Criminal Procedure and Investigations Act 1996

Sections 3–11 CPIA 1996 set out a new three-stage procedure for the pre-trial disclosure of evidence which will apply to any type of criminal investigation except a summary trial where the accused intends to plead guilty.

Under s3 CPIA 1996 the first stage of the new procedure is known as the 'primary prosecution disclosure' stage and requires the prosecution to disclose to the accused all unused material which might in the prosecution's opinion undermine the prosecution case. This will be in the nature of a continuing duty throughout the prosecution of the case. The duty includes the obligation to provide the accused with a schedule of all other unused but possibly relevant material. The police are already obliged to make all material available to the Crown Prosecution Service, so that most decisions on pre-trial disclosure will rest with the CPS, although occasionally they will rest with others, for example customs and excise prosecutors.

The prosecution may apply to the court for permission to withhold relevant but sensitive material on the ground that it would not be in the public interest to disclose such material, for example on grounds of confidentiality or public interest immunity. It should be noted that the prosecution is under a duty not to disclose information obtained by warrants of interception issued under the Interception of Communications Act 1985.

Under s5 CPIA 1996 the second stage of pre-trial disclosure is known simply as 'defence disclosure' and requires the defence to provide the prosecution with a written statement setting out the general nature of the defence, the matters on which it takes issue with the prosecution, and the reasons why it takes such issue. The defence is not obliged to disclose the names and addresses of the witnesses intended to be called unless the defence consists of alibi evidence, in which case disclosure of alibi details is already required by s11 Criminal Justice Act 1967, which is replaced by s5(7) CPIA 1996. (The amendment simply brings the procedural requirements for the disclosure of alibi evidence into line with the new requirements for the disclosure of other evidence.)

Defence disclosure under s5 CPIA 1996 is mandatory for Crown Court trials, and appropriate inferences (including adverse inferences) may be drawn if the defence does not comply or fails adequately to comply with the disclosure requirements. Defence disclosure is voluntary for cases tried by magistrates' courts, presumably because of the more straightforward nature of summary trials.

Under s7 CPIA 1996 the third and final stage of pre-trial disclosure is known as 'secondary prosecution disclosure' and requires the prosecution to disclose any additional unused material which might reasonably assist the defence in the light of the defence disclosure under s5. Again, as under s3, the prosecution may apply to withhold sensitive material on the ground that it would not be in the public interest to disclose it.

The defence can apply at both primary and secondary prosecution disclosure stages for disclosure of specific unused prosecution material. Again the prosecution has the right to apply to withhold such material on the public interest ground.

Section 23 CPIA 1996 requires the Home Secretary to prepare a Code of Practice regulating the handling of unused material for prosecution disclosure and its preservation by the police. Such a Code also contains guidance on the handling of sensitive material, such as names of informants, and on the relevance of public interest immunity (no changes to the substantive law of public interest immunity are made by the 1996 Act).

Several notorious miscarriages of justice had been revealed during the 1980s and early 1990s and had resulted at least in part from the failure by the prosecution to disclose helpful and relevant material to the defence, a notable example being the care of Judith Ward who served 18 years in prison before her conviction was quashed on the basis of medical evidence which ought to have been disclosed by the prosecution at the time of her trial. In this case the Court of Appeal formulated common law duties of pre-trial disclosure: *R v Ward (Judith)* [1993] 2 All ER 577.

The effect was very favourable to defendants since it was for the defence to decide what unused material might prove helpful. The new duties were very onerous on the Crown Prosecution Service, which was faced in some cases with a huge administrative task in compiling and preserving all material connected with the case in question, whether the material appeared to be relevant or not. Dame Barbara Mills, the former head of the CPS, also voiced the fear of the police and prosecution that there were inadequate safeguards protecting sensitive material from being disclosed to the defence.

Consequently the changes made by the CPIA 1996 are designed to deal with the problems caused by the common law requirements on disclosure. It was felt appropriate for the prosecution to determine the relevancy of material to the defence because otherwise defendants would be able to make unreasonable demands for disclosure as a tactical ploy or as a 'fishing expedition' hoping to fasten upon some technical flaw in the prosecution case. The changes made by the 1996 Act should ease the heavy administrative burden shouldered by the investigating and prosecuting authorities as well as providing a procedure for the protection of sensitive information.

However, it was the proposal for defence disclosure which caused the most controversy as this change was said to undermine further the traditional rights of silence and the privilege against self-incrimination. In support of defence disclosure was the argument that defendants who were guilty should not be acquitted because of 'ambush' defences which could not be properly tested or refuted when sprung at the last minute in the court room. A miscarriage of justice occurred just as much when the guilty were acquitted as when the innocent were convicted. Defence disclosure was likely to encourage earlier resolution of cases through more pleas of guilty. Further, in some cases defence disclosure might persuade the prosecution to withdraw its case because the prosecution would realise the weakness of its hand from the details disclosed of the defence case. Hence both sides stood to benefit from the early identification of issues. Both sides would be encouraged to indulge in earlier and better preparation of their cases, thus enhancing the efficiency of the trial process.

Nevertheless some critics of the proposed new law argue that the changes simply 'turn the clock back' and raise once again the spectre of a miscarriage of justice of the kind that occurred to Judith Ward: see especially Murray 'Fair Is Foul and Foul Is Fair' [1996] NLJ 1288.

15.5 The trial procedure

If a plea of not guilty is entered the trial must proceed. The trial procedure is as follows.

Empanelling a jury

At each Crown Court on each day a 'jury panel' is summoned, which consists of approximately 20–25 people. As soon as the defendant has pleaded not guilty the panel is brought into court. The clerk of the court has the name of each member of the panel written on a separate card; he shuffles the cards and picks out twelve at random, one at a time. Jury challenging may take place at this stage: this is discussed in Chapter 5. If a juror is unchallenged, he takes his place in the jury box and takes the juror's oath:

'I swear by Almighty God that I will faithfully try the several issues joined between our Sovereign Lady the Queen and the prisoner at the bar and give a true verdict according to the evidence.'

Once twelve jurors are sworn in, the defendant is 'put in their charge'.

The prosecution case

The prosecution case begins with an opening speech by prosecution counsel. As the jury is likely to be unfamiliar with criminal procedure, the speech is likely to be explanatory of what they will see and hear and what their role is. The speech must also give the jury (and the judge) an 'overview' of the case against the defendant.

The prosecution must then call its evidence. The same procedure applies as it does in the magistrates' court (see Chapter 14, section 14.4). In general, witnesses must give their evidence orally in answer to questions split into examination-in-chief, cross-examination and re-examination.

The prosecution must call as witnesses all those who were called at the committal proceedings and all those who made written statements tendered under s102 of the Magistrates' Courts Act 1980. They may call further evidence provided the defence has been given notice of the same.

Evidence may be received by video link, a live television link, from two categories of witnesses, namely, those who are outside the United Kingdom and children under 14 in cases where the charge involves violence and/or sexual misconduct.

Submission of 'no case to answer'

A submission of 'no case to answer' may be made on the same basis as in the magistrates' court. There is no case to answer if the prosecution has failed to adduce evidence on which a jury, properly directed by the judge in his summing up, could properly convict.

In the Crown Court a submission of no case to answer is made in the absence of the jury and is a matter for the judge. If the judge decides there is no case to answer, the jury is called back in and directed to deliver a verdict of not guilty. If there is a case to answer – the trial continues. After the judge has ruled that there is a case to answer, the prosecution cannot be discontinued, or a plea to a lesser charge accepted, without his consent: see *R v Grafton* [1992] 4 All ER 609.

The defence case

The defence evidence is presented in the same way as the prosecution evidence after the defence opening speech. Where the defendant himself is being called, he should be called as the first witness for the defence.

When a decision is taken by a defendant not to go into the witness box it should be the invariable practice of counsel to have that decision recorded and to cause the defendant to sign the record giving a clear indication of (i) the fact of his having, of his own accord, decided not to give evidence and (ii) that he had done that bearing in mind the advice, regardless of what it was, given to him by counsel.

Closing speeches

Both sides have a right to a closing speech. The prosecution closing speech is delivered first. He may review the evidence but may not comment on the fact that the defendant has not given evidence if that be the case. Prosecuting counsel should not comment on the potentially serious consequences to police officers of their evidence being disbelieved, even where a police officer has raised the matter in his evidence.

Finally, the defence makes its closing speech. Where part of the evidence against an accused is that he had told lies, defence counsel, in his closing speech, is entitled to suggest explanations for such lies, even beyond his client's version of the case, provided that there is other evidence in the case to support such hypotheses.

The summing up by the judge

At the end of the cases presented by the prosecution and defence the judge 'sums up' the trial to the jury. The following matters must be dealt with:

1. The functions of the judge and jury – the judge decides all questions of law and the jury all questions of fact.
2. The burden and standard of proof – the prosecution must prove that the defendant is guilty and the jury must be 'satisfied so that they are sure'.
3. An explanation of the law concerning the offence charged – the jury must accept the judge's directions on the law.
4. Any particular points concerning the evidence, for example, that the evidence of an 'accomplice' must be corroborated otherwise it is unreliable.
5. A review of the evidence actually given – the judge must give a fair summary and reminder to the jury of all material evidence given by witnesses for both sides. This will also include an appraisal of the defence put forward by the defendant.
6. In a case of any seriousness, the defendant's good character.
7. The judge must direct the jury to appoint one of their number as 'foreman' and to retire and reach a unanimous verdict.

The verdict

After the judge's summing up the jury retires to the jury room to reach their verdict. It is for the judge, not the jury, to say when they will retire: *R* v *Hawkins* (1993) The Times 29 June (concern expressed by the Court of Appeal that the judge had left it to the jury to decide whether to retire in the late afternoon or following morning).

The decision of guilt or innocence is theirs alone and must be reached on the basis of the evidence they have heard and their own experience of life. Whilst doing so the jury is kept in the custody of the 'jury bailiff' (but he does not retire with them).

The jury is able to ask questions of the judge by passing him a note via the jury bailiff. The judge must show the question to counsel and if it can be answered by the judge he should do so in open court, the jury being brought back in for that purpose.

If the jury is able to reach a unanimous verdict they may return to court where their foreman will announce that verdict. The following verdicts may be returned:

1. Guilty.
2. Not guilty.
3. Not guilty as charged, but guilty of an alternative, 'lesser' offence.

However, the jury may be unable to reach a unanimous verdict. By s17 of the Juries Act 1974 the jury may acquit or convict by a majority verdict as follows:

Jury number	Majority required
12	11 to 1 or 10 to 2
11	10 to 1
10	9 to 1
9	Must be unanimous

The judge may only direct the jury that he would be willing to accept a majority verdict after the jury has been deliberating for at least two hours. The time period thereafter is within the judge's discretion.

If, despite sufficient time for deliberation, the jury is unable to reach a verdict, the judge must discharge the jury from giving one.

15.6 Sentencing

After the defendant has pleaded or been found guilty of the offence charged, the sentence procedure begins, that is, the procedure by which the punishment is fixed.

Sentencing involves a four-stage procedure: that is, the facts of the offence, the defendant's antecedents, reports on the defendant, and a plea in mitigation.

The facts of the offence

This stage is necessary only when the defendant has pleaded guilty: if he has been found guilty the judge is well aware of the facts of his offence from having listened to the evidence in the trial.

The 'facts' are given by the prosecution and, therefore, are the prosecution's version of events. However, by pleading guilty the defendant has admitted their truth.

It is necessary for the judge to know the facts of the offence in order to be able to fix the sentence. Many offences vary in their degree of seriousness; for example, a plea of guilty to theft may be a plea of guilty to stealing £10,000 from an employer's safe or to shoplifting a newspaper on the spur of the moment. The degree of seriousness of the particular offence must be reflected in the sentence given.

It is also important that the details of what happened are known generally; otherwise the justice of the sentence passed may not be checked.

The prosecution gets the facts of the case from the statements and proofs of evidence of the witnesses who would have been called by them had there been a trial.

The prosecution must not ask for any particular sentence to be passed nor should they comment on how severe or lenient the judge should be.

The defendant's antecedents

These involve previous convictions, recorded cautions, and other personal or relevant details pertaining to the convicted person.

It should be noted that any previous convictions which are 'spent' must be marked as such on the antecedents. Under the Rehabilitation of Offenders Act 1974, as amended, it is possible for a conviction to be 'spent' after a specified period of time – the rehabilitation period. The Act provided that a person need not declare a spent conviction for certain purposes (eg when applying for certain jobs). However, although a spent previous conviction must be marked as such on the defendant's antecedents, a judge is entitled to take account of it in fixing sentence for a subsequent offence.

Reports on the defendant

Reports on the defendant are often prepared for the judge in the Crown Court (magistrates rarely see any when sentencing in the magistrates' court).

The types of reports which may be prepared are as follows.

Pre-sentence reports

Prepared by a court welfare officer (or local authority social worker), after interviewing the defendant. It deals with the defendant's circumstances and income and any social problems he may have. The conclusion is a recommendation as to how the defendant could be dealt with. The officer who prepared the report may be required to give evidence and may be cross-examined by the defence.

Medical and psychiatric reports

There must be consideration of medical reports before a defendant may be ordered to be detained in a mental hospital.

Plea in mitigation

Finally, a plea in mitigation may be delivered by the defence. The purpose of the plea is to persuade the judge to pass as lenient a sentence as can be justified in all the circumstances. In order to so persuade the judge, the defence will usually deal with the following aspects of the defendant and the offence.

The offence itself
The defence should put forward any factor which shows the offence up in a less serious light. For example, its commission was unplanned.

Explanation of the offence
There may be factors which explain why the offence was committed. For example, the defendant is young and inexperienced and was led astray by older people, or the defendant stole when he was in great financial difficulty.

The defendant's future
Factors such as a new job, becoming engaged to be married or other indications of a stable domestic background may be put forward as indicating that it is unlikely that the defendant will offend again.

Finally, if the defendant has no previous convictions, co-operated with the police after arrest pleaded guilty and shown remorse, all these factors may be put forward in favour of the defendant.

Sentences

A wide range of sentencing options, including fines and imprisonment, are available to the Crown Court judge.

16

Criminal Appeals

16.1 Appeals following a summary trial

16.2 Appeals following a trial on indictment

16.3 Miscarriages of justice: the historical position

16.4 The Criminal Cases Review Commission (CCRC)

16.1 Appeals following a summary trial

Appeal to the Crown Court

A defendant may appeal from the magistrates' court to the Crown Court: on conviction and sentence if he pleaded not guilty; and on sentence only if he pleaded guilty. No leave to appeal is required. The prosecution has no right of appeal against an acquittal or an unduly lenient sentence.

There is no right of appeal against a committal to the Crown Court for sentencing.

The procedure for appeal is as follows:

1. Defendant gives notice of appeal within 21 days after the day on which the decision of the magistrates was given, to the magistrates' clerk and to the prosecution.
2. The hearing before the Crown Court is a complete rehearing of the case. Therefore, the prosecution must prove its case afresh by calling its witnesses. New evidence may be tendered without leave of the court.
3. On appeals against conviction, the Crown Court may confirm, reverse or vary the decision of the magistrates' court. This includes the power to increase the sentence to whatever the magistrates had the jurisdiction to impose.
4. On appeals against sentence, the Crown Court may impose any sentence which the magistrates' court could have passed.
5. By s48(2) of the Supreme Court Act 1981 the Crown Court may 'make such other order in the matter as the court thinks just, and by such order exercise any power which the said authority might have exercised.'
6. Remit the matter with its opinion to the magistrates' court.

Appeals against conviction are allowed on one broad ground, namely that the conviction was against the weight of the evidence.

A Crown Court sitting in an appellate capacity has to give reasons for its decision, ie enough to show that it had identified the main contentious issues and how it had resolved each of them. A refusal to give such reasons could amount to a denial of natural justice and lead to the quashing of the decision: *R v Harrow Crown Court, ex parte Dave* [1994] 1 WLR 98.

Appeal to the Queen's Bench Division of the High Court by way of case stated

By s111(1) of the Magistrates' Courts Act 1980, any person who was a party to proceedings before or aggrieved by the decision of the magistrates, may appeal against the proceeding on the ground that it is wrong in law or in excess of jurisdiction by applying to the magistrates' court to state a case for the opinion of a Divisional Court of the Queen's Bench Division.

Application must be in writing, made within 21 days after the date of the decision of the magistrates and indicating the point of law on which the opinion of the High Court is sought.

The 'case' to be stated by the magistrates must include the arguments which they heard, the facts found by them and their decision. In settling a statement of the case the parties should also be consulted.

At the hearing before the High Court the parties will (usually) be represented by counsel and the court will determine the questions of law raised. The magistrates themselves are not usually represented, although they may file an affidavit dealing with any matters they consider to be of importance and relevance.

The High Court may:

1. Reverse, affirm or amend the magistrates' decision.
2. Remit the matter to the magistrates with its opinion.
3. Make such other order as it sees fit, eg, order a re-hearing by the same or a different bench: *Griffith v Jenkins* [1992] 2 WLR 28.

In *Tucker v Director of Public Prosecutions* [1992] 4 All ER 901 the Divisional Court stressed that a severe sentence imposed at the discretion of justices would be varied on an appeal to the Divisional Court only if it appeared to be astonishing by any acceptable standards. In all but the most exceptional circumstances the appropriate course for those dissatisfied by the sentence imposed by magistrates was to go to the Crown Court for a re-hearing.

Any order, judgment or other decision of the Crown Court may be questioned by any party to the proceedings, on the ground that it is wrong in law or is in excess of jurisdiction, by applying to the Crown Court to have a case stated by that court for the opinion of the High Court: s28(1) of the Supreme Court Act 1981. The power of the High Court to review decisions of the Crown Court is limited to the provisions of ss28 and 29 of the Supreme Court Act 1981. The general power of judicial review in s31 is subject to those sections: *R v Chelmsford Crown Court, ex parte Chief Constable of Essex Police* [1994] 1 WLR 359.

Appeal to the House of Lords

An appeal to the House of Lords may be made from the Divisional Court of the Queen's Bench Division. In order to do so there must be a certificate from the Divisional Court that a point of law of general public importance is involved. Further, there must be leave to appeal either from the Divisional Court or from the House of Lords itself.

16.2 Appeals following a trial on indictment

Introduction

The position is governed by the Criminal Appeal Act 1968, as amended by the Criminal Appeal Act 1995. Appeal is to the Court of Appeal (Criminal Division). The changes made by the 1995 Act give effect to many of the recommendations of the Royal Commission on Criminal Justice (1993) Cmnd 2263, and are designed to deal with some of the problems which caused notorious miscarriages of justice, such as the cases of the Birmingham Six, the Guildford Four, Judith Ward and the 'Bridgewater Three' (three men released after serving 18 years in prison, convictions being quashed because of forged confessions concocted by a corrupt police unit. The three men, together with a fourth man who died in prison in 1981, had been wrongly convicted of the murder of a newspaper delivery boy, Carl Bridgewater, in 1979). It is hoped that the reforms introduced by the 1995 Act will eliminate or at least minimise the risk of further such miscarriages of justice in future years.

Appeal against conviction: the ground of appeal

There may be an appeal against conviction based on:

1. a question of law alone; or
2. a question of fact alone; or
3. a question of mixed law and fact.

Leave to appeal is required from the Court of Appeal, unless the trial judge certifies that the case is fit for appeal: s1(1) of the 1995 Act.

Even if the defendant pleaded guilty, there may be an appeal against conviction if the court is satisfied that a ground of appeal is established: *R v Lee* [1984] 1 WLR 578. However, for this purpose the plea of guilty must have been tendered mistakenly or without intention to admit the truth of the offence charged. Sometimes such a plea may be tendered as a result of an erroneous ruling by the trial judge which appeared to make an acquittal legally impossible; in such circumstances an appeal against the conviction is available. However, it is not available if the plea of guilty was not founded upon such a ruling, eg where the ruling may have made the case against the defendant appear factually overwhelming but not legally conclusive. There is no appeal available against a plea of guilty tendered in those circumstances: *R v Chalkley; R v Jeffries* [1998] 2 All ER 155 (CA). Under the 1968 Act there were three grounds of appeal:

1. that the conviction was unsafe or unsatisfactory;
2. that there had been a wrong decision by the trial judge on any question of law; and
3. that there had been a material irregularity in the course of the trial: s2(1) of the 1968 Act.

Even if grounds (2) and (3) were established, the Court of Appeal had discretion to dismiss the appeal if it considered that no miscarriage of justice had actually occurred: the 'proviso' to s2(1) of the 1968 Act. The use of the proviso was controversial since it required the appeal judges to ask themselves whether a reasonable jury, properly directed, would still have reached the same verdict: *R v McIlkenny* [1992] 2 All ER 417; *R v Maguire* [1992] 2 All ER 433. Yet this was logically impossible since, whereas a jury sees and hears all the witnesses, the appeal judges rely mainly on the transcript of the trial and submissions from appeal counsel, and only rarely receive new oral evidence from witnesses. It was feared that the appeal judges, perceived to be part of the 'Establishment', would be reluctant to set aside convictions and, in order to reassure public opinion, it was made clear that the appeal should be allowed if the appeal judges had a 'lurking doubt' about the safety of the conviction: *Stafford v DPP* [1974] AC 878; [1973] 3 All ER 762 (HL).

Nevertheless, criticism continued of the narrow grounds of appeal, which were said to be a 'strait jacket' fettering the exercise of discretion by appeal judges. The Royal Commission on Criminal Justice (1993) Cm 2263 recommended the substitution of one broad ground of appeal, namely that the conviction is 'unsafe or may be unsafe'. The reform enacted by s2(1) of the 1995 Act substitutes a single ground of appeal, namely that the conviction 'is unsafe'. Whilst the reform has been welcomed by some as creating a broader ground of appeal than under the 1968 Act, it has also been criticised for not following the wording recommended by the Royal Commission. Is the omission of the words 'or may be unsafe' an indication that the appeal judges need no longer apply the 'lurking doubt' principle? This possibility was suggested by Professor J C Smith ([1995] NLJ 533 and 572) and his view has been confirmed by the Court of Appeal: *R v Farrow* (1998) The Times 20 October. In this case it was said that the new test of 'unsafeness' under the amended s2(1) of the 1968 Act has the advantages of brevity and simplicity and that it would not be appropriate to place a gloss on that test in the form of the 'lurking doubt' concept.

The basis of an appeal contending an unsafe conviction will usually be a misdirection of law by the trial judge, either during the course of the trial or in the summing-up to the jury. In a recent notorious miscarriage of justice case the conviction of a man executed for murder in 1953 was quashed 45 years later because the Court of Appeal was at long last persuaded that the trial judge's summing-up was so defective and biased that the accused had been denied a fair trial: *R v Bentley* (1998) The Times 31 July (CA).

Apart from misdirection it is possible that other matters that would have been classified as 'material irregularities' under the unamended 1968 Act will today form the basis of an appeal based simply on the unsafeness of the conviction under s2(1) of the amended 1968 Act, eg constant interruptions by the trial judge which prevent the fair presentation of a witness's testimony or of the defence case as a whole.

In *R v Clinton* [1993] 2 All ER 998 it was argued that the negligence of defence counsel in the presentation of the defence could constitute a material irregularity but it was held that only 'flagrantly incompetent' advice or advocacy could constitute a ground of appeal. The Royal Commission had recommended that a mistaken decision of defence counsel, eg in not calling a particular witness, should be a basis for appeal, but this view was rejected in *R v Satpal Ram* (1995) The Times 7 December, where it was held that a 'reasonable' decision of defence counsel, even though mistaken or unwise in hindsight, could not form a basis for appeal since otherwise the adversary system of justice, which depended heavily on the honest and independent judgment of counsel, would be undermined.

It is perhaps not surprising that in view of the notorious reluctance of appeal judges to set aside convictions some critics still contend that, even after the reforms introduced by the 1995 Act, the appeal judges will continue to be difficult to persuade of the need to allow an appeal. This view appears to be confirmed by the approach adopted in *R v Chalkley; R v Jeffries* [1998] 2 All ER 155, where the appellants had contended, inter alia, that the Court of Appeal should consider not only the safeness of the conviction but also whether it was a 'satisfactory' conviction (the language used in the unamended 1968 Act). The contention was rejected – under the amended s2(1) of the 1968 Act the sole ground for appeal is the safety of the conviction and it is not open to the Court of Appeal to consider whether a 'safe' conviction might in some other respect be 'unsatisfactory'. The former tests of 'unsatisfactoriness' and 'material irregularity' are no longer available as grounds of appeal, although they can be used as aids to determining the safety of a conviction.

Appeal against conviction: fresh evidence

Section 23 of the 1968 Act empowered the Court of Appeal to receive fresh evidence which was 'likely to be credible': see further *R v Gilfoyle* [1996] 3 All ER 883. Critics argued that the Court of Appeal interpreted this power too narrowly by displaying a sceptical attitude toward such evidence, in line with its general reluctance to overturn convictions. Section 23 is amended by s4(1) of the 1995 Act, ostensibly to try to deal with this problem. The new power to receive fresh evidence is made subject to a duty to consider the same factors as under s23 of the 1968 Act, namely:

1. credibility;
2. relevance to the safety of the conviction;
3. admissibility at trial; and
4. reasonableness of the explanation for any failure to adduce evidence at trial.

The change brought in by s4(1) of the 1995 Act is in the wording of the test on credibility: the appeal judges are encouraged to receive fresh evidence which is 'capable of belief' rather than 'likely to be credible'. The change was apparently designed to encourage the appeal judges to take a broader, more sympathetic approach to the issue of fresh evidence, but some critics have argued that it is a semantic change which will make no difference. Only time will tell, but in view of the need to restore public confidence in the appeal system after several notorious miscarriages of justice it would be surprising and disappointing if in future the Court of Appeal does not display a more sympathetic treatment of fresh evidence. It appears that the Court of Appeal will be reluctant to receive fresh *expert* evidence, either because the appellant should have been aware of its availability at the time of the trial or because the new test of credibility is more appropriately applied to *factual* evidence: R v *Jones (Steven Martin)* (1996) The Times 23 July.

Appeal against conviction: powers of the Court of Appeal in disposing of an appeal

The Court of Appeal may either:

1. allow the appeal and quash the conviction: or
2. allow the appeal, quash the conviction but substitute a conviction of some other offence and sentence the defendant accordingly. This power is contained in s3(1) of the 1968 Act and should be exercised only where the appeal judges are satisfied that the jury could have found the defendant guilty of the other offence on the facts presented at the trial: R v *Graham (HK) and Others* [1997] 1 Cr App R 302. The power is not available if the defendant pleaded guilty to offences prior to being put in charge of the jury because s3(1) of the 1968 Act expressly contemplates a verdict from a jury: R v *Horsman* [1997] 3 All ER 385 (appellant had pleaded guilty to obtaining property by deception but successfully appealed on the basis of the reinterpretation of law that occurred in R v *Preddy* [1996] 3 All ER 481; his conviction had to be quashed, the s3(1) power being unavailable); or
3. allow the appeal, quash the conviction but order a retrial if it is in the interests of justice to do so, bearing in mind the lapse of time since the trial, the continuing availability of witnesses, etc: s53 Criminal Justice Act 1988 and R v *Grafton* [1992] 4 All ER 609; or

4. dismiss the appeal. If the Court of Appeal takes the view that the appeal was frivolous it can order that any time spent by the defendant in custody pending the appeal, which normally would count as part of the sentence, shall not count as part of the sentence. Apart from this, the Court of Appeal has no power to increase a sentence when dismissing an appeal against conviction.

It should also be noted that, although the prosecution has no right of appeal against an acquittal, there is a right of appeal on a point of law to enable the Court of Appeal to deal with a misdirection without affecting the jury's verdict of not guilty: s36 Criminal Justice Act 1972. There is also a new power to set aside an acquittal obtained by intimidation: see Chapter 5, section 5.2, *The jury in criminal cases: the verdict.*

Appeal against sentence

The defendant may appeal against the sentence passed by the Crown Court, but only with the leave of the Court of Appeal or the Crown Court judge: s9 and s11, as amended, CAA 1968. There is no appeal against a sentence fixed by law.

The Court of Appeal will not interfere with the discretion of the judge below and will only interfere if the sentence is wrong in principle or manifestly excessive. It has power to reduce the sentence or substitute one form of detention for another.

On the recommendation of the Attorney-General the prosecution may appeal against an unduly lenient sentence to the Court of Appeal: ss35, as amended, and 36 of the Criminal Justice Act 1988. This measure was introduced following an outcry in the media at the sentences imposed in certain cases. It has been applied, for example, to substitute detention for two years, pursuant to s53(2) of the Children and Young Persons Act 1933, for a non-custodial sentence passed on a 15-year-old boy convicted of rape (*R* v *W* (1993) The Times 16 March) and to increase a sentence for careless driving causing death having consumed alcohol above the prescribed limit: *Attorney-General's Reference (No 14 of 1993)* [1994] RTR 49.

Until 1 March 1994 s36 of the 1988 Act applied only to cases where the offence was triable on indictment only. Since that date it has applied also to three triable either way offences, ie indecent assault, cruelty to or neglect of children and making threats to kill. However, these extended rights of appeal apply only where the case was heard, or sentence was passed, in the Crown Court.

Appeals to the House of Lords

Either the prosecution or the defence may appeal from the Court of Appeal to the House of Lords if both the following requirements are satisfied:

1. The Court of Appeal certifies that a point of law of general public importance is involved in the decisions.
2. Either the Court of Appeal or the House of Lords gives leave on the ground that the point in issue is one which ought to be considered by the House of Lords.

The House of Lords may exercise the same powers as those exercised by the Court of Appeal: *R* v *Mandair* [1994] 2 All ER 715.

Once a criminal appeal has been decided by the House of Lords, either dismissing the defendant's appeal or directing that his conviction be restored, it is not open to him to apply to the Court of Appeal to have his appeal relisted for the hearing of grounds of appeal not considered by the House of Lords: *R* v *Berry (No 2)* [1991] 1 WLR 125. However, the House of Lords may remit a case to the Court of Appeal where a ground of appeal had not been disposed of by the Court of Appeal: see *R* v *Mandair*, above.

Further, in exceptional cases the House of Lords has inherent jurisdiction to set aside an earlier ruling of the House if it has caused injustice. Whilst the House is naturally reluctant to re-open an appeal it will do so if a party has been subject to an unfair procedure. Apart from such exceptional cases there is no right of appeal from decisions of the House: *Re Pinochet Urgarte* [1999] NLJ Rep 88.

16.3 Miscarriages of justice: the historical position

Section 17 of the 1968 Act enabled the Home Secretary to refer to the Court of Appeal any conviction which the Home Secretary had reason to believe might be unsafe. This referral power was an important device for ensuring reconsideration of cases since, once an appeal had been dismissed, no further appeals could be brought under s2 of the 1968 Act: *R* v *Pinfold* [1988] 2 All ER 217. However, the Home Office only had limited resources to investigate petitions alleging miscarriages of justice, and even where a case was referred the Court of Appeal demonstrated its traditional reluctance to interfere with convictions, notably on such cases as the Birmingham Six, who were the subject of several referrals before the Court of Appeal was persuaded to quash the convictions.

The Royal Commission on Criminal Justice recommended the abolition of the Home Secretary's role in appeals and the establishment of an independent Criminal Cases Review authority to take its place. The implementation of this proposal by the 1995 Act forms the centrepiece of the new appeal system.

16.4 The Criminal Cases Review Commission (CCRC)

The Commission was established by ss8–14 of and Schedule 1 to the 1995 Act and began its work on 1 April 1997. At the time of writing the CCRC is chaired by Sir Frederick Crawford, former Vice-Chancellor of Aston University, and has in total 14 members of whom there is a lay majority who have some experience of the criminal justice and complaints system. However, there appear to be no members with specific knowledge of or experience in criminal defence work and miscarriages of justice, and this omission has caused some criticism of the likely effectiveness of the new body. Members are appointed for terms of five years by the Queen on the advice of the Prime Minister. The Home Secretary's referral powers are abolished by s3 of the 1995 Act.

The CCRC is expected to deal with an estimated average of 800 cases each year. It may consider on broad grounds any allegation of a miscarriage of justice resulting from either a conviction or sentence in either the Crown Court or the magistrates' court, either upon a referral with leave of the Court of Appeal (which may wish to have the matter investigated in an inquisitorial manner) or after the dismissal of an appeal. The CCRC can receive complaints direct from members of the public and has power to interview all applicants, including prisoners. However, legal aid is not available to such applications.

Section 13 of the 1995 Act provides that the CCRC shall not refer a case to the Court of Appeal unless it considers that there is a 'real possibility' that the conviction will be quashed by the Court of Appeal.

The CCRC enjoys an annual budget of approximately £4 million to provide support resources, including a staff of approximately 60, comprising lawyers, forensic scientists and other advisers (including approximately 25 case workers). However, the CCRC has no investigators of its own and must rely on the police, though it has a discretion to supervise police enquiries. Since some of the notorious miscarriages of justice had been caused and covered up by police misconduct, this continuing reliance on police investigations has been criticised by some as a 'fatal flaw' in the new system, undermining the apparent independence of the CCRC from the police.

Decisions of the CCRC are final, although disappointed applicants will be free to try again. The determination of referrals from the CCRC will continue to be a matter for the Court of Appeal acting on the usual adversary principles. The Home Secretary retains his power to pardon offenders under the royal prerogative of mercy and may be assisted by the CCRC for this purpose: s16 of the 1995 Act.

Generally the reforms introduced by the 1995 Act have been welcomed by the Bar, the Law Society and civil liberties groups although, as seen above, criticisms of some aspects of the reforms have been voiced. The Commission enjoyed its first high profile success when referring the case of Derek Bentley to the Court of Appeal. Bentley had been convicted of the murder of a policeman and had been executed in January 1953. The circumstances of his conviction gave rise to a long campaign by his family and a feature film was made of the case (*Let Him Have It*, 1993). Eventually a Royal Pardon was granted, but in respect of the sentence only. The family continued their campaign for the conviction itself to be quashed and they persuaded the Commission to refer the case to the Court of Appeal, which quashed the conviction on the ground of a defective summing-up by the trial judge: *R* v *Bentley* (1998) The Times 31 July. However, it remains to be seen whether the Commission will have success with lower profile referrals.

Part VI: European Legal Systems

17

The European Community and the European Union I

17.1 Introduction

17.2 The institutions of the European Union

17.3 The sources of European Community law

17.1 Introduction

The European Union, as it is has been called since 1992, can trace its origins back to the immediate post-war era of the late 1940s and early 1950s. Europe had been ravaged by two World Wars, and there was a political will to ensure that such a catastrophic breakdown in diplomatic relations, with consequent loss of life and systematic abuse of human rights, should not be allowed to recur. The belief was that the more the individual states of Europe became integrated and interdependent, the less likely it would be that any one state would resort to armed force against another. In May 1950 the French Foreign Minister, Robert Schuman (working closely with Jean Monnet) outlined the aims and methods of the so-called 'Schuman' plan, which sought to integrate the coal and steel industries of those Western European countries wishing participate in the scheme. It will be noted that the coal and steel industries were central to any country having militaristic ambitions, hence the impetus to achieve integration in these areas. The result was the European Coal and Steel Community (ECSC), formally established in 1951 when six countries – Belgium, France, the Federal Republic of Germany, Italy, Luxembourg and The Netherlands – signed the Treaty of Paris 1951. Common institutions were established to govern the operation and development of the coal and steel industries in the member states. The establishment of the ECSC was seen by many as the first step towards greater unity in Europe, the intention being that, following the integration in areas of coal and steel production, economies as a whole of the member countries would be integrated. Once economic integration was completed it was thought that the way might be open to the formation of a United States of Europe. In 1957, the process of integration was taken a step further with the signing of the Treaty of Rome establishing what was, until 1992, known as the European

Economic Community (EEC). This period also saw the formation of the European Atomic Energy Community (Euratom), to encourage co-operation in the peaceful use and development of nuclear energy.

Terminology

Following the signing of the Treaty on European Union (TEU) 1992 or 'Maastricht Treaty', the term 'European Economic Community' (EEC) was dropped in favour of 'European Community' (EC). The TEU 1992 also made it clear that the original Treaty of Rome, as amended by the Single European Act (SEA) 1986 and the TEU 1992, was henceforth to be known as the EC Treaty. Other terminological changes flowing from TEU 1992 are as follows: the Council of Ministers becomes the 'Council of the European Union'; the Commission becomes the 'European Commission'. The Treaty on European Union (TEU) 1997 or 'Amsterdam Treaty' provides that the EC is itself now part of a wider entity, the European Union (EU). The EU is based on three 'pillars': (i) the EC, including the European Coal and Steel Community and Euratom; (ii) the common foreign and security policy; and (iii) co-operation in the fields of justice and home affairs. EC institutions have no jurisdiction in relation to (ii) and (iii) unless the Council of the EC decides otherwise. Matters in (ii) and (iii) are governed by inter-governmental co-operation at a national level.

Although there is a tendency to use the terms 'EU law' and 'EC law' interchangeably, it is technically incorrect to use the former expression as the EU does not actually enact legislation. In the technical sense the expression 'Community law' should now only be used in respect of law arising under the EC Treaty.

The objectives of the European Union

The EC has as its aim the welding of Europe into a single prosperous area by abolishing restrictions affecting the movement of people, goods and capital; in effect an internal market without internal frontiers in which the free movement of goods, persons, services and capital can be achieved. Article 2 of the EC Treaty provides:

> 'The Community shall have as its task, by establishing a common market and progressively approximating the economic policies of member states, to promote throughout the Community a harmonious development of economic activities, a continuous and balanced expansion, an increase in stability, an accelerated raising of the standard of living and closer relations between the states belonging to it.'

Article 3 of the Treaty details the means by which these aims are to be achieved. This includes, for example, the elimination of customs duties and quantitative restrictions on the import and export of goods between member states. With the abolition of all customs duties between member states there will be a single European market of approximately 270 million customers available to producers in Europe, and European manufacturers will be able to produce goods more cheaply on the scale that is practised for example in the United States. Article 3 also envisages the establishment of a common commercial policy, an internal market characterised by the abolition, as between member states, of obstacles to free movement of goods, persons, services and capital. Under the common agricultural policy, designed to keep the price of foodstuffs at a sufficiently high level to ensure an adequate return for farmers without the need for subsidies, foodstuffs entering member states from outside the European Union have levies placed upon them to make them as expensive as those offered for sale by producers in the EC. Prices are not allowed to fall to their natural level because producers can insist on designated national authorities intervening to buy foodstuffs at a certain price – the 'intervention' price fixed each year by the Council. Provision is also made in art 3 for the approximation of laws of member states to the extent required for the proper functioning of internal market; development of a policy on environmental matters; and a common policy on transport. In all the above the EC aims to eliminate inequalities and to promote equality between men and women.

In 1973 the original six member countries were joined by Denmark, Ireland and the United Kingdom. In January 1981 Greece joined the Community and Spain and Portugal also became members on 1 January 1986. With effect from 1 January 1995 membership increased to 15, with the addition of Austria, Finland and Sweden. Following the Amsterdam Summit in 1997 negotiations are in train to admit Poland, Hungary, the Czech Republic, Slovenia, Estonia and Cyprus to an enlarged EU. The preconditions for membership are: stable democratic political institutions; observance of the rule of law; respect for human rights; and a viable market economy able to withstand competition from other member states.

Towards a federal Europe: the Maastricht and Amsterdam Treaties

Following a meeting of heads of government of members states in Maastricht in December 1991, the TEU 1992 (the 'Maastricht Treaty') was signed by all member states, with certain exceptions being made by the United Kingdom, on 7 February 1992. The Treaty accelerated the move towards a federal, unified, Europe, providing, for example, that every national of each member state was to be granted the status of citizen of the EU, in addition to national citizenship. The TEU 1992 laid down a timetable for monetary union, with the aim that a single currency (the ECU) should be in circulation by 1999.

As with previous EC treaties, and in accordance with constitutional requirements, the TEU 1992 had to be incorporated into United Kingdom law by means of domestic legislation, hence the enactment of the European Communities (Amendment) Act 1993. The Conservative government of the day sought an opt-out for the United Kingdom as regards certain aspects of the TEU 1992 'package' (eg limitation upon working hours etc), but the Labour government elected in May 1997 has agreed that the United Kingdom should be bound by them.

The ratification of the TEU 1992 prompted an application for judicial review in *R v Secretary of State for Foreign and Commonwealth Affairs, ex parte Rees Mogg* [1994]

2 WLR 115. The applicant sought a declaration that any such ratification would be unlawful on the ground (inter alia) that the establishment of a common foreign policy (under Title V of TEU 1992) would involve a loss of prerogative power, which could only be achieved by way of statutory enactment. Dismissing the application, the court held that, on the facts, the ratification of Title V of the Maastricht Treaty did not involve a diminution of prerogative power as it would be open to the United Kingdom to renege on its obligations under the Treaty, and re-assert the prerogative power to formulate and execute foreign policy in the areas affected.

Building upon progress made with the TEU 1992, negotiations commenced in Turin on 29 March 1996, culminating in the signing of the TEU 1997 (the 'Amsterdam Treaty') by the leaders of every member state of the European Union on 17 June 1997. The TEU 1997, which takes effect once it has been ratified in each member state, seeks to consolidate each of the three pillars of the EU put in place by the TEU 1992. In addition to addressing issues related to strengthening the operation of the EU institutions (as to which see below), specific matters addressed by TEU 1997 are:

Rights of EU citizens

The EU will co-ordinate policies aimed at reducing unemployment, via the European Investment Bank. With the signing of the Treaty the United Kingdom has accepted the agreement on social policy providing for a maximum working week and a minimum wage. Under the Treaty the EU will monitor the extent to which member states adhere to their obligations under the European Convention on Human Rights. The TEU 1997 contains a non-discrimination clause that allows the EU to take action against all forms of discrimination.

Removing remaining obstacles to freedom of movement and strengthening security

In accordance with the 1990 Schengen Agreement, identity checks will be abolished at internal frontiers with the exception of the borders of Ireland and the United Kingdom. Controls at external frontiers and ports will remain in place. The TEU 1997 also envisages a harmonisation of rules on the issuing of visas and the granting of asylum to those arriving from outside the EU. Minimum European norms will be established regarding facilities provided for asylum seekers. The role of Europol will be expanded and developed in respect of its data-gathering activities and investigative roles. There is no proposal that it should take over any of the policing functions of the forces of member states. Note that the TEU 1997 moves some aspects of justice and home affairs, such as asylum and immigration, from the third pillar of the EU to the first, thus bringing them within the jurisdiction of the EC institutions, notable the European Court of Justice.

17.2 The institutions of the European Union

The Council of the European Union

The Council is the EC's principal decision-making body. The government of each of the 15 nations in the European Union has a seat on the Council. The foreign minister is usually a country's main representative, but a government is free to send any of its ministers to Council meetings. The Council's membership thus varies with the subject scheduled for discussion. Finance ministers will attend for discussion of economic issues, transport ministers for discussion of transport policy, agriculture ministers for discussion of the common agricultural policy, and so on. Unlike the European Commission, the Council's members represent their national interests first and foremost. The presidency of the Council rotates between the member governments at six-monthly intervals.

Under art 202 EC Treaty (formerly art 145) the functions of the Council are stated as being to ensure that the objectives of the EC Treaty are attained, and to ensure the co-ordination of economic policies of member states. The Council carries out these functions by making policy decisions, issuing regulations and directives, and acting upon proposals from the Commission.

The Council can determine issues by a simple majority vote, by qualified majority voting, or by means of a unanimous decision, depending on the procedure required by the EC Treaty, as amended. The provisions regulating the voting procedures of the Council attempt to fulfil two aims: first, to ensure that the Council cannot easily take a high-handed approach to Commission proposals; and, second, to ensure that important proposals aimed at promoting greater integration of member states should not be held back by the veto of one member state. Hence the Council may be able to accept Commission proposals by a qualified majority, but unanimity is required if it seeks to amend a Commission proposal against the wishes of the Commission. For some particularly important decisions, such as acceptance of a new member state or changes in the number of Commissioners, unanimity is required.

As art 205 EC Treaty (formerly art 148) explains, under the system of qualified majority voting the votes of members are 'weighted' according to population. In effect a country will be allocated roughly one vote for every six million of population, although there are anomalies in respect of the smaller nations so as to ensure that their views are not totally marginalised. The entry into the European Union of Austria, Finland and Sweden has increased the total number of votes to 87, and the number of votes needed to form a 'blocking minority' has increased proportionately to 25. The use of qualified majority voting has gradually increased through measures introduced in the SEA 1986, and more recently in the TEU 1997, the latter extending its use to areas such as social exclusion, public health, equal opportunities and employment incentives.

Although in theory it should become more difficult for any one member state to exercise a power of veto by opposing a measure in Council, in reality the Council has recognised that there may be a heavy political price to pay for enforcing on a member state a measure that it bitterly opposes, and which is likely to cause widespread anti-EC sentiment within that member state. Hence, under what is known as the Luxembourg Accord (the Luxembourg Agreement of 1966) the Council will not normally impose a decision on a member state by way of qualified majority voting if a member state can show that the decision would be detrimental to its vital national interests. The Luxembourg Accord has no legal status but has proved an important factor in negotiations between member states. The Council is not bound to accept an assertion by a member state that a matter ought not to be decided by qualified majority voting on the grounds that a vital national interest is affected. The ultimate decision rests with the Council.

Although the Council has a shifting membership, some stability and consistency is ensured by the work of the Committee of Permanent Representatives of Member States (COREPER), which not only undertakes the preparatory work for Council meetings but also co-ordinates meetings of senior civil servants from member states. COREPER is organised on a committee basis, with work being split between the first committee dealing with social affairs and transport, and the second dealing with economic and foreign affairs. Agricultural issues fall under the responsibility of a separate agriculture committee.

The European Commission

The treaties assign the European Commission a wide range of duties. It is the guardian of the treaties setting up the EC and is responsible for seeing that they are implemented. It is the initiator of Community policy and oversees the execution of policy initiatives. The Commission can investigate instances of member states failing to fulfil treaty obligations, and if necessary deliver a reasoned opinion. Non-compliance with such an opinion will result in the Commission referring the matter to the European Court of Justice: see art 226 EC Treaty.

The European Commission, an independent body with executive powers and responsibility, comprises 20 Commissioners chosen for their all-round capability by agreement between the governments of the member states. At present Germany, United Kingdom, France, Italy and Ireland have two commissioners each. A Commissioner is obliged to act in the Community's interests as opposed to the interests of the country of which he or she is a national. Throughout their four-year term of office Commissioners remain independent of their respective governments and of the Council. The Council cannot remove any Commissioner from office; only the European Parliament can compel the European Commission to resign as a body by passing a motion of censure. The number of Commissioners is likely to be reviewed prior to further enlargement of EU membership.

The Commission as a whole is headed by a President, appointed by the Commission in consultation with member states. Each Commissioner heads a department with special responsibilities for one area of Community policy, such as economic affairs, agriculture, the environment and transport. Regular discussions are held between a Commissioner's department and interested parties. As a result of these discussions the relevant Commissioner formulates draft proposals which he believes will help to improve the quality of life of Community citizens. The draft proposals are discussed by all the Commissioners who then decide on the nature of the final proposal. Decisions are taken on a collegiate basis.

The TEU 1997 expands the scope of the European Commission's competence as regards policy initiatives in areas such as employment and health.

Economic and Social Committee

In addition, there is also a body known as the Economic and Social Committee that plays a consultative role in the decision-making processes of the Council and Commission. The committee represents a wide spectrum of European Community interests, such as those of workers, consumers and farmers.

The European Parliament

The EC Parliament is not to be equated with the Westminster model. It cannot legislate in its own right and does not possess any form of parliamentary sovereignty. It does, however, exercise a limited, but growing, supervisory power in relation to legislative measures. In particular the Parliament:

1. Advises the Council of the European Union on Commission proposals.
2. With the Council of the European Union, determines the budget for the EC.
3. Exerts some political control over the Council and Commission.
4. By debate can attract publicity to issues that then have to be considered by the European Commission or the Council.

The European Parliament now has 626 members who represent the citizens of the European Union. Members are directly elected and serve for a period of five years. The composition of Parliament makes it a fully integrated Community institution, as the members do not sit in national groups but in political party groups. The six main political party groups at present are the Communists, Socialists, European People's Party, European Progressive Democrats, European Democrats and the Liberal and Democratic Group. The United Kingdom has 87 MEPs.

The European Parliament meets on average once a month, for sessions which last up to a week. It has 18 standing committees that discuss proposals put forward by the European Commission under the consultation procedure. The committees present reports on these proposals for debate by the full Parliament. The Commission is not obliged to act upon the recommendations of these committees. Similarly, the Parliament can put forward its own policy initiatives, but the Commission is under no obligation to act upon them.

Direct elections have given the European Parliament greater political authority and new prestige both inside and outside the European Union. It has the right to question members of the European Commission and Council and is therefore able, to a limited extent, to monitor the work of these institutions. It also has the power to dismiss the European Commission by a two-thirds majority vote, and can similarly reject the Council's proposals for the Community budget.

The role of the Parliament has been strengthened by the provisions of the SEA 1986, the TEU 1992 and the TEU 1997. As a result the Parliament has a power of co-decision in relation to a wide range of matters such as freedom of movement, non-discrimination, transport policy, social security, rights of establishment of foreign nationals and rules governing professions. The Parliament considers the Council of Ministers' proposals, within a strict time limit, and can adopt, amend or reject them. Rejection or amendment requires an absolute majority of members. In the event of rejection or amendment the conciliation procedures come into play whereby a conciliation committee, comprised equally of Parliament and Council members, seeks to achieve agreement. If agreement cannot be reached the measure in question is dropped.

The European Parliament now has an effective power of veto over applications for EU membership, and the appointment of the EU president will require the endorsement of the Parliament.

The EC Ombudsman

In the wake of the 1994 European Parliament elections an Ombudsman for the EC was appointed by the European Parliament, pursuant to art 195 (formerly art 138e) of the EC Treaty, to investigate allegations of maladministration made by any EU citizen or resident against any EC institution other than the European Court of Justice. Complaints considered by the EC Ombudsman do not have to pass through an MEP filter (he can act on his own initiative), and are not subject to any specific time limit. Given that serious violations of EC law can be pursued by individuals taking cases to the European Court of Justice, it seems likely that the EC Ombudsman will be concerned with less serious cases, perhaps where there may be no obvious judicial remedy, and where political pressure to achieve a settlement or redress is more appropriate. The only sanction available to the EC Ombudsman in the event that he finds an institution guilty of maladministration is the making of an adverse report to the European Parliament. Jacob Soderman, the first European Ombudsman, presented his first report in October 1996, covering the last three months of 1995. During this period he received 298 complaints and carried out 16 investigations. Most of the complaints were found to be outside his jurisdiction.

The Court of Justice of the European Communities

The Court is the European Union's supreme judicial authority; there is no appeal against its rulings. Each of the treaties establishing the European Communities uses the same broad terms to define the specific responsibilities of the Court of Justice, which are to ensure that in the interpretation and application of these treaties the law is observed. The Court therefore interprets and applies the whole corpus of EC law from the basic treaties to the various implementing regulations, directives and decisions issued by the Council and the European Commission.

Although its jurisdiction is principally concerned with EC law, the Court is not cut off from national law, since it draws its inspiration from the legal traditions that are common to the member states. This ensures respect both for the general principles of law and for fundamental human rights in so far as they have been incorporated into the European Community legal order.

The 15 judges of the Court are appointed by common accord of the governments of the member states. The treaties require them to be chosen 'from persons whose independence is beyond doubt and who possess the qualifications required for appointment to the highest judicial offices in their respective countries or who are jurisconsults of recognised competence'. There is no specific nationality requirement, but at the present time the Court has one judge from each member state. The judges select one of their number to be President for a renewable term of three years. Members of the Court hold office for a renewable term of six years. Every three years there is a partial replacement of the Court's membership: five or six judges and two or three advocates-general are replaced alternately. This ensures continuity of the Court's decisions, especially as most of the judges have had their term of office renewed at least once and sometimes twice. The independence of the judges is guaranteed by their status and is based on three fundamental rules of procedure: their deliberations are secret; judgments are reached by majority vote; and judgments are signed by all the judges who have taken part in the proceedings. Dissenting opinions are never published.

The Court is assisted in its work by the advocates-general who are appointed on the same terms as the judges, although nationality is immaterial. According to art 222 (formerly art 166) EC Treaty the functions of the advocates-general are to act with complete impartiality and independence, and to make, in open court, reasoned submissions on cases brought before the Court, in order to assist the Court in the performance of the tasks assigned to it. The advocates-general do not represent the Communities and cannot initiate proceedings themselves. At a separate hearing, some weeks after the lawyers have addressed the Court, the advocate-general comments on the various aspects of the case, weighs up the provisions of EC law involved, compares the case in point with previous rulings, and proposes a legal solution to the dispute. The advocate-general does not participate in the Court's deliberations.

Since 1988 the European Court has been assisted in its work by the Court of First Instance, comprising 12 judges, created under the SEA 1986. Advocates-general may assist the Court of First Instance but there are none specifically assigned to it. The role of the Court of First Instance is to deal with cases that turn primarily on issues of fact, rather than law, brought by natural or legal persons, rather than member states. Initially its caseload was limited to disputes related to production quotas, competition law and staff cases, but since 1993 its jurisdiction has been extended to all matters, other than cases involving anti-dumping proceedings. Appeal on a point of law lies to the European Court of Justice.

There are a variety of ways in which legal disputes can be brought before the European Court of Justice. A distinction is made between direct actions, which involve disputes between parties, and requests for preliminary rulings, which take the form of questions put by national judges. Direct actions may be divided into four categories:

1. proceedings against a member state for failure to fulfil an obligation;
2. proceedings for annulment;
3. proceedings for failure to act; and
4. proceedings to establish liability.

As indicated above, if the Commission considers that any part of the administration of a member state has not honoured an EC obligation, it asks that member state to make its comments and then issues a reasoned opinion. If the member state does not act on the opinion within the time allowed, the Commission may refer the matter to the Court on the basis that the member state has failed to act as required: see art 226 (formerly art 169) EC Treaty. If the Court agrees that the case is well founded, it declares that an obligation has not been fulfilled: see for example *EC Commission* v *Italy* Case 39/72 [1973] ECR 101. All the authorities of the member state concerned are required to take the necessary measures to comply with the Court's judgment in their respective areas of competence. If a state does not comply with the initial ruling, new proceedings may be brought for a declaration by the Court that the obligations arising from its first decision have not been complied with. *EC Commission* v *Italy* [1989] 3 CMLR 25 makes it clear that the member state's duty in such cases is to make the necessary amendments to its domestic law. The TEU 1992 provided a framework for the introduction of a system of fines imposed upon member states for non-compliance with EC obligations: see art 68 (formerly art 73p) EC Treaty. The European Commission has agreed that fines are to be imposed on a sliding scale, related to the 'wealth' of member states.

Proceedings for annulment under art 230 (formerly art 173) EC Treaty are a way of reviewing the legality, under the treaties, of Community acts, Commission decisions and regulations, and of settling conflicts between the institutions over their respective powers under the treaties. The proceedings, which can be instigated by a member state, the Council or the Commission are directed against binding Community acts, be they general regulations and directives or decisions addressed to individuals, taken by the Council and the European Commission. The basis of such a challenge is that the impugned acts are unlawful because of lack of legal competence, infringement of an essential procedural requirement, infringement of the EC Treaty or any rule of law relating to its application, or misuse of powers. A notable recent example was the unsuccessful attempt by the United Kingdom to challenge the validity of the adoption of the 'working time directive' which sought to limit the average working week to 48 hours' duration: see further *United Kingdom* v *Council of the European Union* Case C–84/94 (1996) The Times 21 November. Because opinions and recommendations do not have binding force, proceedings may not be brought in respect of them.

Private citizens, companies and non-EC member states may also initiate proceedings for annulment, but only against decisions which are specifically addressed to them or which, despite being in the form of regulations or decisions addressed to another person, concern them directly and individually. If the Court regards the action as well founded, it declares the act in question void and of no effect and the act then ceases to have any legal force as from the date when it originally took effect.

Proceedings for failure to act (under art 233 (formerly art 175) EC Treaty) provide a means of penalising inactivity on the part of the Council or the European Commission. Should the Council or the European Commission infringe the EC Treaty by failing to act, the member states and the other institutions of the Community may bring an action before the Court of Justice to have the infringement established. Such actions are admissible only if the institution in question has previously been called upon to act. If it has not acted within two months of being invited to do so, an action may be brought within a further two months. Proceedings for failure to act can also be brought under identical conditions by private individuals or firms, who can accuse a Community institution of having failed to take a binding decision (ie one other than a recommendation or opinion) concerning them. Admissibility is subject to the same conditions as those that apply to actions for annulment – the act not taken must have been of direct and personal concern to the party initiating the proceedings.

Finally, the civil liability can be imposed by the Court for damage caused by EU institutions or servants in the performance of their duties in accordance with the general principles common to the laws of the member states. The treaties confer on the Court of Justice the exclusive jurisdiction to order the EC to pay damages because of its actions or its legislative acts, on the principle of non-contractual liability. In exercising its unlimited jurisdiction, the Court decides the basis on which liability is to be determined, whether the damage is due to Community action, the amount of damage caused and the sum to be paid in compensation. By contrast, the EC's contractual liability is subject to the general law of the member states and to the jurisdiction of their courts.

The European Court of Justice is, by its very nature, the supreme guardian of Community law. But it is not the only court that has the power to apply and interpret this body of law that is common to all the member states. Unlike most classical forms of international treaty, there is a mass of provisions set out in the treaties themselves and in the secondary legislation of the Council and the European Commission, and in agreements entered into by the Community that are directly and immediately applicable in the legal systems of all the member states. These acts have a direct effect in that they can confer individual rights on nationals of member states (see below for an explanation of direct effect). Private individuals may invoke them in their national courts in relation to the national authorities and, in some circumstances, in relation to other private individuals and companies. The courts in each member state have thus become, in a sense, 'Community courts'. To avoid differing and even conflicting interpretations, art 234 (formerly art 177) EC Treaty introduced a system of preliminary rulings that can be requested in order to test the validity of acts adopted by the institutions, and to provide clarification regarding the extent to which the domestic law of a member state is at variance with the dictates of EC law.

Under the EC Treaty, where a national court from which appeals be made finds there is a problem regarding the interpretation of the treaties or of measures taken by the institutions, or some question arises as to the validity of these measures, it *may* apply, under art 234, to the European Court for a preliminary ruling if it considers that it needs to do so in order to come to its judgment. When a problem or question of this type arises in a national court against whose decisions there is no judicial remedy under national law (eg the House of Lords), that court *must* refer the matter to the Court of Justice. This system has resulted in valuable collaboration between the Court of Justice and national courts in ensuring the uniform application and interpretation of Community law.

In *Srl CILFIT* v *Ministry of Health* [1982] ECR 3415 the Court defined the extent and limits of the obligation on courts of final instance to request preliminary rulings. The Court stated that national courts did not need to refer questions if: the question raised was irrelevant, as, for instance, if it could have no possible influence on the outcome of the dispute; the Community rule in question had already been interpreted by the Court (whatever the circumstances and without the matters in dispute necessarily being absolutely identical); and there was no reasonable doubt about how the question should be answered.

Opinions vary on the authority enjoyed by preliminary rulings and particularly on whether they have general effect or are binding only on the parties concerned. However, three points seem to have been accepted regarding references for interpretation: the interpretation given by the Court is binding on the judge who requested it – he can refer the matter back to the Court if he considers that there is still a question to be answered; the interpretation serves as a basis for applying the relevant law in any subsequent case and other courts may invoke it without further reference to the Court of Justice; and a judge may always ask the Court of Justice for a new interpretation. A preliminary ruling may only be applied for by a national court or tribunal and not by the parties to the case. Once a ruling has been given the matter is taken back to the domestic court that made the reference for that court to give its ruling in the light of the European Court's decision.

As a consequence of the fact that any domestic court can, in theory, refer a case for consideration under art 234, concern is increasing at the extent to which the process is becoming overburdened by the number of cases so referred. At present the average length of time taken in dealing with a reference is 18 months. One possible reform that may be considered is to only permit the exercise of the right to make references once all domestic appeal procedures have been exhausted.

Given that the EC Treaty reflects its continental legal origins in the way in which it is drafted, as does the output of the Council in terms of other sources of EC law, it is not surprising to find that the approach of the European Court to the interpretation of the EC Treaty and other measures is markedly different from the approach adopted by UK courts when interpreting domestic legislation. As Lord Diplock observed in *Henn and Darby* v *DPP* [1981] AC 850 (at p852):

> 'The European Court, in contrast to English courts, applies teleological rather than historical methods to the interpretation of the treaties and other Community legislation. It seeks to give effect to what it conceives to be the spirit rather than the letter of the treaties; sometimes, indeed, to an English judge, it may seem to the exclusion of the letter. It views the Community as living and expanding organisms and the interpretation of the provisions of the treaties as changing to match their growth.'

The Council of Europe and the European Council

The Council of Europe exists quite independently of the EU, being the creation of the Treaty of Westminster in 1949. It has a much larger membership than the EU, comprising many states that, for political or economic reasons, find the concept of EU membership unacceptable or unattainable. The Council of Europe operates essentially as an inter-governmental organisation, that from time to time generates conventions on key aspects of international law. Its most notable achievement is the European Convention on Human Rights. A possible consequence of failing to comply with the Convention's requirements is expulsion from the Council of Europe. In 1967 Greece had its membership suspended following the military takeover and attendant human rights abuses. Similarly, in April 1995, the Council of Europe approved a resolution ordering Turkey's suspension unless it showed progress in withdrawing from Northern Iraq where it had intervened in relation to the Kurds.

The European Council has existed since the early 1970s and is comprised of the heads of EC member states and the President of the European Commission. Although it originally existed as an ad hoc organisation, its existence has now been formerly recognised by the SEA 1986, and has had its status increased by virtue of the TEU 1997. The European Council provides a forum for discussion of strategic issues related to EU policy, such as economic and social matters, constitutional issues, and for reviewing the operation of the EU. Meetings, normally held three times a year, are chaired by the head of the member state currently holding the Presidency of EC.

17.3 The sources of European Community law

There are three main sources of EC law: the Community treaties; the Acts of the Community institutions; and the decisions of the Court of Justice of the European Communities. Essential to the effective operation of the EC is the principle that its primary law, the treaties, applies to the same extent in the legal system of each member state, and that it takes precedence over the domestic law of any member state, to the extent that there is any conflict between the two.

Article 10 (formerly art 5) of the EC Treaty provides:

> 'Member states shall take all appropriate measures, whether general or particular, to ensure fulfilment of the obligations arising out of this Treaty or resulting from action taken by the institutions of the Community. They shall facilitate the achievement of the Community's tasks. They shall abstain from any measure which could jeopardise the attainment of the objectives of this Treaty.'

The 'appropriate measures' for the implementation of the Treaty depend upon the nature of the member state's legal system. Where it is monist, the Treaty will automatically become part of domestic law that can be relied upon in the courts of that member state (to the extent that it creates rights for individual litigants, as to which see below). Where the member state has a dualist system, as is the case with the United Kingdom, the Treaty has to be incorporated into domestic law in order to be effective: see the European Communities Act 1972, the impact of which (as regards UK parliamentary sovereignty) is considered further in Chapter 18.

As regards the secondary legislation of the European Union, namely regulations, directives and decisions, art 249 (formerly art 189) of the EC Treaty provides:

> 'A regulation shall have general application. It shall be binding in its entirety and directly applicable in all Member States. A directive shall be binding, as to the result to be achieved, upon each member state to whom it is addressed, but shall leave to the national authorities the choice of form and methods. A decision shall be binding in its entirety upon those to whom it is addressed. Recommendations and opinions shall have no binding force.'

Decisions of the Court of Justice may be treated as a secondary source of EC. The Court is not bound to follow its previous decisions and they may therefore be treated as persuasive rather than binding authority.

Any doubt as to the primacy of EC law over national law was resolved by the European Court of Justice in *Costa* v *ENEL* [1964] ECR 585 where the Court stated:

> 'By creating a Community of unlimited duration, having its own institutions, its own personality, its own legal capacity of representation on the international plane and, more particularly, real powers stemming from a limitation of sovereignty or a transfer of powers from the states to the Community, the member states have limited their sovereign rights, albeit within limited fields, and have thus created a body of law which binds both their nationals and themselves. The integration into the laws of each member state of provisions which derive from the Community, and more generally the terms and spirit of the Treaty,

make it impossible for the states, as a corollary, to afford precedence to a unilateral and subsequent measure over a legal system accepted by them on a basis of reciprocity. ... The executive force of Community law cannot vary from one state to another in deference to subsequent domestic laws, without jeopardising the attainment of the objectives of the Treaty set out in art 5(2) and giving rise to the discrimination prohibited by art 7. The obligations undertaken under the Treaty establishing the Community would not be unconditional, but merely contingent, if they could be called in question by subsequent legislative acts of the signatories ...'

The primacy of EC law prevails even where the domestic law is penal in nature, thus creating a defence of reliance on European Community law: see *Pubblico Ministero* v *Ratti* Case 148/78 [1979] ECR 1629.

Direct applicability

It will be seen, therefore, that provisions contained in the treaties and regulations enacted by the Council are of 'direct applicability', by which is meant that they become part of the law of a member state without further intervention by the member state: see further *Van Duyn* v *Home Office* Case 41/74 [1974] ECR 1337 and *Re Export Tax on Art Treasures (No 2)* [1972] CMLR 699. As indicated above, proceedings can be brought in the European Court by any member state against another member state failing to fulfil its obligations under the treaties. Directives, by contrast, are not directly applicable in that they require further enactment by a member state before they can take effect within its domestic law. Member states have no discretion as regards the object to be achieved by the implementation of the directive, but do have discretion as to how that objective is to be achieved. In the United Kingdom, for example, the implementation of a directive may take the form of primary or delegated legislation as appropriate. As to the consequences of an EC directive creating a conflict with existing UK primary legislation: see Chapter 18.

Direct effect

The extent to which the primacy of EC law is made effective depends largely upon the degree to which compliance is policed. Clearly, large-scale failure by a member state to comply with the requirements of EC law would be raised by the European Commission, or other member states. It is through the empowerment of individual EU citizens, however, that the monitoring process is made most effective, and this has been achieved by the European Court's development of the concept of 'direct effect'. In basic terms, if a given provision of EC law is held to have the characteristic of direct effect it can be invoked by a individual against a member state in the courts of the relevant member state.

This form of direct effect is sometime referred to as 'vertical' direct effect to distinguish it from 'horizontal' direct effect (considered below) where an individual seeks to invoke a provision of EC law against another private party.

Broadly, the criteria to be satisfied before a provision can be regarded as having direct effect are that it is sufficiently precise in its terms to be said to be creating individual rights, and does not require any further implementation in order to become effective in law.

That Treaty provisions can have direct effect, where they are found to be sufficiently precise and unconditional in their effect, was established in *Van Gend en Loos* v *Nederlandse Administratie der Belastingen* [1963] ECR 1, where the court observed that:

> 'The objective of the EEC Treaty, which is to establish a Common Market, the functioning of which is of direct concern to interested parties in the Community, implies that this Treaty is more than an agreement which merely creates mutual obligations between the contracting states. This view is confirmed by the preamble to the Treaty, which refers not only to governments but also to peoples. It is also confirmed more specifically by the establishment of institutions endowed with sovereign rights, the exercise of which affects Member States and also their citizens. Furthermore, it must be noted that the nationals of the states brought together in the Community are called upon to co-operate in the functioning of this Community through the intermediary of the European Parliament and the Economic and Social Committee ... the task assigned to the Court of Justice under article 177 [now art 234], the object of which is to secure uniform interpretation of the Treaty by national courts and tribunals, confirms that the states have acknowledged that Community law has an authority which can be invoked by their nationals before those courts and tribunals. The conclusion to be drawn from this is that the Community constitutes a new legal order of international law for the benefit of which the states have limited their sovereign rights, albeit within limited fields, and the subjects of which comprise not only member states but also their nationals. Independently of the legislation of member states, Community law therefore not only imposes obligations on individuals but is also intended to confer upon them rights which become part of their legal heritage. These rights arise not only where they are expressly granted by the Treaty, but also by reason of obligations which the Treaty imposes in a clearly defined way upon individuals as well as upon the member states and upon the institutions of the Community ...'

See further *R* v *Secretary of State for the Home Department, ex parte Flynn* (1995) The Times 23 March.

The same reasoning can be applied to regulations, provided the preconditions for direct effect are met: see *Politi* v *Ministry of Finance* [1971] ECR 1039.

The question of the extent to which directives can have direct effect was considered by the European Court of Justice in *Van Duyn* v *Home Office* Case 41/74 [1974] ECR 1337. The United Kingdom government allowed the Church of Scientology to operate in England, but sought to limit its activities by not granting work permits to foreign nationals seeking to take up employment with the church in England. Ms Van Duyn, a Dutch national offered employment by the church in England, was refused a work permit by the Home Office. She sought a declaration that the minister's prohibition was in contravention of what was art 48 (now art 36) of the EC Treaty, and was not permitted under Council Directive 64/221. Amongst the questions referred under what is now the art 234 procedure, the court asked whether the directive in issue was directly applicable so as to confer rights on individuals enforceable by them in the courts of a member state. The European Court of Justice, holding that the directive could have direct effect, observed:

> 'If ... by virtue of the provisions of article 189 [now art 249] regulations are directly applicable and, consequently, may by their very nature have direct effects, it does not follow from this that other categories of acts mentioned in that article can never have similar effects. It would be incompatible with the binding effect attributed to a directive by article 189 to exclude, in principle, the possibility that the obligation which it imposes may be invoked by those concerned. In particular, where the Community authorities have, by directive, imposed on member states the obligation to pursue a particular course of conduct, the useful effect of such an act would be weakened if individuals were prevented from relying on it before their national courts and if the latter were prevented from taking it into consideration as an element of Community law. Article 177 [now art 234], which empowers national courts to refer to the Court questions concerning the validity and interpretation of all acts of the Community institutions, without distinction, implies furthermore that these acts may be invoked by individuals in the national courts. It is necessary to examine, in every case, whether the nature, general scheme and wording of the provisions in question are capable of having direct effects on the relations between member states and individuals.'

Hence the doctrine of direct effect can be applied to directives despite the fact that, technically, they have to be implemented in order to become part of the domestic law of member states. A further factor to be taken into account was highlighted by the court in *Francovich (and Others)* v *Italian Republic* (see below), where the Court noted (at paras 11 and 26) that:

> 'Wherever the provisions of a directive appear, as far as their subject matter is concerned, to be unconditional and sufficiently precise, those provisions may ... be relied upon as against any national provision which is incompatible with the directive or in so far as the provisions of the directive define rights which individuals are able to assert against the state ... [but] ... even though the provisions ... [are] sufficiently precise and unconditional as regard[s] the determination of the persons entitled to the guarantee and as regards the content of that guarantee, those elements [may not be] sufficient to enable individuals to rely on those provisions before the national courts. [If] those provisions do not identify the person liable to provide the guarantee ... the state cannot be considered liable on the sole ground that it has failed to take transposition measures within the prescribed period.'

On this basis the Court of Appeal, in *Mighell* v *Reading and Another; Evans* v *Motor Insurers Bureau; White* v *White and Another* (1998) The Times 12 October held that the Second Council Directive (84/5/EEC) (OJ 1984 L8/17), which dealt with the approximation of the laws of EU member states regarding civil liability arising from the use of motor vehicles, was not of direct effect as it left it to the United Kingdom government to determine who should provide the scheme of compensation for those suffering losses caused by uninsured drivers: see Chapter 20, section 20.1.

What is a public body for the purposes of 'vertical' direct effect?

As has been noted above, the term vertical direct effect has been used to describe the position where a directive can be invoked by an individual against a member state. The scope of vertical direct effect depends, therefore, on the extent to which defendant bodies are perceived to be emanations of the state, eg the armed forces, the police, regulatory bodies, colleges and universities etc. The extent to which an employer could be regarded as falling within the sphere of public law (and hence amenable to the doctrine) was considered in *Marshall* v *Southampton and South West Hampshire Area Health Authority* (below) and *Johnstone* v *Chief Constable of the Royal Ulster Constabulary* [1987] QB 129, where the European Court of Justice ruled respectively that employees of the National Health Service, and those of constitutionally independent authorities responsible for maintaining law and order, could invoke provisions contained in directives against their employers on the basis that they were agents of the national authority. In *Foster* v *British Gas* [1991] QB 405 the European Court of Justice suggested that:

'... a body, whatever its legal form, which has been made responsible pursuant to a measure adopted by the state, for providing a public service under the control of the state and which has for that purpose special powers beyond those which result from the normal rules applicable in relations between individuals is included in any event among the bodies against which the provisions of a directive capable of having direct effect may be relied upon.'

Following this ruling the House of Lords proceeded on the basis that British Gas was a state body for the purposes of vertical effect. Similarly, in *National Union of Teachers and Others* v *Governing Body of St Mary's Church of England (Aided) Junior School and Others* (1996) The Times 16 December, the Court of Appeal held that the governing body of a voluntary aided school was an emanation of the state, for the purposes of the direct enforceability of a European Community directive. Citing *Foster*, Schiemann LJ noted that voluntary schools, once they chose to come within the state system, were subject to a considerable degree of control and influence by the Secretary of State, such that they could be regarded as coming within the 'control' of the state. In contrast see *Doughty* v *Rolls Royce* [1992] CMLR 1045 (ownership by the Crown not the sole determining factor).

Horizontal direct effect

Given the development of the doctrine of vertical direct effect, the question has arisen as to the extent to which Treaty provisions, regulations and directives can have 'horizontal' direct effect, in the sense that they can be invoked by one individual against another natural or private legal person in the courts of member states.

The horizontal direct effect of Treaty provisions has been recognised by the European Court of Justice in decisions such as *Walrave and Koch* v *Union Cycliste Internationale* [1974] ECR 1405 and *Defrenne* v *SABENA* [1976] ECR 455, where it has been seen as a necessary step towards ensuring that the objectives of the Union are not thwarted by private law bodies exercising their rights to legal autonomy. A distinction has been drawn, however, between Treaty provisions and regulations on the one hand, that are directly applicable and hence become part of domestic law without further enactment, and directives on the other, that require the state to which they are addressed to carry out the necessary procedures for implementation. Whilst it might be justifiable to permit proceedings against a private party for non-compliance with a Treaty provision or regulation, should that private party be at risk of litigation because of the member state's failure to implement a directive? In a number of cases, most notably *Marshall* v *Southampton and South West Hampshire Area Health Authority* [1986] QB 401 and *Faccini Dori* v *Recreb Srl* Case C–91/92 [1995] CMLR 833, the European Court of Justice has ruled that directives cannot have horizontal direct effect so as to impose liabilities and duties on individuals and private companies. As the court observed, recognising the limits of the scope of Community law in *Faccini Dori* v *Recreb Srl*:

> 'The effect of extending ... to the sphere of relations between individuals [the case law on horizontal direct effect to directives] would be to recognise a power in the Community to enact obligations for individuals with immediate effect, whereas it has competence to do so only where it is empowered to adopt regulations.'

See also *R* v *Secretary of State for Employment, ex parte Seymour Smith* (1997) The Times 14 March and *El Cortes Ingles* v *Rivero* [1996] 2 CMLR 507.

The unwillingness of the European Court of Justice to recognise the horizontal direct effect of directives has, however, to be seen in the light of two other factors: the doctrine of indirect horizontal effect and the availability of damages against member states for failure to implement directives.

Indirect effect

Although the European Court of Justice has balked at the prospect of openly recognising horizontal direct effect in respect of directives, not least because they are addressed to member states and not individuals, it has developed a doctrine, sometimes referred to as indirect effect, whereby the responsibility of the member state for the application by its courts of EC law is regarded as being the means by which they can be compelled to ensure that the objective of a given directive is achieved in the resolution of disputes in domestic courts.

In two cases, *Von Colson* v *Land Nordrhein-Westfalen* [1984] ECR 1891 and *Harz* v *Deutsche Tradex GmbH* [1984] ECR 1921, the plaintiffs sought compensation having had their job applications turned down on grounds of gender. Under German law the rejection of their applications was lawful, and their only entitlement was to reimbursement of their travelling expenses. The plaintiffs claimed that there had been a breach of art 6 of the Equal Treatment Directive. The European Court held that, notwithstanding whether the Directive gave rise to direct effect, the German state was obliged, under art 10 (formerly art 5) of the EC Treaty, to ensure that its domestic courts interpreted domestic law in such a way as to secure compliance with the objectives of the Directive. Hence, even if the Directive was not one having direct effect, by this means it could be given indirect effect. Note that although Von Colson was pursuing her action against a public body (the German prison service), the claim in *Harz* was against a private company. This is significant because it means that the doctrine of indirect effect can operate vertically and horizontally.

Indirect effect places UK courts in a particular dilemma as the traditional approach is to give domestic legislation its ordinary and everyday meaning. How far should UK courts now go in attempting to interpret domestic law so as to ensure conformity with directives? In *Lister* v *Forth Dry Dock & Engineering Co Ltd* [1990] 1 AC 546 the House of Lords was willing to disregard the prima facie meaning of a statutory instrument in order to ensure compliance with a directive, notably because it was felt that the statutory instrument had been introduced specifically to ensure compliance with the directive (note also that this was litigation against a private party). Even where domestic legislation has not been enacted to secure compliance with a directive, the courts are still likely to strive for a meaning that ensures compatibility provided this can be done without doing undue violence to the terms of the domestic law: see *Webb* v *EMO Air Cargo Ltd (UK) (No 2)* [1995] 1 WLR 1454. Where no such accommodation is possible, the plaintiff would be advised to pursue a claim in damages against the member state for non-compliance: see below.

In *Marleasing SA* v *La Comercial Internacional de Alimentacion SA* [1992] 1 CMLR 305 the doctrine of indirect effect was developed further to cover the situation where a directive had not been implemented. The plaintiff company had sought the nullification, in the Spanish courts, of the creation of the defendant company, on the basis that it had been formed with the sole purpose of defrauding creditors. The plaintiff's legal challenge was based on the provisions of Spanish law (sections 1261 and 1275 of the Civil Code) which rendered invalid contracts which were without legal purpose or caused unlawful consequences. The defendants called in aid art 11 of Council Directive 68/151 claiming that it listed exhaustively the circumstances in which the nullity of a company could be declared, and that the ground relied upon by the plaintiff was not listed therein. The Directive had not, at the time this issue came before the Spanish courts, been incorporated into the domestic law of Spain. The question referred to the European Court of Justice was as to whether the article in question was directly applicable so as to preclude a declaration of nullity of a public limited company on a ground other than those set out in the article. The European Court of Justice ruled that, whilst directives were not of themselves capable of having direct effect between individuals, the national courts of member states were obliged to interpret domestic law so as to ensure conformity with EC directives, whether the domestic law originated before or after the incorporation of the directive. The effect of the decision was to prevent the Spanish court from declaring the defendant company to be a nullity on any ground other than one listed in the relevant directive: see further *Faccini Dori* v *Recreb Srl* (above). Note again that the decision gives rise to a measure having horizontal indirect effect. If it is simply impossible for the domestic court to interpret existing domestic law so as to achieve conformity with the objectives of the directive, the member state may be liable in damages: see further *Wagner Miret* v *Fondo de Garantia Salaria* [1993] ECR 1–6911.

Remedies for non-compliance with Community law

The failure of a member state to ensure compliance with the provisions of the EC Treaty or other Community legislation, or indeed to implement directives accurately and within given time limits, may give rise to a right in damages on the part of an individual adversely affected by the failure. The development of this form of state liability is of particular significance where there is no relevant domestic law upon which a plaintiff can base a legal claim. The possibility of such liability being imposed was recognised by the European Court of Justice in *Francovich (and Others)* v *Italian Republic* [1992] IRLR 84. A number of Italian workers who had been made redundant found that, following their employer's insolvency, there were insufficient funds to pay their salaries. The workers complained that the Italian government had failed to implement legislation, required by a directive, to guarantee that such salary arrears should be paid by the State. The European Court of Justice held that, even in situations such as presented by the case under consideration where (because of uncertainties relating to implementation) the directive in question could not be regarded as one having direct effect, member states were obliged to provide protection for clearly defined individual rights granted by EC law to specific groups, and a failure to provide such protection, if resulting in economic loss to individuals within those groups, rendered the member state in question liable in damages.

The Court based its reasoning on the ground that the full effectiveness of EC law might be called into question, and the protection of the rights which they conferred would be weakened, if individuals could not obtain compensation where their rights were infringed by a breach of EC law for which a member state was responsible. In other words, a member state should not be able to hide behind its own failure to implement a directive when defending such proceedings. The Court identified three precondition to liability: the directive had to be one conferring individual rights; the rights had to be identifiable on the basis of the provisions of the directive; and there had to be a causal link between the member state's failure and the damage suffered. For these purposes a directive will generally be regarded as conferring individual rights if it is intended to provide protection for economic welfare (eg as regards consumer contracts), health (eg drinking water standards) or safety (eg product liability). In many ways this development is a logical extension of the doctrine that compliance with Community law will be most effectively policed by individuals within member states. It simply provides them with a financial incentive to bring instances of non-implementation before the courts.

The European Court of Justice has since gone on to extend this right to damages to other instances of non-compliance by member states, notably in *Brasserie du Pêcheur SA* v *Federal Republic of Germany* Case C–46/93; *R* v *Secretary of State for Transport, ex parte Factortame Ltd and Others (No 4)* Case C–48/93 [1996] 2 WLR

506. The first case concerned an action brought by a French beer producer in respect of losses caused through not being able to export its beer to Germany, following a ruling by the German authorities that its products did not comply with the German beer purity laws. The restriction imposed by the German authorities had, in previous proceedings, been found to be in contravention of EC Treaty articles seeking to eliminate quantitative restrictions on imports. The second case was brought by Spanish trawlermen seeking damages for losses caused by the enactment of Part II of the Merchant Shipping Act 1988 that had prevented them from operating fishing vessels that could be registered in the United Kingdom and thus permitted to fish against the British quota under the Common Fisheries policy. The 1988 Act had, in previous proceedings, been found to be in breach of Community law, in particular of the EC Treaty provisions ensuring freedom of establishment. The European Court ruled that the principle established in *Francovich* applied equally where the non-compliance was caused by any organ of government of the state, including the state's legislature, provided three conditions were met:

1. the rule of law infringed must be intended to confer rights on individuals;
2. the breach must be sufficiently serious; and
3. there must be a direct causal link between the breach of the obligation resting on the state and the damage sustained by the injured party.

On the facts the Court was satisfied that condition (1) was clearly satisfied in both cases. As regards condition (2), the test was whether or not a member state had manifestly and gravely disregarded the limits on its discretion regarding the measures to be taken in ensuring compliance, due regard being had to factors such as whether the breach was intentional or voluntary, whether an excusable error of law had been made, whether the action of any Community institution might have contributed to the breach, and whether or not there were previous decisions of the European Court making clear the incompatibility of the domestic law in question. The issue of causation was to be determined by the domestic courts of member states. See further *R v Secretary of State for Social Security, ex parte Sutton* (1997) The Times 25 April.

Exemplary damages could be awarded in respect of such claims, provided they could be awarded on a similar basis under the domestic law of a member state, subject always to the proviso that domestic law should not operate so as to make the obtaining of such reparation excessively difficult or impossible. In this regard, the requirement of English domestic law, to the effect that damages would only be recoverable in cases of misfeasance, was a measure that made the recovery of damages excessively difficult, if not impossible, given that the action that was the subject matter of the claim for damages was that of the legislature. Under EC law, the only permissible fault requirement for the award of damages was that there had been non-compliance with EC law. The measure of damages awarded had to be commensurate with the nature of the loss and damage suffered by the plaintiff, due regard being had to the extent to which the plaintiff had shown due diligence in mitigating the extent of any loss. In this respect, the proper protection of EC rights militated against the exclusion of a right to recover damages for loss of profit. Note that the court rejected the contention that the right to damages should be limited to losses occurring only after the ruling by a competent court that there had been a violation of EC law.

The matter returned to the domestic courts of the UK in *R v Secretary of State for Transport, ex parte Factortame Ltd and Others (No 5)* (1998) The Times 28 April, where the Court of Appeal upheld the ruling of the Divisional Court to the effect that breaches of EC law by the United Kingdom in implementing the Merchant Shipping Act of 1988 were sufficiently serious to give rise to liability in damages, but not exemplary damages. Lord Woolf MR made the following observations: a violation of EC law alone was not sufficient to give rise to liability; lack of clarity as regards the relevant EC law could be a factor in determining a state's liability for non-compliance (particularly where the meaning attributed to the relevant provision of EC law by the UK legislature was one shared by other member states acting in good faith: see further *R v HM Treasury, ex parte British Telecommunications plc* [1996] 3 WLR 203); the view of the European Commission as to how a law should operate was highly persuasive, but not decisive of the matter; where there was doubt about the validity of a domestic measure as regards conformity with EC law, a member state ought to be guided by the Commission; any legislation brought into effect following advice to the contrary from the Commission was likely to result in an inexcusable and manifest breach of Community law; a breach could be manifest and serious without being intentional or the result of negligence; and the seriousness of any breach had to be viewed objectively, taking all factors into account. Where, as in the present case, there was evidence of a fundamental right under EC law (the right not to suffer discrimination on grounds of nationality) had been violated, it was almost inevitable that liability in damages would arise. See Chapter 20, section 20.1, for further details.

As Lord Woolf MR observed, a breach of EC law is likely to be regarded as inexcusable and manifest if a member state proceeds with action it knows to be of dubious legality, or where the Commission has made its opposition plain: see further *R v Ministry of Agriculture, ex parte Headley Lomas (Ireland) Ltd* [1996] 3 WLR 787, where the United Kingdom ban on the export of live sheep to Spain, on the basis that methods used in Spanish slaughterhouses were not consistent with those required by Council Directive 74/577/EEC, was held to give rise to a right to damages because art 34 (quantitative restriction on imports) created individual rights, and the breach of that article had been serious (there was no evidence that the slaughterhouses used by applicants were breaching the directive).

As to the availability of punitive or exemplary damages, the Divisional Court at first instance in *ex parte Factortame Ltd and Others (No 5)* recognised that there should be no discrimination in domestic law between claims for damages based on breaches of domestic law as against claims based upon breaches of EC law. Where a claim for breach of EC law by the United Kingdom was made it should be viewed on the same basis as an action for breach of statutory duty: see *Bourgoin SA and Others* v *MAAF* [1986] QB 716. On this basis, unless the relevant statute provided for punitive damages, only compensatory damages would be available. The court rejected the submission that breach of EC law by a Crown servant was to be equated with misfeasance. As to what would be required to establish an action based upon the tort of misfeasance (and hence open up the possibility of punitive damages): see further *Three Rivers District Council* v *Bank of England (No 3)* [1996] 3 All ER 558.

Where a causal link cannot be established between the failure to implement Community law and financial loss on the part of the applicant, declaratory relief will be more appropriate: see *R* v *Secretary of State for Employment, ex parte Equal Opportunities Commission and Another* [1994] 2 WLR 409 and *R* v *Secretary of State for Employment, ex parte Seymour Smith* (above).

18

The European Community and the European Union II

18.1 EC law in the United Kingdom

18.2 EC law and United Kingdom sovereignty

18.3 Conclusion

18.1 EC law in the United Kingdom

The United Kingdom became a member of the European Communities with effect from 1 January 1973, by virtue of the Treaty of Accession 1972. Given the dualist nature of the United Kingdom's legal system it was necessary for the Treaty of Accession and the Community treaties to be incorporated into domestic law in order for them to have effect in the domestic courts. This was achieved by the European Communities Act 1972, as amended.

With the benefit of hindsight it might be said that what the politicians of the day, and most voters, thought that they were agreeing to was membership of an enlarged free trade area. It is clear that the true legal implications of membership were not grasped at the time, in particular the consequences for parliamentary sovereignty. The level playing field required for fair competition between manufacturers and suppliers in member states brings with it many restraints that go beyond the prohibition of anti-competitive tariffs. The institutions of the European Union have turned their attentions to related matters such as conditions of working, equal opportunities, sex discrimination, pollution, etc. As will have been seen from Chapter 17, a central tenet of the European Union's philosophy is that EC law should apply to the same extent within each member state. Inevitably, therefore, situations have arisen where the United Kingdom's domestic law has been found to be in conflict with the provision of EC law. Given the provisions of the European Communities Act 1972 (considered below), the courts have had to try and resolve these conflicts, constrained by the doctrine of parliamentary sovereignty on the one hand and the realities of EU membership on the other.

What the European Communities Act 1972 provides

Section 1 of the 1972 Act defines the Community treaties to which the Act relates and includes the treaties entered into by the Communities prior to 22 January 1972. Any subsequent treaties entered into by the Communities may be incorporated into United Kingdom law by Order in Council. Section 2(1) is arguably the most important provision of the Act in that it provides that:

> 'All such rights, powers, liabilities, obligations and restrictions from time to time created or arising by or under the Treaties, and all such remedies and procedures from time to time provided for by or under the Treaties, as in accordance with the Treaties are without further enactment to be given legal effect or used in the United Kingdom shall be recognised and available in law, and be enforced, allowed and followed accordingly; and the expression enforceable Community right and similar expressions shall be read as referring to one to which this subsection applies.'

The effect of this subsection is that all the provisions of EC law which are, in accordance with EC law, intended to take direct effect in the United Kingdom, are given the force of law. This applies to EC law made both before and after the coming into force of the Act. Section 2(2) provides that where EC law requires legislative implementation in the United Kingdom, for example, directives, this may be achieved by means of delegated legislation.

Section 2(4) addresses the issue of conflict between domestic legislation and EC law by providing that:

> 'The provision that may be made under subsection (2) ... includes, subject to Schedule 2 to this Act, any such provision (of any such extent) as might be made by Act of Parliament, and any enactment passed or to be passed, other than one contained in this Part of this Act, shall be construed and have effect subject to the foregoing provisions of this section; but, except as may be provided by an Act passed after this Act, Schedule 2 shall have effect in connection with the powers conferred by this and the following sections of this Act to make Orders in Council and regulations.'

The 'foregoing provisions' for these purposes include s2(1), which states that directly applicable EC law shall have effect in the United Kingdom. Therefore, s2(4) seems to amount to a statement that United Kingdom Acts of Parliament shall be construed and have effect subject to directly applicable EC law.

Section 3(1) provides that, for the purposes of all legal proceedings, any question as to the meaning or effect of any of the treaties or as to the validity, meaning or effect of any Community instrument, shall be treated as a question of law (and if not referred to the European Court of Justice) be for determination as such in accordance with the principles laid down by the European Court of Justice.

18.2 EC law and United Kingdom sovereignty

Despite Lord Denning's words in *Bulmer* v *Bollinger* [1974] Ch 401, to the effect that:

'... when we come to matters with a European element the [T]reaty is like an incoming tide. It flows into the estuaries and up the rivers. It cannot be held back ...'

there are several possible interpretations of s2(4) European Communities Act 1972.

It could be seen as amounting to a statement that all United Kingdom legislation shall only take effect to the extent that it is consistent with EC law, however clearly it may appear from the United Kingdom legislation that it is intended to have effect notwithstanding any EC law to the contrary. It is clear both from the Treaty and from statements made by the European Court of Justice, that the Community view is that EC law should prevail over national law in all circumstances. The European Court of Justice, in *Costa* v *ENEL* [1964] CMLR 425, stated that accession to the European Communities has as a corollary the impossibility, for the member state, to give preference to an unilateral and subsequent measure against a legal order accepted by them on a basis of reciprocity. In *Re Export Tax on Art Treasures (No 2)* [1972] CMLR 699 the European Court of Justice stated:

> 'The grant to the Community by the member states of the rights and powers envisaged by the provisions of the Treaty implies in fact a definitive limitation of their sovereign powers over which no appeal to provisions of international law of any kind whatever can prevail.'

This makes it clear that, as far as the European Court of Justice is concerned, any United Kingdom constitutional law doctrine of the legislative sovereignty of Parliament is irrelevant.

A third approach to s2(4) is to treat it as amounting to a rule of interpretation that there shall be a presumption that the United Kingdom Parliament, in passing legislation, intends to legislate consistently with EC law. This approach differs from the first since it allows that if the United Kingdom Parliament were to make it clear in an Act that it intended to legislate contrary to EC law, or that it intended the legislation to take effect notwithstanding any provision of EC law to the contrary, then the United Kingdom legislation would prevail to the extent that it was in conflict with EC law. This is the approach that was favoured by the Court of Appeal in *Macarthys Ltd* v *Wendy Smith* [1979] 3 All ER 325. A man had been employed as a stockroom keeper at £60 per week. Subsequently a woman was employed in this position at £50 per week. She took the matter to an industrial tribunal on the grounds that this was contrary to law. Three main questions arose: first, was this arrangement contrary to the Equal Pay Act 1970 as amended by the Sex Discrimination Act 1975?; second, if it was not, was it contrary to art 119 of the Treaty of Rome (now art 141 EC Treaty) which provides: 'Each member state shall ... ensure and ... maintain the application of the principle that men and women should receive equal pay for equal work'?; third, in the event of a conflict between the United Kingdom legislation and art 119 (now art 141) EC Treaty, which should prevail in the United Kingdom courts? The employment appeal tribunal held that the 1970 Act provided Ms Smith with the right to equal pay where she had performed identical duties in succession to a male employee. The employers appealed to the Court of Appeal. It was held (per Lawton and Cumming Bruce LJJ) that the Equal Pay Act 1970, as amended by the Sex Discrimination Act 1975, only required equal pay for men and women employed in like work contemporaneously, and thus afforded no protection for the female plaintiff in the present case. There was uncertainty, however, as to whether or not art 119 covered the situation where a woman was employed on certain work that had previously been performed by a man. Since the proper interpretation of art 119 was uncertain, the matter was referred to the European Court of Justice under art 177 (now art 234) EC Treaty for a preliminary ruling.

It is interesting to note the views that were expressed by Lord Denning MR regarding the primacy of EC law:

> 'It is unnecessary, however, for these courts to wait until all that procedure has been gone through. Under s2(1) and (4) of the European Communities Act 1972 the principles laid down in the Treaty are without further enactment to be given legal effect in the United Kingdom; and have priority over any enactment passed or to be passed by our Parliament. So we are entitled and I think bound to look at art 119 [now art 141 EC Treaty] ... because it is directly applicable here; and also any directive which is directly applicable here: see *Van Duyn v Home Office (No 2)*. We should, I think, look to see what those provisions require about equal pay for men and women. Then we should look at our own legislation on the point, giving it, of course, full faith and credit, assuming that it does fully comply with the obligation under the Treaty. In construing our statute, we are entitled to look to the Treaty as an aid to its construction, but not only as an aid but as an overriding force. If on close investigation it should appear that our legislation is deficient or is inconsistent with [EC law] by some oversight of our draftsmen then it is our bounden duty to give priority to [EC law]. Such is the result of s2(1) and (4) of the European Communities Act 1972 ... I pause here, however, to make one observation on a constitutional point. Thus far I have assumed that our Parliament, whenever it passes legislation, intends to fulfil its obligations under the Treaty. If the time should come when our Parliament deliberately passes an Act with the intention of repudiating the Treaty or any provision in it or intentionally of acting inconsistently with it and says so in express terms then I should have thought that it would be the duty of our courts to follow the statute of our Parliament. I do not however envisage any such situation.'

Thus Lord Denning put forward the view that if Parliament in an Act stated an express intention to legislate contrary to EC law or notwithstanding EC law, then in that one situation the United Kingdom court would give preference to the United Kingdom legislation over the EC law. The other members of the court expressed the same view, Lawton LJ saying:

> '... I can see nothing in this case which infringes the sovereignty of Parliament ... Parliament by its own act in the exercise of its sovereign powers has enacted and followed in the United Kingdom (s1(1) European Communities Act 1972) and that any enactment passed or to be passed ... shall be construed and have effect subject to (s2 in accordance with s2(4) of the Act). Parliament's recognition of [EC law] and the jurisdiction of the European Court of Justice by one enactment can be withdrawn by another. There is nothing in the Equal Pay Act 1970 as amended by the Sex Discrimination Act 1975, to indicate that Parliament intended to amend the European Communities Act 1972, or to limit its application ...'

On the reference under art 177 (now art 234), the European Court of Justice ruled that art 119 (now art 141) did not require contemporaneous employment (*Macarthys Ltd v Smith* [1980] ECR 1275), and the case was referred back to the Court of Appeal for the implementation of this interpretation: *Macarthys Ltd v Smith* [1981] QB 180. Although his comments were obiter Lord Denning took the opportunity afforded by the second hearing to state the following view:

> 'Art 119 [now art 141 EC Treaty] now takes priority over our English statute ... [EC law] is now part of our law; and, whenever there is any inconsistency, [EC law] has priority. It is not supplanting English law. It is part of our law which overrides any other part which is inconsistent with it.'

This 'rule of construction' approach, whereby domestic law is always interpreted in a manner that ensures its compliance with EC law, amounts to a retention of the doctrine of express repeal of earlier law by later legislation, but involves the abandonment of the doctrine of implied repeal as far as EC law is concerned. In this approach it is neither consistent with the traditional United Kingdom doctrine of the sovereignty of Parliament, nor with the Community doctrine of the supremacy of EC law over national law.

The matter was considered further by the House of Lords in *Garland v British Rail Engineering Ltd* [1983] 2 AC 751. The appellant was a female employee of the respondent company. Employees enjoyed (ex gratia) free travel on British Rail. Upon retirement male employees continued to enjoy this benefit for themselves and their families. In the case of retiring female employees, the benefit did not extend to their families. The appellant contended that this discrimination was not permitted by s6(4) of the Sex Discrimination Act 1964, and was in breach of art 119 (now art 141) EC Treaty. The complaint was dismissed by an industrial tribunal, allowed on appeal to the employment appeal tribunal, and the respondent employers appealed successfully to the Court of Appeal. On appeal to the House of Lords, the issue was referred to the European Court of Justice, which held that the discrimination was in breach of art 119 (now art 141) EC Treaty, which was directly applicable where a domestic court found such discrimination to exist. On reference back to the House of Lords the decision of the employment appeal tribunal was restored. Lord Diplock observed that:

> '... it is a principle of construction of United Kingdom statutes, now too well established to call for citation of authority, that the words of a statute passed after the Treaty has been signed and dealing with the subject matter of the international obligation of the United Kingdom, are to be construed, if they are reasonably capable of bearing such a meaning, as intended to carry out the obligation, and not to be inconsistent with it. A fortiori is this the case where the Treaty obligation arises under one of the Community treaties to which section 2 of the European Communities Act 1972 applies ...'

To some extent Lord Diplock side-stepped the key question of when, if ever, domestic law would be allowed to prevail where it was in conflict with EC law. He expressed the view that:

'The instant appeal does not present an appropriate occasion to consider whether, having regard to the express direction as to the construction of enactments to be passed which is contained in section 2(4), anything short of an express positive statement in an Act of Parliament passed after 1 January 1973, that a particular provision is intended to be made in breach of an obligation assumed by the United Kingdom under a Community treaty, would justify a [domestic] court in construing that provision in a manner inconsistent with a Community treaty obligation of the United Kingdom, however wide a departure from the prima facie meaning of the language of the provision might be needed in order to achieve consistency.'

As will have been seen in Chapter 17, the growing influence of the doctrine of indirect effect means that domestic courts are now expected to interpret domestic law to achieve conformity with EC law, regardless of whether the measure in question is directly applicable or of direct effect: see again *Von Colson* v *Land Nordrhein-Westfalen* [1984] ECR 1891, *Harz* v *Deutsche Tradex GmbH* [1984] ECR 1921 and *Marleasing SA* v *La Comercial Internacional de Alimentacion SA* [1992] 1 CMLR 305. These decisions have had some influence on the courts of the United Kingdom, as evidenced by their willingness to interpret domestic legislation to ensure compliance with directives, even if this means straining the natural language of the domestic law: see further *Pickstone* v *Freemans plc* [1989] 1 AC 66; *Lister* v *Forth Dry Dock & Engineering Co Ltd* [1990] 1 AC 546; and *Webb* v *EMO Air Cargo Ltd (UK) (No 2)* [1995] 1 WLR 1454. Where the United Kingdom courts have drawn the line is in refusing to give retrospective effect to domestic law enacted to give effect to a directive, in the absence of clear evidence that Parliament intended the domestic law to operate retrospectively: see *Duke* v *GEC Reliance Ltd* [1988] 1 All ER 626.

A situation where there is an irreconcilable conflict between domestic law and EC law, in the sense that there has been a deliberate attempt by the United Kingdom legislature to repudiate its international obligations under EC law, may seem a remote possibility, but where a conflict arises that cannot be resolved by means of an 'elastic' approach to the interpretation of domestic law to ensure compliance, the United Kingdom courts will have little option but to refer the matter to the European Court of Justice under art 234 (formerly art 177) EC Treaty. Pending the consideration of the reference by the European Court of Justice, questions arise as to the legal position of those litigants who claim that their rights under EC law are being infringed by the courts giving effect to domestic law. If domestic law is applied until the European Court of Justice rules that it is in conflict with the proper application of EC law, the litigant may have suffered financial loss. If such loss is to be prevented, the operation of the domestic law will have to be suspended by the domestic court pending the European Court of Justice's ruling.

Such a situation arose in *R* v *Secretary of State for Transport, ex parte Factortame (No 2)* [1990] 3 WLR 818. Fishing quotas were introduced by the EC to prevent overfishing. The United Kingdom Parliament enacted the Merchant Shipping Act 1988 (Part II) to protect British fishing interests by restricting the number of vessels whose catch could be counted against the British quota. The Secretary of State issued regulations under the Act that required any vessel wishing to fish as part of the British fleet to be registered under the 1988 Act. Registration was contingent upon a vessel's owner being a British citizen or domiciled in Britain. In the case of companies, the shareholders would have to meet these requirements. The applicants were British-registered companies operating fishing vessels in British waters. These companies now found it impossible to obtain registration because their shareholders and directors were Spanish. The applicants contended that the regulations effectively prevented them from exercising their rights under EC law to fish as part of the British fleet. The Secretary of State contended that EC law did not prevent the United Kingdom from introducing domestic legislation determining which companies where 'British nationals' and which were not.

The applicants sought judicial review of the minister's decision that their registration should cease; the minister's determination that they were no longer 'British' ships; and the relevant parts of the Act and regulations which would have the effect of preventing them from fishing. In terms of remedies the applicants sought a declaration that the minister's decision should not take effect because of its inconsistency with EC law; an order of prohibition to prevent the minister from regarding the ships as de-registered; damages under s35 of the Supreme Court Act 1981; and an interim injunction suspending the operation of the legislation pending the ruling of the European Court of Justice.

As regards the interpretation of EC law, the Divisional Court requested a preliminary ruling under art 234 (formerly art 177) so that the questions relating to the applicant's rights could be resolved. Pending that ruling, the court granted the applicants interim relief in the form of an injunction to suspend the operation of the legislation by restraining the minister from enforcing it, thus enabling the applicants to continue fishing. The Secretary of State sought to challenge the order for interim relief, which was set aside by the Court of Appeal. On appeal the House of Lords held that domestic courts had no power to grant interim relief to prevent the operation of a statute passed by Parliament, unless it could be shown that there was some overriding principle of EC law which provided that member states must provide such relief. The question of whether such a principle existed was referred to the European Court of Justice under what is now art 234 EC Treaty.

In responding to the House of Lords' reference, the European Court of Justice held that EC law required the courts of member states to give effect to the directly enforceable provision of EC law, such EC laws rendering any conflicting national law inapplicable. A court that would grant interim relief, but for a rule of domestic law, should set aside that rule of domestic law in favour of observing EC law. On the reference back, the House of Lords held that, in determining whether interim relief by way of an injunction should be granted, the determining factor should not be the availability of damages as a remedy, but the balance of convenience, taking into account the importance of upholding duly enacted laws. Damages are not available against a public body exercising its powers in good faith. The court should not restrain a public authority from enforcing an apparently valid law unless it is satisfied, having regard to all the circumstances, that the challenge to the validity of the law is prima facie so firmly based as to justify so exceptional a course being taken. On the significance of this litigation, Lord Bridge observed (at p857):

> 'Some public comments on the decision of the European Court of Justice, affirming the jurisdiction of the courts of member states to override national legislation if necessary to enable interim relief to be granted in protection of rights under [EC law], have suggested that this was a novel and dangerous invasion by a Community institution of the sovereignty of the United Kingdom Parliament. But such comments are based on a misconception. If the supremacy within the European Community of [EC law] over the national law of member states was not always inherent in the EEC Treaty (Cmnd. 5179–11) it was certainly well established in the jurisprudence of the European Court of Justice long before the United Kingdom joined the Community. Thus, whatever limitation of its sovereignty Parliament accepted when it enacted the European Communities Act 1972 was entirely voluntary. Under the terms of the Act of 1972 it has always been clear that it was the duty of a United Kingdom court, when delivering final judgment, to override any rule of national law found to be in conflict with any directly enforceable rule of [EC law]. Similarly, when decisions of the European Court of Justice have exposed areas of United Kingdom statute law which failed to implement Council directives, Parliament has always loyally accepted the obligation to make appropriate and prompt amendments. Thus there is nothing in any way novel in according supremacy to rules of [EC law] in those areas to which they apply and to insist that, in the protection of rights under [EC law], national courts must not be inhibited by rules of national law from granting interim relief in appropriate cases is no more than a logical recognition of that supremacy.'

The limits of applicability

It should be obvious from the foregoing that domestic courts will only have to apply EC law in the form of treaty provisions, regulations or directives where it is relevant to the issue that is the subject of the litigation. The more subtle question of whether the fundamental principles of EC law, such a proportionality, equal treatment and non-discrimination are of general application in domestic law was considered by the Divisional Court in *R* v *MAFF, ex parte First City Trading and Others* (1996) The Times 20 December. Following the ban placed on the export of British beef by the European Commission, the Ministry of Agriculture Food and Fisheries (MAFF) had introduced a scheme of financial aid – the Slaughtering Industry (Emergency Aid) Scheme 1996 – to assist exporters who had been adversely affected. The applicants sought, unsuccessfully, to challenge the legality of the scheme on the basis that it discriminated against those exporters who lacked their own slaughtering and cutting up facilities, and was thus in breach of fundamental principles of EC law, namely the principles of equal treatment and non-discrimination. In dismissing the application, Laws J observed that the fundamental principles of EC law referred to had been developed by the European Court of Justice in the course of deciding cases raising issues regarding the interpretation of the key Community treaties. Hence they were only relevant where an issue of EC law was under consideration. EC law might be under consideration where a member state took action required by EC law, or acted under domestic law in an area that fell within the scope of the EC law. The scheme in question, however, had not been implemented at the behest of the European Community and the United Kingdom government had not had to seek the permission of the European Community prior to its implementation. The fact that the scheme had been introduced in response to action taken by the European Commission was irrelevant. Hence the principles evolved through the case law of the European Court of Justice were not binding upon a domestic court assessing the legality of the scheme.

18.3 Conclusion

The United Kingdom Parliament appears to have forfeited its sovereignty by enacting the European Communities Act 1972, which provides for the direct applicability of EC law in the United Kingdom, and the enforceability of rights arising under EC law before United Kingdom courts. It may be, however, that this apparent forfeiture of sovereignty is, in reality, limited and partial. The European Communities Act 1972 is not entrenched. Parliament can, in theory, repeal the Act at any time and thus regain its full supremacy as a sovereign legislature. With the passage of time, however, this regaining of sovereignty becomes more theoretical and less practical. The political realities of the situation will dictate that the greater the degree of integration in terms of economic, monetary, and commercial union, the more difficult it will be for any United Kingdom government to extricate itself from the European Union. As successive generations grow up not having known anything of life prior to membership, it may be unlikely that any prospective United Kingdom government would receive a mandate for withdrawal. Monetary union in particular marks something of a political and economic 'point of no return'.

The view expressed by Hoffmann J in *Stoke-on-Trent City Council* v *B & Q plc* [1991] 2 WLR 42 displays increasing realism on the part of the judiciary. His Lordship stated (at p45):

> 'The EEC Treaty is the supreme law of this country, taking precedence over Acts of Parliament. Our entry into the European Economic Community meant that (subject to our undoubted but probably theoretical right to withdraw from the Community altogether) Parliament surrendered its sovereign right to legislate contrary to the provisions of the Treaty on matters of social and economic policy which it regulated.'

See further Jacobs 'Public Law – the Impact of Europe' [1999] PL 232.

19

The European Convention on Human Rights

19.1 Introduction: the political background

19.2 The rights protected under the ECHR

19.3 The Strasbourg machinery for enforcement

19.4 The place of the ECHR in English law

19.5 The Human Rights Act 1998

19.1 Introduction: the political background

Although the Bill of Rights 1689 has been a feature of the British constitutional landscape for over 300 years, it would be quite inappropriate to contend that it provides anything like the comprehensive protection for basic individual rights and freedoms that one normally associates with a modern Bill of Rights. The British constitution has traditionally looked to the common law to ensure that individual rights are recognised and upheld, but this has operated in an essentially negative fashion. Hence citizens have been entitled to do as they please, subject to the restrictions imposed by common law and statute, rather than being able to point to positive legal rights to such things as freedom of expression, association or privacy.

While the protection of fundamental rights and freedoms on the international plane has proved a slow and difficult process (witness the implementation of the Universal Declaration of Human Rights since 1948), the protection of human rights on the regional level among groups of states sharing common ideals and standards has been more effective. One of the most highly regarded of the regional conventions for the protection of human rights is the European Convention on Human Rights (hereinafter the ECHR). The ECHR is very much a product of the determination amongst the Allies in the immediate post-war years to ensure that the widespread atrocities, witnessed during the Second World War, and the concomitant violations of human rights should not be repeated in mainland Europe. There was a realisation that the way in which individual states treated their citizens was no longer a purely domestic matter. The evidence was all too clear that any state that started out by denying the basic rights of its own citizens would, in all likelihood, be only too willing to treat inhabitants of neighbouring states in a like fashion if the opportunity arose. The essential concept underpinning the ECHR is that signatory states should police each other and, where applicable, the nationals of signatory states should be able to draw attention to violations.

The United Kingdom was one of the original signatories of the ECHR, on 4 November 1950, and of its First Protocol on 8 March 1952. The instruments of ratification of the ECHR and its First Protocol were deposited with the Secretary-General of the Council of Europe on 8 March 1951 and 3 November 1952, respectively. The ECHR entered into force on 3 September 1953. On 23 October 1953 a declaration was made under art 63(1) extending the ECHR's force to certain territories for whose international relations the United Kingdom was responsible. On 14 January 1966, the United Kingdom recognised the competence of the European Commission of Human Rights (hereinafter the Commission) to receive individual applications, and recognised the compulsory jurisdiction of the European Court of Human Rights. With the enactment of the Human Rights Act 1998 those rights have now been 'brought home' with the effect that, from a date to be appointed in 2000, certain Convention provisions will have direct effect as part of the domestic law of the United Kingdom (see section 19.4 below)

19.2 The rights protected under the ECHR

Article 2: Right to life

Article 2 provides as follows:

> '(1) Everyone's right to life shall be protected by law. No one shall be deprived of his life intentionally save in the execution of a sentence of a court following his conviction of a crime for which this penalty is provided by law.
> (2) Deprivation of life shall not be regarded as inflicted in contravention of this Article when it results from the use of force which is no more than absolutely necessary:
> (a) in defence of any person from unlawful violence;
> (b) in order to effect a lawful arrest or to prevent the escape of a person lawfully detained;
> (c) in action lawfully taken for the purpose of quelling a riot or insurrection.'

Article 3: Prohibition of torture

Article 3 provides that 'No one shall be subjected to torture or to inhuman or degrading treatment or punishment.'

Article 4: Prohibition of slavery and forced labour

Article 4 provides that 'No one shall be held in slavery or servitude', and that 'No one shall be required to perform forced or compulsory labour.' For these purposes the term 'forced or compulsory labour' does not include:

'(a) any work required to be done in the ordinary course of detention imposed according to the provisions of art 5 of this Convention or during conditional release from such detention;
(b) any service of a military character or, in case of conscientious objectors in countries where they are recognised, service exacted instead of compulsory military service;
(c) any service exacted in case of an emergency or calamity threatening the life or well-being of the community;
(d) any work or service which forms part of normal civic obligations.'

Article 5: Right to liberty and security

Article 5 seeks to ensure that deprivation of liberty should only occur where sanctioned by law and following the correct procedure. It provides thus:

'(1) Everyone has the right to liberty and security of person. No one shall be deprived of his liberty save in the following cases and in accordance with a procedure prescribed by law:
(a) the lawful detention of a person after conviction by a competent court;
(b) the lawful arrest or detention of a person for non-compliance with the lawful order of a court or in order to secure the fulfilment of any obligation prescribed by law;
(c) the lawful arrest or detention of a person effected for the purpose of bringing him before the competent legal authority on reasonable suspicion of having committed an offence or when it is reasonably considered necessary to prevent his committing an offence or fleeing after having done so;
(d) the detention of a minor by lawful order for the purpose of educational supervision or his lawful detention for the purpose of bringing him before the competent legal authority;
(e) the lawful detention of persons for the prevention of the spreading of infectious diseases, of persons of unsound mind, alcoholics or drug addicts or vagrants;
(f) the lawful arrest or detention of a person to prevent his effecting an unauthorised entry into the country or of a person against whom action is being taken with a view to deportation or extradition.'

Further safeguards provided under art 5 are that: 'Everyone who is arrested shall be informed promptly, in a language which he understands, of the reasons for his arrest and of any charge against him' (5(2)); 'Everyone arrested or detained in accordance with the provisions of paragraph 1(c) of this article shall be brought promptly before a judge or other officer authorised by law to exercise judicial power and shall be entitled to trial within a reasonable time or to release pending trial. Release may be conditioned by guarantees to appear for trial': 5(3).

The right of anyone who is deprived of his liberty by arrest or detention to 'take proceedings by which the lawfulness of his detention shall be decided speedily by a court and his release ordered if the detention is not lawful' (5(4)), was found to have been violated by the United Kingdom in respect of its procedures for detaining juveniles convicted of murder during Her Majesty's pleasure (ie for an indeterminate period at the discretion of the Home Secretary).

Under art 5(5), everyone who has been the victim of arrest or detention in contravention of art 5 should have an enforceable right to compensation. See, further, *Steel and Others* v *United Kingdom* (1998) The Times 1 October: Chapter 20, section 20.2.

Article 6: Right to a fair trial

Article 6 is effectively a 'due process' clause designed to ensure that both civil and criminal proceedings provide adequate protection for the parties involved. Article 6(1) provides:

> 'In the determination of his civil rights and obligations or of any criminal charge against him, everyone is entitled to a fair and public hearing within a reasonable time by an independent and impartial tribunal established by law. Judgment shall be pronounced publicly but the press and public may be excluded from all or part of the trial in the interest of morals, public order or national security in a democratic society, where the interests of juveniles or the protection of the private life of the parties so require, or to the extent strictly necessary in the opinion of the court in special circumstances where publicity would prejudice the interests of justice.'

Under art 6(2) everyone charged with a criminal offence shall be presumed innocent until proved guilty according to law.

Article 6(3) lists the minimum rights of an individual charged with a criminal offence as being:

> '(a) to be informed promptly, in a language which he understands and in detail, of the nature and cause of the accusation against him;
> (b) to have adequate time and facilities for the preparation of his defence;
> (c) to defend himself in person or through legal assistance of his own choosing or, if he has not sufficient means to pay for legal assistance, to be given it free when the interests of justice so require;
> (d) to examine or have examined witnesses against him and to obtain the attendance and examination of witnesses on his behalf under the same conditions as witnesses against him;
> (e) to have the free assistance of an interpreter if he cannot understand or speak the language used in court.'

On police powers and procedures generally see Chapter 12.

Article 7: No punishment without law

Article 7 provides for a prohibition on retrospective legislation creating any criminal offence or increasing the penalty for an offence, by providing that:

> 'No one shall be held guilty of any criminal offence on account of any act or omission which did not constitute a criminal offence under national or international law at the time when it was committed. Nor shall a heavier penalty be imposed than the one that was applicable at the time the criminal offence was committed.'

This prohibition is modified by art 7(2) to the extent that it should apply without prejudice to the possibility of a person being tried and punished for any act or omission which, at the time when it was committed, was criminal according to the general principles of law recognised by civilised nations.

Article 8: Right to respect for private and family life

Article 8 provides that: 'Everyone has the right to respect for his private and family life, his home and his correspondence' (8(1)); and that under 8(2):

> 'There shall be no interference by a public authority with the exercise of this right except such as is in accordance with the law and is necessary in a democratic society in the interests of national security, public safety or the economic wellbeing of the country, for the prevention of disorder or crime, for the protection of health or morals, or for the protection of the rights and freedoms of others.'

Article 9: Freedom of thought, conscience and religion

Article 9 provides that:

> '(1) Everyone has the right to freedom of thought, conscience and religion; this right includes freedom to change his religion or belief and freedom, either alone or in community with others and in public or private, to manifest his religion or belief, in worship, teaching, practice and observance.
> (2) Freedom to manifest one's religion or beliefs shall be subject only to such limitations as are prescribed by law and are necessary in a democratic society in the interests of public safety, for the protection of public order, health or morals, or for the protection of the rights and freedoms of others.'

Article 10: Freedom of expression

Article 10(1) provides that:

> 'Everyone has the right to freedom of expression. This right shall include freedom to hold opinions and to receive and impart information and ideas without interference by public authority and regardless of frontiers. This article shall not prevent states from requiring the licensing of broadcasting, television or cinema enterprises.'

Limitations upon this right are envisaged by art 10(2), which goes on to provide that:

> 'The exercise of these freedoms, since it carries with it duties and responsibilities, may be subject to such formalities, conditions, restrictions or penalties as are prescribed by law and are necessary in a democratic society, in the interests of national security, territorial integrity or public safety, for the prevention of disorder or crime, for the protection of health or morals, for the protection of the reputation or rights of others, for preventing the disclosure of information received in confidence, or for maintaining the authority and impartiality of the judiciary.

Note that the article allows what is referred to as a margin of appreciation to contracting states regarding restrictions upon the right to free expression.

Article 11: Freedom of assembly and association

Article 11 provides that:

'(1) Everyone has the right to freedom of peaceful assembly and to freedom of association with others, including the right to form and to join trade unions for the protection of his interests.
(2) No restrictions shall be placed on the exercise of these rights other than such as are prescribed by law and are necessary in a democratic society in the interests of national security or public safety, for the prevention of disorder or crime, for the protection of health or morals or for the protection of the rights and freedoms of others. This article shall not prevent the imposition of lawful restrictions on the exercise of these rights by members of the armed forces, of the police or of the administration of the state.'

Article 12: Right to marry

Men and women of marriageable age have the right to marry and to found a family, according to the national laws governing the exercise of this right.

Article 14: Prohibition of discrimination

The enjoyment of the rights and freedoms set forth in the Convention are to be secured by the contracting states without discrimination on any ground such as sex, race, colour, language, religion, political or other opinion, national or social origin, association with a national minority, property, birth or other status.

Article 16: Restrictions on political activity of aliens

Nothing in arts 10, 11 and 14 should be regarded as preventing the contracting states from imposing restrictions on the political activity of aliens.

Article 17: Prohibition of abuse of rights

Nothing in the Convention may be interpreted as implying for any state, group or person any right to engage in any activity or perform any act aimed at the destruction of any of the rights and freedoms set forth in the Convention or at their limitation to a greater extent than is provided for in the Convention.

The First Protocol

There are a number of protocols to the ECHR that states can sign up to as they see fit. In effect they are 'optional extras' on the human rights menu. The First Protocol, to which the United Kingdom is a signatory, provides (under art 1) that:

'Every natural or legal person is entitled to the peaceful enjoyment of his possessions. No one shall be deprived of his possessions except in the public interest and subject to the conditions provided for by law and by the general principles of international law.
The preceding provisions shall not, however, in any way impair the right of a state to enforce such laws as it deems necessary to control the use of property in accordance with the general interest or to secure the payment of taxes or other contributions or penalties.'

Article 2 details a right to education:

> 'No person shall be denied the right to education. In the exercise of any functions which it assumes in relation to education and to teaching, the state shall respect the right of parents to ensure such education and teaching in conformity with their own religious and philosophical convictions.'

Note that the United Kingdom has filed a reservation in respect of art 2 to the first Protocol to the effect that the principle affirmed in the second sentence of art 2 is accepted 'only so far as it is compatible with the provision of efficient instruction and training, and the avoidance of unreasonable public expenditure' (reservation dated 20 March 1952).

As the White Paper *Rights Brought Home: The Human Rights Bill* (Cm 3782) indicates (para 4.5):

> 'The reservation reflects the fundamental principle originally enacted in the Education Act 1944, and now contained in section 9 of the Education Act 1996, "that pupils are to be educated in accordance with the wishes of their parents so far as that is compatible with the provision of efficient instruction and training and the avoidance of unreasonable public expenditure". There is similar provision in Scottish legislation. The reservation does not affect the right to education in art 2. Nor does it deny parents the right to have account taken of their religious or philosophical convictions. Its purpose is to recognise that in the provision of State-funded education a balance must be struck in some cases between the convictions of parents and what is educationally sound and affordable.'

Article 3 provides for a right to free elections:

> 'The High Contracting Parties undertake to hold free elections at reasonable intervals by secret ballot, under conditions which will ensure the free expression of the opinion of the people in the choice of the legislature.'

Other protocols

Protocol 4 prohibits deprivation of liberty on grounds of inability to fulfil contractual obligations; provides a right to liberty of movement; a right to non-expulsion from the home state; a right of entry to the state of which a person is a national; and a prohibition on the collective expulsion of aliens. The United Kingdom signed Protocol 4 in 1963 but has not subsequently ratified it because of concerns regarding the compatibility of domestic law. Protocol 6 prohibits the death penalty. Again this has not been ratified on the basis that the issue of whether or not to retain the death penalty has always been regarded as one best determined by individual MPs as a matter of conscience. Protocol 7 prohibits the expulsion of aliens without a decision in accordance with the law or opportunities for review; a right to a review of conviction or sentence after criminal conviction; a right to compensation following a miscarriage of justice; a prohibition on double jeopardy in criminal cases; and a right to equality between spouses. The present government intends to ratify Protocol 7 once certain aspects of domestic law have been rationalised.

Limitations, restrictions and derogations

A number of articles contain express exemption provisions. For example, arts 11(2), 8(2), 9(2) and 10(2). As regards derogation in time of war or public emergency art 15 provides:

> '(1) In time of war or other public emergency threatening the life of the nation any High Contracting Party may take measures derogating from its obligations under this Convention to the extent strictly required by the exigencies of the situation, provided that such measures are not inconsistent with its other obligations under international law. But:
> (2) No derogation from art 2, except in respect of deaths resulting from lawful acts of war, or from arts 3, 4(1) and 7 shall be made under this provision.'

The United Kingdom applied for a derogation in respect of art 5(3) in the light of that fact that:

> 'There have been in the United Kingdom in recent years campaigns of organised terrorism connected with the affairs of Northern Ireland which have manifested themselves in activities which have included repeated murder, attempted murder, maiming, intimidation and violent civil disturbance and in bombing and fire raising which have resulted in death, injury and widespread destruction of property. As a result, a public emergency within the meaning of art 15(1) of the Convention exists in the United Kingdom.' (derogation notification of 23 December 1988)

In the White Paper referred to above, the government has indicated that it is considering replacing judicial for executive authority for extensions, enabling the derogation to be withdrawn. As explained below, when the Human Rights Act 1998 becomes law, derogations will become time-limited, expiring after five years if not renewed.

19.3 The Strasbourg machinery for enforcement

What follows is an examination of the machinery existing under the ECHR for dealing with claims that its provisions have been violated by a signatory state. With the enactment of the Human Rights Act 1998 individuals will be able to pursue such claims before the courts of the United Kingdom from a date to be specified. The procedure to be followed in pursuing a claim before the United Kingdom courts is considered below at section 19.4.

Article 1 of the ECHR provides that the High Contracting Parties shall secure to everyone within their jurisdiction the rights and freedoms defined in the ECHR. To help achieve compliance with this objective the ECHR established a procedure for enforcement (arts 19–56). As originally enacted this enforcement process comprised a Commission on Human Rights, a Committee of Ministers and a Court of Human Rights. The Commission itself comprised a number of members equal to that of the High Contracting Parties, with members elected by the Committee of Ministers of the Council of Europe for a period of six years. Inter-state applications could be received by the Commission, and individual applications were accepted where a signatory state accepted the right of individual petition. Approximately 90 per cent of the petitions submitted by individuals under art 25 were declared inadmissible by the Commission at this stage, which suggests that there was still widespread misunderstanding of the scope and purpose of the ECHR.

The Commission, on accepting a petition referred to it, would then ascertain the facts and try to secure a friendly settlement of the matter on the basis of respect for human rights as defined in the ECHR. If a solution was not reached the Commission would draw up a report on the facts and state its opinion as to whether the facts found disclosed a breach by the state concerned of its obligations under the ECHR. The report was forwarded to the Committee of Ministers, together with such proposals as the Commission thought fit. Absenting any settlement the case would have been referred, in due course, to the European Court of Human Rights.

With an increasing number of states accepting the right of individual petition it became evident that the effective protection offered by the Commission and the Court was in danger of being undermined by its inability to deal with the ever-growing caseload. Between 5,000 and 6,000 applications were received each year, of which approximately 1,600 were registered, and approximately 200 declared admissible. Between 1959 and 1973 only 11 cases where referred to the European Court of Human Rights. In 1991 alone 93 cases were referred. The backlog of unconsidered cases as a whole reached over 1,500. The average time taken for an application to reach the European Court of Human Rights had stretched to five years. With Eastern European countries applying to join the Council of Europe the prospect emerged of some 800 million citizens having the right to have recourse to the European Court of Human Rights.

The new procedure under Protocol 11

In response to these pressures the text of what is referred to as Protocol 11 was opened for signature in April 1994. The purpose of the Protocol is to completely overhaul the procedure for dealing with applications under the Convention. Because the Protocol alters the provisions of the Convention itself it could not come into force until all states had signed – a process that was completed in time for it to come into effect in November 1998. The changes introduced by Protocol 11 had been trailed by limited reforms introduced in 1990, with Committees being used to rule on admissibility, and Chambers determining routine cases. There was a resultant improvement in processing rates, but concerns about the system being overwhelmed continued.

Protocol 11 is more radical. It provides for a new permanent European Court of Human Rights, replacing the current structure of the Commission and Court. With effect from 1 November 1998 Protocol 11 replaces the existing arts 19–56 of the ECHR. The new Court comprises 40 judges (one from each member state) allocated to Committees (three judges to each Committee), Chambers (comprising seven judges) and a Grand Chamber of 17 judges. The Court will be assisted by a single Registry comprising the Commission secretariat and the Court secretariat (around 100 lawyers in total).

The right of individual petition to the new Court becomes mandatory upon member states. The ECHR is itself restructured so that Section I deals with the rights protected; Section II with the machinery for enforcement; and Section III with miscellaneous matters.

The new procedure involves an applicant filing his application with the Court's Registry, which assigns it to a Chamber and a judge rapporteur who has responsibility for overseeing the progress of the application. A Committee, or tribunal, of judges considers the admissibility of the application, and provided at least one of the three considers it to be admissible, the ruling is communicated to the member state against whom the application has been made. If a friendly settlement cannot be reached the Chamber (seven judges) will give its judgment. The procedure also applies to applications between states. The authors of these reforms envisage that an application will only need to be referred to the Grand Chamber in exceptional cases, and a panel of five Grand Chamber judges will decide whether there are grounds for re-examination, unless the case is one where the Chamber itself has relinquished jurisdiction. It may be a number of years before this new single-tier system becomes operational. The Committee of Ministers becomes responsible for overseeing the enforcement of the Court's rulings.

It is hoped that the time taken for a case to be dealt with can be reduced from five years to two.

See further Mowbray 'The Composition and Operation of the New European Court of Human Rights [1999] PL 219.

19.4 The place of the ECHR in English law

Historically the approach of United Kingdom governments and courts has, to a large extent, been that incorporation of the ECHR was unnecessary, given the track record of the United Kingdom in respecting human rights, and the ability of the common law to respond to changing circumstances. As indicated above, the Human Rights Act 1998 marks a significant milestone in the protection afforded to fundamental human rights under the law of the United Kingdom. It has the effect of incorporating certain of the rights provided for under the ECHR into the law of the United Kingdom. The enactment of the 1998 Act was necessary because the United Kingdom legal system is dualist in nature. Whilst the Crown has power to enter into treaty obligations on the international plane, such treaties can only resound in domestic law if incorporated by Act of Parliament. Hence although the ECHR and its First Protocol have (subject to derogations and reservations) been signed and ratified by United Kingdom governments they could not become part of domestic law without first being enacted in an Act of Parliament. This mirrors the position regarding the Treaty of Rome (as it was then known) and the European Communities Act 1972. By contrast, many other signatory states have monist legal systems, whereby the ECHR became part of their domestic law once ratified.

The pre-incorporation era

Until such time as the provisions of the Human Rights Act 1998 come into effect the position, technically at least, remains that the ECHR cannot be directly relied upon in domestic courts as a binding source of law. The courts have always been willing, however, to use the ECHR to resolve ambiguities in domestic legislation, on the basis that it is presumed that Parliament would not have legislated in contravention of those obligations without clearly flagging that fact. What, historically, United Kingdom courts have refused to do is recognise rights created by the ECHR where no such corresponding right exists in domestic law.

For example, in *Uppal* v *Home Office* (1980) 3 EHRR 391, the applicants, illegal immigrants, applied for declarations that they should not be deported from the United Kingdom until the European Commission on Human Rights had determined whether deportation would contravene their right to respect for family life under art 8 of the ECHR, and argued that deportation would hinder the effective exercise of the right of individual petition. In his judgment Sir Robert Megarry doubted the validity of this argument, but in any event held that obligations in international law which were not enforceable as part of English law could not be the subject of declaratory judgments or orders. Subsequently, when considering the legality of telephone tapping in *Malone* v *Metropolitan Police Commissioner* [1979] Ch 344, he reaffirmed his decision in *Uppal* after full argument on the point.

Whilst Lord Denning MR in *R* v *Home Secretary, ex parte Bhajan Singh* [1976] QB 198 observed that the executive should have regard to the ECHR in exercising its discretion because it was, in his view, only a statement of the principles of fair dealing, the House of Lords made it clear in *R* v *Secretary of State for the Home Department, ex parte Brind* [1991] 2 WLR 588 that public bodies exercising discretion were not bound to take into account the terms of the ECHR as a precondition of acting intra vires. The House of Lords recognised that to have accepted such a contention would have amounted to the incorporation of the ECHR via the 'back door'. This was true whether the power in question was one derived from statute, or the prerogative: see *R* v *Secretary of State for the Home Department, ex parte Ahmed and Others* (1998) The Times 15 October.

Elsewhere the courts have tended to adopt the view that the common law and the ECHR provide, in any event, the same rights and freedoms. For example, in holding that a local authority could not use the law of defamation against a newspaper that had been critical of its conduct in certain financial matters, the House of Lords appeared to regard any argument based on art 10 of the ECHR as redundant. Whilst Balcombe LJ, in the Court of Appeal, had felt that domestic law was uncertain on the point and observed that 'where the law is uncertain, it must be right for the court to approach the issue before it with a predilection to ensure that our law should not involve a breach of art 10', Lord Keith expressed the view that he had reached his conclusion based on the common law of England, adding only that it was 'consistent with obligations assumed by the Crown under the Treaty in this particular field': see *Derbyshire County Council* v *Times Newspapers Ltd and Others* [1993] 2 WLR 449.

A more positive approach to reliance on the ECHR was expressed in *Rantzen* v *Mirror Group Newspapers (1986) Ltd* [1993] 3 WLR 953, where the Court of Appeal held that to allow juries to award unlimited amounts of damages to successful plaintiffs in defamation actions could amount to a breach of art 10, in the sense that as a restriction on free speech the threatened sanction of a large award of damages had to be shown to be necessary in a democratic society, and 'prescribed by law'. Like the House of Lords in the *Derbyshire* case the Court expressed the view that art 10 reflected the rules of the common law in relation to freedom of expression.

The Human Rights Act 1998: the debate over incorporation

The twenty-year period prior to the enactment of the Human Rights Act 1998 saw growing support for the notion that the United Kingdom should 'bring human rights home' by incorporating the ECHR into domestic law. Significantly the Labour Party, which won the May 1997 general election with a huge majority, included a commitment to incorporating the ECHR at the earliest opportunity as part of its manifesto. In observance of this promise, the Human Rights Bill was duly introduced into the House of Lords in November 1997, at the same time as the publication of the White Paper *Rights Brought Home: The Human Rights Bill* (Cm 3782).

Various arguments were advanced in favour of incorporation. Essentially they stressed the following: that it was better for the United Kingdom's reputation (as a nation that taking human rights seriously) for human rights issues to be determined by domestic courts; that the provision of domestic remedies would provide litigants with cheaper and speedier legal redress; and that was illogical for the United Kingdom to agree to protect various rights in an international treaty but not extend that protection by incorporation into its domestic law.

As the White Paper stated:

> 'It is plainly unsatisfactory that someone should be the victim of a breach of the Convention standards by the state yet cannot bring any case at all in the British courts, simply because British law does not recognise the right in the same terms as one contained in the Convention.' (para 1.16)

Further there was the view, expressed by Lord Irvine LC, introducing the Human Rights Bill in the House of Lords, that an unwritten constitution could not provide the citizen with adequate protection from abuses of state power that infringe human rights.

The proposals for incorporation were, at least superficially, seductive, particularly to those who equating the provision of rights with some form of political empowerment. They marked a shift from rights being associated with freedoms, towards rights being seen as entitlements given by the state. On the other hand, traditionalists, such as Lord Donaldson, argued that incorporation was 'constitutionally unacceptable' and that Parliament's right to govern should not be curtailed by Strasbourg. Other objections raised were that: the ECHR was out of keeping with the traditional style of domestic legislation; it represented an imported written constitution, whereas it would be preferable for the United Kingdom to be devising its own; it was undemocratic, because it sought to transfer power from the elected legislature to the courts; and that if enacted as domestic law, it could cause an unnecessary increase in litigation. Lord Mackay, speaking during a two-day debate on the constitution in the House of Lords in July 1996, expressed the view that the common law offered sufficient protection, and warned of judges being dragged into political controversy.

The statistics concerning cases brought against the United Kingdom were frequently relied upon to support the contention that the human rights of United Kingdom citizens were not sufficiently safeguarded by United Kingdom law, and that justice could only be obtained by resort to Strasbourg, or by incorporation of the ECHR. It is true that, in the period from 1990–1995, the United Kingdom was the subject of over 3,000 claims lodged by individuals with the Commission, of which approximately 600 were declared admissible, and that the United Kingdom has lost over 50 cases at Strasbourg. Few signatory states, other than Turkey and Italy, have suffered a higher rate of successful challenge. Against this, some argued that many of the cases involved what some might regard as peripheral human rights issues, as opposed to dealing with matters of life and death, and many cases turned upon issues in relation to which perfectly reasonable persons could agree to differ without either forfeiting the right to be described as reasonable. Furthermore, the frequency with which a signatory state was cited as a respondent before the court at Strasbourg did not necessarily have any correlation with its having incorporated the ECHR, as the track records of Turkey and Italy indicated.

19.5 The Human Rights Act 1998

The rights protected

The Human Rights Act 1998 received the Royal Assent in early November 1998, with ss18, 20 and 21(5) coming into effect on enactment, and the remaining sections to be brought into effect in due course. The Act seeks to give effect to the European Convention on Human Rights in the domestic law of the United Kingdom, but the actual Convention rights to be incorporated are stated in s1 as being: arts 2–12 and 14 of the Convention, arts 1–3 of the First Protocol, and arts 1 and 2 of the Sixth

Protocol, as read with arts 16–18 of the Convention. This restricted definition of Convention rights must also be read in the light of the derogations and reservations claimed by the United Kingdom in respect of art 5(3) and art 2 of the First Protocol.

Procedure for enforcement

The Act does not expressly create a new procedure for raising alleged violations of Convention rights. Section 7(1) envisages that individuals will be able to bring proceedings (or a counterclaim) against a public body in the appropriate court or tribunal 'as may be determined in accordance with rules': s7(2). Section 7(9) provides that these rules are to be made by the Lord Chancellor. Alternatively litigants will be allowed to 'rely on the Convention right or rights concerned in any legal proceedings' (s7(1)(b)), legal proceedings including, for these purposes 'proceedings brought by or at the instigation of a public authority; and ... an appeal against the decision of a court or tribunal': s7(6)(a) and (b). Only the 'victim' of the alleged unlawful act is permitted to bring proceedings or rely on the Convention in legal proceedings: s7(1). It is clear that many of the cases involving reliance on Convention rights will take the form of applications for judicial review – given that the Act is of direct application to public bodies (see below). The result is that a narrower test for locus standi will be applied in applications alleging a breach of Convention rights, as compared to applications for review generally. As s7(3) makes clear: 'If the proceedings are brought on an application for judicial review, the applicant is to be taken to have a sufficient interest in relation to the unlawful act only if he is, or would be, a victim of that act.' 'Victim' for the purposes of s7 is defined as 'a victim for the purposes of art 34 of the Convention if proceedings were brought in the European Court of Human Rights': s7(7). In particular, whereas pressure groups are increasingly seen as having 'sufficient interest' for the purposes of applying for judicial review, it will be difficult for them to satisfy the 'victim' test adopted by the Act. Section 7(5) provides for a time limit of 12 months for the bringing of proceedings where it is claimed that a public authority has acted in breach of Convention rights, time running from the date on which the act complained of took place. Beyond this a court or tribunal will have a discretion to allow proceedings outside this time limit if it considers it equitable to do so having regard to all the circumstances. This time limit would apply subject to any rule imposing a stricter time limit, hence, the three-month rule in relation to applications for judicial review would still apply.

Significantly the Act makes no provision for a Human Rights Commission to oversee compliance with the Act and bring proceedings in respect of non-compliance. This omission has drawn criticism from some quarters, particularly where comparisons have been drawn with the work of the Equal Opportunities Commission and Commission for Racial Equality in overseeing legislation dealing with discrimination on the grounds of gender and ethnicity.

Who can be the subject of these proceedings?

By virtue of s6(1) it becomes unlawful for a public authority to act (or fail to act – see s6(6)) in a way which is incompatible with a Convention right. A public body for these purposes includes a court or tribunal, and 'any person certain of whose functions are functions of a public nature, but does not include either House of the [United Kingdom] Parliament or a person exercising functions in connection with proceedings in the [United Kingdom] Parliament': s6(3). The term 'Parliament' as used in s6(3) does not include the House of Lords in its judicial capacity. By contrast the Scottish Parliament and the Welsh Assembly, as subordinate legislatures, are bound by the 1998 Act. Section 29(2)(d) of the Scotland Act 1998 provides that the Scottish Parliament does not have legislative competence to enact legislation that is incompatible with Convention rights, and Sch 4 to the 1998 Act further provides that no Act of the Scottish Parliament can modify the Human Rights Act 1998. Section 107 of the Government of Wales Act 1998 imposes similar restraints on the Welsh Assembly, subject to the fact that the Assembly is not, in any event, empowered to enact primary legislation.

A 'person is not a public authority by virtue only of subs(3)(b) if the nature of the act is private.' It seems likely that the courts will be influenced by the jurisprudence built up in relation to applications for judicial review in determining whether non-statutory bodies can be regarded as public authorities for these purposes: see for example *R v Panel on Take-overs and Mergers, ex parte Datafin plc* [1987] 2 WLR 699; *R v Disciplinary Committee of the Jockey Club, ex parte The Aga Khan* [1993] 1 WLR 909; and *R v Insurance Ombudsman Bureau and the Insurance Ombudsman, ex parte Aegon Life* (1994) The Independent 11 January. It is possible that bodies such as the BBC, the Church of England and other religious bodies, universities, the governing bodies of various sports, self-regulatory bodies, and any organisation that has taken over what was previously a public law function, such as running prisons, could come within the scope of 'public authority' for the purposes of the Act, as regards their public law functions. The press will presumably not come within the scope of the Act, raising the possibility of different approaches being taken to the right to privacy under article 8 depending on whether it is a television broadcast or newspaper article that is complained of. The Press Complaints Commission (PCC) will, it is submitted, be regarded as a public body. If the PCC fails to safeguard the right to privacy, or indeed the right to freedom of expression as defined in the ECHR, it could find itself involved in lengthy litigation.

Where the claim of unlawfulness under s6 is based upon a judicial act, proceedings under s7(1)(a) may only be brought by exercising a right of appeal, making an application for judicial review, or by following such procedure as may be laid down in rules made from time to time: s9(1). So-called 'ouster' clauses that seek to remove rights of appeal or exclude judicial review would not be affected by this requirement: see s9(2).

Section 6(1) effectively creates a new 'head' of ultra vires as regards applications for judicial review of public bodies. If a public body fails to pay due regard to the terms of the Convention, or indeed the jurisprudence of the European Court of Justice, in exercising its discretion, prima facie grounds for review will exist. In particular the notion of proportionality as developed by the European Court of Human Rights becomes a facet of domestic law to which reviewing courts will now be obliged to have regard.

Section 6(2) restricts the scope of s6(1) by providing that the latter does not apply if, as the result of one or more provisions of primary legislation, or because of the way in which subordinate legislation has to be applied in the light of primary legislation, the public body alleged to have acted unlawfully could not have acted differently. If such a situation arises the court may still be willing to make a declaration of incompatibility, as to which see below.

Further, no action will lie against a minister for not laying a proposal for legislation before Parliament or for not making any primary legislation or remedial order: see s6(6)(a) and (b), and below.

Given that it includes the courts and tribunals, the definition of public authority in s6 creates the possibility of the Convention having indirect 'horizontal' effect. Although the 1998 Act does not expressly create any obligation on the part of private individuals to abide by the terms of the Convention, proceedings could be brought against a court that failed to uphold a Convention right in proceedings between private individuals. An example might be an allegation that a newspaper had invaded the privacy of an individual. There is no common law right to privacy as such. Article 8 of the Convention is now part of domestic law, but appears only to apply to public authorities, not newspapers. If a court were to strike out proceedings brought by a private individual against a newspaper alleging invasion of privacy as disclosing no cause of action, the court might itself then become the focus of an action for not upholding Convention rights. It remains to be seen how the courts will deal with such claims.

What is required of a court considering a case involving an allegation that a Convention right has been violated?

A court or tribunal called upon to do so, must interpret primary legislation and subordinate legislation 'in a way which is compatible with the Convention rights': s3(1). This duty applies whether the legislation was enacted before or after the coming into force of the Human Rights Act 1998.

Section 2(1) of the 1998 Act makes it clear that any court or tribunal determining a question arising in connection with a Convention right must take into account: any judgment, decision, declaration or advisory opinion of the European Court of Human Rights; any opinion of the Commission given in a report adopted under art 31 of the Convention; any decision of the Commission in connection with arts 26 or 27(2) of the Convention; or any decision of the Committee of Ministers taken under art 46 of the Convention, 'whenever made or given, so far as, in the opinion of the

court or tribunal, it is relevant to the proceedings in which that question has arisen.'
It may also be the case that the courts take into account rulings of the Privy Council in appeals concerning constitutional rights for those countries having written constitutions incorporating terms similar to those found in the ECHR: see for example *DPP* v *Tokai* [1996] AC 856 and *Robinson* v *The Queen* [1985] AC 956.

It seems inevitable that the courts are going to have to adopt a new approach to statutory interpretation where Convention rights are concerned, rather than stick rigidly to the traditional 'rules' of interpretation. The tradition of the European Court of Human Rights is to be more flexible and evaluative in its exercise of its interpretative functions. Thus, domestic judges will have a more explicit role in assessing the merits of executive decision-making (ie its legitimacy within the context of the ECHR), whereas their role to date, at least in theory, has been limited to scrutinising the legality of executive action by means of judicial review.

As Lord Irvine LC observed:

'[Once the ECHR is incorporated in domestic law] The courts' decisions will be based on a more overtly principled, indeed moral, basis. The court will look at the positive right. It will only accept an interference with that right where a justification, allowed under the Convention, is made out. The scrutiny will not be limited to seeing if the words of an exception can be satisfied. The court will need to be satisfied that the spirit of this exception is made out. It will need to be satisfied that the interference with the protected right is justified in the public interests in a free democratic society. Moreover, the courts will in this area have to apply the Convention principle of proportionality. This means the court will be looking substantively at that question. It will not be limited to a secondary review of the decision making process but at the primary question of the merits of the decision itself.

In reaching its judgment, therefore, the court will need to expand and explain its own view of whether the conduct is legitimate. It will produce in short a decision on the morality of the conduct and not simply its compliance with the bare letter of the law.' (Tom Sargant Memorial Lecture, December 1997)

During the passage of the Human Rights Bill great concern was expressed by religious organisations as to the effect of incorporation on their rights to act in accordance with their religious beliefs, and by sections of the media concerned at the impact of a right to privacy on the common law notion of free speech. Section 11 provides that the incorporation of the Convention should not be regarded by a court as necessarily restricting any other rights and freedoms conferred on an individual by common law or statute. Section 12 goes on to deal more specifically with the issue of free speech by providing (in s12(4)) that the courts must have:

'... particular regard to the importance of the Convention right to freedom of expression and, where the proceedings relate to material which the respondent [ie person against whom the application for relief is made] claims, or which appears to the court, to be journalistic, literary or artistic material (or to conduct connected with such material), to –
(a) the extent to which –
(i) the material has, or is about to, become available to the public; or
(ii) it is, or would be, in the public interest for the material to be published;
(b) any relevant privacy code.'

Where a court is considering whether to grant any relief which, if granted, might affect the exercise of the Convention right to freedom of expression, and the respondent is neither present nor represented, no such relief should be granted unless the court is satisfied: '(a) that the applicant has taken all practicable steps to notify the respondent; or (b) that there are compelling reasons why the respondent should not be notified': s12(2)(a) and (b). Further, 'no such relief is to be granted so as to restrain publication before trial unless the court is satisfied that the applicant is likely to establish that publication should not be allowed': see s12(3).

Section 13 provides that a court determining a question arising under the 1998 Act that 'might affect the exercise by a religious organisation (itself or its members collectively) of the Convention right to freedom of thought, conscience and religion' must 'have particular regard to the importance of that right.'

The usefulness of both ss12 and 13 must be questioned. They seek to assist the courts in the interpretation of domestic legislation and Convention rights, but ultimately the United Kingdom courts will be bound by the jurisprudence of the European Court of Human Rights as regards the 'hierarchy' of rights (ie whether freedom of expression outweighs the right to privacy). If domestic courts restrict the scope of Convention rights in a manner that is contrary to the rulings of the European Court of Human Rights, the way lies open to have the matter determined at Strasbourg with the prospect of the United Kingdom being found in breach of its Convention rights, notwithstanding incorporation.

Judicial remedies

A court dealing with an application for judicial review of subordinate legislation would be able to declare it to be ultra vires if it was found to incompatible with the Convention rights. The courts have no such power in relation to primary legislation, however. Indeed, s3(2)(b) expressly provides that the section 'does not affect the validity, continuing operation or enforcement of any incompatible primary legislation'. Further the section cannot be relied upon to invalidate incompatible subordinate legislation if '(disregarding any possibility of revocation) primary legislation prevents removal of the incompatibility: s3(2)(c). Where an irreconcilable issue of compatibility arises before the House of Lords, the Judicial Committee of the Privy Council, the Courts-Martial Appeal Court, or the High Court or the Court of Appeal, that court will be empowered to grant a declaration of incompatibility. In relation to subordinate legislation the power to make such declarations will arise provided (disregarding any possibility of revocation) the primary legislation concerned prevents removal of the incompatibility. Where such a declaration is made it does not 'affect the validity, continuing operation or enforcement of the provision in respect of which it is given; and ... is not binding on the parties to the proceedings in which it is made': s4(6). The Crown can be joined as a party to the proceedings if a court is considering whether to make a declaration of incompatibility: s5(1).

It could be argued that the 1998 Act is further evidence of the steady erosion of parliamentary sovereignty. Although a declaration of incompatibility does place a minister under a duty to take remedial action (see below), the political pressure to do so will be intense. It suggests more clearly than ever before that it is the judiciary that are to be the protectors of minority groups, not a legislature that represents, by definition, the interests of majority groups.

Whilst the 1998 Act does not provide for any new judicial remedies (other than the declaration of incompatibility), a court finding that a public authority as acted unlawfully within the terms of s6 'may grant such relief or remedy, or make such order, within its powers as it considers just and appropriate': s8(1). In particular there is no new power to award damages simply because Convention rights have been violated: see s8(2). Even if a power to award damages exists an award should only be made if, having taken into account all the circumstances of the case, including 'any other relief or remedy granted, or order made, in relation to the act in question (by that or any other court), and ... the consequences of any decision (of that or any other court) in respect of that act, the court is satisfied that the award is necessary to afford just satisfaction to the person in whose favour it is made': s8(3). A court should also have regard to 'the principles applied by the European Court of Human Rights in relation to the award of compensation under art 41 of the Convention' in determining whether to make an award and in determining quantum.

Remedial action by ministers

Where a declaration of incompatibility has been made and rights of appeal have been exhausted, abandoned or become time-barred, or it appears to a minister that (in the light of a finding of the European Court of Human Rights) a provision of legislation is incompatible with obligations under the Convention, a minister may, if he considers that there are compelling reasons for so doing, make orders to amend the relevant legislation to the extent that considers necessary to remove the incompatibility: see s10(1) and (2).

Note the far-reaching effect of these provisions. A minister will be able to amend primary legislation by means of a statutory instrument: s20(1). Amendments can be retrospective in effect (but not so as to create criminal liability): see Sch 2 paras 1(1)(b) and 1(4). Schedule 2 provides for two types of procedure for the making of remedial orders, depending upon the urgency of the situation. In most cases a minister will prepare a 'document' comprising the draft order and other details required by Sch 2 para 5 (ie details of the incompatibility to be removed and the reasons for proceeding under s10). There then follows a 60-day consultation period during which period representations can be made both inside and outside Parliament. Following this period of consultation the minister lays before Parliament the draft remedial order together with a summary of the representations made and details of any revisions made to the order in the light of those representations. To come into effect the draft order must have been laid before Parliament for 60 days and must then be approved by Parliament. In urgent cases a minister will be able to bring an order into effect without parliamentary approval. The safeguards take the form of requirements that the minister should then lay the 'made' order before Parliament with the details required by Sch 2 para 5. Once 60 days have passed the minister must lay before Parliament a summary of the representations made and details (if any) of revisions made to the order in the light of those representations. At the end of a period of 120 days from the date when the order was first laid before Parliament it will cease to have effect unless approved by both Houses of Parliament. The failure by Parliament to affirm such an order does not affect the validity of actions taken pursuant to that order within the 120-day period.

Pre-enactment procedures

Section 19 places the relevant minister in charge of a Bill under a duty to 'make a statement to the effect that in his view the provisions of the Bill are compatible with the Convention rights', or to make a statement to the effect that 'although he is unable to make a statement of compatibility the government nevertheless wishes the House to proceed with the Bill.' Such statements must be made before the Second Reading of a Bill, must be in writing and should be published in such manner as the minister considers appropriate. Presumably a statement of non-compliance would only ever be made where the government had already secured derogations or reservations in respect of certain Convention provisions, or had at least indicated that it intended to do so. Otherwise Parliament would be being invited to enact legislation acknowledged to be in breach of the Convention. Were such legislation to be enacted the courts would then be in a position to grant declarations of incompatibility to litigants alleging that action taken on the basis of the non-compliant legislation was unlawful. If no remedial order was forthcoming, the litigant would presumably take his case to the European Court of Human Rights and have the United Kingdom found to be in breach of its obligations.

Alternative mechanisms for entrenching rights

The Human Rights Act is a cleverly worded compromise between the demands of those who wished to see the courts being given the power to invalidate primary legislation found to be incompatible with Convention rights, and those who feared that the Act would, almost by default, mark a serious erosion of parliamentary sovereignty. It is nevertheless instructive to examine briefly the alternative strategies that could have been adopted to ensure that the courts accord special status to human rights provisions. First, the Act could have avoided any reference to incompatibility altogether, and simply allowed existing constitutional principles to apply. This would clearly have been unsatisfactory for a government wanting to be seen to take the incorporation of the Convention seriously. The resulting Act would have taken precedence over previous incompatible legislation by virtue of implied repeal, but would have been a the mercy of any subsequent legislation. Second, at the other extreme, the model provided by the Canadian Charter of Rights and Freedoms could have been adopted, whereby the Canadian courts have been given the power to disapply incompatible legislation, unless the legislation in question expressly states that it is to apply notwithstanding any such incompatibility. In practice this means that the Canadian courts 'read in' the missing rights, or make it clear that, for certain purposes, a statute no longer applies. The Canadian Parliament remains at liberty to amend legislation as it sees fit following such a ruling. Third, the government could have copied the approach taken following the incorporation of the Treaty of Rome (as it then was), whereby the European Communities Act 1972 operates to make certain aspects of EU directly part of domestic law: see Chapter 2. This latter proposal was rejected, however, on the basis that it is a prerequisite of EU membership that member states give priority to EC law, whilst becoming a signatory to the Convention creates no such obligations.

The approach adopted for the incorporation of the ECHR in the United Kingdom bears close similarity to the New Zealand Bill of Rights Act 1990, which adopts what is known as an 'interpretative' approach, requiring courts to strive for an interpretation which gives effect to the human rights legislation, but leaving intact legislation that cannot be complied in a manner consistent with those rights. Defending the adoption of this method the White Paper states:

> 'The government has reached the conclusion that courts should not have the power to set aside primary legislation, past or future, on the ground of incompatibility with the Convention. This conclusion arises from the importance that the government attaches to parliamentary sovereignty. In this context, parliamentary sovereignty means that Parliament is competent to make any law on any matter of its choosing and no court may question the validity of any Act that it passes. In enacting legislation, Parliament is making decisions about important matters of public policy. The authority to make those decisions derives from a democratic mandate. Members of Parliament in the House of Commons possess such a mandate because they are elected, accountable and representative. To make provision in the Bill for the courts to set aside Acts of Parliament would confer on the judiciary a general power over the decisions of Parliament which under our present constitutional arrangements they do not possess, and would be likely on occasions to draw the judiciary into serious conflict with Parliament. There is no evidence to suggest that they desire this power, nor that the public wishes them to have it. Certainly, this government has no mandate for any such change.' (para 2.13).

The ECHR and EC law

The ECHR does not form part of EC law in the strict sense, but it is accepted that respect for fundamental human rights is a precondition for the lawfulness of Community acts: see comments in *Opinion No 2/94* [1996] ECR 1–1759. The preamble to Single European Act 1986 also makes express reference to the need to respect such fundamental rights, and similar commitments to respect fundamental human rights are to be found in art 6 EC Treaty (formerly art F of TEU 1992) and art 7 (formerly art F.1 of TEU 1997). In *Opinion No 2/94*, the opinion of the

European Court of Justice was sought on the question of whether the accession of the European Community to the ECHR would be compatible with the EC Treaty. Whilst the Court declined to answer the question as posed, it held that, as EC law presently stood, the Community had no competence to accede to the ECHR. Notwithstanding the provisions of art 308 of the EC Treaty empowering the Council to take appropriate measures to ensure that the Community was empowered to achieve its objectives, there was no specific Treaty power that enabled the Community institutions to enact rules relating to human rights or to become a party to international conventions on human rights. In the Court's view, accession to the ECHR would effectively make its provisions part of Community law, with profound consequences for the institutions of the Community and for member states, and would hence involve changes of such constitutional significance that it could only be brought about by amendment of the EC Treaty.

An individual asserting that the domestic legislation of a member state is in breach of the ECHR, and thus EC law, will not succeed before the ECJ where the domestic legislation does not deal with a matter falling within the field of application of Community law, and has not been enacted by a member state so as to ensure compliance with Community law: see further *Kremzow* v *Republik Osterreich* [1997] ECR 1–2629. There remains the possibility of the ECHR being indirectly invoked where the application of EC law having direct effect is held, by the European Court of Justice, to require reference to, and conformity with, provisions of the ECHR: see for example *R* v *Kirk* [1984] CMLR 522.

20

Recent Cases

20.1 The European Community and the European Union

20.2 The European Convention on Human Rights

20.1 The European Community and the European Union

Mighell v *Reading and Another; Evans* v *Motor Insurers Bureau; White* v *White and Another* (1998) The Times 12 October Court of Appeal (Civil Division) (Hobhouse, Swinton Thomas and Schiemann LJJ)

Directive – whether of direct effect – conditions for direct effect

Facts

In the first two appeals the plaintiffs sought damages from the Motor Insurers' Bureau (MIB) in respect of losses caused by uninsured drivers. Compensation was, in principle, payable by the MIB by virtue of the Motor Insurers' Bureau (Compensation of Victims of Uninsured Drivers) Agreement 1988, but in both cases the courts had found against the plaintiffs on the basis that they had known, or ought to have known, that the driver in question was uninsured. In the third appeal the MIB sought to overturn the ruling at first instance that compensation was payable, notwithstanding that the plaintiff had known the driver concerned was uninsured, because the terms of the Motor Insurers' Bureau (Compensation of Victims of Uninsured Drivers) Agreement 1988 offended against the Second Council Directive (84/5/EEC) (OJ 1984 L8/17), which dealt with the approximation of the laws of EU member states regarding civil liability arising from the use of motor vehicles.

Held

The appeals brought by Mighell and Evans were dismissed. The appeal brought by the MIB was allowed. The court was willing to assume for the present purposes that the directive (which required member states to amend their laws by 31 December 1987) had not been properly implemented by the United Kingdom. In such cases damages might be available under the *Francovich* principle either because the MIB was an emanation of the state, or directly from the United Kingdom on the basis that it had failed to implement the directive. In *Francovich* v *Italian Republic* [1991] ECR 1–5337, the court had noted (at para 11) that:

> 'Wherever the provisions of a directive appear, as far as their subject matter is concerned, to be unconditional and sufficiently precise, those provisions may ... be relied upon as against any national provision which is incompatible with the directive or in so far as the provisions of the directive define rights which individuals are able to assert against the state ...'

But as Schiemann LJ explained, the European Court of Justice went on (at para 26) to hold that:

> 'Even though the provisions ... were sufficiently precise and unconditional as regard the determination of the persons entitled to the guarantee and as regards the content of that guarantee, those elements were not sufficient to enable individuals to rely on those provisions before the national courts. Those provisions do not identify the person liable to provide the guarantee, and the state cannot be considered liable on the sole ground that it has failed to take transposition measures within the prescribed period.'

Further, in *Wagner Miret* [1993] ECR 1–6911 it was held that the doctrine of direct effect could not be used to obtain compensation where it had been left to the state to identify the one or more guarantee institutions against which the remedy was to be available.

As the MIB had been nominated to provide the compensation for those claiming in respect of losses caused by uninsured drivers the doctrine of direct effect could not, therefore, operate to provide a right to compensation.

Comment
Note that the issue of whether or not the MIB was actually an emanation of the state for the purposes of direct effect did not fall to be considered by the court.

R v *Secretary of State for Transport, ex parte Factortame Ltd and Others (No 5)* (1998) The Times 28 April Court of Appeal (Civil Division) (Lord Woolf MR, Schiemann and Robert Walker LJJ)

Breach of EC law – whether punitive damages available

Facts
The applicants, Spanish owners and managers of fishing trawlers operating in United Kingdom waters, sought damages in respect of losses alleged to have arisen from the implementation of the Merchant Shipping Act 1988. Under the 1988 Act restrictions were introduced to prevent foreign nationals from fishing against the United Kingdom fishing quota (so called 'quota-hopping'). The legislation was eventually declared to be in breach of EC law (see *R* v *Secretary of State for Transport, ex parte Factortame Ltd and Others* [1990] 2 AC 85; *R* v *Secretary of State for Transport, ex parte Factortame Ltd and Others (No 2)* [1991] 1 AC 603; *R* v

Secretary of State for Transport, ex parte Factortame Ltd and Others (No 3) [1992] QB 680) and in *Brasserie du Pêcheur SA* v *Federal Republic of Germany* Case C–46/93; *R* v *Secretary of State for Transport, ex parte Factortame Ltd and Others (No 4)* Case C–48/93 [1996] 2 WLR 506 the European Court of Justice held that the applicants could recover damages provided three conditions were met:

1. the rule of law infringed must be intended to confer rights on individuals;
2. the breach must be sufficiently serious; and
3. there must be a direct causal link between the breach of the obligation resting on the state and the damage sustained by the injured party.

The European Court of Justice concluded that condition (1) was clearly satisfied. As regards condition (2), the test was whether or not a member state had manifestly and gravely disregarded the limits on its discretion regarding the measures to be taken in ensuring compliance, due regard being had to factors such as whether the breach was intentional or voluntary, whether an excusable error of law had been made, whether the action of any Community institution might have contributed to the breach, and whether or not there were previous decisions of the ECJ that made clear the incompatibility of the domestic law in question. The issue of causation was to be determined by the domestic courts of member states.

The court went on to note that exemplary damages could be awarded in respect of such claims, provided they could be awarded on a similar basis under the domestic law of a member state, subject always to the proviso that domestic law should not operate so as to make the obtaining of such reparation excessively difficult or impossible. In this regard the court found that the requirement of English domestic law, to the effect that damages would only be recoverable in cases of misfeasance, was a measure that made the recovery of damages excessively difficult, if not impossible, given that the action that was the subject matter of the claim for damages was that of the legislature. Under Community law, the only permissible fault requirement for the award of damages was that there had been non-compliance with Community law. The measure of damages awarded had to be commensurate with the nature of the loss and damage suffered by the plaintiff, due regard being had to the extent to which the plaintiff had shown due diligence in mitigating the extent of any loss. In this respect, the proper protection of Community rights militated against the exclusion of a right to recover damages for loss of profit.

In the light of this ruling the applicants commenced an action in the Queen's Bench Division for compensation in respect of the losses caused by the United Kingdom's breaches of EC law, and in particular sought punitive damages given the nature of the breach. At first instance the Divisional Court held that the breaches of EC law by the United Kingdom, in implementing the Merchant Shipping Act 1988, were sufficiently serious to give rise to liability in damages, but the applicants were not entitled to exemplary damages from the Secretary of State. The court proceeded on the basis that the test for whether or not a breach of EC law was sufficiently serious was whether there had been manifest and grave disregard of whatever discretion the member state might possess. Applying *Mulder and Others* v *Council and Commission* [1992] ECR 1–3061 the Divisional Court took the view that it should assess the following:

1. the importance of the principle infringed and the seriousness of the breach;
2. the fact that the disregard affected a clearly defined and limited number of commercial enterprises;
3. the fact that damages suffered by the applicants went beyond what could be expected in the normal course of economic risk taking; and
4. the lack of justification for the infringement.

The Divisional Court determined that of these factors the only live issue was that of justification for the infringement, and proceeded to determine that issue in favour of the applicants. On appeal by the Secretary of State:

Held
The appeal was dismissed. Noting that the breach of Community law had been conceded, and that causation had been established, Lord Woolf MR made the following observations:

1. A violation of Community law alone was not sufficient to give rise to liability.
2. Lack of clarity as regards the relevant Community law could be a factor in determining a state's liability for non-compliance.
3. The view of the European Commission as to how a law should operate was persuasive, but not decisive of the matter.
4. The breach of Community law resulting from the enactment of the 1988 Act was too grave and serious to avoid the conclusion that there should be a right to damages.

20.2 The European Convention on Human Rights

Steel and Others v *United Kingdom* (1998) The Times 1 October European Court of Human Rights

Articles 5(1), 6(3) and 10 ECHR – whether violated by domestic law on arrest for breach of the peace

Facts
In 1992 Helen Steel was arrested whilst protesting at the scene of a grouse shoot. She walked in front of members of the shoot in order to stop them firing their guns. She was charged with causing a breach of the peace and detained for 44 hours prior to her appearance in court. Having refused to be bound over to keep the peace Ms Steel was committed to prison for 28 days.

In the second case Rebecca Lush was arrested after she stood in front of a JCB digger in order to prevent building work on a new road. She was charged with conduct likely to cause a breach of the peace and detained for 18 hours before appearing before a court. She too refused to be bound over to keep the peace and was committed to prison for seven days.

In the third case three protestors, David Polden, Andrea Needham and Christopher Cole, were arrested outside an arms manufacturers' conference in London. They had been handing out leaflets and holding up banners protesting about the sale of arms. They were arrested on the grounds that a breach of the peace was apprehended and detained for seven hours. Proceedings against them were discontinued after the prosecution decided to offer no evidence.

The applicants alleged that their treatment involved violations of arts 5(1), 6 and 10 of the European Convention on Human Rights (ECHR). The European Commission on Human Rights, having failed to secure a friendly settlement, concluded that there had been a violation of art 10, the right to freedom of expression, as regards Cole, Needham and Polden, but concluded that there had been no other violations of the ECHR's provisions. Before the European Court of Human Rights the applicants reasserted their claim that the arrests and detentions had been in violation of art 5(1) because the process was not prescribed by law, and that there had been violations of their rights under art 10.

Held

There had been no violation of the ECHR rights of the first two applicants, Steel and Lush. As regards Cole, Needham and Polden there had been breaches of arts 5(1) and 10.

The court noted that although breach of the peace was, technically, not an offence under English law, it amounted to an offence for the purposes of art 5 of the ECHR. The requirement under art 5 was that an offence should be prescribed by law with sufficient clarity so that an accused person would be able to foresee the legal consequences of any given action. The Court was satisfied that, through case law, the concept of breach of the peace had been clarified in English law to the extent that it could be defined as arising when a person caused harm to, or appeared likely to do so, persons or property or acted in a manner the natural consequence of which was to provoke others to violence. There was also a clear power of arrest in such circumstances. On the facts the Court was satisfied that the behaviour of the applicants Steel and Lush had warranted arrest for breach of the peace as defined. Further, the binding over orders issued in respect of the first two applicants made it sufficiently clear that they were being asked to refrain from committing similar breaches of the peace within the following 12 months. In respect of Cole, Needham and Polden, however, the Court concluded that, as their protest had been entirely peaceful, there had been no basis for their being arrested for breach of the peace, hence there had been a violation of art 5(1).

As regards the alleged violations of art 10, the Court concluded, as regards the first two applicants, that although the detention following arrest had resulted in an interference with the applicants' right to freedom of expression under art 10, the interference was not disproportionate in the circumstances. In particular, the Court was persuaded by the fact that the protests were dangerous and were likely to continue if the applicants were not detained. As regards Cole, Needham and Polden, the court concluded that there had been a breach of art 10. As with their claims under art 5(1), given that their protests were peaceful, the interference with their rights under art 10 had been disproportionate to the aim of preventing disorder and protecting the rights of others. Article 10(2) required any interference with the right to freedom of expression to be prescribed by law.

Comment
It will be interesting to see whether the government responds to this decision with a codification of the law relating to breach of the peace. To date its vagueness has made it a useful weapon for police officers involved in the policing of public protest.

Index

ABWOR, *120–121*
Alternative dispute resolution, *114–116*
Alternative legal services, *127–129*
Anton Piller orders, *7, 141*
Appeals
    bail, and, *228–229*
    civil. *See* Civil appeals
    criminal. *See* Criminal appeals
Arbitration, *113–114, 163–164*
Arrest, *189–197*
    appearance before magistrates following charge, *201*
    arrestable offences, for, *189–190*
    fingerprinting following, *207–208*
    information on, *196–197*
    offences not arrestable, *194–196*
    powers of, *189*
    procedure following, *198–200*
    right to legal advice, and, *201–205*
    searches following, *205–207*
Arrestable offences, *189–190*
    arrest for, *190–194*
Assizes, *4–5*

Bail, *224–230*
    appeal, *228–229*
    challenges, *228–229*
    conditions, *227–228*
    imprisonable offences, *226*
    non-imprisonable offences, *227*
    procedure, *224–225*
    reconsideration of decision *228*
    reporting, *228*
    residence, *228*
    restrictions, *228*
    right to, *225–227*
    sureties, *227*
Barristers, *92–97*
    cab-rank rule, *97*
    continuing education, *94*
    discipline, *96*
    functions, *95*
    qualification, *92–93*
    Queen's Counsel, *94*
    regulation, *96*

Barristers (*contd.*)
    relationships with clients, *96–97*
    rights of advocacy, *95*
    rights of audience, *95*
Bye-laws, *21*

Case law, *21–23*
Caution, use of, *209–212*
Circuit judges, *64–65*
Citizens' advice bureaux, *128*
Civil appeals, *166–170*
    Court of Appeal, to, *167–170*
    courts of first instance, from, *166–167*
    House of Lords, to, *170*
Civil law, criminal law distinguished, *10–11*
Civil procedure in the county court, *158–165*
    from 26 April 1999
        allocation, *164–165*
        costs, *165*
        effect on precedents, *165*
        jurisdiction, *164–165*
        pre-trial, *165*
        trial, *165*
    prior to 26 April 1999
        automatic directions, *161*
        bringing proceedings, *160*
        enforcement of judgments, *162*
        interlocutory applications, *161–162*
        issue of proceedings (action) and service, *160–161*
        jurisdiction, *159–160*
        pleadings, *161*
        proceedings ending before trial, *162*
        small claims, *162–164*
        trial, *162*
Civil procedure in the High Court, *135–157*
    from 26 April 1999
        allocation stage, *153*
        Civil Justice Council, *150*
        costs, *156*
        defence response, *153*
        disclosure, *153–154*
        effect on precedents, *157*
        interest, *156*
        interlocutory applications, *154*

Index

Civil Procedure in the High Court, from 26 April 1999 (*contd.*)
    issue and service of proceedings, *152*
    judges as trial managers, *151–152*
    judgment, *156*
    jurisdiction, *150*
    listing questionnaire, *154*
    pre-action protocols, *151*
    proceedings ending before trial, *154*
    sanctions, *155*
    terminology, *156–157*
    trial, *156*
  prior to 26 April 1999
    acknowledgement of service, *137–138*
    costs, *144*
    discovery, *140*
    enforcement of judgments, *144–145*
    exchange of pleadings, *138–140*
    interest, *144*
    interlocutory applications, *140–141*
    issue and service of writ, *136–137*
    judgment, *144*
    jurisdiction, *136*
    new approach, *145–146*
    proceedings ending before trial, *141–143*
    summons for directions, *140*
    trial, *143*
Classification of offences, *230–231*
  indictable, *230–231*
  summary, *231*
  triable either way, *231*
Codification, *57–58*
Committal proceedings, *234–237*
  alibi warning, *236*
  bail, *236*
  legal aid, *236–237*
  sending case for trial, *237*
Common law, *3–5*
Conditional fees, *125–127*
Confessions, *208–209*
Contract, *11–12*
Costs
  High Court, *144, 156*
  legal aid, and, *124–125*
Council of Europe, *283*
Council of the Inns of Court, *96*
County courts, *111*
Court of Appeal, *53–55, 107–108*
  appeals to, *167–170*
    Civil Appeals Office, *167–168*
    powers of court, *169*
    procedure, *168–169*
    reform, *169–170*

Court structure, *105–117*
  civil, *105*
  common law, *106*
  courts of record, *105*
  criminal, *105*
  diagrams of, *116–117*
  divisions, *105–106*
  equity, *106*
  inferior courts, *105*
  superior courts, *105*
Criminal appeals, *260–268*
  against conviction, *262–267*
  against sentence, *267*
  Crown Court, to, *260–261*
  House of Lords, to, *262, 266–267*
  Queen's Bench Division of High Court, to, *261–262*
  summary trial, following, *260–262*
  trial on indictment, following, *262–267*
Criminal Cases Review Commission, *267–268*
Criminal law, civil law distinguished, *10–11*
Crown Court, *110*
Crown Prosecution Service, *97–99*
  constitution, *98*
  origin, *97–98*
  reorganisation, *98–99*
  rights of advocacy, *99*
  rights of audience, *99*
Curia Regis, *4*
Custom, *14–16*
  certainty, *16*
  creation, *16*
  definition, *15*
  enjoyment, *16*
  essential elements, *15–16*
  obligatory, *16*
  reasonable, *15–16*
  time immemorial, *15*
  uninterrupted, *16*

District judges, *65*
Divisions of English law, *3–13*

Enforcement of judgments, *162*
Entry, search and seizure
  police powers, *182–188*
  without warrant, *185–188*
Equity, *5–10*
European Community law, *23, 295–303*
  direct applicability, *285*
  direct effect, *285–287*
  ECHR, and, *324–325*
  horizontal direct effect, *288–289*

European Community law (*contd.*)
  indirect effect, *289–291*
  recent cases, *326–329*
  sources, *284–294*
  United Kingdom, in, *295–296*
  UK sovereignty, and, *296–303*
  remedies for non-compliance, *291–294*
  vertical direct effect, public body for the purposes of, *287–288*
European Convention on Human Rights, *23, 304–325*
  Commission, *311–322*
  Court, *312*
  derogations, *311*
  Euopean Community law, and, *324–325*
  Human Rights Act 1998, *316–325*
    action by ministers, *322–323*
    alternative mechanisms, *323–324*
    judicial remedies, *321–322*
    pre-enactment procedures, *323*
    procedure for enforcement, *317*
    rights protected, *316–317*
    subject of proceedings, *318–319*
    violation of Convention rights, *319–321*
  incorporation into English law, *315–316*
  limitations, *311*
  machinery for enforcement, *311–313*
  place in English law, *313–316*
  political background, *304–305*
  recent cases, *329–331*
  restrictions, *311*
  rights protected under, *305–310*
European Council, *283*
European Court of Human Rights, *50*
European Court of Justice, *50, 278–283*
  advocates general, *279*
  Court of First Instance, *279–280*
  judges, *279*
  proceedings for failure to act, *281*
  proceedings for annulment, *280–281*
  proceedings for failure to fulfil obligation, *280*
  proceedings to establish liability, *281*
  references under art 234, *282–283*
European Union, *23, 271–294*
  Amsterdam Treaty, *274*
  Council of the European Union, *275–276*
  Court of Justice of the European Communities, *278–283*
  EC Ombudsman, *278*
  Economic and Social Committee, *277*
  European Commission, *276–277*

European Union (*contd.*)
  European Parliament, *277–278*
  Maastricht Treaty, *273–274*
  objectives, *272–273*
  origins, *271–272*
  terminology, *272*
  Treaty of Rome, *271–272*
Evidence, challenging the admissibility of, *212–218*

Family mediation, *115–116*
Fines, *259*
Fingerprinting, arrest, following, *207–208*
Free legal services, *127–129*
Free Representation Units, *128–129*

General Council of the Bar, *96*
General Eyre, *5*
Green form scheme, *119–120*

Hansard, *36–37*
High Court, *55–56, 108–109*
  Chancery Division, *109*
  Family Division, *109*
  Queen's Bench Division, *109*
High Court judges, *64*
House of Lords, *50–53, 106–107*
  appeals to, *262, 266–267*

Imprisonment, *259*
Indictable offences, *230–231*
Indictment, trial on, *247–259*
  disclosure, *252–254*
  plea, *248–252*
  plea bargaining, *251–252*
  procedure, *254–257*
  representation, *248*
  verdict, *256–257*
Injunctions, *141*
Inns of court, Council of the, *96*
Inquiries, *112–113*
Interrogation of suspects, *201–205*

Judiciary, *61–72*
  appointment, *66–68*
  career, *61–62*
  functions, *71–72*
  immunity, *69–70*
  impartiality, *70–71*
  independence, *70*
  offices, *62–66*
  removal, *69*
  retirement *69*

Judiciary (*contd.*)
    statistics, 62–66
    training, 68–69
Jury system, 76–85
    arguments for and against retention, 84–85
    civil cases, 76–77
        assessing compensation, 77
        composition, 76
        suitability, 76–77
    criminal cases, 78–83
        composition, 78
        deliberations, 82
        empannelling, 79–80
        qualifications, 78–89
        random selection, 80–82
        verdict, 82–83
    reform, 85

Law centres, 127–128
Law Commission 39
    reports, 36, 39
Law Society, 89, 91
Legal advice centres, 128
Legal aid, 118–125
    ABWOR, 120–121
    civil, 121–122, 124–125
        financial requirements, 121–122
        merits test, 122
        scope, 121
    costs, and, 124–125
    criminal, 122–124, 125
        financial requirements, 123
        merits test, 123–124
        scope, 122–123
    green form scheme, 119–120
    proposed reforms, 129–131
    scheme, 118–119
Legal expenses insurance, 125
Legal profession, 86–102
    divided, 86–87
    fusion, 87–88
    reform, 100–102
Legislation, 17–21
    codification, 19
    consolidation, 19
    form, 18
    functions, 18–19
    history, 17
    operation, 19–20
    modern, 17–18
    social, 19
    subordinate, 20–21
Lord Chief Justice, 63
Lord Chancellor, 62

Lord Justices of Appeal, 64
Lords of Appeal in Ordinary, 63–64

Magistracy, 72–75
    lay, 72–75
    magistrates' clerk, 74–75
    stipendiary, 75
Magistrates' courts, 111–112
Mareva injunctions, 7, 141
Master of the Rolls, 63
Mediation, 115–116
Ministerial regulations, 21
Miscarriages of justice, 267
Mode of trial, determining, 231–234
    criminal damage offences, 234
    reform, 234

Obiter dicta, 46–47
Offences triable either way, 231
Orders in Council, 21

Pleadings, 138–140, 161
Police
    entry, search and seizure, 182–185
        without warrant, 185–188
    prosecutors, as, 220
    stop and search, 175–178, 179–180
Police and Criminal Evidence Act 1984
    conduct of searches, 178–179
Precedent, doctrine of, 42–58
    certainty, 44
    codification, and, 57–58
    fairness, 44
    flexibility, 44
    operation within hierarchy of courts, 49–56
    predictability, 44–45
    reform, 56–58
President of the Family Division, 63
Property, 12–13
Prosecution, 219–224
    commencing, 223–224
    Crown Prosecution Service, 220
    decision to, 221–223
    police, 220
    private, 220–221

Queen's Counsel, 94

Ratio decidendi, 45–46
Recorders, 65
Reform, 38–41
    ad hoc committees, 39
    examples, 39–40
    ministry of justice, 40–41

Reform *(contd.)*
  standing committees, *38–39*
Road checks, *180–182*
Royal Commissions, *39–40*

Search
  arrest, following, *205–207*
  police powers, *175–178*
Seizure, powers of, *188*
Sentencing, *257–259*
  antecedents, *258*
  facts of offence, *257–258*
  plea in mitigation, *259*
  reports on defendant, *258*
  sentences, *259*
Silence, right to, *209–212*
Small claims, *162–165*
Solicitors, *88–92*
  discipline, *90–91*
  functions, *88–89*
  liability to third parties, *92*
  qualification, *88*
  regulation, *90–91*
  relationship with clients, *91–92*
  rights of advocacy, *89–90*
  rights of audience, *89–90*
Sources of law, *13–23*
  formal, *14*
  historical, *14*
  legal, *14*
  literary, *14*
Stare decisis, *45–49*
  distinguishing, *47*
  overruling, *47–48*
  per incuriam, *48–49*
  persuasive authority, *47*
  reversing, *48*

Statutes. *See* Legislation
Statutory interpretation, *24–37*
  conflicting provisions, *33*
  eiusdem generis, *32*
  external aids, *35–37*
  golden rule, *29*
  impact of Human Rights Act 1998, *37*
  influence of European Convention on Human Rights, *37*
  internal aids, *34–35*
  judges, and, *37*
  literal rule, *26–29*
  mischief rule, *30–31*
  presumptions, *32–33*
  purposive, *31*
  statute should be read as a whole, *31–32*
  statutory history, *35*
Stop and search, police powers, *175–178, 179–180*
Subordinate legislation, *20–21, 33*
  classification, *20–21*
Summary offences, *231*
Summary trial, *238–246*
  attendance, *239–241*
  information, *241*
  procedure, *241–245*
  representation, *241*
  sentencing, *245–246*

Tort, *11*
Tribunals, *112–113*

Vice-Chancellor, *63*
Voluntary attendance at police station, *197–198*

Woolf Report, *146–149*
  reactions to, *149*

Criminal Justice and Penology Textbook

**Michael Doherty, BA, MA Criminology,
Senior Lecturer in Law, University of Glamorgan**

An up-to-date and well illustrated account of the key stages of the criminal justice system is provided. The text analyses a plethora of areas relating to the imposition of punitive measures upon criminals in modern English society, including: an exploration of the prospects for crime prevention, evaluation of the role of the police and examination of bail and prosecution decisions. No stage or aspect of the system is left untouched.

What is the impact of the jury system and what is it's importance today? What are the factors that influence sentencing decisions in English courtrooms? How do courts decide between the use of custodial and non-custodial measures? What is the role of prisons and do they fulfil that purpose? A comprehensive and thought-provoking text which encourages its readers to think much more deeply about the philosophies that lie behind the criminal justice system.

For further information on contents or to place an order, please contact:

Mail Order
Old Bailey Press
200 Greyhound Road
London
W14 9RY

Telephone No: 020 7385 3377
Fax No: 020 7381 3377

ISBN 1 85836 372 1
Soft cover 246 x 175 mm
272 pages   £11.95
Due September 2000

Law Update 2000

Law Update 2001 edition – due February 2001

An annual review of the most recent developments in specific legal subject areas, useful for law students at degree and professional levels, others with law elements in their courses and also practitioners seeking a quick update.

Published around February every year, the Law Update summarises the major legal developments during the course of the previous year. In conjunction with Old Bailey Press textbooks it gives the student a significant advantage when revising for examinations.

Contents

Administrative Law • Civil and Criminal Procedure • Commercial Law • Company Law • Conflict of Laws • Constitutional Law • Contract Law • Conveyancing • Criminal Law • Criminology • English Legal System • Equity and Trusts • European Union Law • Evidence • Family Law • Jurisprudence • Land Law • Law of International Trade • Public International Law • Revenue Law • Succession • Tort

For further information on contents or to place an order, please contact:

Mail Order
Old Bailey Press
200 Greyhound Road
London
W14 9RY

Telephone No: 020 7385 3377
Fax No: 020 7381 3377

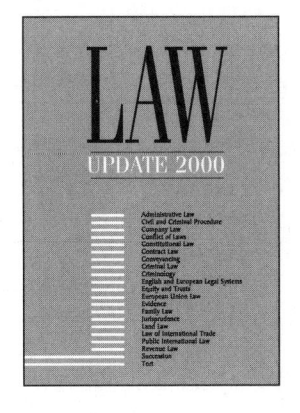

ISBN 1 85836 347 0
Soft cover 246 x 175 mm
392 pages   £9.95
Published February 2000

Old Bailey Press

The Old Bailey Press integrated student law library is tailor-made to help you at every stage of your studies from the preliminaries of each subject through to the final examination. The series of Textbooks, Revision WorkBooks, 150 Leading Cases/Casebooks and Cracknell's Statutes are interrelated to provide you with a comprehensive set of study materials.

You can buy Old Bailey Press books from your University Bookshop, your local Bookshop, direct using this form, or you can order a free catalogue of our titles from the address shown overleaf.

The following subjects each have a Textbook, 150 Leading Cases/Casebook, Revision WorkBook and Cracknell's Statutes unless otherwise stated.

Administrative Law
Commercial Law
Company Law
Conflict of Laws
Constitutional Law
Conveyancing (Textbook and Casebook)
Criminal Law
Criminology (Textbook and Sourcebook)
English and European Legal Systems
Equity and Trusts
Evidence
Family Law
Jurisprudence: The Philosophy of Law (Textbook, Sourcebook and
    Revision WorkBook)
Land: The Law of Real Property
Law of International Trade
Law of the European Union
Legal Skills and System
Obligations: Contract Law
Obligations: The Law of Tort
Public International Law
Revenue Law (Textbook,
    Sourcebook and Revision
    WorkBook)
Succession

Mail order prices:	
Textbook	£11.95
150 Leading Cases/Casebook	£9.95
Revision WorkBook	£7.95
Cracknell's Statutes	£9.95
Suggested Solutions 1998–1999	£6.95
Law Update 2000	£9.95
The Practitioner's Handbook 2000	£54.95

To complete your order, please fill in the form below:

Module	Books required	Quantity	Price	Cost
		Postage		
		TOTAL		

For Europe, add 15% postage and packing (£20 maximum).
For the rest of the world, add 40% for airmail.

ORDERING

By telephone to Mail Order at 020 7385 3377, with your credit card to hand.

By fax to 020 7381 3377 (giving your credit card details).

By post to:

Mail Order, Old Bailey Press, 200 Greyhound Road, London W14 9RY.

When ordering by post, please enclose full payment by cheque or banker's draft, or complete the credit card details below. You may also order a free catalogue of our complete range of titles from this address.

We aim to despatch your books within 3 working days of receiving your order.

Name

Address

Postcode   Telephone

Total value of order, including postage: £

I enclose a cheque/banker's draft for the above sum, or

charge my   ☐ Access/Mastercard   ☐ Visa   ☐ American Express
Card number

☐☐☐☐ ☐☐☐☐ ☐☐☐☐ ☐☐☐☐

Expiry date   ☐☐☐☐

Signature: ....Date: ....